TEACHING
BUSINESS
SUBJECTS

Prentice-Hall Education Series

PRENTICE-HALL INTERNATIONAL, INC., *London*
PRENTICE-HALL OF AUSTRALIA, PTY., LTD., *Sydney*
PRENTICE-HALL OF CANADA, LTD., *Toronto*
PRENTICE-HALL OF INDIA (PRIVATE) LTD., *New Delhi*
PRENTICE-HALL OF JAPAN, INC., *Tokyo*

Second Edition

TEACHING BUSINESS SUBJECTS

Lloyd V. Douglas
*Head of the Department of Business Education
and Professor of Business Education
State College of Iowa*

James T. Blanford
*Professor of Business Education
State College of Iowa*

Ruth I. Anderson
*Professor of Business Education
North Texas State University*

Prentice-Hall, Inc., Englewood Cliffs, N. J.

LIBRARY OF CONGRESS CATALOG CARD NO.: 65-13454

PRINTED IN THE UNITED STATES OF AMERICA

89144-C

PREFACE

The reader will find this book is developed around three major and basic concepts of learning and teaching:

1. Learning is mostly an individual matter. Although certain general laws of adaptation, growth, conditioning, and learning are known, the many influencing factors present in the heritage and environment of each individual are so complex that each individual learner presents a different problem.

2. Hence, teaching combines both an art and a science. Good teaching must be *based on* psychological principles known to be sound and must be *achieved through* techniques that are efficient and effective; to this extent it is a science. But the good teacher must be a true artist in *selecting and applying* these principles and techniques in accordance with the ever-changing needs of students, both as groups and as individuals.

3. New teaching techniques and new facts about learning are constantly being discovered and perfected. Modern teachers must be (and are) competent to intelligently choose from and add to this growing body of knowledge.

Thus, this book is not limited to presenting *a method* or *a best technique* for teaching various business subjects under specified conditions; it goes further than that. In the belief that teaching is both an art *and* a science, it also directs attention to many alternate and supplementary techniques, procedures, and devices which teachers may choose to use in appropriate situations.

The result of these basic concepts is a book that the authors are proud to present as a methods *text* for all business education students and as a handy reference or *handbook* for all business teachers and educators interested in ever-improving methods of teaching business subjects. It places carefully chosen emphasis on those known facts and established methods which the authors believe to be most helpful for all teaching of the various business subjects—a characteristic which will be greatly appreciated by the inexperienced teacher. Yet, it also encourages the future development and strengthening of the individual teacher as a true artist in the teaching profession by presenting numerous alternate and supplementary suggestions—and arranges it all under a readily understood plan of parts, chapters, and subheadings to form a most useful handbook for constant future reference.

An especially valuable feature of this book is the inclusion of special materials reviewing the learning process and its phases most important in teaching the skill subjects and the nonskill subjects. These materials provide welcome "bridges" between basic psychology and education courses and more advanced applications to the specific teaching situations in the business subjects.

Part Four, "Extending Learning Beyond the Classroom," brings into this single volume a treatment of that *professional extra* which so frequently is the difference between an ordinary business education program and one that achieves distinctly superior results. It is the belief of the authors that these three final chapters deal with three aspects of good education that are destined to become of ever-increasing importance.

An especially valuable group of projects and questions for discussion and case problems has been included for each chapter. These carefully selected questions and problems can readily form the basis for discussions that will both review and give greater meaning to the text material, as well as *extend* the learning to new related areas.

Finally, the authors wish to give credit to Dr. Harland E. Samson, Teacher-Educator in Distributive Education, formerly at the State College of Iowa and now at the University of Wisconsin, for contributing the chapter "Cooperative Part-Time Business Education Programs."

L. V. D./J. T. B./R. I. A.

CONTENTS

I INTRODUCTION 1

1. The Business Teacher   3

The Former Setting, 4. The Changed Setting, 5. Areas of Subject-Specialization, 6. General and Liberal Arts Preparation, 7. Minor Subject-Specializations, 7. Professional Preparation, 9. Personal Development, 9. Extracurricular Activities, 10. Business Experience, 11. The Business Teacher in the Small High School, 12. The Business Teacher in the Larger High School, 13. The Business Teacher in Post-High-School Work, 14. Adult and Evening Classes, 15. Acquiring Professional Stature, 16. Professional Stature for the Business Teacher, 17. Future Career Possibilities, 19. Projects and Questions for Discussion, 20. Case Problems, 21. Suggested Readings, 23.

2. The Business Education Curriculums   24

The Goals of Secondary Education, 25. The Broad Field of Business Education, 27. The Basic Twofold Classification, 28. General Objectives of Business Education, 30. The High-School Program, 32. The Small High School, 34. Business Education in a Medium-Size City, 37. Projects and Problems for Discussion, 41. Case Problems, 42. Suggested Readings, 44.

3. The Business Teacher Looks at the Learning Process   46

Learning as Individual Growth, 47. Motivation, 49. Attention, Interest, and Desire, 53. Knowledge of Results, 58. Whole Versus Part Learning, 59. Rivalry and Competition, 61. Goals and Subgoals, 62. Skill Development, 63. Problem-Solving, 65. Individual Differences, 66. Projects and Questions for Discussion, 68. Case Problems, 69. Suggested Readings, 70

4. Teaching Techniques Applied to the Learning Process   72

The Business Teacher as a Person, 72. The Teacher as a Technician, 75. Planning, 82. Evaluation and Grading, 91. Methodology, 102. Projects and Questions for Discussion, 104. Case Problems, 105. Suggested Readings, 106.

II THE SKILL SUBJECTS 109

5. Teaching Typewriting   111

The Typewriting Room, 112. Objectives in Typewriting, 114. The Psychology of Typewriting, 115. Length of the Typewriting Course, 120. Course Content in Typewriting, 121. Introducing the Keyboard, 127. Teaching Machine Parts, 129. Developing Correct Techniques in Typewriting, 129. Speed and Accuracy in Typewriting, 134. Drills in Typewriting, 136. Teaching Figures and Symbols, 151. Analysis of Typewriting Errors, 154. Proofreading, 158. Related Knowledges in Typewriting, 160. Composition at the Machine, 162. Erasing, 164. Production Typewriting, 165. Standards in Typewriting, 170. Teaching Electric Typewriting, 176. Projects and Questions for Discussion, 179. Case Problems, 181. Suggested Readings, 185.

6. Teaching Shorthand and Transcription   187

Shorthand, 187. Objective of Teaching Shorthand, 188. The Shorthand Teacher, 189. The Shorthand Student, 190. The Shorthand System, 191. The Shorthand Course—One Year or Two? 192. Shorthand Methods—Manual or Functional?, 194. Classroom Procedures, 198. Use of the Blackboard, 200. Teaching Shorthand Theory, 202. Reading Shorthand Plates, 203. Homework Assignments, 205. Penmanship Practice, 208. Good Dictation Practices, 209. Shorthand Dictation Equipment, 224. Testing in Shorthand, 228. Pretranscription Training, 229. Shorthand Standards, 230. Transcription, 234. Projects and Questions for Discussion, 256. Case Problems, 259. Suggested Readings, 261.

7. Teaching Clerical Practice and Stenographic Practice **264**

Clerical Practice, 267. Automation and Clerical Work, 268. Duties Performed by Clerical Workers, 270. Objectives of the Course, 273. Prerequisites for Enrollment, 274. Units to Be Included in Clerical Practice, 275. Equipment and Supplies Needed, 277. Methods of Teaching Clerical Practice, 279. State and City Programs in Office and Clerical Practice, 284. Specific Teaching Suggestions, 292. Basic Units for a One-Semester Course, 301. Stenographic or Secretarial Practice, 307. Objectives of Stenographic Practice, 308. Units in Stenographic Practice, 309. Specific Teaching Suggestions for Stenographic Practice, 311. Evaluation, 313. Projects and Questions for Discussion, 315. Office Case Problems, 317. Case Problems, 321. Suggested Readings, 322.

III THE NONSKILL SUBJECTS **325**

8. Teaching General Business **327**

The Subject, 327. Subject-Matter Units Typically Taught in a General Business Course, 329. Instructional Materials, 330. Methods of Teaching General Business, 333. The Discussion, 335. Classroom Discussion, 337. Question-and-Answer Method, 343. Miscellaneous Techniques, 345. Evaluation and Measurement, 348. Economic Education, 352. Projects and Questions for Discussion, 355. Case Problems, 356. Suggested Readings, 358. Bibliographies of Free and Inexpensive Material for Use in Teaching Business Education Subjects, 358.

9. Teaching Bookkeeping **359**

The Subject, 359. Units of Content, 364. Instructional Materials, 364. Basic Concepts of Teaching Bookkeeping, 366. Specific Methods of Teaching Bookkeeping, 367. Teaching General Topics in Bookkeeping, 370. Manual and Machine Bookkeeping, 382. Miscellaneous Problems in Teaching Bookkeeping, 383. Visual Aids and Motivation Devices for Teaching Bookkeeping, 386. Suggestions for Teacher-Made Visual Aids in Bookkeeping, 387. Evaluation in Bookkeeping, 389. Projects and Questions for Discussion, 392. Case Problems, 393. Suggested Readings, 395.

10. Teaching the Distributive Subjects **396**

Distributive Occupations Defined, 397. Distributive Subjects, 398. Distributive Education, 399. Purpose of Course, 401. Measuring Achievement, 402. Group Discussion, 404. Demonstration, 404. The Sales Talk, 406. The Sales Skit, 407. Case Studies, 408. Shopping Tours and Shopping Reports, 409. Posters and Displays, 410. Field Trips and Speakers, 411. Case Studies of Local Businesses, 412. Other Instructional Aids, 413. Cooperative Part-Time Programs, 413. Projects and Questions for Discussion, 414. Case Problems, 414. Suggested Readings, 416.

11. Teaching Other Business Education Subjects   417

Data Processing in the Business Education Curriculum, 418. Selected Bibliography of Data-Processing Information, 419. General Electives, 422. Business Law, 424. Consumer Business, 428. Business Arithmetic, 431. Other Business Education Courses, 435. Projects and Questions for Discussion, 437. Case Problems, 437. Suggested Readings, 439.

IV   EXTENDING LEARNING BEYOND THE CLASSROOM   441

12. Cooperative Part-Time Business Education Programs   443

The Nature of Learning in Cooperative Part-Time Training, 448. Techniques in Providing General Related Learnings, 454. Techniques in Providing Occupational Group Learnings, 456. Techniques in Providing Specific Job Learnings, 463. Procedure for Providing On-the-Job Learnings, 467. In Conclusion, 470. Projects and Questions for Discussion, 470. Case Problems, 471. Suggested Readings, 473.

13. Adult Programs in Business Education   475

Adult Education in General, 476. Applied Psychology for Adult Business Education, 480. Special Administrative Considerations, 486. Business Classes for Adults, 489. Projects and Questions for Discussion, 495. Case Problems, 496. Suggested Readings, 497.

14. Business Student Organizations   499

The Psychology of Student Organizations, 500. Worth-while Concomitant Learnings, 506. Objections to Student Organizations, 507. National Organizations for Business Students, 509. Projects and Questions for Discussion, 520. Case Problems, 521. Suggested Readings, 522.

Index   **524**

I INTRODUCTION

The first four chapters of this book are intended to serve four major purposes:

1. To aid business teachers and prospective business teachers in "raising their sights" and broadening their professional horizons as they start this study of methods of improving their teaching

2. To provide a brief orientation to the entire field of business education and the emerging organizational environment in which the business teacher seems likely to work during the coming years

3. To provide a brief review of important psychological principles and educational procedures already studied by most business teachers and advanced students of education

4. To assist in making these same psychological principles *meaningful* to the business teacher and thus to establish an important foundation for future chapters and related studies

Thus, from Part One should be gained both general insight and understanding, and specific professional knowledge.

1

1

The Business Teacher

A successful business teacher occupies an unusually favorable position in the teaching profession, since preparation automatically qualifies him for either of two careers—one in business or one in teaching. The experience he gains in either career usually strengthens his qualifications for both careers, because his work, the dynamic, interesting, ever-changing subject-matter—modern business, keeps him acquainted with his local business community and aids him to become a respected leader in it. In addition, his students are usually those extremely interested in their work and their future careers.

The modern business teacher is far removed from the too-frequently painted picture of the stern pedagogue who devoted a great share of his time to being a drillmaster, a disciplinarian, and a penny-pinching character living in a twilight zone of citizenship. Occasionally one of the old school of relatively unprepared "commercial teachers" may have come close to fitting such a picture; such a teacher is comparatively rare today, however.

Instead, the successful business teacher of today is a happy, highly respected, and well-known leader in his school and community. Besides teaching his classroom work he is an active member of local social and civic clubs and organizations. He not only knows and visits in the homes of his students' parents, but is similarly personally acquainted with the business people of his community. In the smaller and medium-sized towns of the nation, at least, he hears his name spoken in friendly greeting as he walks down the street. Everywhere he is treated with respect. Frequently citizens and business people seek his advice.

Although he occupies a position of importance in his local school and community, his activities and personal acquaintances are not limited to this one locality. Through his memberships in professional and in business organizations he is an active member of many larger "communities" that are state-wide and national in scope. Through his state business education association and state education association he gains professional friends throughout the state; he meets and talks with them at conventions each year. Similarly, through his membership in the NEA and in his own department of the NEA (The National Business Education Association) as well as in regional professional groups, he extends this pleasant and profitable experience to include the entire nation.

In brief, then, the successful business teacher of today has much to be happy about and much to look forward to throughout life. Let us now take a look at some of the many factors that help to give us a more complete picture of this career.

The Former Setting

Business education is a relative newcomer in the field of education. Like many of its predecessors, including even the field of science, in its infancy it was a "stepchild," not being completely accepted by the entire educational family and often quite uncertain of its own status. Thus, as historically has been true of various new areas of education, within the memory of many of us yet living there often existed a connotation of unrespectability when the term *commercial education* was used in educational circles. In a very few localities this may still exist today, but it is the exception rather than the rule.

Perhaps, too, there was good reason for questioning the real values of "commercial education" in those earlier days. Admittedly the value of any study or group of studies pursued in schools is influenced by the ability, skill, and preparation of its teachers—and when a study is new to education it seems self-evident that really competent teachers for it must necessarily be scarce or nonexistent.

Thus, it was but natural that high-school advisers of students frequently counseled their better students to study the more respectable, time-proven, "academic" or college-entrance subjects— leaving the commercial subjects quite largely for those pupils who for one reason or another were deemed unsuitable for any sizable amount of formal classroom education.

The result often tended to be a combination of relatively poorly prepared teachers holding classes that often were labeled the "dumping ground" of the school. The achievements in those classes often suffered when compared (loosely and unscientifically, perhaps!) with achievements attained in the more customary and standard academic classes with their more select group of students under the guidance of better-prepared teachers.

Actually, this setting has completely changed today—although some people, even in the education profession, still vividly recall the "dumping ground" era and still can hardly believe it already is a phase of history.

The Changed Setting

The setting in which the business teacher of today works is vastly improved over that of a quarter of a century ago. In fact, it probably was mostly in order to better overcome the impeding connotations attached to the term *commercial education,* and to permit the development of understandings and related implications more in accordance with existing conditions, that the use of the term *business education* came into common use. Commercial education is now officially considered to be an *obsolete* educational term.[1]

Details of the present-day business *education curriculums* appear in subsequent pages (see Chapter Two). It is recognized that this setting influences the picture of today's business teacher. It is sufficient at this time to state that business education no longer is limited to relatively narrow skills. Instead, it encompasses (*a*)

---

[1] Carter V. Good, *Dictionary of Education* (New York: McGraw-Hill Book Company, 1959), p. 112.

information and abilities of personal and citizenship value to everyone, and also (*b*) relatively complete vocational education for each
of several distinct career-areas in our modern American business
economy.

Thus, the business teacher of today carries the responsibility of
assisting in the total education of all young people, *plus* responsibility for the vocational preparation of a more limited number of
young people in one or more selected areas of work in the world
of business.

Areas of Subject-Specialization

The business teacher must either prepare to teach a rather wide
variety of subjects or else decide to choose one or more areas within
business education in which to specialize. This is not an easy decision to make, since many factors must be considered. Perhaps of
most importance in guiding the teacher's preparation is the question of the location, size, and type of school in which the teaching
is to be done. For practical reasons, this frequently means the type
of school in which the first teaching position is likely to be secured.

Thus, if the first position is likely to be in a one-business-teacher
school, it is quite obvious that the teacher must be prepared to
teach *all* business subjects commonly offered in such schools. In
some states, such as those in the Midwest, these schools are very
common. Perhaps it should be noted, however, that the present
trend is toward larger schools having more than one business
teacher.

In general there are three main areas of subject-specialization
within the field of business education: (*a*) the secretarial and related office knowledges, abilities, and skills; (*b*) the accounting,
bookkeeping, and related business management and office knowledges, abilities, and skills; and (*c*) the selling, retailing, merchandising, and related business management and store knowledges,
abilities, and skills. Although the terms are not completely accurate,
these frequently are referred to as the Secretarial, the Accounting,
and the Distributive Education areas.

It is not to be inferred that all secondary business education is
or should be classified under these three classifications; such is not
the case. For instance, certain phases of the above areas of preparation may be combined into a pattern of education designated as a

Clerical Curriculum. Likewise the area known as General, or Basic, Business Education is and should be of major importance in the high school; most of this, too, is derived from subject-matter found in the three major areas of subject-specialization.

Frequently the business teacher finds it desirable to be able to teach *all* business subjects offered in the school in which he secures his first teaching position. Thus, there is much to be said for the policy of making the undergraduate major in business education a relatively broad one, leaving a portion of the more highly specialized preparation for work on the graduate level. However, there is no one best answer to this problem for all students and for all situations; usually the student's college adviser is in a position to offer best advice on this point.

General and Liberal Arts Preparation

Like all teachers, the business teacher must be an educated person. It seems quite evident that the better informed one is about everything associated with life the better his chances are of being an excellent and valuable teacher. Today nearly every degree-granting college specifically provides for this phase of the student's education, and it need not be discussed at length here. The business teacher should realize, however, that this *is* an important part of his preparation for becoming an outstanding teacher.

One should not make the mistake, however, of believing that abstract ability to reason and make judgments always can be successfully transferred to some other field of thinking once it has been successfully developed in one field of thinking. Sound reasoning must be based on knowledge and mastery of facts upon which to base the reasoning! Thus, one cannot afford to use too much of his college time in broad, liberal studies to the detriment of his knowledge of the field of study to which he proposes to devote the major portion of his career.

Minor Subject-Specializations

Most colleges, although not all, require degree students to have one or more "minor" areas of specialization or the equivalent. There probably is no one minor area that is *especially* to be recommended for all business teachers. The selection of the minor or minors *should* vary with such factors as:

1. The interests, aptitudes, and abilities of the individual student
2. The area of major specialization of the student
3. The previous education and experience of the student
4. The probable demands of the schools in that section of the nation in which the student expects to teach
5. The student's plans for future graduate work.

Here again the student's adviser is most likely to be in the best position to assist him in making his choice. However, there are three related ideas that the prospective business teacher might well consider in evaluating or selecting his minor preparation. First, there is a growing trend for the teacher with a major in business education to be called upon to teach very little, if anything, outside of his major area. This is true because the smaller schools that offer very little true vocational business education and that have need for only one part-time business teacher tend to prefer (and *should* prefer) teachers with majors in the more academic subjects; one with minor preparation in the field may be able to teach the business subjects in such schools. The significance of this statement will be better understood by the reader after completing the following chapter.

Secondly, somewhere there are schools and situations in which the business teacher who desires can *also* teach in the field of almost any "normal" minor. Thus, regardless of what one's minor preparation may be, it is quite possible to find use for it in the teaching profession as a business teacher.

Third, the business education major should give due consideration to assuring himself of a good understanding of the field of economics. In some colleges and universities this may mean that a minor specialization in the field of economics is advisable; in others this becomes a part of the business education major.

The Minor in Business Education. Many business teachers have majors in other subject-fields with only minor specialization and preparation in the field of business education. This often proves to be an excellent preparation for the teaching profession, and certainly it is to be especially encouraged for those teachers who expect to start their careers in the smaller high schools but who perhaps feel that eventually they would prefer to teach in some subject-field other than business education.

Obviously most business education minors cannot be prepared

to teach in all phases of business education. Thus, they usually find it advisable to confine their specialization mostly to one of the three main areas of subject-specialization already mentioned as composing the field of business education. Again, the college adviser should be in the best position to assist in making this choice. It might be pointed out, however, that by far the largest student enrollment in any business subject is to be found in typewriting.

Professional Preparation

State certification requirements usually are basic in determining the amount and kind of special professional preparation a business teacher must have for entering the teaching profession. The student usually has but little choice in this.

However, it is worth noting that most of this preparation (commonly referred to as Education and Psychology) actually consists of learning how to understand, deal with, control, and lead other people. This is the basic study needed for success in the entire field of human relations—and is especially valuable for *all* who hold leadership positions, since any leadership position normally indirectly involves teaching or controlling others.

Thus, we can understand why the professional preparation of the business *teacher* also serves a unique function in at the same time *better* preparing that same individual for service and leadership in positions in the business world. It is small wonder that many large businesses, looking for young people with high managerial potential, frankly admit that they especially like to find business teachers for such positions.

Personal Development

Some whose professional, general, and specialized subject-matter preparation in college seems to be about as perfect as possible turn out to be failures as teachers; others enjoy extremely successful careers. Likewise it may be said that many with relatively inferior college subject-matter preparation become extremely successful teachers. Why is this?

Almost invariably the key to a successful career lies in the individual as a person. This does not mean that proper subject-matter and professional preparation is unimportant; on the contrary, it is distinctly important. Yet it is quite widely agreed that the individual as a person (or as a personality) has more influence on teaching success than has the individual as an educated product of the subject-matter classroom!

Certainly the business teacher is no exception to this. Owing to his customary work with his business community and thus with a more diverse group of adults and students, it probably is especially important for the business teacher to be ever alert to develop himself personally in every way possible.

Extracurricular Activities

Various group activities customarily referred to as extracurricular hold special significance for the business teacher. First, they provide him with one of his best and most practicable means of personal development while a student and also after graduation. Secondly, he will find they may be effectively used to assist in achieving the personal growth and development objectives that he desires for the youth whom he teaches.

The most successful business teacher today is likely to be one who has participated rather widely and intensively in college activities providing opportunities for group participation and leadership experience, and who sees to it that the students under his guidance also have adequate opportunity for a similar type of participation.

As a citizen and member of his community, the business teacher is likely to have opportunity to participate in community groups such as the Chamber of Commerce, the Junior Chamber of Commerce, the Business and Professional Women's Club, service clubs such as Lions International, Rotary International, Kiwanis, and others. As a business teacher he will be called upon to give leadership and guidance as a sponsor for various organizations and groups of students.

Although most extracurricular activities sponsored by high schools provide important experience opportunities for students, the business teacher perhaps should have his attention especially directed to two national organizations for business students. These are FBLA (Future Business Leaders of America) and DECA (Distributive Education Clubs of America).

The Future Business Leaders of America is a youth organization sponsored by the business teachers of America through their national professional organization, the National Business Education Association. This association, NBEA, is one of the departments of the National Educational Association, and is the world's largest association of business teachers.

Already charters have been issued to more than 2,000 chapters of FBLA throughout the nation and in Hawaii and Puerto Rico. Over thirty states now have organized state chapters and hold annual state conventions from which representatives for various purposes are chosen to attend the annual national FBLA convention. The organization already has its own magazine, the *FBLA Forum,* which is received by its 60,000 members. It is a highly democratic type of organization open to all business students in public and parochial high schools and is growing rapidly; business teachers should become fully informed about it and its services for business students.[2]

The Distributive Education Clubs of America enroll as members only those students who are enrolled in regularly approved courses in distributive education. These courses are organized under relatively high standards maintained partially because of financial backing received through the federal George-Barden Act. They have the expert guidance of specially qualified state supervisors and teacher-trainers working through similarly qualified local coordinators and teachers. The DECA activities are distinctly well organized and these clubs tend to be distinct assets to the school systems and departments in which they exist.[3]

Business Experience

Actual business experience for pay should be a part of the professional preparation of every business teacher. This is one of the principles adopted by the National Association for Business Teacher Education,[4] and a number of state and city requirements for fully approved business teachers include it in some form.

The preferred business experience is that which is procured

---

[2] For complete information consult NBEA publications or write to National Business Education Association, 1201 16th Street, N.W., Washington 6, D.C.

[3] For further information consult your own State Supervisor of Distributive Education if you have one.

[4] For a summary of details pertinent to such experience, see *Criteria for Certification of Business Teachers,* NABTE Bulletin No. 56, 1952.

under the planned supervision of a regular business teacher training college or university; many of them now have such programs in effect as a recognized part of the professional preparation of business teachers.

However, there is much to be said in favor of such actual business experience as the business teacher may gain on the job either part time or full time prior to graduation, or during summer vacations after graduation. The important factor is that the business teacher who has had such actual business experience gains in know-how, in understanding of the requirements of the practical business world, in self-confidence, and in ability to win and hold the full confidence of his students.

It is to be preferred that business experience gained be in positions directly related to the subject-area that is to be taught, and that it include positions in different firms and involving both technical skills or knowledges and some degree of managerial or administrative responsibility.

The Business Teacher in the Small High School

In some parts of the nation, as in the Midwest, there are many small high schools. A high school that is considered "small" in the East, for instance, might well be considered "large" in other areas. Thus, in the state of Iowa in 1955 there were 819 separate high schools but the *median* enrollment for all high schools was only around eighty-five students—which means that half of the high schools had *less* than eighty-five students! However, a few rather small high schools are to be found in nearly all parts of the nation. (*Note:* the trend is toward reorganizing them into larger units; in Iowa in 1964, for instance, there were but 500 separate high schools, but the median enrollment was 120 students.)

One may wonder how the one business teacher commonly found in such schools can possibly do well the task of teaching all the different business subjects that are or seemingly should be offered in the high school. However, frequently the work of that one business teacher is looked upon by the community as being a major contribution of its high school.

The standards of vocational proficiency reached by students in certain technical subjects may be relatively limited as compared with the achievements of students in those schools which are able to provide more specialized vocational curriculums. Yet these business subjects often provide the *only* readily marketable education that the smaller school has to offer its students—and thus become quite important for that school and community.

Also, it must be remembered that in the small high school the business teacher has a *much* better opportunity to become personally acquainted with individual students, their backgrounds, their abilities, their needs, and their hopes and ambitions. It must be remembered that usually it is the personal characteristics of the individual *as a person* that count most heavily in his future success. Thus frequently the business teacher in the small high school is able to prepare students who, though somewhat inferior in certain aspects of technical and skill development, have actually acquired a relatively superior type of personal development and ambition which enables them to compete successfully in the business world.

The Business Teacher in the Larger High School

As soon as a high school becomes sufficiently large to require the services of two business teachers instead of one, each teacher tends to specialize in some major area of the work. Thus in a two-business-teacher high school, one teacher is likely to teach mostly subjects such as typewriting, shorthand, and secretarial training, while the other one teaches subjects such as general business, bookkeeping, business law, or distributive education.

As the size of the staff increases, the scope of the subject offerings also tends to expand and the degree of specialization of each teacher to become more in evidence. Thus the business teacher in the larger high schools customarily becomes quite specialized in one or more subjects, *i.e.*, bookkeeping, retailing, general business, typewriting, secretarial subjects, and so on (further details appear in Chapter Two).

Accordingly, one who plans for a professional career as a business teacher in a large high school, or in a high school of commerce in a metropolitan area, should give special consideration to the following factors in his career planning:

1. Sound undergraduate preparation including broad general education and also a broad base of business education on which to build special preparation later

2. The necessity for a master's degree or equivalent graduate study, including additional preparation in the chosen specialized area of business education

3. The need for realistic, actual (paid) business experience in preparation for the career desired (Usually it is safe to estimate that this should be about one year of full-time business experience or its equivalent. Customarily greater importance is attached to such experience when it is secured under competent college supervision.)

4. The frequent requirement that other teaching experience be gained prior to entering a more specialized position in the larger high school (This often has the effect of causing business teachers to start their careers in smaller one-business-teacher high schools.)

5. Taking advantage of every possible opportunity to develop personal leadership abilities

In return for this special preparation, the position of business teacher in a larger high school customarily offers superior rewards in terms of salary, security, and living conditions.

The Business Teacher in Post-High-School Work

For most of us the smaller high school offers a real opportunity for acquiring early experience in a setting where we can fully understand the many facets of education at work. Moreover it offers us much in the way of opportunity for personal development through assuming broader school and community responsibilities. For some business teachers it provides a most satisfying permanent career.

Yet for most business teachers the challenge and appeal of a career in a larger high school in due time becomes even more attractive. Often the same can be said about the career opportunities offered by junior colleges, community colleges, four-year colleges, business colleges, and other forms of post-high-school education.

Thus the business teacher should be fully aware of the many opportunities that eventually will unfold for him. Certainly he has an unusually wide selection of possible careers within the field of business education from which to choose. To this, of course, may be added an even wider variety of potential careers of comparable nature in the business world itself should later experience indicate the wisdom of making the change away from the teaching profession.

It must be recognized that success in most of these post-high-school careers in the field of business education requires much special preparation. The master's degree customarily is the minimum educational requirement, and today we find many business teachers employed in high-school and college positions who hold the doctor's degree.

Because of the great encouragement provided by the federal government in the Vocational Education Act of 1963, for instance, a very rapid growth in the number of "area vocational schools" may be anticipated. Since this same congressional act specifically includes "business and office" occupations *for the first time* among the federally recognized "vocational" fields, well-qualified business teachers will be in great demand in these new area schools.

Adult and Evening Classes

Contrary to popular notions, education does not stop with the granting of a diploma or a college degree. In recognition of this, modern society is now providing many means of assisting individuals to secure this needed additional education. Evening classes, adult classes, forums, extension classes, and clinics of many varieties are to be found in abundance today throughout most parts of the nation.

The business teacher perhaps has greater opportunity to participate in these forms of education than has any other teacher. Even in the smallest communities evening classes, when offered, customarily include such subjects as typewriting, shorthand, and bookkeeping. Usually a demand exists for many other special courses for local citizens and business people, and is dormant only because a qualified instructor is not available. The list of special adult and evening classes offered in larger cities sometimes includes thirty or more separate subjects in the field of business education.

Often these special forms of additional education provide real opportunities attractive to the business teacher owing to factors such as these:

1. Substantial extra pay usually is received for the work involved.
2. Valuable experience is gained in working with adults.
3. The business teacher gains a better insight into the business education activities and needs of adults in his community.
4. The work and abilities of the business teacher become more widely known and respected among the parents and citizens of the community, with resulting high prestige for the business teacher and for business education.
5. In many cases the business teacher thereby has an opportunity to continue serving and improving the vocational abilities of his pupils who have graduated from school, resulting in greater pride in his work and in his product.
6. Not infrequently the contacts made with these adults in evening classes aid materially in the placement of students on suitable jobs in the future. (Such contacts have been known to assist the teacher, also, in securing summer or permanent employment in the business world!)

Whenever possible, the student preparing to become a business teacher should include in his program of studies appropriate preparation for organizing and teaching adult and evening classes. Frequently these classes require the use of special materials and methods adapted to shorter courses and to adult students.

Acquiring Professional Stature

Teaching is today considered one of the world's important professions. As is true of other professions, within the teaching profession there exist various levels of professional attainment and various areas of professional work. Within each area of work, such as business education, an important part of the satisfaction derived by the professional worker is evidenced by his level of professional attainment, or his stature within the profession.

Acquiring a certificate as a business teacher actually constitutes admission into the teaching profession. In most states two or more types, or levels, of certification are available to business teachers. Thus, one type of certificate may be granted on the basis of the bachelor's degree with appropriate professional education, but a higher-level certificate may be granted on the basis of the master's degree or thirty semester hours of graduate credit, satisfactory teaching experience, or other considerations. It appears, then, that one route by which the business teacher may advance to a higher standing in his profession is through the securing of appropriate graduate credit. This method is recognized and used almost universally.

But of perhaps even greater importance to the teacher in terms of personal satisfaction, prestige, and promotions is the attainment of *professional stature* through participation and work within the teaching profession itself. It is assumed, of course, that basic to this is a "job well done" at all times in the classroom. But for true professional success it is equally important that the teacher join hands with others in the profession in constantly guarding and improving the work and standards of the profession.

Here in America it is proper and fitting that such professional associations be democratically formed on a completely voluntary basis, and that has become customary in all professions. Thus, here in the United States members of the teaching profession have voluntarily joined together into one national association known as the National Education Association (NEA); every teacher in the nation is eligible for membership in this professional association which has been in existence over a century and now numbers around a million members.

Professional Stature for the Business Teacher

There are many, many opportunities for the business teacher to profit from and gain stature in his profession, and we can only briefly indicate a few of them here. For an average voluntary outlay of but two or three dollars per month (far less than the common laborer often pays in union dues in order to work at his trade!) the business teacher may belong to his own local, state, regional, and national professional associations and attend and participate in their many conferences and conventions, and have his own monthly, quarterly, and special professional magazines and bulletins currently on his desk. This is where he needs them and where he will *use* them.

Of special importance to business teachers is their own *department* in the NEA, the National Business Education Association. The NBEA has a full-time executive director and staff working in

Washington, D.C. on behalf of business education throughout the nation. It provides many services to business teachers, including typewriting tests, monthly and quarterly and special professional magazines, regional representative assemblies, National Business Entrance Tests, and awards and certificates. It also is sponsor of the national organization Future Business Leaders of America with chapters located throughout the nation. Most state business education associations are affiliates of NBEA.

Business education students preparing to become business teachers should take advantage of the opportunity offered them by most of their professional associations to secure student membership at half price. For instance, two years of student comprehensive membership in the NBEA would, at low cost, provide a professional library of sixteen issues of the *Business Education Forum,* eight or more issues of the *National Business Education Quarterly,* and two issues of the *American Business Education Yearbook.* In addition there would be the satisfaction of a two-year history of professional membership plus opportunities of attending conventions and other professional meetings.

It should not be inferred that professional membership alone will result in recognized professional stature; such is not the case. However, if one will systematically read the professional literature that such memberships bring to him he will be assured of "keeping up" with his profession and thus of being in a good position to attain the desired stature. To this should be added attendance at conventions and meetings held by his professional associations, with active participation in discussions, programs, and forums whenever opportunity is presented.

Perhaps the following list of suggestions will be found helpful as a guide in better preparing for real achievement in the teaching profession as a business teacher:

1. Maintain your professional memberships, always; start early. This should include at least the NEA, NBEA, your state education association and state business education association, your local association if there is one, and the American Vocational Association (AVA) if you are to teach vocational aspects of business education.
   (*Note:* NBEA membership automatically includes state and regional association membership in all regions.)

2. Subscribe for one or two good professional business education monthly magazines in addition to your association literature.

3. Systematically read the literature that reaches you relative to your profession.

4. Attend *and participate* in the professional conferences, forums, and conventions that are available to you.

5. When you feel that you have achieved notably in your teaching efforts, or that you have an especially valuable idea for the teaching profession, share it with others in the profession by submitting it in written form for publication.

6. Acquire recent and appropriate business experience.

7. Continue working to meet requirements for any advance-level certification that may remain available to you; among other things, this normally includes graduate study.

8. Continue your *personal* development as an individual; this may well include participation in and acceptance of leadership responsibilities in your local community civic groups.

Future Career Possibilities

No one is competent to completely and accurately predict the future. It is true that many excellent careers were available a generation ago that no longer exist. Rapid changes are to be expected during the next generation, and, of course, career opportunities likewise will change. However, the well-prepared business education student would seem to have unusual assurance of excellent and dependable, career opportunities of many varieties during his lifetime; he has basic preparation for two of the major fields of endeavor known to mankind, the education profession and the business world.

In the field of education all indications point toward a continuous scarcity of personnel eligible for professional certification at least through 1970—and probably for many more years thereafter. One has only to glance at the recent acceleration of our increase in population to know that a tremendous task faces the teaching profession, for we are not going to deny our youth the advantages of a good education.

Moreover it should be recognized that our high schools even today are increasing in size rapidly; this means greater opportunities for more of the special curriculums such as those provided by business education. It likewise means relatively greater opportunities for business teachers to teach only their major area of specialization. And as the years go by the tendency definitely is for a greater percentage of youth to secure post-high-school education, which already is directing attention to the coming need for more teachers with the advanced preparation needed for teaching in these post-high-school positions—a tendency which will continue to give the business teacher excellent opportunities for ever-expanding and growing careers in the teaching profession.

Finally, it must be remembered that our entire American economy is primarily a *business* economy. So long as we remain dedicated to the philosophy of democracy and freedom and respect for the individual we are going to maintain our American system of free competitive enterprise based on property rights and the profit motive; and that is the other major field of endeavor into which the business education teacher stands constantly ready to enter. Its opportunities likewise appear relatively unlimited.

Projects and Questions for Discussion

1. Investigate and report on the size, organization, and services of the National Education Association.

2. Prepare a chart or an outline showing the regions, divisions, and services of the National Business Education Association.

3. Secure the names and locations of the officers of your own state business education association, and report on the services of this association. Is it affiliated with NBEA? With AVA?

4. Investigate and report on the number and locations of FBLA and DECA chapters in your own state.

5. Prepare a display of current professional publications of special interest to business teachers.

6. Investigate and report on the services offered by your own State Department of Public Instruction for business education.

7. "A good business education teacher should have sufficient breadth of training to teach any business subject. For this reason all prospective business teachers should be required to be qualified to teach shorthand as well as basic business subjects." Do you agree or disagree? What problems are connected with the points raised in the statement?

8. A state legislature recently passed a law requiring all students graduating from high school in that state to complete two units of foreign language; two units of history; three units of English; two units of science; and two units of mathematics. The typical high school requires sixteen units for graduation. Thus, the above law would permit students to have approximately four units of electives. Do you believe this law is a good one? Why or why not?

9. The coming years will find that schools are faced with increased enrollments and a shortage of qualified teachers. What are some of the practical things that a business teacher can do to overcome some of the problems he will face in this situation?

10. A teacher stated, "Why should I go to the trouble of starting a business club in my high school—I have all I can do now in preparing my lessons properly and teaching well the classes to which I am assigned. If I sponsor a business club for my students then surely my classroom teaching will suffer." Does this teacher have a valid argument?

11. Two teachers are discussing the relative merits of professional organizations for teachers *vs.* the merits of the American Federation of Teachers which is affiliated with the American Federation of Labor. One teacher believes that teachers will obtain more benefits from a professional organization while the other favors the teachers union. What are your points of view concerning the relative merits of the two types of organization for teachers?

12. A superintendent of schools has stated: "I will never employ a beginning teacher; the poorest teaching is done during the first two years of teaching. A teacher really comes into his own after he has obtained several years experience." Do you believe this to be true? Why or why not?

Case Problems

1. William Lloyd, a beginning business teacher, was employed for the coming year in Harlin high school. Prior to accepting the position he was informed by the superintendent of schools that he would be assigned to teach only business subjects. Lloyd was quite happy with this arrangement as he did not wish to teach outside his major field even though he was theoretically qualified to do so because he had a minor in sociology.

When Lloyd reported to his school in the fall he found that (without his knowledge) he had been assigned to teach a class in Social Problems, a senior sociology course. He talked with the superintendent and reminded him of his statement during the employment interview that he would not be required to teach outside his major field. The superintendent regretted that he had to assign Lloyd to the Social Problems class but scheduling difficulties made this necessary.

Lloyd feels that he is being treated unfairly and his sense of justice tells him that he should resign in protest. Discuss the pros and cons of this situation.

2. John Samson, an undergraduate business education major in a teachers college, has just had a conference with his faculty adviser. The adviser has been concerned with John's grade-point average which is just above the minimum required by the college for graduation. John is a student with above-average ability, but his grades do not reflect his ability because of his interest and participation in extracurricular activities at the college. Time spent in these activities has been taken away from his studies.

John tells his adviser that he is not too concerned about his grades because he feels that it is important for a teacher to be able to get along well with people and that his extracurricular activities are helping him greatly in this respect. "It is just as important," says John, "for a prospective teacher to have a solid social background as it is to have a solid academic background." Do you believe John is correct? What are all of the factors to consider in this case?

3. Harold Swanson is a student in a methods course concerned with specific methods of teaching business subjects. Harold feels quite bitter about the professional education courses which he has had to take as a part of the requirements for graduation. He expresses the point of view in class that he would be much better off if he were permitted to take more specialized courses in business rather than the fifteen semester hours he has been required to take in educational psychology, introduction to education, and problems in education.

Although he does not say so there is the implication that he also includes the professional business education courses in this category. He feels that these courses have been a waste of time and are too impractical. Is Harold right? What arguments could you give in support of his point of view? What arguments could you present in contradiction?

4. Mr. James Sloan is a beginning business teacher in the town of Van Horne, population 4,000. One day during the noon hour while lunching with a colleague he complains bitterly about the community and the townspeople in the community. Mr. Sloan's complaints center about the coolness of the townspeople toward the teachers in the school.

School has been in session about two months and not once have people in the community taken the trouble to invite him into their homes or even bothered to introduce themselves to him. Mr. Sloan feels that since he is a newcomer to the community it is proper etiquette for the townspeople to make the overtures toward making him feel a member of the community. He believes that it is not up to him to make any effort to become better acquainted.

Should be continue to wait or should he take the initiative in becoming acquainted? If he does take the intiative will he not be considered too forward? Perhaps he is right—the townspeople are cold and unfeeling and perhaps he should leave this community at his earliest opportunity. What do you think?

Suggested Readings

Blanford, James T., "Some Problems of Beginning Teachers," *Journal of Business Education,* January, 1953.

Douglas, Lloyd V., ed., *The Business Education Program in the Expanding Secondary School,* NBEA, 1957. *Note:* also a bulletin of the NASSP.

Herndon, Frank M., "A Career in Teaching the Business Subjects," *Business Education Forum,* January, 1964, p. 7.

Kessel, Robert M., "The Critical Requirements for Secondary School Business Teachers Based on an Analysis of Critical Incidents," *DPE Journal,* September, 1959. The 1958 DPE Research Award Study.

Muse, Paul F., "Dare We Be Professional?" *Business Education Forum,* January, 1964, p. 1.

———, "Work, What Is It?" *Business Education Forum,* October, 1963, p. 1. Editorial.

"National: Know the NBEA Publications and Meet the NBEA Editors," *Business Education Forum,* March, 1963, pp. 28-30.

"NAVBE Is New Division of NBEA," *Business Education Forum* (March 1964), p. 27. *National News.*

Olson, Milton C., "Encouraging Professional Growth," *National Business Education Quarterly,* May, 1962, pp. 54-59.

Policies Commission for Business and Economic Education, "Business Education for the College Bound Student," *Business Education Forum,* May, 1964, pp. 21-22.

Robek, Mary F., "Cause and Cure of Business Teacher Obsolescence," *Business Education Forum,* February, 1964, p. 16.

Rosenberg, R. Robert, "Ask Yourself: How Do I Rate as a Teacher?" *Business Education World,* February, 1964, pp. 24-25.

Thistlethwaite, Robert L., "To Beginning Teachers—Some Words of Counsel, Caution, and Encouragement," *Business Education Forum,* March, 1963, p. 17.

2

The Business Education Curriculums

The business teacher works mostly within the framework of an organized educational group, usually the high school. His objectives form a part of the objectives of the high school itself. At the same time, he must achieve these objectives through a planned organization of his own area of work within the school. Frequently this planned organization of the work of business education in a school system is referred to as the *business education curriculum* or the *business education curriculums;*[1] it will vary from school to school with varying needs, objectives, facilities, and desires of the various communities being served. Since methods of instruction used by the business teacher will be materially influenced by (*a*) the objectives of the school and curriculum within which he teaches and

---

[1] The term *business education* quite commonly is used in preference to the term *business* (alone) in order to avoid confusion with the function of caring for the business transactions of the school itself. Thus a school may have a "business office" which is quite apart from the instructional department performing the function of "business education."

by (*b*) that phase of the curriculum in which he is teaching at any given time, it is the purpose of this chapter to present some of the curriculum settings that the business teacher is likely to encounter. The best curriculum is the one that has been intelligently planned to meet the needs of a specific school and community; there is no one curriculum that is "best" for all schools. Yet intelligent planning must be based on knowledge of the experience of others. In order to succeed in his professional work as a teacher the business teacher must be prepared to offer constructive advice and suggestions relative to the organizational plan within which he is to work.

The Goals of Secondary Education

The field of work of the business teacher extends from the junior high school through the senior high school, the junior college, various types of adult and post-high-school work, and college and university and post-college education. However, we are most concerned here with teaching students of the adolescent age; in general this encompasses grades seven through fourteen, commonly known as *secondary education.* The major portion of the work of the business teacher with which we are here concerned is to be found in grades nine through twelve in our American education system. Thus, it is appropriate that we briefly review the main objectives or goals of secondary education, of which business education forms a part.

A relatively brief yet practical and authoritative statement bearing on this question is to be found in the *Ten Imperative Needs of Youth,* as set forth by the National Association of Secondary School Principals in *Planning for American Youth.*[2] Actually these ten "imperative needs" are a portion of this NASSP summary of *Education for All American Youth,*[3] a publication of the Educational Policies Commission of the NEA. The business teacher will do well to keep these ten imperative needs in mind as a background and framework within which to pursue his professional career.

---

[2] *Planning for American Youth, An Educational Program for Youth of Secondary School Age* (Washington, D.C.: National Association of Secondary School Principals, 1944), p. 43.

[3] Educational Policies Commission, *Education for All American Youth,* (Washington, D.C.: National Education Association, 1944).

Ten Imperative Needs
of Youth of Secondary-School Age

1. All youth need to develop salable skills and those understandings and attitudes that make the worker an intelligent and productive participant in economic life. To this end, most youth need supervised work experience as well as education in the skills and knowledge of their occupations.
2. All youth need to develop and maintain good health and physical fitness.
3. All youth need to understand the rights and duties of the citizen of a democratic society, and to be diligent and competent in the performance of their obligations as members of the community and citizens of the state and nation.
4. All youth need to understand the significance of the family for the individual and society and the conditions conducive to successful family life.
5. All youth need to know how to purchase and use goods and services intelligently, understanding both the values received by the consumer and the economic consequences of their acts.
6. All youth need to understand the methods of science, the influence of science on human life, and the main scientific facts concerning the nature of the world and of man.
7. All youth need opportunities to develop their capacities to appreciate beauty in literature, art, music, and nature.
8. All youth need to be able to use their leisure time well and to budget it wisely, balancing activities that yield satisfactions to the individual with those that are socially useful.
9. All youth need to develop respect for other persons, to grow in their insight into ethical values and principles, and to be able to live and work cooperatively with others.
10. All youth need to grow in their ability to think rationally, to express their thoughts clearly, and to read and listen with understanding.

Although many books and articles have been written in attempts to clearly explain the goals of secondary education, we believe that no better or clearer guide can be found for the business teacher than these ten "imperative needs" set forth by our Educational Policies Commission of the NEA and by the principals of our American secondary schools through their own NASSP. It is urged that

they be studied carefully and thoughtfully for the purpose of helping to identify readily those phases of business education which
may well contribute to some, several, or all of these needs of youth.

The Broad Field of Business Education

Business education is but one of the many areas into which the
entire secondary-school program is divided in our efforts to plan
suitable media through which to achieve our American educational
goals. The final success of our entire secondary program must be
measured in terms of accomplishments for each individual student,
and we must never overlook the fact that usually every departmental
area of the secondary school is actively contributing, in varying
degrees, to the educational development of each individual student.

Thus, the business teacher who is concerned especially about the
education of certain young people who profess a special interest in
the business subjects must always realize that the entire school
faculty is endeavoring to assist him, each in his own special sphere
of work—the speech teacher is employing his specialized ability to
help improve the speech habits of this business student; the English
teacher is doing the same for his English habits; the physical education teacher for his health habits; the social studies teacher for his
citizenship habits; the science teacher for his understanding of "the
influence of science on human life"; the music and art teachers for
his appreciation of the beauties of his heritage; and so forth throughout the entire school faculty. Hence, instead of attempting to *himself* achieve for his students the entire gamut of educational goals,
the successful business teacher concentrates major attention on those
objectives which he is best prepared to assist the student to reach—
although always being careful to also do his best to help assist and
reinforce the work of his fellow teachers in their efforts to help this
same student achieve other "imperative needs." Thus the major objectives of business education are most appropriately stated in terms
of, and limited to, the special work of the business teacher.

Perhaps it should be pointed out, too, that likewise each of the
other members of the school faculty must necessarily depend to
some extent upon the business teacher for assistance in completing
the education of students who may profess greatest interest in educational areas other than business education. Thus, the typewriting
teacher may furnish the would-be author or journalist with a skill

invaluable to his future career, and through various business classes the business teacher may well provide all youth with business knowledges, skills, and understandings invaluable to them as future homeowners, consumers, parents, and citizens exercising their voting responsibilities in our American free-enterprise economy.

Thus all business education endeavor may best be first broadly divided into two classes of goals or general objectives, namely, *vocational education* and nonvocational or *general education*.

Vocational business education has been defined as "a program of education which equips the student with the marketable skills, knowledges, and attitudes needed for initial employment and advancement in business occupations." [4] *General business education,* on the other hand, "provides the student with information and competencies which are needed by all, in managing personal business affairs and in using the services of the business world." [5] The goals in vocational business education include the coverage of such areas as:

1. Stenographic and secretarial work
2. Bookkeeping, accounting, and data-processing work
3. Clerical and general office work
4. Distributive education and store work
5. Business-management and ownership responsibilities

The goals in general business education include:

1. Consumer information, guidance, and education
2. Business understanding for management of personal business affairs
3. Business and economic understanding for intelligent citizenship
4. Common business skills for personal use

The Basic Twofold Classification

It is important that the business teacher and the school administrator fully recognize the existence and importance of these two main classifications of business education, the *vocational* and the *general*. Too frequently there is a tendency to think of business education wholly in terms of its vocational significance and goals, a view-

---

[4] *Definitions of Terms in Vocational and Practical Arts Education* (Washington 5, D.C.: American Vocational Association, 1954), p. 7.
[5] *Ibid.*

point which limits the value of business education to only that portion of youth who evidence interest and/or aptitudes for employment and potential careers in the world of business. Better methods of instruction might be adopted were it fully recognized that certain portions of the business education program in the secondary school are of vital significance in providing for the "imperative needs" of *all* youth aside from the need for vocational or occupational preparation.

Perhaps this concept of the twofold classification will become clearer if we take time for a look at some of the outstanding characteristics of each classification.

Characteristics of Vocational Business Education

1. It usually encompasses a series or sequence of related courses and subjects extending through two or more years of the secondary school and culminating at or near the time of graduation.

2. This series of courses or subjects usually constitutes a fairly well-defined separate pattern for each of the four main employment areas of business education, *i.e.*, the stenographic,[6] the bookkeeping, the clerical, and the distributive areas, although the pattern may vary somewhat from school to school. Each often is referred to as a *curriculum*.

3. It properly is provided for only a portion of youth of secondary-school age, appropriately selected on the basis of such criteria as aptitudes, interest, and ability.

4. Final measurement and grading of the student should be based heavily (and possibly totally) on the student's ability to meet employment standards of the business world.

5. Although by no means slighting more intangible mental understandings and abilities, instructional methods must be adapted to the extra task of also developing ability "to do" in terms of marketable skills and abilities and applied knowledges.

------

[6] Since most high-school graduates enter stenographic work, as distinguished from secretarial work, the term *secretarial* is best reserved to describe post-high-school education in this area.

Characteristics of General Business Education

1. The various elements usually may be adequately learned through the media of *individual* business subjects and courses.
2. Thus, there usually is no separate curriculum recognized as pertinent to the achievement of this objective of business education.
3. It properly is so arranged as to provide for *all* youth of secondary age.
4. Final measurement and grading of the student may properly be based heavily (and possibly totally) on the extent to which the individual student has profited from the course or subject in accordance with his individual abilities and needs.
5. With the exception of the area of personal-use skill, instructional methods devote major attention to the development of understandings and knowledges as differentiated from marketable skills, abilities, and applied knowledges.

A comparison of these five major characteristics for each of the two classifications of business education purposes, or goals, seems to clearly indicate that the successful business teacher needs to know in which area his endeavors are being focused at any given time, and to adapt his instructional procedures and evaluations accordingly.

General Objectives of Business Education

It is not enough that we get an overview of the nature of business education, such as that presented in the preceding portion of this chapter; we also need to look at it from another viewpoint, namely, that of the purposes it hopes to accomplish. It is true that a classification of the types of business education has inherent in it considerable connotation as to its purposes; yet educators find it also helps them to better guide their instructional activities if they carefully analyze and state the major purposes or objectives of the work they are doing.

In preparing a list of such objectives we must keep in mind that they are not intended to apply to only one subject or course but to the entire field of business education. Other statements of objectives, more specific in nature, ordinarily are prepared for each of the separate business subjects and courses.

The following list of eight general objectives for all business education was worked out after much discussion by a representative committee of Iowa business teachers and is used as a guide by business teachers and school administrators in the state of Iowa:

1. To provide for *all students* exploratory opportunities and introductory information relating to business.
2. To assist in developing occupational intelligence on the part of *all students*.
3. To develop the ability to choose discriminatingly and to use wisely all goods and services which business has to offer.
4. To develop in a practical way an understanding and appreciation of the functioning of our economic system.
5. To enable students to acquire certain knowledges and skills in business subjects for personal use.
6. To prepare students to handle business activities common to many professional, commercial, industrial, agricultural, service, and homemaking activities.
7. To prepare students to enter and succeed in a business occupation as a beginner who expects to follow business as a career.
8. To prepare students for more effective study in the field of business beyond the secondary level.[7]

To assist Iowa business teachers and others in fixing these eight objectives in mind, they are identified by these eight descriptive words or phrases:

Exploratory	Occupational intelligence
Consumer education	Economic understanding
Personal use	Semivocational
Vocational	College preparatory

It is to be recognized that some educators would question the wisdom of including "college preparatory" among the objectives of business education. Traditionally business subjects have not been included in recommended college-preparatory courses; however, research evidence strongly indicates that this discrimination is unwarranted. Success in college definitely is not dependent upon any

---

[7] *Business Education—Secondary Schools,* Iowa Secondary School Cooperative Curriculum Program, Volume XII (Des Moines, Iowa: Department of Public Instruction, 1950), p. 17.

particular pattern of subject-matter studied in the secondary school. Moreover, today's relatively large enrollments of college students in the fields of business, commerce, and business education indicate a distinct need for having many high-school students include business subjects as a part of their college-preparatory work. Today the college or university is indeed rare that will not permit a reasonable number of business subjects to be included as acceptable college-preparatory work completed in high school.

Many business education handbooks and guides have been prepared for use in various states and cities and, in one form or another, they all set forth statements of the main goals or objectives of business education. Usually the objectives stated are to be found in the eight concepts presented by the Iowa business teachers. As a further illustration, here are eight objectives of business education as prepared by a committee of South Dakota business teachers, working under the joint sponsorship of their State Department of Public Instruction and the University of South Dakota:

1. To give all students a background of information relating to business.
2. To develop an understanding and appreciation of the functioning of our economic system.
3. To develop personality for effective human relations in society and in business.
4. To assist students to use goods and services for intelligent consumer activity.
5. To enable students to acquire certain knowledge and skills in the business subjects for personal and semivocational use.
6. To help students acquire occupational intelligence and explore the requirements of specific business occupations.
7. To assist students to acquire *marketable* skills sufficient for the initial position, and with understanding of means of growing in vocational competency after employment.
8. To give students background for study in business beyond the secondary schools.[8]

The High-School Program

In America the local school district is rather proud and a bit jealous of its right to determine its own offerings. Frequently states do require schools within their respective borders to teach specified

---

[8] *A Handbook in Business Education for South Dakota,* Bulletin No. 61 (Pierre, South Dakota: State Department of Public Instruction, 1953), p. 3.

subjects, but this requirement usually is very limited in scope. As a result the offerings and the requirements of high schools vary widely from state to state and from district to district.

At the same time, however, there always is the factor of current educational leadership at work tending to establish a degree of uniformity since we all do look to recognized leaders for guidance. One may outline certain characteristics of the high-school offerings throughout the nation today with reasonable assurance that the deviations therefrom by the individual high school will seldom be great. The beginning teacher must realize, though, that the school in which he secures his first teaching position will not necessarily fit the pattern that such an outline suggests. Nevertheless, it is helpful to refer to a somewhat typical pattern in our endeavor to better understand how the business education curriculums may best fit into and become a part of the comprehensive high-school offerings.

One standard that is recognized nation-wide is that high-school graduation requires of the student the successful completion of sixteen Carnegie units of education. A Carnegie unit is represented by one full-time subject pursued throughout the entire school year of nine months. Thus if the student carries four subjects each year he will earn four units each year or the total of sixteen required for graduation by the end of four years in high school.

It is not unusual for a given high school to specify the content, or subject-matter, of which a sizable portion of these units *must* be composed in the case of each individual student. These contents, or subjects, often are referred to as *constants* or *required subjects.* Thus in a high school having a typical subject curriculum[9] it is relatively common to find the requirement of three or four units of English, three or four of social studies, one or two of mathematics, and one or two of science. Obviously this uses from eight to twelve of the sixteen units, leaving only four to eight of the units available for all other studies. Such requirements may, of course, severely restrict the amount and kind of business education that may be offered in those schools.

In practice, these required subjects would be distributed in a specified manner over the four years of high school. Thus we might find the *required* units to be as follows:

---

[9] Similar situations would exist in schools using fused, correlated, broad-fields, core, and experience curriculums although a different terminology would be in use.

9th grade	*10th grade*	*11th grade*	*12th grade*
English	English	English	Social Studies
Social Studies	Social Studies		
Mathematics	Science		

Only eight units are specifically required in the above illustration, leaving eight for "electives" to be distributed one in each of the first two years and three in each of the last two years; frequently fewer than eight units remain as electives.

It must be remembered that these eight "elective" units must now be made to serve the needs of the student for *all* other subjects, including homemaking, industrial arts, business education, foreign language, art, music, agriculture, and many others that might be mentioned! Obviously the number of units that students may justifiably use for business education is likely to be considerably less than eight; perhaps a *maximum* of four or five units would be about right for most high schools. This will vary considerably with the needs of the students and the community and the size of the high school.

It should be observed that *most* of the elective work will come during the last two years of high school. This is especially favorable to vocational education since it should be completed as near as possible to the time at which it will be put into use.

The Small High School

A high school that is considered small in some parts of the nation would be considered large in other parts. In the more densely populated urban sections a high school enrolling but 500 to 600 students might be considered small, whereas in the sparsely populated rural states in the plains of the Midwest some high schools may have less than 100 students enrolled. In some of these states only from one-fourth to one-third of the high schools will have more than 100 students; enrollments of less than 40 may still be found.[10]

It seems obvious that the very small high school must limit its offerings to relatively unspecialized areas of instruction that may seem appropriate for all or nearly all of its students. This means that students in those schools will have little if any choice of preparation

---

[10] Rapidly increasing population coupled with a current desire to improve administrative efficiency of school districts is causing the size of all high schools to rise rather rapidly, however.

in the areas of vocational education; in fact, true vocational education does not exist in any form in many of these high schools. When the student body and the teaching staff are so small that all (or nearly all) students *must* study whatever subjects are offered, the problem of program planning becomes an important one for the school administrator; he must choose carefully and wisely the few subjects to be offered.

Therefore, it may be unwise (and practically impossible) to include business education courses that would permit students to secure vocational preparation for either the stenographic, the clerical, the distributive, or the bookkeeping field. In fact, it is doubtful that complete vocational preparation can be justifiably offered in any one of these areas of business education, since to do so might easily force *all* high-school students to prepare for this one field of employment. Certainly it would be unwise, for instance, to construct a high-school program that would, in effect, require all students to study shorthand!

On the other hand, in order to meet the "imperative needs" of its students as well as possible such a school might very well feel justified in including general business, typewriting, and consumer education in its program; these courses or subjects contain information and objectives that *should* be a part of the high-school education of *all* youth. Thus for the very small school we might have this situation:

Minimum Basic Business Education Program
(General Education)

General Business (one or two semesters in 9th or 10th grade)
Typewriting (one or two semesters; any grade desired)
Consumer Education (one or two semesters in 11th or 12th grade)

These three business subjects can hardly be said to constitute a business education curriculum; rather, they constitute a basic offering in the field of business education of a type that every high-school youth may well include in his general education. Probably these three subjects (or subjects of comparable materials offered under other names) should be a starting point of minimum business education to be included in the program of every American high school.

Vocational Curriculums in the Small High Schools? As already indicated, it is questionable whether the smaller high schools can and should attempt true vocational education; the exact answer must depend on the individual school situation—its size and purposes, and the needs of the community and young people it serves. However, there are innumerable reasons why such schools do wish to do "the best they can" at providing vocational preparation for their students, and as a result we typically do find them offering some type of education best classified as vocational. (In many cases the *name* of the subject or course offering would imply a vocational objective, but checking into the local objectives and procedures used would indicate an uncertainty in the minds of the teachers, and the school administrators which probably results in hazy, fluctuating, multiple-purpose objectives. This situation is not likely to result in effective teaching and learning.)

We must remember, though, that in America the local school district has final control over the offerings of its own school. Thus the business teacher, although cognizant of the difficulties of attempting vocational business education in the small school, should not take it upon himself to try to dictate the policies of the school. Rather, if some form of vocational business education is desired, he should strive to use his very best judgment in recommending that which will best serve the needs of his pupils and of his community. This should be based on the best *factual* information obtainable, both as to the accepted or recommended curriculum practices and as to the needs of his community and pupils.[11]

Obviously the choice must be one or more of the main employment areas of business; these customarily are referred to as the *stenographic,* the *clerical,* the *bookkeeping,* and the *distributive education* fields or curriculums. Space in this chapter does not permit discussion of the relative values of each for the smaller high school, and the reasons therefore. It may be pointed out, however, that the two areas in which the *largest numbers* of high-school graduates constantly find employment throughout the nation are general office work (clerical, filing, typewriting, and simple record keeping) and work in stores (selling, wrapping, delivering, stock work, and similar

---

[11] It is not within the province of this book to discuss methods of obtaining such facts, but it is pointed out that many colleges offer excellent graduate work in business education and are prepared to assist business teachers in answering such questions. Appropriate research either has found or can find most of the needed answers.

beginning duties). Both boys and girls are employed in each and both find careers in each.

Business Education in a Medium-Size City

Although local community and school history, needs, philosophy, administration, and other influencing conditions will cause some variations among communities, it will be worth our time to briefly review the exact situation relative to business education offerings in at least one public high school in a city of medium size. Such a school offers opportunity for a reasonably diverse and complete offering in the various areas of business education. It would customarily maintain a relatively stable and relatively well-qualified staff of teachers and administrators, and thus it might be expected to more nearly approach a program of studies that would be educationally justifiable in terms of the needs of its students and its community. In all probability its administrators and its business teachers would be rather well informed about the local business needs and opportunities.

For illustrative purposes the public high school of Austin, Minnesota, may be chosen as such a school. Austin is a growing Midwestern city of around 30,000 population with customary diversified businesses and an important meat-packing industry. It maintains two three-year junior high schools, a three-year senior high school, and is the location of an area vocational technical school. A two-year junior college also is to be found in Austin; until August 1964, it was an integral part of the city public school system, but since then has become one of the Minnesota state-supported junior colleges.

For the 1964-1965 school year, the two junior high schools enrolled approximately 1,800 students, and the senior high school enrolled 1,700. A total of fifteen business teachers were employed in Austin, four of them in the junior college.

Table 2.1 gives an over-all picture of the "constants," or required subjects, as presented to the school's students and advisers for the 1964-1965 school year. The first opportunity for an "elective" subject (one subject) is offered in the ninth grade, but thereafter there is opportunity for at least two elective subjects each year.

The specific business subjects offered at Austin include these:

General Business. (One year, grade nine.) Students are handed the following information about this course:

This is a valuable course for every ninth grader. It is especially helpful for those students who plan to follow the business course in high school, but it also will help every student with business knowledges that he needs for everyday living. Every citizen needs to know about such things as methods of communication and transportation, income taxes, insurance, how to use the services of a bank, how to buy merchandise wisely, and how to budget and save money. All of these topics are studied in this course.[12]

Typewriting. (One year, grade ten, eleven, or twelve.) Students who plan to take shorthand in the eleventh grade are advised to take typewriting in the tenth grade.

Bookkeeping. (One year, grade eleven or twelve.) Students who follow the business course in high school are advised to include this course. Also, those who intend to follow a business course (Business Administration) in college are told that they should register for this course.

Shorthand I. (One year, grade eleven or twelve.) Typewriting must precede or accompany this course. Only students who have

TABLE 2.1

A Summary of Requirements by Grades, Austin, Minnesota 1964-1965

7th	*8th*	*9th*	*10th*	*11th*	*12th*
English	English	English	English	English	English
Social Studies	Social Studies	Civics	Amer. Hist.	World History	Social Studies
Mathematics	Mathematics	Mathematics			
Science & Reading	Science & Reading	Science			
Phys. Ed.	Phys. Ed.	Phys. Ed.	Phys. Ed.		
Shop or H. Econ.	Shop or H. Econ.				
Art & Music	Art & Music				
(No elective)	(No elective)	(1 elective)	(2 electives)	(2 electives)	(2 or 3 electives)

Note: Electives are available in speech, agriculture, mathematics, the sciences, Latin, German, Spanish, journalism, home economics, industrial arts, woodwork, carpentry, metals, auto mechanics, printing, nursing, music, and other subjects *as well as* the various business subjects.

Source: Charting Your Course, grades 9-10-11-12 (Austin, Minn.: Austin Public Schools, 1964-1965); pp. 7-8. Mimeographed guide to registration.

---

[12] *Charting Your Course,* grades 7-8-9, Austin, Minn.: Austin Public Schools, 1957-1958, p. 5. Mimeographed guide to registration.

made a "C" average in all subjects in the ninth and tenth grades ordinarily register for this subject; they also must have a good background in English and are expected to continue with Shorthand II and Secretarial Training.

Merchandising. (Also Part-Time Occupational Experience in Retail Selling. One year each, grade twelve.) Students taking merchandising also earn one credit for correlated work experience. Registration for this work is dependent upon advance approval by the distributive education coordinator.

Clerical Office Practice. (One year, grade twelve.) Typewriting is a prerequisite. This is for students who have not had shorthand, and includes mimeographing, duplicating, filing, comptometry and voice-writing as well as additional typewriting.

Shorthand II and Secretarial Training. (One year *each*, grade twelve.) A student cannot enroll in one course without the other. Prerequisites are Shorthand I and Typewriting. Two credits are given for the two courses. Secretarial Training includes transcribing, duplicating, voice-writing, filing, calculating machines, personal grooming, and personality development.

Office Occupations. (One year, grade twelve.) This is the part-time cooperative work-experience program for selected students enrolled in Shorthand II and Secretarial Training; applications for enrollment must be approved during the junior year by the office occupations coordinator. It will be observed that seniors *may* be given approval to register for five full-credit courses.

Economics. (One year, grade eleven or twelve.) This course includes the usual economic topics and concepts; however, it also places emphasis on practical, applied economics for everyday living, saving, investing, and making other economic decisions as consumers.

Occupational Relations. (One year, grade twelve.) This course is intended for the beginning worker, and students enrolled in it are placed on part-time jobs in local retail stores. They also must register at the same time for the course in Merchandising.

It should be pointed out that vocational business training, including secretarial training and merchandising, also is available as a part of the work in the Austin Junior College.

Thus, with a relatively simple listing of separate courses, we see that it *is possible* (although not required) for every student to elect to take a course in General Business and one in Economics and also to acquire ability in typewriting for his personal use. At the same time, there also is adequate provision for real vocational preparation in the major areas of job and career opportunities in business.

Vocational Curriculums in business education, although not "set" in the actual illustration just presented, nevertheless very definitely are observable to the experienced eye of a qualified adviser. Thus the ninth-grade student and his adviser *might* choose to outline in advance a proposed program similar to any of the following leading toward preparation for specific jobs and careers in business. (The "constants" already presented are omitted here.)

(Grade)	Stenographic Preparation	General Office Preparation	Distributive Education
9th	General Business	General Business	General Business
10th	Typewriting	Typewriting	Typewriting
11th	Shorthand I Bookkeeping	Economics Bookkeeping	Economics Bookkeeping
12th	Shorthand II Secretarial Training Office Occupations	Clerical Office Practice	Merchandising Occupational Relations

On the other hand, it is quite possible that the student may prefer to elect only a portion of the business subjects listed in one of these proposed programs, and to use a portion of his electives for some other course or courses that he and his adviser feel will be of more aid in achieving his special needs and goals. For instance, he might decide it will be best to take the Typewriting in grade eleven in order to elect Geometry, or Home Economics, or Auto Mechanics, or Biology, or some other subject in grade ten. For the *best* planning it is essential that the student constantly have good guidance. Today's schools are making distinct progress in the task of providing students with appropriate guidance aid.

Again, let us remember that the work of the business teacher in preparing students for intelligent use of the business world as consumers and citizens or for successful future employment and careers in various phases of business is but one small portion of the entire preparation of that student that is being cared for in the secondary school. It has been observed that perhaps three-fourths of the education given a business student while in high school—all of which is for the purpose of helping to equip him better for his own personally chosen future and career—is given by other teachers, each of whom is better equipped to perform his special function than would be the business teacher. Frequently the work of these teachers has more far-reaching effects on the success of the business education graduate than does the work of any one business teacher.

With this background of understanding of the characteristics of the business teacher of today (Chapter One) and of the characteristics and functions of the curriculums and programs of study with which he must work (Chapter Two), we are now ready to direct our attention to the actual process of teaching. Teaching has the purpose of complementing, fostering, and aiding the learning process. Thus we are now ready to deal with the learning process, and Chapter Three will take us directly into that as the business teacher finds it. This will be followed by a study of the basic teaching techniques commonly used by the business teacher.

Projects and Problems for Discussion

1. Investigate and report on any business education handbook or suggestions which may be distributed by your own State Department of Public Instruction.

2. Procure and report on the business education curriculums in one or more small, medium, and large high schools in your state.

3. Prepare appropriate bulletin boards to illustrate each of the five vocational education goals or areas outlined in this chapter.

4. Hold a panel discussion about the suitability of business subjects as a part of preparation for college.

5. Report on assigned or selected readings suggested at the end of this chapter.

6. Can you defend this statement: "Shorthand should not be taught in any school unless there is an opportunity in the community for the graduates to use this skill."

7. Your superintendent wishes to require all students in your high school to take typewriting. Would you deter him or encourage him? Why?

8. Develop the minimum program of business education you would recommend for a high school located in a rural area with an enrollment of 100 students. Defend your recommendations.

9. Do you believe that business education can contribute to the general education of students in the secondary school? In what way? Do you believe that it should?

10. What do you believe the future holds for the business education curriculum in the secondary school? Suggest possible subjects or ideas for the curriculum of 1975.

11. It has been said that the secondary school should not train students vocationally. This type of training can be done more efficiently and economically on the job. Can you agree with this idea? Why or why not?

12. The "personal use" objective is quite important in the minds of some business educators as an integral part of the present-day business education curriculum. What do you believe?

13. Should the preparation of business education students in the secondary school consist of preparing more for the distributive occupations than for the secretarial or general business? Defend your arguments.

Case Problems

1. Mr. Charles Coleman is a business teacher who has been teaching in the secondary schools for ten years. He is a superior teacher and has always been highly conscientious about his teaching. At present he is very discouraged about the future of business education in the secondary school. He believes that automation is going to play such an important role in the future that there is going to be little need for business teachers. He is convinced that bookkeeping, shorthand, and typewriting will all be eliminated and that machines will perform the work formerly done by people with these skills. He is considering leaving the teaching profession and seeking other types of employment that will have a more secure future. What advice do you have for Mr. Coleman?

2. Miss Jane Connoley is an enthusiastic and excellent business education teacher. Her main interest is in teaching shorthand, typewriting, and secretarial practice. Although she recognizes that general business and consumer education (among others) are classified as business education subjects, nevertheless she is convinced that the only valid objective for teaching business subjects in the secondary schools is for vocational use. Consequently she has stated publicly that unless a business subject can be justified on purely vocational grounds that subject has no place in the business curriculum. She refuses to recognize that general business or consumer education can be taught for other than vocational goals.

Miss Connoley is quite influential with the superintendent of schools and has convinced him she is right. She is advocating that the business curriculum should consist of two years of shorthand, two years of typewriting, two years of bookkeeping, and one year of secretarial practice. Would you attempt to thwart Miss Connoley? If so, what arguments would you use? Can you support your arguments by facts rather than opinion or logic?

3. You are a business teacher in Manson High School. You have been teaching bookkeeping, typewriting, and general business in this school for several years. A new superintendent has been employed for the present school year. Shortly after the beginning of the second semester he calls you into his office and tells you that he plans to recommend to the board of education that the subject of bookkeeping be dropped from the business education curriculum. He is convinced that the subject of bookkeeping has little effect in the training of bookkeepers and if the subject does not have this value then he cannot see any need for retaining it in the curriculum.

However, he states to you that he has an open mind and is willing to listen to your reasons for retention of the course and if you can convince him, he will not make the recommendation to the board. What would you do?

4. Max Sherrill is a business teacher in Columbus, a small city of 8,000 population, which is a trading center for several counties. His superintendent has just returned from a professional meeting at which he spent a large amount of time talking with the State Director of Vocational Education. This director has interested the superintendent in the advantages of a cooperative distributive education program for Columbus High School. The superintendent has asked Sherrill to investigate the possibilities of such a program for the high school and report back to him in approximately two weeks. What steps would you recommend for Max to take in completing this assignment?

5. Miss Sheldon is an excellent secretarial teacher in the Rutland High School. However, she is finding that for some reason her secretarial graduates of this high school are not as good as were the ones where she formerly taught. Yet Rutland seems to be a normal community with average-type people and families. The school offers two years of typewriting and two years of shorthand, both starting in the junior year. The first year of each also is open to seniors. The courses are open to all juniors and seniors who care to take them. Miss Sheldon feels sure she is working as conscientiously as she ever did, and actually feels that she is trying very hard to do a top-flight job of teaching these subjects. What do you feel may well be some of the causes of her lack of success at this high school?

Suggested Readings

"Business Classroom Equipment," *Business Education World,* 1963 and 1964. Special March issues.

Catherine, Sr. M., O.S.F., "What Does Automation Mean to Our High School Program?" *Business Education World,* June, 1964, p. 22.

Conant, James B., "Recommendations for Improving Public Secondary Schools," in *The American High School Today.* New York: McGraw-Hill Book Company, 1959.

Douglas, Lloyd V., *Business Education,* pp. 1-4 and 21-45. Englewood Cliffs, N.J.: The Center for Applied Research in Education, Inc., 1963. A volume of *The Library of Education.*

————, "The Effect of the '50's in the '60's," *National Business Education Quarterly,* May, 1960, pp. 5-12.

————, "Today's Educational Tragedy," *Balance Sheet,* May, 1961, pp. 389-91.

Educational Policies Commission, *The Central Purpose of American Education,* NEA, 1961, 2 pp.

Lomax, Paul S., *et al.,* "The Business Program for the Superior Student," *Business Education Forum,* January, 1962, pp. 11-14.

National Business Education Association, *Business and Economic Education for the Academically Talented,* 1961, 80 pp. A publication for the NEA project on the academically talented student.

"Summary of Provisions of the Perkins VOCATIONAL EDUCATION ACT," *American Vocational Journal,* January, 1964, p. 6. Prepared by U.S. Office of Education.

Velie, Lester, "Why Johnny Can't Get a Job," *Reader's Digest,* January, 1963.

Wanous, Samuel J., "Let's Break the 'Egghead' Stranglehold on Business Education," *Balance Sheet,* November, 1960, 7 pp.

Warmke, Roman F., "Are Economic Understandings Developed through Business Courses?" *Business Education Forum,* March, 1964, pp. 7-9.

Career pamphlet series produced by FBLA and PBL, published by the National Business Education Association in 1964:

Calver, Gordon and Elsie M. Jevons, "A Career in the Secretarial Occupations."

Carlson, Arthur E., "A Career in Bookkeeping and Accounting."

Meyer, Warren G. and Harold O. Toupin, "A Career in the Distributive Occupations."

Robek, Mary F., "A Career in Data Processing."

Pamphlet series produced by the Policies Commission for Business and Economic Education, published by the National Business Education Association starting in 1963:

"This We Believe About Business Education in the High School."

"A Proposal for Business-Economic Education for American Secondary Schools."

"The Counselor and Business Education."

3

The Business Teacher Looks at the Learning Process

Learning is a continuous and a very personal process. Every individual is in the process of learning at all times—at school, in the home, at the store, in the daily work at the factory—in all economic, social, religious, and other activities in which the individual may engage. Teaching is partially a viewpoint toward learning. Teaching encompasses all factors in the learning process and attempts to guide and control those factors to provide a learning situation giving maximum effectiveness and efficiency. Teaching is the art of applying scientifically determined facts about learning, often referred to as *educational psychology*, in order to assist the learner in his learning.

Basically the individual is a creature of emotions whose responses to stimuli (including environment and motives) are largely the result of conditioning of his natural inherited powers, abilities, and tendencies. Thus the best teacher must be one who is thoroughly familiar with the field of educational psychology and the learning process, and who has adequate maturity of judgment and control (*a*) to interpret intelligently the present developmental status of

46

the student, and (*b*) to be a true artist in providing for the student the appropriate learning situation.

The present chapter is a review of major aspects of educational psychology and of the learning process as they apply to the work of the business teacher.

Is it true that "If the learner hasn't learned the teacher hasn't taught?" How do I know when I'm doing the right thing? How do I know which of many factors is of most importance? What do I do when things go wrong?

Questions such as the above are almost sure to be in the minds of all business teachers; in fact, they frequently enter the mind of every business teacher who is worth his pay! There definitely is no one simple answer to such questions. The best answer always is going to be one based on (*a*) a complete knowledge and understanding of the individual student or students involved (*b*) by a teacher who is well versed in educational psychology and factors influencing learning and (*c*) prepared in pertinent subject-matter or skills and (*d*) who has sufficient maturity of judgment and control to arrive at and carry through wise decisions.

Probably the most complicated single thing known to man is the human being. Over the years we have learned much about ourselves and "what makes us tick"; yet we still have much to learn and probably never will be able to reduce that learning to an all-inclusive body of definite statements as may be done in some of the more exact sciences. New knowledge about the human being as an individual and as a learner is being brought to light every year through continued research. That is why the successful teacher continues throughout his teaching career to subscribe to and to read and study the literature of his profession. And that also is why it is wise for us at this time to briefly review some of the major factors in the teaching-learning process on which educators quite generally agree.

Learning as Individual Growth

When the business teacher faces a class, he must realize that he actually has before him as many individual learning situations as there are students in the class. Each was born into this world endowed with a central nervous system capable of automatically producing various muscular responses throughout the body in answer to various internally produced and exteriorly received stimuli. These responses, however, both verbal and otherwise, were largely of a random nature.

As the teacher faces the class, though, he now has before him individuals whose responses have been conditioned over perhaps from fourteen to twenty or more years. Owing to home environments, outside associates, sickness, successes, frustrations, previous formal learning situations—and innumerable other conditioning factors—there are bound to be wide differences in the development or learning status of the various students in every class. Although all students in typical business classes have now attained a high-order level of response, probably even including problem-solving ability, each has attained it through a different maze of influences. Thus, owing to previous conditioning, each can be depended upon to have different learning responses to each teaching situation.

In addition, it must be realized that each individual student also possesses native ability and characteristics different from those of each of the others; this refers primarily to inherited physical qualities and characteristics. One phase of this (but one phase only) may be measured in an individual in terms of intelligence quotient or in terms of mental age. Other phases may be measured in terms of various aptitudes, in terms of physiological growth, in terms of reaction time, or in terms of such measurements as number ability, or perceptual speed, or spatial-relations-recognition ability.

Thus the business teacher is cautioned against the pitfall of oversimplification of his concept of learning and of teaching. A class, for instance, may consist entirely of girls and lead the inexperienced teacher to conclude that he has a "homogeneously grouped" class which will simplify his teaching procedures. Or it may be a class of "high-I.Q." students, or of "below-normal" students, or of students carefully selected for high aptitudes and interests in a given subject such as shorthand, or of students all coming from apparently similar home backgrounds. The teacher should never make the mistake of believing that, therefore, a given teaching procedure or technique will apply equally well to every student in the class! Such is not the case—and for very good reasons.

In summary, then, in every business class the task of the teacher is to teach individual students. (And to teach means to give assistance to the student in his learning—not to "pour" or otherwise transfer the teacher's learning into the student!) Learning is an individual matter. Thus the good business teacher makes his efforts student-centered as opposed to subject-matter- or class-centered.

Motivation

In general it is true that we learn well only that which we want to learn well. Or, stated in other words, if one wants sufficiently strongly to learn something he is very likely to do so. Yes—he is even likely to do so in spite of the impediment of a poor teacher!

In the education profession we refer to this desire to learn, or to do something, as *motivation*. It is something that must always be present for efficient and effective learning. It is the drive that causes students to soar to real heights in learning. And it is one of the very major functions of the good business teacher, or of any teacher, to see that each individual student goes about his learning possessing the highest possible motivation.

Again it should be realized that motivation is an individual matter. That which motivates Mary to work until she has achieved a dictation speed of 140 words per minute in shorthand may be of no interest whatsover to Tom. And that which motivates Richard to spend many interesting hours at the library and interviewing people downtown in order to prepare a report for his class on the subject of insurance may have no effect whatsoever on Marvin, who finds he would rather play hooky that day and go fishing. Yet, if he wanted to, Tom might develop higher shorthand speed than Mary, and Marvin might well outdo Richard in learning about insurance!

And so it goes throughout all learning—and throughout life. And the business teacher asks, "How can I possibly have the understanding and the time to provide the best motivation for each of the many individuals in my classes?"

To be honest, the answer probably is "you can't." At least you probably never can have the understanding and the time to be 100 per cent effective in having the work of each student become the result of the highest possible motivation of which the student is capable. But as a skilled teacher you can, in various ways, assist each student in materially raising his motivation—his desire to succeed well in the learning process or problem with which he is faced.

Kind of Motivation. Broadly speaking, all motivation may be classed as either real or artificial. Where a real motivation appears to be lacking on the part of the student, it is the teacher's role to discover and provide learning situations that will develop or engender a real motivation on the part of each student. To some extent, owing to the individual differences existing among the students, this becomes a trial-and-error procedure. Yet the skillful teacher avoids an undue waste of learning time by artificially motivating the class constantly and by various means while permitting time for individual students to develop real interest and motivation.

The offering of prizes or pins or certificates to typewriting or shorthand students is illustrative of one type of artificial motivation. Desire for and pride in personal recognition and approval by one's associates is a common characteristic of all of us. This may almost be looked upon as an "inborn trait"; it is not something that we consciously reason out for ourselves and thereafter adopt as a characteristic because we reason that it is a good thing! Mother Nature has taken care of this for us and endowed us with this "built-in" response as a result of the functioning of the autonomic division of our central nervous system. Only through a conditioning process can we change it.

Artificial motivation, such as the use of pins and certificates, should be recognized for what it is—a means toward an end and not the ultimate goal. It is more desirable when the student feels an inward burning desire to achieve this same degree of skill (as in typewriting or shorthand) because he knows and feels that this skill is something that makes him, as an individual, happy and satisfied with himself; that will make him proud of himself throughout life as an individual possessing an ability that others do not have; that will make him feel more secure in his ability to earn his way through life successfully. Yet, if the possibility of earning a certificate or pin will help motivate him to at least "make a start," is it not worth considering?

This should not be construed as advocating indiscriminate use of pins and certificates as the best artificial motivation. The teacher should be an "artist" in skillfully selecting the best from the countless types of somewhat artificial motivation that may be available and in selecting that which seems to best suit his teaching personality, his teaching situation, and his students. Yet we must realize that such motivation does appeal to our deep-seated desire for recognition and, therefore, does tend to help increase our efforts.

For instance, the authors have observed (and happily participated in!) occasions at which adult professional and business men and women of a community have been called forward in meetings such as a service-club banquet to have bestowed upon them appropriate pins in recognition of such relatively minor achievements as perfect attendance for one year, or continuous membership for ten, fifteen, or twenty years. And these people gave silent testimony to the pleasure it gave them by constantly wearing the pins thereafter! Moreover, they customarily thereafter made an even greater effort to continue to maintain and improve the records they had set.

Thus the business teacher should not belittle so-called artificial motivation. Make use of it. Choose intelligently, however. Recognition for achievements may also be given in many other ways, such as through the posting of names of those students making "greatest improvement," the posting of especially fine work; publication in school and local papers of names of those achieving any of countless types of success; arranging for individual students to display their various abilities before local community groups, or through radio or television programs; posting or publishing pictures of students engaged in giving top-ranking sales talks, taking dictation, transcribing from dictaphones, or giving reports in any business class; publicly announcing the names of those elected to membership in student groups, such as the Future Business Leaders of America; and in literally thousands of other ways which the alert business teacher is capable of devising.

Praise and Encouragement. Far too often does the teacher attempt to motivate through criticism, punishment, or grades. Far too seldom does the teacher motivate through deserved praise and encouragement.

It is true that both "reward" and "punishment" are recognized as potential means of motivating learning. Moreover, criticism is essential. However, the human being is known to respond better and to secure greater motivation from praise than from punishment. The skillful business teacher makes certain that he judiciously gives praise when it is deserved and that he typically makes his criticism of a constructive and encouraging nature. He reserves punishment and a destructive type of criticism for very, very few cases and then only when it is decided upon as a last resort after thorough, deliberate consideration of the individual toward whom it is to be directed. Administering it before other students usually results in more damage than good.

It has been claimed that the most powerful single drive in human nature is the desire to gain recognition. This might also be described as the desire to be appreciated. At times it takes the form of desire to be loved, to "belong," to be heard, to be seen, and various other modifications. This should constantly be recognized by the teacher in all business classes. The drive is always present in each student.

Moreover, should a given student fail to obtain this desired recognition in a desirable or approved manner he will tend to be driven to obtaining it in some other manner. This usually accounts for the boisterousness, the "paper wads," the shuffling of feet, the loud whispers, the interference with others, and the innumerable other petty annoyances sometimes encountered by teachers and referred to as *discipline situations.* One of the best means of avoiding such situations, and of motivating desired learning at the same time, is to be sure each individual student receives deserved praise and encouragement.

Thus, it may be that a bookkeeping student arrives at an incorrect net profit for his set of books or for a problem. Perhaps he has incorrectly classified a debit entry as an asset when it should have been considered an expense. Some teachers might comment to him somewhat as follows: "Dick, you are careless. You've been warned that you must be accurate at all times. Apparently you haven't followed instructions, so it's your own fault. You deserve the 'F' you'll get on this—and you'll now have to do it over besides."

It may be that Dick needed criticism on some of these points. Yet it hardly is possible that he had done everything wrong! Wasn't there anything in all of his work that deserved a word of encouraging recognition or praise? A more skillful teacher might have commented more like this: "I'm sorry, Dick, but your final net profit is wrong; you've prepared this more neatly and in better form than you sometimes do, and it's too bad to let some error creep in and cheat you. I presume you've checked your arithmetic already. Do you suppose you've made an error in judgment in analyzing some transaction? Would you like to look this over again and see if you can find it so I can give you full credit for your work? It really appears to be quite well done otherwise."

Comments more like the second one let Dick know that you are "on his side"; that you, as a teacher, stand ready and eager to give him credit and recognition when deserved; that you do recognize something good and worth-while in his efforts; and that you have at least some degree of confidence in his ability to "come through." Yet at the same time there is the critical attitude toward his arithmetic and toward the use of judgment in analyzing transactions—but given in a constructive and friendly manner.

It requires only a moment of reflection to understand that the first type of comment to Dick, which fails completely to give him any recognition for whatever he may have done indicating improvement for him, could only help make Dick feel "rebellious" and perhaps turn to other means of gaining attention and recognition—helping to make of him a so-called discipline problem. And on the other hand, the second type of comment gave him opportunity to feel that his efforts were appreciated and that he was on the road to deserved recognition; it would be much more likely to encourage and motivate him to continued and improved learning.

Attention, Interest, and Desire

Recently a student in a salesmanship class was observed presenting a demonstration or practice sales talk before his classmates. He apparently had learned his principles of good salesmanship well and had prepared his demonstration sales talk carefully, for in it he demonstrated clearly the importance of first gaining favorable attention, of then using that attention to develop a real interest, and finally, of encouraging and developing that interest until it became a desire—in that case a desire on the part of his prospect to purchase the item that was for sale.

In a way this student condensed into a twenty-minute class demonstration an excellent illustration of the entire process through which the business teacher must take his students in motivating and achieving real learning. First, of course, it is necessary to secure favorable attention of the students. Usually this is not too difficult to do. It is somewhat more difficult, however, to develop a real interest even though the teacher may have the attention of the students. The real evidence of a top-ranking teacher comes, however, when he can get that interest to develop into a real desire for learning! Let us consider briefly what happened in this demonstration sales talk.

The student-salesman saw to it that he immediately got favorable attention. In the first place this applied to himself; he appeared neat and well groomed, pleasant, and confident. At the same time he was polite and thoughtful in dealing with his prospect. And in the second place he assured attention (at least) to his merchandise by casually placing it conspicuously on the table before his prospect. The fact that it was still covered by a beautiful display case which was closed merely aided in arousing curiosity and assuring continued attention while the student-salesman had an opportunity to "get under way" in his prepared sales talk. (Every time a teacher enters a classroom to face a class he encounters this same challenging situation; if he is well prepared, he will in some manner be duplicating this sales situation. And the good teacher is well prepared every time he enters the classroom!)

As the student-salesman proceeded then to develop interest he was careful to constantly keep before himself his prospect's viewpoint. It was obvious that the information he was giving was all directed toward the interests of his prospect. He encouraged his prospect to talk, to answer questions, and to ask questions. Moreover, he had his prospect actively participating by taking the merchandise (in this case a power drill) in his own hands, examining it, and then "trying it out" on a piece of wood which the salesman had ready for that purpose! Is it any wonder that the attention of the prospect was gradually changed into a real interest in the drill and, finally, to a desire to possess it? (Similarly, the teacher develops real interest on the part of his students by constantly keeping before himself his students' viewpoint, by encouraging them to ask and to answer questions, and by having them actively engaged in the many activities, both physical and mental, that are associated with learning. It is through this same method that the teacher develops a real desire to learn!)

In brief, then, in order to promote real learning it is necessary first to secure the attention of the students and then to hold it and at the same time to develop interest; when his interest in the subject-matter at hand can be sufficiently expanded and becomes a real part of the student's activities and thinking the chances are good that he will also develop a desire to learn about it. The teacher who achieves this outcome consistently and repeatedly is in fact a real "Master Teacher."

Attention-Killers. Psychology teaches us (as does experience) that it is relatively easy to get attention. All it takes is a bright light, a moving object, a bright color, a loud noise, something new or unusual, something attractive, a pleasant odor, or any of many, many other stimuli. The skillful teacher quickly becomes adept at securing attention.

However, holding attention may be more difficult. It must be remembered that any of these same multitudinous stimuli can just as easily steal the attention away from the teacher. This happens whenever there is some unusual noise or other sound either inside or outside the classroom; whenever a class is interrupted by the entrance of a tardy student; whenever "unruly" students attract attention to themselves; or whenever a student is called out of class.

What can the teacher do about this? How can the teacher prevent "attention-killers" from interrupting and interfering with the learning process of his students? In general, there are two things that the master teacher does: he plans to eliminate as many of them as possible and he keeps alert to counteract the others.

Every business teacher certainly should be businesslike in conducting all his business classes. This may seem to be a trite statement, yet it is the very heart of the success of many business teachers. If a class is conducted in businesslike manner—from the very moment the class is scheduled to start until the moment when it is dismissed—the number of attention-killers in that class automatically will be drastically reduced. In general, this means making maximum use of every second of class time. It means "starting" promptly—and making that a habit that becomes automatic with the students. It means entering the classroom with a well-laid plan of procedure each day. It means advance planning to see that roll-call and other clerical duties are taken care of automatically and efficiently; that needed equipment and supplies are in place and in working order; that the classroom is "in order," properly heated, properly lighted, properly ventilated, and relatively free from outside distractions; and that advance cooperation of the administration has been arranged to cut to a minimum undesirable interruptions over which the teacher can have no control.

Yet, in spite of advance planning to be businesslike in all ways, unwanted interferences must be expected. This is where the master teacher demonstrates that he is a true "artist" in applying his knowledge of human psychology. He must then quickly but artfully use good judgment in counteracting the unwanted influence of such attention-killers. He must manage to motivate his students (perhaps almost unrealized by them) to redirect their attention to the problem of learning that currently is before the class. In doing this, he may of course choose from innumerable procedures potentially available. He may refer to some chart or other visual aid in resuming the discussion or explanation or summarization or other step in the learning process that was under way at the time of the interruption; he may make use of the chalk board for this purpose; he may ask some student to continue the discussion, or explanation, or summarization, or to consider a pertinent question or problem posed by the teacher; or he may use other procedures seemingly well suited to the occasion, his students, and his own personal preferences.

It should be noted, however, that the master teacher does not simply exhort his students to "now forget" about the interruption! This probably would merely tend to continue to fix the attention on the interruption. Instead, through actively redirecting the attention to the desired topic, the master teacher has helped his students "forget" the interruption—and without even realizing they are doing so.

Fatigue and Boredom. It is quite possible, however, that interruptions and even "attention-killers" may be turned into real advantages by the master teacher. Thus the teacher should not permit himself to become overly concerned about them. Just as the alert salesman is prepared to accept objections and then to move immediately forward toward an advantage, so, also, should the alert teacher be prepared to accept interruptions and then to make use of them. After all, we all know that at times we become "fatigued" and sometimes "bored" —and that at such times almost any kind of a "pause" or "interruption" can enable us to then pursue our objective with renewed vigor and interest.

In some class work, such as that in beginning typewriting or early shorthand writing, the fatigue that quickly sets in is largely of a physical nature. Muscles are clumsily performing new tasks and fatigue quickly until they become accustomed to these new activities. It is then that the business teacher should apply counteracting principles learned in his educational psychology. For instance, he may recall that in controlled experiments, the ergograph has clearly shown the adverse effects on both quantity and quality of output resulting from fatigue. (No wonder the beginning typewriting student tires, slows down, and makes errors if he tries hard for more than a minute or so at a time!) And he may also recall that less "work" time with appropriately spaced periods of complete physical relaxation will result in an actual increase in output—and of a better quality. (Small wonder, then, that even the very thought of facing a "double-period" typewriting class may cause the beginning typewriting student to "give up" and start saving himself from the beginning of the class period!)

In class work involving the learning of new skills (something the business teacher often faces) constant care must be taken to permit the students (perhaps without fully realizing it) to sit back and relax and physically rest. Sometimes the best means of doing this is to have them relax physically while they watch the teacher as he explains or demonstrates something new to them. Certainly, though, it is necessary that they rest and counteract developing physical fatigue.

It is to be remembered that this matter of fatigue applies especially to the beginning stages of learning a skill. In due time it may be desirable to so develop the skill that the advent of physical fatigue is delayed for rather long periods. As muscles become more skillful at new tasks this ability will gradually develop.

Perhaps of even greater importance than actual physical fatigue is the matter of a general mental feeling of fatigue, often bordering on or becoming boredom. This is common to all life situations, and thus is present in all classroom work, in both skill courses and non-skill courses. Thus it is quite possible that it may be in any class—bookkeeping, general business, typewriting, salesmanship, consumer education, shorthand, retailing, business law, or others—that the business teacher detects the presence of a "feeling of fatigue" (or is it boredom?).

What should he do about it? Give them a rest? In a way, the answer is "yes." However, that which may best be a "rest" for his students is then likely to be merely a "change." In brief, the real cure for boredom is motivation. It is probable that the particular technique of learning in use in class at the moment needs to be changed. Are the students getting bored or "fatigued" from listening to too much talking by the teacher? Perhaps from listening to a long and uninspired report by a fellow student? Perhaps from sitting idly by while the teacher goes through a long explanation, or argument, or chastisement, primarily for the benefit of some one student? Perhaps from an unnecessary repetition of something they already know and understand? Or perhaps merely because the teacher has used the same old technique day after day in that class?

It is especially true that at times such as these almost any "interruption"—even an ordinarily undesirable "attention-killer"—may actually be used to advantage by the teacher!

A recent article in a professional education magazine, written by a nationally known business educator, advocated "Change for the Sake of Change!" There was much merit in this man's advice. He would forestall feelings of fatigue, developing feelings of boredom, and general tendencies toward lack of interest, through a widespread use of the principle of "change." It is well to apply this idea constantly to motivation and teaching techniques. It may also be profitably applied to other factors, such as the teacher's clothing and appearance and to the physical arrangements within the classroom.

Perhaps a word of caution is well, however. The master teacher discovers procedures and techniques that he is sure achieve high motivation and achievements when he consistently uses them. He is entirely justified in making repeated use of these procedures and techniques—subject, undoubtedly, to the occasional need for variations.

Knowledge of Results

Many business teachers are accused of having a strong preference for teaching skill subjects, such as typewriting and shorthand, and of having a dislike for teaching the sociobusiness subjects, such as general business and business law. Perhaps this is true. If so, at least one reason arises from the fact that both students and teacher get satisfaction from being able to actually see and measure the progress that is being made. If progress is not being made, this also is readily discernible and that tends to spur each to greater effort—again likely to be followed by satisfying results.

This illustrates another well-established psychological truth. A learner achieves more when he can know "how he is doing" than he does when kept in the dark as to the results of his efforts. Thus keeping the student well informed about the results of his efforts is an important psychological means of motivation. It should be noted, moreover, that this is a highly individualized factor in motivation, and thus aids the student in realizing and in feeling that the learning going on in the classroom is a very personal thing for him.

At the same time, and probably as a result of its motivational value, knowledge of how he is doing materially retards the feeling of fatigue. Thus a double value accrues from keeping the student well informed about the results of his learning endeavors.

The business teacher has many opportunities for conveying this knowledge to the student. In typewriting, frequent timed writings checked by the students themselves accomplish the purpose admirably. Over longer periods of time this may be reinforced through individual progress charts—also kept by the students themselves. In various cooperative part-time programs students similarly are likely to know very well how they are doing since they are on the job and actually producing. In secretarial classes they may have the self-measurement of mailable letters transcribed. In bookkeeping, success or failure in correctly analyzing, recording, and summarizing business transactions is again quite evident to the student—often at the time he prepares his trial balance or work sheet, and certainly when he "checks" his final results.

The master business teacher sees to it that each individual student in each class is kept fully aware of the extent to which he is progressing in his learning. This is best done when it can be an integral part of the learning process itself, as just illustrated. It also can be done by direct comments (preferably deserved praise) by the teacher, by appropriate problems and exercises, and by reasonably frequent tests and "checks" of various kinds.

Although tests and examinations (evaluations) graded by the teacher have an important place in education, it should be noted that in many ways the student may be enabled to make this evaluation of his own progress for himself. Another excellent example of this technique is to be found in certain "study guides" (often used in business law, for instance) in which case it takes but a minute or two in class for the teacher to have each student check his own understandings and thereby to spot immediately any errors or inadequacies in his own learning. This can be used effectively in real motivation of individual students.

Whole Versus Part Learning

Imagine for a moment, if you can, a student who has never seen or heard about a typewriter but who has been advised to learn how to typewrite. He has no knowledge of what this is, of what the machine can do, or how large or small it may be, or of the purpose of the machine. He therefore procures for himself a special tutor—an expert typist who, as it happens, has had no preparation as a teacher.

Wishing to be very thorough in his new role as a teacher (for which he is not qualified), this tutor decides to begin with a detailed study of the typewriter itself. He also decides to make it "simple," and to break the learning down into small segments. Accordingly, he completely dismantles a typewriter and proceeds to present to his student only one part at a time! First, he happens to select the bell; he takes it to the pupil and proceeds to teach all he can think of about the typewriter bell. The student examines it and handles it and takes careful notes on the tutor's lecture, and that night diligently studies for hours trying to memorize all he has been told.

And so the learning process (if it could be called that!) might proceed for many, many days. What a horrible waste of time and effort!

Yet this might well exemplify teaching by a *part method*, or from the "simple to the complex." It would lack, however, one extremely important requisite of effective learning, namely, learning by the *whole method*—or learning through gaining some understanding of the "complete meaning" or the "ultimate goal" toward which the learner is striving. How much simpler and how much more effective it would have been for the tutor to sit down at a typewriter and demonstrate the complete process of typewriting! Then—and only then—would the student be ready to effectively attack the problem of learning the simple things and progressing to the more complex. Without some understanding of the whole process and the relations of its parts to each other the learner is confused, can have no clear goal toward which to work, finds himself constantly rebelling inwardly—and is likely soon to give up.

Today all master teachers make use of this principle of teaching parts in proper relation to the whole to which they belong. That is why nearly all bookkeeping today begins with a study of the final bookkeeping reports and the bookkeeping equation. That is why typewriting and shorthand students no longer spend long hours practicing the writing of single unrelated words or letters. That is why many typewriting teachers now have students writing complete sentences during the first day in class.

Each business subject offers its own peculiar need for having the student first gain some knowledge of "where he is going" and "what it is all about." Without this early understanding of the "whole," motivation soon deteriorates and learning is impeded seriously.

Rivalry and Competition

Almost everyone loves to compete. When rivalry or competition is present we put forth more effort and enjoy doing so; at the same time the feeling of fatigue is seldom noticed. We are motivated more highly by the anticipation of "winning," and of receiving recognition as a member of our group. Competition is a device frequently used effectively by most teachers.

The factor of rivalry is present in many teaching techniques commonly used by business teachers. No student in a typewriting or shorthand class can be striving to attain a record of a given number of words per minute without being aware that a spirit of competition and rivalry exists. He at all times is, in a sense, competing with other members of his class. Of even more importance from the viewpoint of "student-centered" teaching is the fact that he always is trying to improve his own record.

On occasion, the alert business teacher may create a situation that makes a game of this rivalry. On other occasions, he may make use of this form of motivation by selecting his better students to represent the class in assembly demonstrations or talks, or to make similar appearances before the Parent-Teacher Association or business and professional groups of the community, or to be announced through the columns of the paper as honor-roll students in business education. At times he may emphasize this same factor through various forms of bulletin-board charts and displays.

Two warnings should be heeded relative to the use of competition and rivalry. *The competition for high achievement records should not focus too much effort and attention on only the few students who are attaining the best records.* This formerly was quite customary during the era of commercial contests. Too often the teacher was made to feel that his promotion in the profession, and sometimes even his job, depended upon winning contests. This caused him to confine his efforts largely to his "team" members, and, accordingly, to give little assistance to the great majority of his students. *Care must be taken not to embarrass or discourage some students.* This can readily happen, for instance, when certain students continue to remain near the bottom of the class in spite of their best efforts— and this is a common occurence. If, in addition, this fact is prominently displayed before everyone in a bulletin-board chart these students may suffer severe psychological damage, become badly frustrated, and even be caused to develop inferiority complexes and very undesirable personalities. (On the other hand, progress charts showing results of "self-competition" can change this into a desirable influence; such charts may be constructed in terms of gain in words per minute, or in terms of points of improvement shown.) Also, it should be remembered that occasionally a very superior student also becomes embarrassed when his superiority is flaunted before his classmates by his teacher.

Goals and Subgoals

Throughout life most of us have goals that we wish to attain and toward which we strive. Our motivation and our efforts are greater when we are aware of such goals. As we approach the attainment of each of these goals we experience increased interest and motivation, have a pleasant feeling of satisfaction, and seldom feel fatigued even though we are increasing our efforts. Once we have attained a given goal we are likely to feel satisfied and confident, and to look for "new worlds to conquer."

Thus in each subject or class it is important that each student have an understanding of the goal (or goals) toward which he is striving in that course. True, this also should fit into the pattern that makes up his longer-term goal or goals for himself and his life. In a way this becomes a part of the "whole" pattern (Gestalt) composing the individual's personality and purpose in life.

Psychologically, however, it is even more important to the learner that the teacher arrange the course or subject so that it also contains many subgoals all along the way. If the student can have a definite subgoal before him that he may reasonably expect to reach each month, or each week, or each day, and toward which he is knowingly striving each day, he can reap over and over again the many motivational advantages of approaching the achievement of his goal.

We find modern textbooks divided into many chapters and sections, each providing a definite subgoal toward which the student may work. In addition the wise business teacher provides each student with a constantly changing pattern of daily "goals" made reasonably achievable in terms of the capacities and developing abilities of each student. Thus the immediate subgoal may be that of learning to identify the common forms of insurance policies, to correctly solve a specific problem, to learn how the seventeenth section of the Statute of Frauds applies to our ordinary business transactions, or to add five correct words per minute to our average typewriting speed.

Make liberal use of the principle of providing the learner with many goals and subgoals that are attainable for him.

Skill Development

Many people, including some teachers, make the mistake of considering learning to be entirely a mental process. Actually all learning is accompanied by and influenced by physiological factors both within and outside the individual who is learning. In some types of learning, known as *skill development,* the physical responses of the individual become much more important. This is true, for instance, in learning to typewrite, or to take dictation in shorthand, or to transcribe from the dictaphone, or to skate, or to ride a bicycle, or to play basketball, or to walk upright and with poise, or to speak before an audience, or to receive callers with poise and charm either in person at the office or over the telephone.

Similarly, many people, including some teachers, make the mistake of considering the learning of skills to be entirely a physical thing. Nothing could be further from the truth.

As a matter of fact, from the viewpoint of the learner, the learning of a skill is a much more complicated and difficult process than is the mere acquiring of knowledge and understanding. Learning a skill usually includes the necessity of acquiring knowledge and understanding, but there is also the necessity, usually, of much effort and time devoted to purposeful and controlled practice. Behind all of this practice usually lies the necessity of fitting together many, many previously learned complex knowledges and understandings into what appears to be a simple skill that can be performed almost automatically! It is quite true that once a high skill is attained in something, the act can be performed automatically, in fact, it must be performed automatically without any "interference" from the higher brain centers.

Perhaps an example will aid in understanding this. A teacher once had in class a girl who was unusually expert in taking dictation on the Stenotype. She quite often was hired to record discussions and proceedings at conventions and important board meetings. She had the reputation of never missing a word in her recording. Yet, while she was recording, she habitually also was reading a book or magazine at the same time! She had developed her skill so highly that it was completely automatized; her fingers reacted instantly when the sound of the voice reached her ears. She had actually found that her records were more accurate when she deliberately kept her mind off her work.

Similarly we sometimes see a demonstration by an expert typist in which he (or she) copies with 100 per cent accuracy from a printed page at an extremely high rate, far over 100 words per minute, while at the same time carrying on a conversation and perhaps computing difficult arithmetic problems mentally. Here again is a skill so highly developed that it has been automatized. Yet, in both of these examples, the learning process while the skill was being developed had necessarily been difficult and had originally required a high order of mental concentration and a very real mental effort to gain the necessary knowledge and understanding.

Let us once more consider an example. The fingers of a secretary may fairly fly as she types a beautiful letter from her shorthand notes. As you watch, though, you are aware that this apparently simple physical skill actually is the culmination of years of study of many separate things, and that now she is skillfully combining a very complex set of factors and previous learnings. First, she had to learn to typewrite. She probably learned to do this through and from the printed word. Later (preferably), she had to learn a complete new "sound language," shorthand. Not only did she have to learn it, but she also had to learn how to write it—and with accuracy, perfection, and high speed. Still later, she then had to "relearn" her typewriting; instead of using the printed page as the stimulus to cause her fingers to type accurately she had to learn to change to the stimulus of her shorthand notes. And these notes constitute a "sound" language; they do not spell out the words as they must be typed. Her eyes now see shorthand characters that represent words, sounds, and phrases but with many, many of the "silent" letters completely omitted! Nevertheless, from this incomplete stimulus she must now have her fingers correctly spell out every word. And in addition—her mind must be ever alert to insert all needed punctuation, to correct any bad English or poor sentence structure, and even to make sure that the dictator has used correct terminology.

These examples help demonstrate two concepts important for

the skill teacher. First is the realization that so-called skill development also has in it an important basis of mental learning, of knowledges and understandings. Thus, this portion of the developmental process is influenced by all the factors and motivations that influence any other type of learning.

Second is the further realization that the development of an expert skill carries the learner beyond the purely mental process and into a status of automation or semiautomation controlled by direct response of the appropriate muscles to the stimulus received. (Psychologists tell us that "short-circuit" responses have been set up which operate without having the stimulus pass through the higher brain center on its way to the responding muscles.) Although this portion of the developmental process may be influenced to some degree by ordinary motivating factors, it is much more dependent upon intense drill.

Problem-Solving

Today's educational philosophy strongly emphasizes the desirability of producing a graduate of our schools who is capable of solving life's problems as he meets them. The final evaluation of the success of an education lies largely in the ability the graduate has to apply his learning in the solving of the problems he will meet. This same philosophy applies to the learning acquired through any given subject or course.

The master teacher, therefore, provides ample and appropriate opportunity for his students to practice applying their learnings to problem-solving. At the same time this media provides them with opportunity to check the results of their learnings, an important factor in motivation. Every course and every bit of learning may be applied in some fashion to the problem-solving situation. The bookkeeping student faces problem-solving constantly. The business law student practices and checks himself through the use of appropriate legal case problems. The general business student and the consumer education student spend much time discussing the problem situations. Every business class provides opportunity for problem-solving in some form.

In any subject, however, it is important that the solving of any particular problem be delayed until the learner is ready for that problem. The beginning bookkeeping student obviously is not yet ready to solve problems involving controlling accounts and subsidiary ledgers, nor is the beginning student in business law yet ready to solve cases dealing with real estate mortgages or decedents' estates. Thus, in general, real problem-solving should constitute a relatively minor portion of the work in the early stages of any learning but become a more major function of the work in the more advanced stages of learning. No definite line of demarcation can be drawn.

In skill subjects it often is especially important to delay certain types of problem-solving until the learner is ready; attempting solutions before the learner is ready causes a great waste of time and inefficient learning. Thus it would be foolish in elementary typewriting to introduce centering and various styles of letters before the student has even developed reasonable ability to type sentences on the keyboard; such a beginning student might get the practice of setting up but one letter during a period of time in which an advanced student might get the practice of setting up a large number of letters.

Individual Differences

We started this review of the learning process with a reminder that all learning should be looked upon as individual growth; that it is each separate student as an individual, and not simply "a class," that the teacher is assisting through a learning process. We have now briefly reviewed some of the major factors entering into a successful teaching-learning process and have given some thought to how they specifically apply to the professional work of a business teacher. Although other factors might be mentioned, probably the ones reviewed are of major importance. It now is appropriate that we finish this review by returning to our original concept that all learning is an individual matter. [*Note:* At this point it is suggested that the reader review the viewpoint expressed at the beginning of this chapter and also the materials under the heading of "Learning as Individual Growth" (p. 47).]

Professional educational literature frequently refers to "providing for individual differences." The pressing problem is that of how to provide suitable learning materials and situations to meet the many varying needs of all the individuals in a class and to get it all done in the limited time available to the teacher.

Obviously there is no one solution. Just as obviously, no teacher can expect to do a 100 per cent perfect job of it. Yet the master teacher always is doing this to an appreciable degree in every class.

In typewriting, for example, are to be found techniques in which the teacher has control of the entire class, as a class, and yet at the same time is automatically adjusting the learning to the individual needs of each student. The "call-the-throw" drills, for instance, are so arranged as to permit each student to almost automatically select his own best practice rate under timed conditions! Again, in shorthand the teacher may dictate the material at several different speeds, permitting each student to transcribe it whenever he is satisfied that he has been able to successfully get it recorded in his shorthand notebook.

Of special significance in caring for the problem of individual differences in subjects such as shorthand and transcription are the recent developments in the use of tapes and records for individual student practice. Today schools rapidly are becoming equipped with "laboratories" or practice rooms where such equipment is made available for student practice at learning levels needed by individual students. At times dictation records may be taken home by the student for home practice with the aid of a record player. An increasing number of schools are being provided with multichannel listening stations served by various types of electronic equipment which provides the necessary controlled dictation. (See Chapter Seven for further details.)

In group discussions the alert teacher is constantly allowing for individual differences in his class as he leads his students in expressing themselves, in asking and answering questions, and in attempting explanations. In addition, the alert teacher is constantly providing individual students with specialized activities, projects, assignments, and suggestions for preparations outside of class that are chosen because they especially fit the needs of the individual student.

Yes—treating the learning process as an individual matter and making appropriate provisions for the needs of differing individuals keeps the teacher busy. It also requires the successful teacher to be a true professional artist. But the satisfactions accruing to the teacher who does this are perhaps unmatched in any other profession.

Projects and Questions for Discussion

1. Interview the sales manager or marketing manager of some large business or industrial firm and inquire about any means he may use for motivating salesmen to increase their sales.

2. Inquire of the secretary or president of some local chapter of an organization such as the Lions Club or Rotary Club and find out whether or not it makes use of any kinds of "awards" for its members; if so, why are the awards used?

3. Check the various factors in the learning process described in this chapter with those presented in the text(s) used in your course in educational psychology; report on any additional factors or elements which you find.

4. Interview the personnel director of some large business; inquire about the individual differences they find among applicants for various office positions.

5. We often hear the statement, "We teach as we have been taught." Do you believe there is any truth in this point of view? Why or why not?

6. Discuss the pros and cons of the following two statements:

"Man in his fundamental nature is everywhere and at all times the same; the apparent differences are of far less importance than the underlying similarities."

"Individual differences, all kinds of differences, are vast and measurable. In educational planning these differences are far more important than are the uniformities."

7. Discuss the statement, "The use of grades is an excellent type of motivation device."

8. Would you say that fear of criticism or fear of punishment would be a stronger motivation for students than praise and encouragement?

9. Should a teacher attempt to gain the attention of his classes through use of such personal techniques as flashy dress, unusual mannerisms, slangy talk, or some other personal element that sets him apart from the usual?

10. When a teacher observes his students showing fatigue or boredom, should he do something to divert them even though the diversion is not a part of the learning process?

11. What are the techniques involved in solving problems? Should these techniques be used in teaching high-school business classes?

12. A teacher has stated, "I never answer questions of students if it is possible for them to find the answers themselves." Do you believe this to be a good procedure?

13. What are the different ways in which people learn? How can these be applied to the teaching of business subjects in the secondary school?

Case Problems

1. It is a Friday afternoon in late April. Miss Arthur, a beginning business teacher, is teaching a class in second-semester typewriting during the last period of the day. It is raining rather steadily outside.

All during the period Miss Arthur has noticed a lethargy on the part of the students. They don't seem to care whether they type well or not. Here and there several students are causing a slight disturbance. During a timed writing Miss Arthur noticed that several of the students stopped to talk briefly even though taking a timed test.

Miss Arthur is becoming somewhat irritated with the seeming indifferent attitude on the part of the class in general. There is still twenty-five minutes remaining in the period and Miss Arthur plans to introduce a new typing problem—manuscript typing with footnotes.

Would you suggest that Miss Arthur is doing something wrong? Normally this class has been very cooperative and there has existed a fine student-instructor relationship. If Miss Arthur were to ask your advice on what she could do to correct the present situation, what might you tell her?

2. You are observing a class in beginning typewriting. You notice that the teacher who has just presented a problem in tabulation to her students is using what you believe to be improper techniques. She gave very few directions to the students on how to proceed in the tabulation problem and now while the students are struggling with the solution the teacher is doing very little if anything to help those students who are having difficulty. In fact, you just noticed that the teacher observed one of the students doing something wrong but did not stop and correct him —she just walked right on by him.

What, if anything, is wrong with this teacher? Is she lazy? Doesn't she know the answers herself? Give your evaluation of this procedure.

3. Two teachers in Sandusky High School are discussing the case of one of their colleagues, a Mr. Bright, who is a business teacher in the high school. It seems that many of the faculty of the school believe that Mr. Bright is an ill-prepared and ineffective teacher. He never appears to be in front to his classes teaching them—it always seems that students are conducting his classes. One or two students have reported that all

they ever seem to do is to sit around and talk. However, there seems to be a high interest in Mr. Bright's classes. The classes never seem to have any direction but wander about and oftentimes do not even appear to be discussing the subject-matter of the course (although in all fairness most often the topics that are being discussed are related to the subject-matter).

The epithet of "progressive" has been attached to Mr. Bright, and several of the other teachers in the school feel that he should be fired at the end of the school year. What course of action do you suggest should be taken? Should Mr. Bright be shown the "error" of his ways? How would you determine whether he is ineffective or not?

Suggested Readings

Blum, Milton L., and Benjamin Balinsky, *Counseling and Psychology: Vocational Psychology and Its Relation to Educational and Personal Counseling*, Chaps. 6, 7, and 8. Englewood Cliffs, N.J.: Prentice-Hall, Inc., 1951.

Broudy, Harry S., *Psychology for General Education*. Longmans, Green & Co., Inc., 1956.

Christensen, G. Jay, "Atmosphere for Learning a Skill: Chaos or Creativity?" *Business Education Forum*, April, 1964, p. 23.

Del Turco, Lorraine, "Handling All Levels of Ability in the Classroom," *Business Education World*, February, 1964, pp. 21-23.

Electronic Dictation Laboratories and Multiple Listening Stations, "Special Section," in *Business Education World*, January, 1964, pp. 7-22.

Lebeda, Agnes, "Teach and Talk About Business," *Business Education Forum*, March, 1964, p. 5. Editorial.

Liles, Parker, "Concomitant Learnings in Business Education," *The Journal of Business Education*, November, 1963, pp. 54-56.

Munn, Norman, *Psychology, The Fundamentals of Human Adjustment* (3rd ed.), Chaps. 2 to 10. Boston: Houghton Mifflin Company, 1956.

Mursell, James L., *Successful Teaching: Its Psychological Principles* (2nd ed.), Chaps. 1, 2, 3, and 4. New York: McGraw-Hill Book Company, 1954.

Musselman, Vernon A., "Meeting Individual Differences," *Business Education Forum*, October, 1964, p. 24.

Sorenson, Herbert, *Psychology in Education* (3rd ed.), Chaps. 5, 12, 14, and 18. New York: McGraw-Hill Book Company, 1954.

Spache, George D., "Psychological Bases for Procedures in Continued and Remedial Learning," *American Business Education Yearbook,* XII (1955), 22-41.

Stolurow, Lawrence M., *Readings in Learning,* Chaps. 3 and 4. Englewood Cliffs, N.J.: Prentice-Hall, Inc., 1953.

Teaching
Techniques
Applied
to the
Learning
Process

4

In Chapter Three is found a discussion of some of the major aspects of the learning process. It is necessary for all teachers to understand thoroughly the fundamentals of the learning process and then to apply these fundamentals in teaching by using sound teaching techniques. Too often teachers overemphasize the importance of techniques of teaching without thoroughly understanding the basic elements of learning. The good teacher first understands the reasons and means by which students learn, and then uses appropriate techniques to accomplish the desired ends. Many of the elements discussed in Chapter Four will be discussed more fully in later chapters as they apply to specific subject-matter courses in business education. In this chapter it is sufficient to point out some of the major techniques used by teachers in applying the fundamentals of the learning process, which are applicable to all business subjects.

The Business Teacher as a Person

Before we can discuss some of the more effective techniques used by successful business teachers we first should consider some of the personal characteristics teachers must have in order to use these techniques effectively.

It is not sufficient for today's business teacher to be a possessor of knowledge alone. He must be able to develop an environment in his classroom that is conducive to making students desire to learn. It does not take one with great ability to use proven and tested teaching techniques in the classroom. Unless the person using the techniques has the proper personality and character traits to use them effectively, they will be of little use to him in developing the learning process in his students. Let us consider, then, what some of these personal traits are that must be present before technical devices can be used to the best advantage.

The Effective Business Teacher Is Dynamic. The business teacher who is vigorous, stimulating, dramatic, and exciting will be the one who is most successful in the classroom. His classes will move swiftly and surely and be free from boredom and monotony. Much of this dynamic atmosphere found in the classroom will stem from the actions of the teacher himself. His personal enthusiasm and interest should be such that it will be absorbed and projected by the students in the class. The teacher should have a flair for the dramatic even to the extent of being somewhat of a "ham" actor. Care should be taken, of course, not to be flashy or superficial or obtain the reputation of being a "screwball"—but the teacher who senses the drama in a particular situation and then uses this to advantage in instruction will be compensated for his actions in having a stimulating and interesting class.

Other simple yet important elements in developing a dynamic climate are the use of gesture, voice, and general mien. Use of expression in speaking, gesturing to emphasize a point—even the use of facial expression—are all necessary. The small yet important item of the clothing of the teacher has a bearing upon the classroom atmosphere. Variety and even color (in good taste) in clothing can do much oftentimes to overcome drabness in surroundings.

Today's business teacher is an adventurer who is always willing to project his thinking beyond what is known—not being afraid of being unusual—being curious and willing to experiment; these are the characteristics of the dynamic teacher.

The Effective Business Teacher Is Scholarly. The outstanding business teacher has a thorough knowledge of the subject-matter he is teaching plus a breadth of knowledge covering many areas of human understanding. He has the ability to interrelate and use this knowledge for effective teaching and living. These are all an integral part of his scholarly achievement. His knowledge of his field and his knowledge of humanity will help him to develop a confidence that will be invaluable to him in the classroom. Students admire and respect scholarly attributes and will respond to teachers with these characteristics. Care must be taken, however, not to flaunt knowledge to the point of being "stuffy." A respect for knowledge coupled with a humble attitude toward its proper uses will aid in making a teacher liked, admired, and respected by students, colleagues, and members of a community.

The Effective Business Teacher Is Realistic. By being realistic the effective business teacher seldom will overestimate his own abilities nor will he misjudge the capabilities of his students. He will realize the limitations that society places on man and the burdens that man places upon society. He will be aware of the inequalities of life, but he will never subjugate his thinking to accept unjust inequalities. He will respect the limitations of the learning process and will use teaching methods that are based on the abilities of his students to acquire knowledge and to develop the qualities of an educated person.

He will realize that teaching can be both an enjoyable and yet a frustrating experience; that often the standards teachers set for themselves with respect to the degree of achievement of their students are higher than their (the teachers') ability to achieve. Because of this the effective teacher will acknowledge the need for relaxing activities so that he can meet his daily tasks without undue strain and concern. He will accept failure and disappointments with the knowledge that upon these things successes are often built.

The Effective Business Teacher Is Democratic. The democratic process is highly important to the effective business teacher. He believes in the inherent right of the individual and he sees and knows the inherent goodness within youth and endeavors to direct the ideas, thoughts, and knowledges of these young people into useful and productive channels. He will understand that we cannot be responsible for our students but that they must learn from themselves; thus he will eliminate from his thinking the paternalism and authoritarianism that is so often found in teachers.

The atmosphere of his classroom will be democratic in that the ideas and opinions of his students are considered of importance even though they may vary from his own. He will respect the views of others and zealously guard their right to believe as they do. He will be constantly seeking the truth and will attempt to develop this concept in the minds of his students. Bigotry and prejudice will have no place in his thoughts and he will express his faith in the democratic process and subscribe wholeheartedly to the American system of government.

The Teacher as a Technician

One of the first elements conducive to learning is the physical and mental atmosphere of the classroom. To a large extent the teacher is responsible for these important items and, although many teachers feel these are relatively unimportant as compared to other factors in teaching, actually inferior physical and mental atmosphere of the classroom can retard learning and cause teaching problems that are difficult to solve. Knowledge of and proper utilization of such factors as physical arrangement, lighting, equipment and supplies, student-teacher relationships, record keeping, and classroom organization may make the difference between a superior or an inferior teacher.

Physical Arrangements. The physical arrangement of the classroom should be a matter of concern and requires much study on the part of the teacher. Such factors as proper lighting, heating, ventilation, and room for both students and teacher to move about must be considered. It is not necessary for the teacher to be an expert in the physical properties of light and heat; the use of good common sense is sufficient. Anyone should be able to tell when a room is properly lighted, or to move desks and tables around to take advantage of available light. Comfort should be the best guide for heat and ventilation. Raising a window to adjust heating and ventilation to sensible proportions is a matter of good judgment. The aid of the school janitor might be sought for suggestions of maximum utilization of existing heating and ventilation facilities. It is an obvious fact that students cannot perform their best work in overheated, underventilated and poorly lighted surroundings. It will not always be possible in many schools to develop these facilities to an ideal, but at least the teacher should be aware of the best physical condition for learners and adapt existing conditions in the classroom to as near the ideal as possible.

Experiments with various room arrangements oftentimes will lead to the solutions of problems that the teacher may at first believe to be insoluble. One teacher in a typewriting class was plagued by students throwing wastepaper at the wastebasket with a resulting messy appearance where the thrown paper missed the mark. She solved her problem by the simple expedient of moving the wastebasket to a more convenient position for the students to use. Another teacher who had difficulty moving about his typewriting room because of crowded conditions solved his problem by arranging the tables of the class in the form of a square, and by so doing gave approximately 25 per cent more space in which to move about and observe the students as they typed.

As high schools become more crowded in the coming years, and with school-building construction lagging behind the increased enrollments, the problem of the physical arrangement of the classroom will become more and more important. Each teacher will be called on to use his ingenuity to solve these problems so that learning can take place in the best of physical conditions.

Classroom Organization. The organization of the classroom with respect to seating of students, the passing out and handing in of instructional supplies and papers, taking attendance and issuing student permits are also important factors for the teacher to consider. Again common sense should be the guide. It will be well for the teacher to determine the practice in the school concerning these matters and then adapt her procedures to this practice. Although there is no set rule with respect to the best method for seating students in class, frequently a simple alphabetic arrangement will prove to be the most feasible. This method oftentimes will separate the "buddies" and the "lovebirds" and thus eliminate at the beginning any minor problem that might arise because of the overfriendliness of certain students. Also, an alphabetic arrangement will facilitate handing out papers and taking roll, and in the early days of the class will facilitate learning students' names.

The teacher should learn the names of students as quickly as possible—usually within a day or two—and should follow the custom of the school with respect to calling students by name. In most schools addressing students by their first names is customary; usually the shortened version of the first name such as Jim, Bill, or Sue, or whatever the student prefers, is best. The more formal Mr. and Miss and the use of the last name only is oftentimes considered too cold and unfeeling.

The teacher should devise a good and fast method for dispensing graded papers, handing in papers, and passing out supplies. Sloppiness and carelessness in these matters can be distracting to both students and teacher and can cause petty annoyances which are not found in the best-organized classes. Care must be taken that classes are not overorganized to the point of highly formalized procedures and not underorganized to the extent of having time-consuming and improper procedures. A little care and preplanning on the part of the teacher can eliminate many minor difficulties which could grow to major ones.

Human Relationships (*Discipline*). The problem of discipline is one that many teachers, both experienced and inexperienced, dread. Actually this problem is not the major one that many teachers feel it is. However, the mental anguish that can be caused by disciplinary problems tends to lead teachers to overemphasize both its importance and its magnitude. Some school administrators have helped to overemphasize this problem because too many principals and superintendents have tended to measure the ability of a teacher by the manner in which he controls his students rather than by the teacher's ability to teach. Superintendents have stated that more teachers fail because of a discipline problem with students than for any other reason. It is doubtful that this is true because too few administrators actually get time to observe the teacher in action. They merely see the results of a discipline difficulty and thus assess the teacher's ability by this factor alone. Recent movies have emphasized the problems caused by recalcitrant students to the extent that many people believe that schools today are a beehive of juvenile delinquency. Radio and television programs about teachers (and written by laymen) have also aided in developing this delusion.

If the truth were actually known, difficulties of teachers with recalcitrant students, in all probability, are a minor part of the typical teacher's problems. In many cases young teachers have difficulty controlling students because of a predetermined fear that all students in the secondary school are a group of rowdies waiting for a chance to eject the teacher from the classroom. Of course, such is not the case.

In any event the management and control of students is one of the requirements of good teaching in order to maintain the proper atmosphere for learning in the classroom. It is difficult for the teacher to teach or for students to learn in a classroom in which an air of suspense is always present. The teacher cannot be at his effective best if he feels that he must be ever watchful for student disturbances. The students cannot be at their effective best if disturbances and distractions are always breaking out to disrupt their thinking.

What, then, is the solution for maintaining good disciplinary relationships in class? There is no one answer to this problem. Some teachers may say "be tough from the very beginning—let them know who is boss." Another will say "don't stand for any nonsense." Still another pet phrase is "be friendly but firm." All of the foregoing expressions may have some merit, but the truth is that each teacher must assess his own personality and the situation in which he is teaching and must then use the procedures that are best suited both to himself and to the situation in which he finds himself.

The foregoing statement will not satisfy the teacher who is looking for a nice, neat answer to the problem of disciplinary control. It is unfortunate, but there is no nice, neat answer. The differences found in people are so pronounced that it would be impossible to give one pat answer for every problem.

There are, however, several basic principles of human behavior that may give some key to the avoidance or elimination of conflicts between students and teacher. If teachers will only put out of their minds the thought that disciplinary problems are inevitable and treat their students with courtesy and respect as they would treat an adult, then the majority of the disciplinary situations will never appear. All teachers, regardless of their ability, are faced with the problem child at some time or another. The main thing to remember is that 99 per cent of secondary-school youngsters are well behaved and cause no difficulty. The other 1 per cent can be controlled usually with patience, understanding, and common sense.

Although there is no one solution to problems arising from disciplinary breakdowns, the following list of suggestions might be considered possible procedures to follow to minimize difficulties of this nature. It should be remembered that this list is not a final solution to problems, but merely suggestion of procedures that may prove useful.

1. Study the seating of the students. Determine, if possible, any trouble spots that may result from students sitting near each other who are "buddies" or "sweethearts." Rearrange the seating of students (as inconspicuously as possible) to eliminate possible trouble spots.

2. Learn the names of your students as quickly as possible and call on students whose attention may tend to waver. Do not use this procedure to embarrass a student, however.

3. Be businesslike in the classroom. Know what you intend to do in each class and get to the task as quickly as possible. An informal businesslike attitude is best.

4. Avoid all suggestions of criticism, anger, or irritation before the students. Be careful not to lose your temper. However, if you do become angry, make every effort to hide your feelings.

5. By your actions let the students know that you are interested in them as human beings as well as students in a class.

6. Stop little disciplinary difficulties before they get out of hand and become major problems.

7. Do not become sarcastic or belittle your students.

8. Do not threaten or harangue individuals or the group.

9. When discussing a disciplinary problem with an individual or the group, be as impersonal as possible. Do not permit favoritism to show in your actions and do not require apologies.

10. When not certain what course of action to take in a disciplinary situation, don't do anything. It is much better to back away from a problem and attack it later than to take too hasty action without careful thought.

11. Handle your own disciplinary problems insofar as possible. However, do not permit a problem to become more complex before you seek aid from others.

12. In the long run the following factors on your part will eliminate many difficulties:

    a. Respect for your students as individuals.
    b. Courtesy.
    c. Your scholarship and preparedness.
    d. Your sense of humor.
    e. Tolerance and understanding.
    f. Fairness.
    g. Enthusiasm.

Specialized Instructional Equipment. Modern science, and especially modern electronics, is providing the business teacher with automatic and mechanical aids which rapidly are becoming an accepted part of the total teaching profession. Technical skill and "know-how" must enter into the preparation of the business teacher who is to make use of them in the classroom. The necessity of teaching larger classes while at the same time giving greater attention to *individual* student needs and achieving more learning in shorter time all add up to a positive need for knowing how to make use of this very helpful modern specialized equipment.

For many years now the more skillful business teachers have been experts in the use of film and filmstrip projectors, opaque projectors, and simple record players. More recently they have discovered the value of the overhead projector—and especially when its use is combined with the use of an aid such as the Thermofax copy machine for quickly preparing transparencies. And today the use of the tape recorder is becoming almost standard practice in many phases of office and secretarial education.

Presently far too few business teachers are making use of the possibility of having students receive instructional materials through the use of headphones. This medium has the triple advantage of: (*a*) concentrating the student's attention on his work through eliminating outside distracting sounds; (*b*) permitting various students or groups of students to each be working on his own needed materials and at his own needed speed; and (*c*) having all these various activities going on in one room at the same time but without each interfering with the other! Frequently it has the added advantage of permitting individual students to study and practice effectively without the need for direct aid from the teacher.

The source of information received via the headphones may be either a single tape or a single record; either one or many students may be receiving the sound simultaneously through "gangs" of headphones. Through the use of two or more record players and/or tape recorders the variety of simultaneously presented instructional materials may be multiplied manyfold—and all may be done in one apparently quiet room with each student hearing only *his own* instructional material! The equipment may be relatively simple or it may be of a more sophisticated type comparable to the well-known foreign-language "laboratories." In the more modern secretarial and typewriting electronic laboratories each student has at his desk his own selector and volume control, which permit him to "tune in" on the particular channel needed for practice at the moment and to individually adjust the volume to his own needs.

Similarly, modern equipment now permits the business teacher to positively control the content and speed of materials being presented visually; such equipment is an adaptation of tachistoscopic training which long has been in use in reading-improvement programs. Ready-prepared film is available for use with such equipment in teaching shorthand, typewriting, transcription, filing, arithmetic, machine calculation, business English, and other phases of business education.

Additional types of such specialized equipment are appearing annually. Just as the modern surgeon must constantly add new technical skills as modern science comes to his aid, so too must the modern business teacher constantly improve and expand his ability as a technician in order to make effective use of the applications of modern science to needs of the teaching profession. Frequently, too, he finds it advantageous to prepare his own tapes, records, and/or film for use with this modern specialized equipment.

Programmed Instructional Materials. Recently much experimentation has been done with, and much has been written about, "teaching machines." *Basic* to the entire concept of teaching machines, however, is the necessity for "programming" instructional materials. It is quite possible to prepare and to use programmed instructional materials without the use of a so-called teaching machine. Some programmed texts and units of instruction are now available in business subjects.

The modern business teacher also should realize that, through the use of an electronic computer today, it is quite possible to completely automate the entire presentation of instructional materials, including the control of such equipment as film projectors, slide projectors, tape recorders, and so forth—all interwoven and automatically presented in proper sequence with appropriate voice and other explanations! Once carefully programmed, such a presentation may be used over and over, either with a single student or with multiple groups of students.

Certainly programmed instruction today still is in its infancy. However, there is much evidence that it is a potentially useful technique whereby much learning can take place on the part of the individual student *without* the physical presence of the teacher. Again it is pointed out that the necessity of teaching *more* students efficiently and with economy of teacher-time makes programmed instructional materials worthy of due consideration.

Planning

The planning of instruction is a highly important aspect of the teacher's work. The superior teacher will not only plan carefully each day's lesson, but will plan even a semester or year ahead.

In the past, lesson planning by teachers took the form of very detailed and formal plans. Each day's lesson was stated in the form of objectives, aims, procedures, and so forth, which necessitated a great deal of laborious thought and work on the part of the teacher. Obviously this type of planning, though it had the advantage of making the teacher think through carefully each day's lesson, nonetheless had many limitations. In spite of the work and time required to prepare such plans, they usually were so detailed and restrictive that they actually had little value. If the work in the classroom were a set pattern that the teacher could forecast, these types of plans would be useful. However, the better teachers have found that learning will best take place when the activity of the classroom is patterned after current situations or stimulated by the interests of the students. The teacher who holds himself within the confines of a detailed lesson plan will not be an effective teacher because he will not be able to use current class situations as a point of departure for teaching. The superior teacher has found that a loosely constructed, flexible lesson plan, but one carefully thought through, is much more effective and applicable to the typical class.

The modern concept of lesson planning, then, is somewhat more liberal and less restrictive than the old-type formal plans. The importance of planning remains as great as before. However, the modern trend of planning permits more flexibility and adaptability on the part of the teacher to meet various learning problems as they are confronted in the class.

The well-prepared teacher usually is a confident teacher and one who commands respect from his students. The time spent in planning and preparing for the class by necessity requires much of the teacher's time. However, this time can be shortened considerably through a few days of concentrated effort.

There are three main stages of planning in teaching that are used today by superior teachers. The first is the long-range stage in which plans are laid for a particular course for a semester or year. The second stage is planning for a shorter period of time, usually for a chapter or a unit of work composed of shorter chapters. The third stage is the day-to-day planning for each of the individual lessons that may have been assigned.

Long-Range Planning. A long-range plan for instruction is usually the first step in the teacher's preparation for a course. This type of plan usually is in outline form and is the basis for future unit or day-to-day planning. The broad topics to be covered, or the units, are listed with an estimated time to be spent on each. The instructional materials that supplement the textbook are also listed with notations of those on hand in the teacher's files and those which must be obtained. The audio-visual aids to be used are planned along with their approximate dates of use. If these materials must be procured, then the name and address of the supplier should be listed. Other resources or instructional materials that may be used also should be listed. Finally, the examinations to be used should be listed together with the approximate date for each.

Although at first glance it would appear that preparing such a long-range plan would be a time-consuming task, it should be remembered that the teacher will only have to do it once during the semester and that the time taken to prepare more detailed plans for units and day-to-day lessons will be cut down accordingly. Below is illustrated in condensed form a long-range plan for teaching general business.

Outline of a
Longe-Range Plan for General Business
(One Semester)

1. Units
    a. The functions of business in society (2 weeks)
    b. Banking services (3 weeks)
    c. Budgeting and spending wisely (2 weeks)
    d. Credit services (3 weeks)
    e. Insurance and social security (4 weeks)
    f. Savings and thrift (2 weeks)
2. Instructional materials (other than text and workbook) to be used for each of the units
    a. List instructional materials and indicate unit in which they will be used.
        (1) Indicate in some manner whether these materials are on hand or must be obtained

3. Audio-visual aids to be used
   a. List which ones
4. Other resources that can be used (field trips, speakers, individual and group projects, and so forth)
5. Examinations (time and type)

Unit Planning. The planning of instruction for a unit of work or for several related chapters is much more detailed than is the long-range plan. In this type of plan the major objectives to be accomplished should be listed primarily to clarify them in the teacher's mind. A detailed outline is needed of the topics to be covered in the unit, the instructional materials, teacher and student references, student activities and projects, teaching techniques, and a tentative examination. Care should be taken in preparing the unit plan, for it is from this plan that daily lesson plans will be developed.

Below is an illustration of a plan for use in teaching a unit in general business.

Unit Plan for General Business *Money*

1. Reasons for Teaching:
   The handling of money is a daily task of paramount importance to everyone. There should be no need to justify including a unit on money in the basic business program when we realize that so many people through lack of information entangle their lives in a hopeless twine of financial difficulties.

   With the rapid changes in our economic system since World War II and those which are to result from a continually expanding economy, it is the job of the schools to attempt to give students an adequate understanding of money economics to insure their financial security as far as possible.
2. Sources of Information and Materials:
   a. Consumer Education Study
      Managing Your Money
      Using Consumer Credit
      You and Our Economic System
   b. Sister M. Virginia, O.P., "Studying Money Can Be Fun," *Business Education World*, XXVII (June 1947).
   c. *How Money Works*, Public Affairs Pamphlet No. 45, 20 cents
   d. *Moneys of the World*, Chase National Bank

e. *Your Money and the Federal Reserve System,* Federal Reserve Bank of Minneapolis, Minnesota

f. Elementary Teachers Guide to Free Curriculum Materials, Educational Progress Service. *Know Your Money*—United States Treasury Department—Secret Service
Money Management—The Budget Calendar—Household Finance Corporation

g. Household Finance Corporation
Men and Money, sound film, twenty-five minutes. The first half of the movie tells about the interest and the history of borrowing money. The last half depicts the activities of a small loan corporation. *Managing the Family Income,* slides, seventeen frames. Principles of borrowing money are illustrated by cartoons.

3. Detailed Topics:
   a. History and Use of Money:
      (1) Suggested Content:
          (a) Purpose of money
          (b) Need for money
          (c) Items that have been used for money
          (d) Where and how money is made
          (e) Characteristics of good money
          (f) Counterfeit money
          (g) Moneys of the world
      (2) Activities and Projects:
          (a) Exhibit: Have students bring to class any samples of foreign money or old American money that they may have.
          (b) Make a poster showing various forms that were used for money in early times.
          (c) Report: "History of Money in the United States."
          (d) Film: *Story of Money.*
   b. Earning Money:
      (1) Suggested Content:
          (a) Wages and salaries in community compared to state or nation
          (b) Economic principles concerning money:
              (*a*) How and why prices fluctuate
              (*b*) How and why wages and salaries fluctuate
      (2) Activities or Projects:
          (a) Students may prepare charts or graphs showing fluctuations of prices and wages over a ten-year period. Use statistical data suggested in sources.

(b) Panel discussion on "Current Prices and Trends in the Near Future."

(c) Committee of students investigates job possibilities within the community and compiles a table of jobs and wages. Several representative firms might be chosen such as a factory, retail store, wholesale house, insurance office.

(d) Prepare a series of charts illustrating the economic principles concerning money.

(e) Business arithmetic might be correlated by giving some problems to illustrate the difference in actual salaries and take-home pay.

(f) Movies: *Money at Work, Men and Money.*

c. Spending Money Wisely:

(1) Suggested Content:

(a) Study of the budget

(b) Importance of wise buying

(c) Best time to buy

(2) Activities and Projects:

(a) Give a short talk before the class on the topic "Is time more important than money?" or "Why budgets will not always work."

(b) Write a paper on the topic "The importance of wise buying and the keeping of budgets."

(c) Debate: "Resolved, Wise spending of money is as important as earning of money."

(d) Bring to class daily newspaper advertisements of sales in which the advertisers indicate why the sales are being held.

(e) Compare prices of articles and calculate percentages saved.

d. How to Make Change:

(1) Suggested Content:

(a) How to make change correctly

(b) Types of machines that make change

(2) Activities and Projects:

(a) Set up an imaginary store of any type. Students take turns being customers and clerks. Purchases should be made for different amounts that require the making of change. Play money can be used.

(b) Report: "How Change-Making Machines Operate."

(c) A committee could be chosen to find out where in the

community change-making machines are used and how they operate.

e. How to Wrap Coins:
  (1) Suggested Content:
      (a) Purpose of wrapping coins
      (b) Coin-wrapping machines
  (2) Activities and Projects:
      (a) Students practice wrapping coins of the different denominations.
      (b) If coin-wrapping machines are used in the local banks have a committee of students visit a bank and report their observation of the machine.

f. Money Substitutes:
  (1) Suggested Content:
      (a) Substitutes provided by the banks, post offices, express agencies, and telegraph companies.
  (2) Activities and Projects:
      (a) Bulletin-board display showing actual copies (if possible) of a check, bank draft, registered check, certified check, application for postal money order, express and postal money orders, postal note, travelers' check, telegraph money-order blank
      (b) Have a committee of students visit the local telegraph office and report to the class the procedure used in wiring money. (See Unit IX—Communication.)
      (c) Committee of students visit the local banks in order to find out amounts that can be sent and fees charged for bank draft, register check, and certified check.
      (d) Committee of students visit the post office and find out what amounts can be sent by postal money order and by postal note and also the fees charged.
      (e) Report: Students who have sent money by any of the methods mentioned report on the procedure.
      (f) Ask students who have had experience using travelers' checks to report to the class.

4. Examination Over Unit.

Daily Lesson Plans. The daily lesson plan is based on the planning developed for the unit. For the experienced teacher it usually can be prepared on 3 x 5 cards which merely serve as a reminder of the planning for the day—a list of questions for discussion, drills to be used, or other elements pertinent to the lesson. No formal planning sheet is necessary. At times it may even taken the form of brief notes. It merely is a reminder for the teacher of elements to be taught that day as a part of the master (unit) plan.

However, it is *extremely important* that there be daily lesson planning, and that it be psychologically sound as well as logical. Thus for the relatively inexperienced teacher and, especially, the apprentice student-teacher, good planning habits are best learned when some type of formal lesson plan is used. There appears to be no one best form. It merely should be so arranged as to *encourage* a well-planned lesson. There probably are four major factors which the expert teacher constantly (and perhaps semiautomatically) gives attention as he prepares and teaches a lesson:

1. The content, topics, subject-matter or "learnings" for the day, and the related sequences in which they are to be presented

2. The various procedures and activities *of the teacher* as he conducts the class and carries through the sequences planned

3. The activities and participations *of the students* as the class period proceeds—for an idle student learns but little

4. An *evaluation* of the success of the plan (How well did it work? Should it be changed before it is used again in the future?)

It is recommended that the beginning teacher adopt a two-, three-, or four-column "form" (as may be preferred) to use in preparing daily lesson plans, and mimeograph or duplicate a big supply (paper is relatively cheap!). These sheets may be punched for a ring notebook, and thus provide a convenient reference while conducting the class. Use sheets liberally and avoid attempting to get too much on one page for quick, convenient reference. The form on page 89 is illustrative of one which might be used for this purpose.

As a further guide to preparing daily lessons and lesson plans, page 90 reproduces more detailed directions which have been used for completing a lesson plan form such as the one shown on page 89.

Team Teaching. Consideration of modern techniques available as a part of good instructional planning would hardly be complete today without mention of team teaching. This modern and increasingly popular practice, simply stated, is based on the idea that two or more "heads" and two or more teachers are better than one!

Team teaching takes many forms, but it means that two or more

LESSON PLAN. Subject:_____ Unit:_____ When to be used:_____ No.:___
(Note: Course and unit objectives, contents, time allotments, etc., must first be fully decided. Daily lesson plans must conform to unit and course plans. Related physical conditions must be checked daily.)

Special materials needed:

Special learnings planned:

Topics and/or learnings to be taught	Teacher procedures and activities	Student activities and participations	Evaluation of the plan

teachers work together in *preparing* and in *teaching* various subjects, courses, and lessons. It is based on a pooling of ideas and a pooling of talents, abilities, and interests. Sometimes two teachers may be working together in a classroom; this may provide better individual assistance or may permit more students to be present in the class. At times several different classes or sections of a given class may be brought together to benefit from the special work of one master teacher. At other times the regular teacher of a course may bring to his students the benefit of hearing from some other teacher who possesses expert knowledge or ability in some unit of study. At all times the "team" of teachers works together in formulating the plans for the entire course and for the various units within the course(s) involved, dividing the work among themselves in accordance with their individual interests, abilities, and preparation. Thus, to a large extent, it is a further application to the teaching profession of the principle of specialization in work. Yet, at the same time, it encourages and attains greater cooperation and mutual assistance among the teacher-specialists. The result: both the teachers and the students profit!

To summarize, there is no substitute for the development of confidence in teaching by being well prepared. It is much better to be overprepared than to have too little preparation. A few hours of hard

THE DAILY LESSON PLAN: First, there are certain "constants" which ALWAYS must be cared for—heat, ventilation, light, proper seating, roll-call, etc. But the MAIN items to be "worried about" in advance essentially are the "variables" from day to day. *Three* of them are always with you: (*a*) that which is being learned—subject-matter or content, objectives, attitudes, knowledges, skills, etc. (*b*) the teacher—as a guiding, directing, motivating force constantly controlling the situation, and (*c*) the students—who *cannot* remain passive and disinterested if they are learning, but who should at all times be engaged in appropriate motivated ACTIVITY of SOME kind. At any one moment the teacher should have *planned control* of all three variables. Hence —What types of notations should go in each of a three-column lesson plan? (*Note:* This is merely a listing; not a lesson plan!)

1 Topics and/or learnings to be taught (Briefly!)	2 Teaching procedures and teacher activities	3 Student activities and participations	4 Evaluation for future
Reminders of: (*In order!*) Major topics or ideas subtopics Skills to be learned Attitudes to develop References to be used: in class in assignments A chart to be shown or prepared A film to be shown A pertinent assignment (reference) Concepts to master Problems to solve More content to be taught	Rather specific brief "guides"—*in the order they are to be used*—to help the teacher be sure to "get going" correctly on each item in lesson Might Include: Questions to assure discussions Explain—using blackboard Drill—using chart, or flashcards, or blackboard, or certain pages in text Demonstrate—as carriage throw Topic for a buzz session Call for a certain report Checking skill techniques Develop a point through questioning, how to get started	Might Include: Listening—attentively Taking notes Asking and answering questions Individual recitations—while group listens Group discussions Panel reports and/or discussions Committee reports Individual reports Practicing on skills Problem-solving Watching, watching and listening	

work at the beginning of the school year will do much to minimize the burden on the teacher of planning and preparing lessons, and the results from careful planning will also eliminate disorganized teaching. A well-prepared teacher is a confident teacher and one whom students respect. Respect from students will eliminate disciplinary problems and oftentimes will stimulate students, because well-planned lessons usually are interesting ones.

Evaluation and Grading

One of the most difficult problems of teachers is that of evaluation of student ability and the assigning of grades. In recent years there has been much dissatisfaction among educators with the systems of evaluation and the subsequent assignment of grades in the public schools. There also have been many attempts made to improve present practices. Notably, in the elementary schools the use of the parent-teacher conference has worked out quite well as a means of informing parents about their child's achievement as well as the development of his personality and character traits. However, this type of evaluation or grading has not yet been introduced successfully into the secondary school.

Some of the questions teachers always ask themselves and others concerning this problem are these:

1. On what basis should grades be given—subject-matter knowledge, attitude, improvement, social development, or what other basis?
2. Should students be compared grade-wise one with the other?
3. Should grades be used as a motivating device? Should a student who earns a high grade be graded lower if his conduct is poor?
4. Should students be failed ever?
5. Is the competition brought on among students to get high grades a good thing?
6. Should grades be based upon test results alone or should such factors as interest, class participation, or industriousness have a bearing?
7. How do you assign a grade to such subjective measurements as attitude, participation, or industriousness?
8. Should everything (every assignment) that a student completes be graded?

These and many other questions are often raised by teachers in their quest for a solution to the problems of evaluation and grading.

If you are looking for answers to these questions then you must look elsewhere than in this book. There is no answer other than the opinion held by each individual. One teacher may believe, for example, that no student should ever fail. The reasons advanced might be that our evaluative devices, at best, are not perfect and thus who are we to say who should fail? Also, perhaps the fact that a student has a poor knowledge of the subject-matter of a course is not the student's fault, but the fault of poor teaching. A further argument might be that failing a student does not accomplish anything other than causing the student to feel inferior. Is it fair, the argument might be stated, to compare a student with a limited intellectual capacity to one with a superior capacity? It isn't his fault that he is "dumb." A final argument might be that there are more important things than subject-matter knowledge, and that although a student might not have the essential knowledges of a subject, nonetheless he is learning how to cooperate with a group; perhaps the fact that he is in school and keeping out of mischief is sufficient reason to pass him so that he will remain in school.

On the other hand, it might be argued that if we do not fail a student who is weak in the subject-matter of a course then we may be doing him a disfavor. When he does get out of school he will have to face the reality of not having the same ability as others. What is wrong, the argument might go, with a student being failed in a course if he doesn't meet the standards set for the course? Are we not detracting from the students who do pass if we fail none? School should be similar to life—in life there are failures which must be overcome, why then should we protect students from knowledge of this fact? Are we not performing a disservice to employers of students if the employer is erroneously permitted to believe a student is capable in a given subject? The purpose of school is to help students learn. If a student does not learn, then he should be failed. And, finally, by passing everyone is there not a danger of destroying the respect and confidence of the public in our schools?

Both of the arguments in the foregoing paragraphs are strong ones. The frustrating thing to teachers is that neither point of view can either be proven or disproven other than by personal opinion. The point is that grading and evaluation is a major problem with many teachers and one that does not lend itself to an easy solution.

It is not the purpose in this book to suggest answers to all the problems arising because of evaluation and grading. Rather, the purpose is to suggest ways that teachers may solve their own problems more easily. Each teacher should formulate his own philosophy as to the purposes of evaluation and grading, and then apply the proper technical procedures to fulfill this philosophy.

In later chapters of this book some of the specific techniques of evaluation and grading will be discussed as they apply to specific subject-matter courses in business education. In this chapter some of the more general procedures will be presented as they apply to all business education courses. No attempt will be made to go into the philosophical bases of evaluation and grading. The subject will be treated in terms of the practical approach with which the problems are confronted by the typical secondary-school business teacher.

These facts about evaluation and grading are known:

1. Grades must be given in secondary schools today.
2. There must be some bases for determining these grades.

First let us examine various bases that might be used by a teacher in assigning a student's grade. The most common are:

1. Examinations
2. Class recitation
3. Student projects

Examinations. There are various types of examinations available to the business teacher for the measuring of a student's ability. Although the types of exams for use in measuring ability in the skill subjects are quite different in form from those used in the nonskill business subjects, they still may be classified under the following categories:

1. Objective examinations (true-false, multiple choice, matching, and so forth)
2. Essay examinations (subjective)
3. Problem examinations
4. Performance examinations

The so-called objective examinations, which are quite commonly found in use in business classes today, have many advantages. The greatest advantage is their ease in scoring, and this is important to the busy teacher of today with large enrollments in the class. Another advantage is elimination of the element of subjectivity. In other words, an answer to a question is either correct or incorrect, and the teacher does not have to make a subjective evaluation of the correctness of an answer as she must do in an essay-type exam. However, the characteristic of objectivity given to this exam does not always hold up under close scrutiny (except in the case of a fully standardized test) because the factor of subjectivity does enter into the picture in the sense that the teacher selects the item about which the question is asked, and by so doing she makes a subjective decision that this item is of sufficient importance to be worth determining whether the student knows the correct answer. However, the supposed objectivity or subjectivity of this type of examination is not of major importance. The important thing is that this type of examination is widely used in courses of the nonskill areas of business, and in certain instances can be effectively used in the skill areas. It is best used, of course, to measure the extent of knowledge of a student in the subject-matter of a course.

This type of examination also has some disadvantages. Students may guess at an answer easily, the exam is difficult and time-consuming to prepare, and it does not always measure a student's ability to think or apply his knowledge.

Many objective tests provided by the publishers of the various textbooks are made available for teachers to use in almost all business courses. For the most part these examinations have been carefully prepared and are probably as good as, if not better than, ones prepared by the teacher. However, the better teachers should try their hands at preparing their own examinations, for in many instances a published examination may not fit the content of a course.

Types of Objective-Test Questions. The best objective-type tests have included in them several different forms of questions. The most commonly used types are:

1. True-false
2. Multiple choice
3. Completion or single answer
4. Matching or master list

A true-false type of question is best used to determine whether students have acquired a misconception about an idea, to determine a single fact that is important for a student to know, or to determine whether a student knows the difference between two related but different concepts such as socialism and government regulation. In the preparation of a true-false question several principles should be kept in mind:

1. The question should be either totally true or totally false.
2. The use of trick questions should be avoided. This most often occurs in the development of a false statement.
3. Use of words such as *always* and *never* should be avoided.
4. Avoid the use of the exact wording found in a textbook.
5. Avoid the use of long questions that are highly involved.
6. Be careful of the placement of the questions on the exam so that they do not follow a specific pattern.

Although true-false questions have been criticized because students find it easy to guess, this can be minimized somewhat by requiring students to write a brief sentence on their reasons for answering a question either true or false. Partial credit may be given for an incorrect answer if the logic used in answering incorrectly is sound. For example, one point might be given for a correct answer to the question and one point for the reason given. Another method advocated by some educators to discourage guessing is to subtract from the right answers the number of wrong answers. In this method a double penalty is given for an incorrect answer and only a single penalty for a question not answered.

Multiple-choice questions can best be used to determine knowledge of cause-and-effect relationships, ability to make comparisons, and ability to differentiate among several possible correct procedures. Principles to keep in mind while constructing a multiple-choice question are:

1. The question should have four or five possible answers.
2. The correct answer should be completely correct. In other words, there should be no danger of two possible answers being too closely related.
3. Long involved answers should be eliminated.
4. It is sometimes good to include several correct answers in one question with one being indicated as the *best* answer.
5. The question should be stated positively rather than negatively.

The single-answer or completion-type question is one of the most difficult types of objective questions for students to answer and is one from which the element of guessing is eliminated. It can best be used for determining single facts, or to replace a question that asks for a definition. For example, instead of developing a question such as "Define insurance," the question might be stated in this way: "The sharing of economic risks is known as―――――――."

In developing single-answer or completion questions, the following points should be kept in mind:

1. Each answer should call for a single—but important—idea that can be stated as one word, a number, a phrase, or a short sentence.
2. Allowance should be made for expressing the same idea in several different ways.
3. Avoid questions with so many blanks that it is difficult to follow the sense of the question.
4. Avoid indefinite questions of such nature that almost any word would apply to the missing blank.

The use of matching or master-list questions has the advantage that it can be applied to almost any type of subject-matter and retain the advantages of any of the other types of questions described. Particular care should be taken in the construction of these types of questions. Factors that should be considered are:

1. The directions should be explicit and clear.
2. Arrangement of the items in the basic list should be at random, such as alphabetic, numerical, or chronological.
3. There should be more items in the basic list than in the secondary list.
4. Not more than fifteen items, nor less than five items, should be included in the secondary list.
5. Directions should be clear as to whether items in the basic list can be used more than once.

Essay-Type Questions. The essay-type question is one that can be used to advantage in evaluating the progress of students in business education courses. The essay question will have more application to measurement of information learned in the nonskill courses than to the skill courses, because this type of question lends itself more readily to the measurement of subject-matter knowledge.

Some of the advantages given for the essay-type question are:

1. Students are required to think before answering the question.
2. Guessing is discouraged.
3. The ability to communicate is emphasized.
4. The questions are comparatively easy to prepare.

Some of the disadvantages are:

1. The essay question is difficult to grade objectively.
2. It takes much longer for the teacher to check.
3. Teachers are unsure as to whether to evaluate the ability to express ideas as well as the content of the answer.
4. Students' handwriting may be poor and thus difficult to read.
5. Only a small body of knowledge can be examined.

Although the disadvantages listed above for using essay-type examination questions should be carefully considered, nonetheless occasional use of this type of question is important in the educational function. The argument that the use of essay questions in an examination is time-consuming for a teacher is a strong one. However, if the questions are carefully prepared, this argument loses much of its weight. The value gained through requiring students to use written expression involving analytical ability is an important one.

In preparing essay-type questions the teacher should consider carefully the type of information desired. If a specific answer is required, then the question should be stated in a specific manner. Be careful in preparing the question to avoid one that can be answered in generalities. In answering a question that is too general in nature a student having limited knowledge can bluff. It is this type of essay question that is difficult to grade.

Broadly speaking, essay questions can be categorized into the following types:

1. *Recall of information*
   "Name four types of risk that everyone has, and suggest a type of insurance that could be used to cover each risk."
2. *Comparison of information*
   "Compare the advantages to a businessman who owns a

grocery store of requiring customers to pay cash rather than extending credit to them."

3. *Cause-and-effect relationships*
"Explain and give reasons why a good credit rating will be of benefit to an individual."

4. *Definition or explanation*
"Explain how mass production increases the standard of living of the people."

5. *Evaluation*
"Which is more serious to the average family whose income is from salary—loss of property or loss of income? Illustrate your answer by giving an example."

6. *Discussion—for or against*
"Discuss the advantages and disadvantages of owning your own home instead of renting your home."

7. *Problem-solving*
"Joe Smith is planning to buy a new car. His old car is four years old and has been driven 30,000 miles. He has been offered a trade on a new car with automatic transmission for $3,100 receiving an allowance of $1,700 on his old car. Cars similar to his old car are selling in used-car lots for $1,300. His old car cost $2,500 new." Joe must finance the purchase of the new car and his payments would be $65 per month for 24 months.
What should Joe do? Give your reasons.

One of the greatest problems in using essay-type questions is that of grading them objectively. The best procedure for a teacher to follow is to set up the answer to the question in terms of a series of points that should be developed by the testee. Each of these points should be weighted, and the final answer given by the student should be compared with the teacher's key. The teacher will have to make a decision (subjective) as to how well the student's answer brings out all of the points desired by the teacher. It is the author's opinion that the ability to communicate his ideas to the teacher in the written paper should also be a factor in the grade received. However, this may or may not be a factor. It is whatever the teacher desires.

Problem Tests. Problem tests can be used most effectively in a course such as bookkeeping, or in the skill subjects of typewriting and shorthand. In this type of test a question is developed around a problem situation and the student is expected to arrive at the correct answer. This type of test is one of the most objective kinds because there is only one correct answer. Either the student works the problem correctly, or he does not. There is no need for a subjective evaluation. An example of this type of question for a bookkeeping examination is given below.

John Smith owns a grocery store. He purchases merchandise costing $500 and is entitled to a cash discount of 2 per cent. What are the entries on the books of Mr. Smith if he pays cash for the merchandise?

Obviously, in this type of question there is only one correct answer. However, the teacher may be confronted with the question of whether or not he should give partial credit for an answer that is partially correct. In the preceding question, for example, what if the student got the account titles correct but made an error in arithmetic? Should partial credit be given? Conversely, if the arithmetic is correct but the account titles are misplaced, what then?

There is still a further difficulty in using this type of examination question. Oftentimes in working a long problem a student will make a mistake early, which in turn will cause several other errors. The teacher is then faced with a decision—is the problem right or wrong? Should an error made early in a problem be followed through and further errors that are caused by this early mistake not be counted?

Other questions oftentimes asked by teachers are: Should an examination of this type have the element of speed in it? Who is the better student—the one who works slowly but accurately, or the one who works swiftly but slightly inaccurately? Teachers will often hear the complaint from students, "I didn't get finished (working the exam) but the problems I did solve were correct. If you would only have given me more time I would have gotten them all finished and correct." This is a difficult problem to solve. For example: Suppose that the teacher gives an examination consisting of four problems of equal weight—each problem is worth a maximum of 25 points and they total 100. One student works two problems correctly during an hour's examination period for a total of 50 points. Another student works all four problems, but has errors on each one that cut his score down to 20 points per problem for a total of 80 points. Which is the better student? Probably it is the student who earned the 80 points. At least the teacher is sure that he has some knowledge of all the areas over which the test was developed, whereas for the student who didn't get finished, the teacher can only speculate. However, these problems give the teacher much cause for reflection in the evaluation of students.

The time element in a problem examination must be included. Ability to think rapidly and accurately rather than just accurately is most important. To eliminate the difficulty of tracing errors through a long problem-type examination, it will be best to develop a series of short problem questions all unrelated to one another. Thus, the teacher can eliminate the dependence of one part of a question on another, and at the same time broaden the examination to cover more areas of information.

Performance Tests. Performance tests are particularly adapted to the subjects of typewriting and shorthand where a student is examined over his ability to type a letter, type straight copy, transcribe from dictation, or set up a tabulated problem either with or without the element of time entering in. Performance-test questions are easy to develop and easy to score—either a student can perform or he cannot.

Because of the relative ease in developing and grading this type of examination, there is danger of using it too much. Timed writings in typewriting are an excellent example of the overuse and abuse of this type of test. Too many teachers use at least one, sometimes two, and even three timed tests daily, recording the student's achievement on each. Performance tests of this nature probably should be given only once each week at the most.

However, it should be made clear that the present discussion refers to *testing.* There are many occasions when the typewriting teacher properly uses short timed writings, perhaps of a repetitive nature, as a drill technique for increasing speed or for other reasons; such timed writings are not in the nature of tests, and when used as learning devices, of course, no grades are recorded. This point will be discussed further in a later chapter of this book.

Although tests are an important instrument in the hands of the teacher as a means of evaluating student ability, the wise teacher will use test results carefully and with a certain amount of skepticism. Test results by themselves will not provide an accurate measure of a student's ability or worth, such as ability to think and solve problems while not under the pressure of an examination. His sense of responsibility in completing assignments, in class recitation, and in completing student projects certainly is another value worth measuring.

Since any teacher can cite examples of students who were poor students in a subject as reflected by their scores on examinations, but yet were successful workers as adults, the teacher should remain humble about this method of evaluation. Use tests wisely to examine not only the ability of students, but the effectiveness of teaching. After the results have been obtained, consider the other factors that may help determine the ability of students to achieve; only by putting all of these factors together can the teacher be partially sure that she has evaluated a student's ability correctly.

Class Recitation and Participation. The measurement of class recitation or participation in discussion as a means of evaluating student achievement is necessary. However, the use of such evaluation has its limitations in that the evaluation must be purely subjective. Because of this factor teachers have not generally placed much emphasis upon classroom participation by students as a measurement device.

It is true, however, that some students can communicate better orally than by written examinations. The ability to think constructively and to express ideas effectively is one that should be developed by teachers. Care should be taken not to confuse intelligent recitation with loquaciousness. Some students will have the ability of eloquence yet not say much. The teacher must also be skilled in the ability to so lead discussion that all students will be encouraged to participate. In large classes this is difficult, but it can be done by using the technique of small-group discussion.

As has been mentioned, the greatest drawback in the measurement of class participation is the inability of the teacher to point to some specific and objective measure of achievement. However, this difficulty should not deter the teacher from attempting some type of measurement. At the conclusion of a class the teacher could make some type of code mark in the grade book relative to the participation of the students. This does not mean that a grade would be given every day. Only those people who had made a worth-while contribution to the class discussion would be checked.

Although using this technique means that the teacher must recall evidences of participation and that there may be some danger of forgetting, nevertheless it is inadvisable to check participation at the actual time. To do so is disconcerting to the students and also makes it necessary for the teacher to withdraw his attention from the class momentarily while some kind of mark is being made. The obviousness of the teacher grading participation at the time of the act will detract and perhaps will even discourage students from contributing for fear of contributing something that may be considered inadequate.

Student Projects. Student projects such as practice sets in bookkeeping, special reports, notebooks, displays, and the like present another means of evaluating student achievement. The bases upon which these projects may be graded will necessarily vary from time to time and from teacher to teacher. The more obvious and important bases are extensiveness of the project, care with which it was developed, originality, and importance to the subject-matter of the class.

Methodology

Although the specific methodology that should be used by business teachers will be discussed in detail in later chapters as it pertains to specific business subjects, it is proper here to mention briefly some of the more general pertinent ideas.

It should be pointed out that there is no one best method or procedure. The method to be used by a teacher will depend upon many things:

1. The objective to be attained
2. The number of students to be taught and their stage of advancement
3. The character or the content of subject-matter used
4. The nature and availability of the resources, such as reading materials, visual aids, and laboratory equipment
5. The place in the course, whether at the beginning, in the middle, or at the end
6. The ability of the teacher to use various methods

The wise teacher will consider all of the factors listed above and adapt his methodology to those situations to which it will be suited best.

The more common methods proper for use in teaching business in the secondary school are discussion, problem-solving, demonstrations, drill, and question-and-answer. Drill, problem-solving, and demonstration will be best suited for the skill type of courses such as typewriting, shorthand, and secretarial practice. The discussion method, question-and-answer (recitation), and problem-solving will be best suited for the nonskill subjects such as bookkeeping, general business, and business law.

An important point to remember in teaching business subjects in the secondary school is to use a method that is student-centered. Learning will be most effective if the methodology used places its greatest emphasis upon the activities and actions of the students rather than those of the teacher. The skillful business teacher will guide and direct the learning of his students while remaining in the background and not being the dominant person in the room.

Thus it would follow that there is little if any place in the secondary school for the lecture method or for excessive illustration, demonstration, or explanation by the teacher. A common fault of many beginning teachers is that they talk too much. Questions too often are so stated that they either call for only a yes or no answer or are answered by the teacher himself. Typing classes have been taught in which the problem method was being used and yet the teacher would not permit the students to solve their own problems; he solved them himself.

Oftentimes a method may be used by a teacher without the teacher's fully understanding the implications or reasons back of the method. *Group dynamics* is a term describing a highly specialized type of discussion technique. In recent years it has received a great deal of attention and "glamour" as a progressive method. Yet this type of procedure can be used only by the teacher who has studied its various ramifications and understands fully its operations. Inexperienced or unwise teachers have attempted to use this type of teaching with sad results.

The superior teacher will assess his own capabilities and will use the method that suits him best as well as that which suits his students best. He will study and plan carefully the methods he will use in a particular situation and will quickly shift or change his procedure if he finds that it is not working. In these ways teaching methodology can be utilized to its greatest effectiveness.

Projects and Questions for Discussion

1. Investigate and report on the EDL Skill Builder and its possible use in teaching business subjects.

2. Prepare a bulletin-board display showing and explaining the use of headphones and multiple-channel electronic equipment in teaching typewriting and/or shorthand.

3. Read and report on some article describing the use of team teaching in some business subject.

4. Choose some unit in a business subject you will be teaching, prepare a brief outline of its contents, and then prepare a detailed lesson plan for teaching one day or more of the unit.

5. Have a committee of class members investigate and report on teaching machines and programmed instructional materials. Try to secure and bring to class actual programmed texts or units of instruction.

6. Do you consider it permissible for a student to call a teacher by his first name outside of school hours? What should the attitude of a teacher be toward his students—friendly, or reserved?

7. Is it ever desirable to use the device of lowering a grade in a class as punishment for a serious disciplinary act? Explain.

8. What action would you take if you found that one of your students was cheating on an examination?

9. May an objective-type examination actually measure a student's ability in the subject-matter of a course, or is there too much opportunity for guessing?

10. Do you believe it is better to grade your students on their ability or on their improvement? If you believe improvement is best, then who is the better typing student—one who improves in a six-week period from sixty words a minute on a five-minute writing to sixty-five or the student who improves from twenty words per minute to forty?

11. Is it necessary to spend much time planning lessons in typewriting when each lesson is planned for you by the organization of the textbook into daily lessons?

12. Is it ever a good idea to use the lecture method in a high-school business class? Why or why not?

13. Do you believe that students should ever be permitted to assist you in planning the activities of a class in general business?

14. Should the element of time ever be introduced into an examination in bookkeeping? If it is, is this fair to the slow student who is very accurate?

15. Would you suggest that it would be a permissible procedure to teach a typewriting class and a bookkeeping class simultaneously in adjacent rooms?

Case Problems

1. The Superintendent of Midvale High School is a firm believer in strong disciplinary control of students in the high school. He has cautioned his teachers time and time again not to permit any rowdyism in their classes. You are the teacher of a typewriting class and the following incident takes place. One of the students (a rather large boy), while taking a timed writing, becomes angry because of the errors he has been making. He tears his paper out of the machine with a large noise before the end of the writing, swears out loud, and then looks at you with a defiant look as if to say "Well, what are you going to do about it!" You have had minor disturbances from this lad several times before and have talked with him, but it has not done any good. What will you do this time?

2. You are the business teacher in a small high school. Every afternoon the room in which you teach your classes becomes very warm from the heat flowing through the radiators. The reason this situation occurs is that your room is nearest the heating system and in order for some of the rooms on the upper floors to be properly heated the furnace must be operated at full steam. There are no valves on the radiators with which you can turn them off. The janitor becomes irritated if you open the windows because he considers it a waste of heat. It becomes so warm most of the time in the afternoon that the students have a difficult time remaining alert or even awake. Is there any solution to this dilemma?

3. After she had given her class an examination, one of Miss Bauer's students complained that copies of the test were being circulated among certain students prior to the exam. The student was certain he would have ranked higher on the test as compared to the other students if the test had not been out. What should Miss Bauer do?

4. At the end of the semester Mr. Johnson was amazed and chagrined to find that 60 per cent of his students in general business had failed the final examination. Prior to this time he had given about a dozen short tests and had the students turn in much homework. On all this work the class had been an "average group." What should he do?

5. Mr. Able, in his freshman class in general business, found that a sizable segment of the class acted genuinely bored with the course. He

tried hard to make the class stimulating but he occasionally had to lecture as the class had thirty-eight students. He found that discussion was difficult in a class of this size. What might be the cause of the boredom? What might Mr. Able do?

Suggested Readings

"Audio Learning Laboratories," *Business Education World*, March, 1964, pp. 19-22.

Banerdt, Jack, "Planning for Multiple Outlets," *Journal of Business Education*, February, 1964, pp. 187-88.

Del Turco, Lorraine, "Handling All Levels of Ability in the Classroom," *Business Education World*, February, 1964, pp. 20-22.

Hamilton, Raymond, "We Can Improve Transcription by Using Dictating Machine Manufacturers' Teaching Aids," *Business Education World*, January, 1962, p. 18.

"How to Use Instrument Training Techniques in Typewriting and Shorthand Programs." Fall, 1963, pp. 1-10. Educational Developmental Laboratories Business Education Report.

Kline, Randall Miller, "Effectiveness of the Skill Builder in Teaching Typewriting." Spring, 1963, pp. 1-11. Educational Developmental Laboratories Business Education Report.

Less, Margaret M., "Bulletin Boards Anyone?—Try These Tips," *Business Education World*, September, 1963, p. 14.

Liguori, Mary, "Dictation Laboratories on the New Frontier," *Business Education World*, March, 1964, p. 8.

Marting, Barbara, "Make Use of an Electronic Classroom in Shorthand," *Balance Sheet*, February, 1962, pp. 249-50.

Nixdorf, Marion E., "A Study to Determine the Effect of Using the Skill-Builder Controlled Reader in the Teaching of Beginning Shorthand," *National Business Education Quarterly*, October, 1963, p. 38.

Patrinos, Chris G., "How We Take Advantage of Our Overhead Projectors," *Business Education World*, June, 1964, pp. 18-19.

Robinson, Charles, "New Horizons for Educational Television," *Journal of Business Education*, January, 1963, pp. 162-63.

Trimpe, Adrian, "Industry Tour—A Motivating Force," *Business Education Forum*, March, 1964, p. 22.

Wallace, William A., "A Philosopher Looks at Teaching Machines," *Catholic Business Education Review*, Winter, 1963, pp. 13-23.

Ward, Ruth B., "Use of the Projector for Motivating, Teaching, and Grading," *Business Education World,* March, 1964, pp. 13-14.

West, Leonard J., "Objective Testing in Bookkeeping," *Business Education Forum,* December, 1963, p. 9.

II

THE
SKILL
SUBJECTS

Important differences exist between methods of teaching to develop skills and those where nonskill outcomes are of major importance. Skills require the development of musculature control and coordination in addition to mental phases of understandings and attitudes. This is the real reason for separating the subjects treated as Part Two from those composing Part Three of this text.

The business teacher must learn to purposefully choose teaching techniques and procedures best calculated to attain the goals and purposes desired. Moreover, he must learn to judiciously divide teaching time among such techniques in accordance with the *major* purposes as compared with the many supplementary or minor purposes to be served.

It will be helpful to recognize at once subjects such as those included in Part Two as ones in which a *major* portion of time and effort must be devoted to skill development. Yet this does not mean that learning other than skill development is absent; on the contrary, it may be basic. But it does mean that in such subjects *more* attention must be given to psychological principles and procedures most useful in the development of skills and abilities—those activities of "doing" as opposed to "understanding" only.

Similarly, the omission of a subject from consideration in Part Two does not mean it contains no "skill-development." Rather, it indicates that to best serve his students and the goals of those courses it is believed that the business teacher should look upon those subjects as requiring relatively less attention to skill-development and more attention to understandings, problem-solving, and similar outcomes.

Thus in the next three chapters the attention of the reader is directed especially to those techniques and procedures especially valuable in developing skills—an important phase of such education for vocational objectives; the subjects under consideration demand this, and probably to a much greater extent than is true of other business subjects.

5   Teaching Typewriting

Today more high-school students are enrolled in typewriting than in any other business subject. In addition, thousands of young people are receiving instruction in typewriting at the junior-high-school level, and recently some interest has been shown in the possibility of teaching typewriting to elementary-school pupils. In 1960-1961 it was estimated that over 1.5 million students were taking typewriting. Typewriting is being identified more and more as general education with the result that the majority of the persons now enrolled in typewriting are interested solely in developing this skill for personal-use purposes. One of the major problems facing school administrators is that of finding some way to make typing instruction available to all those students desiring it. In many areas, a shortage of typing teachers, equipment, and funds is necessitating the introduction of new procedures in typing instruction. In some schools short, intensive typing courses have been included in the summer-school curriculum for those wishing to develop a personal-use skill. In other schools administrators are experimenting with team teaching of classes ranging in size from 75 to 125 or more students. The typing teacher should be thoroughly familiar with these developments and be ready to cope with the problem of increasing enrollments in this field.

The first typewriter was patented in 1868 by Christopher Shoals, a printer and editor, and Carlos Glidden, an attorney. However, these two men did not have sufficient capital to perfect the machine. At this point James Densmore, a Pennsylvania oil man, agreed to finance the project; in 1873, he was successful in persuading E. Remington & Sons to begin manufacture of the Type-Writer. Today there are many different typewriters on the market, including standard, noiseless, portable, and electric machines.[1] The young person planning to enter the business world may find himself seriously handicapped if he cannot type. Certainly he will find that the person who is a good typist has a skill that will help him gain entrance into the business office. In this chapter are discussed those techniques and devices which are generally recognized today as being effective procedures in the teaching of typewriting.

The Typewriting Room

The typewriting room should be located on either the first or second floor, away from outside noise and distractions. In many instances it is desirable to have the room situated near the shorthand and office-machine rooms and also near the administrative offices. Because of the space required for typewriting tables or desks, the typing room ordinarily needs to be 1½ times the size of a regular classroom. Preferably the room should be deeper than it is wide and should accommodate a maximum of thirty to thirty-five students. Twenty-five to 30 square feet should be allowed for each typewriter. The ceiling should be of acoustical material to partially absorb the noise of the machines. The room should be so located that it is possible to take advantage of all natural light available, with the light coming from the back or from the right.

The equipment in the typing room will vary from school to school. Most typing rooms are equipped with individual tables or desks which should be so arranged that the teacher has easy access to

---

[1] A "simplified" typewriter keyboard was developed by August Dvorak and W. L. Dealey in 1932. According to Dvorak and Dealey, on the universal keyboard the left hand does 56 per cent of all the stroking while on their scientific keyboard the left hand does only 46 per cent of the stroking. However, the Dvorak keyboard has not been widely accepted.

each student for demonstration purposes and individual assistance. It is recommended that the tables or desks be adjustable and free from vibration. A table 22 inches wide and 36 inches long will give the student space for his typing material and text. L-shaped tables are also excellent, but they require more floor space than other types of desks. If the tables or desks are adjustable, the teacher will need to see that the students adjust them to the correct height each day. Because adjustable desks are more expensive than other types, some schools purchase desks of varying heights. In this case most of the desks will need to be 28 to 30 inches in height with only a few ranging from 26 to 27 inches. (Desks for some makes of electric typewriters need to be slightly lower than the desks for manual machines.) The desk is the correct height for the student if his arms slope at approximately a 30-degree angle. This is the same slope as the keyboard. Schools that use the typing classroom for other classes often purchase drop-head desks. These desks are satisfactory for the other classes meeting in the typing room, but they are not suitable for the typing class. The typewriters are much too low to develop correct typing techniques.

Teachers do not agree about the advisability of using adjustable chairs in the typing room. All too often these chairs are not easily adjusted, and no attempt is made to change the height once the chairs are installed. Many teachers believe it is better to take care of any adjustments needed through the use of adjustable tables or desks. The chairs should not be fastened to the floor.

Much has been written regarding the advisability of using electric versus manual typewriters in the classroom. If a school has more than one typing room, then the room in which personal-use or first-year typing is taught is frequently equipped with one make of manual typewriters, with lettered keyboards and preferably elite type, since this is the size of type used by most businesses today. Few persons taking typing for personal-use purposes will purchase electric typewriters. Hence it is logical to provide instruction for such persons on manual machines. The advanced typing classroom is then equipped with electric typewriters, frequently of several different makes. In planning the layout of a typing room, electrical outlets should be provided at each typing station to permit the use of electric typewriters.

The teacher in the small school system having only one typing room must decide whether the room should be equipped with several makes of manual typewriters and perhaps three or four electrics or whether to limit the equipment to only one make of machine. Obviously it is easier to teach beginning students in a room equipped with one kind of typewriter, but there is also the problem arising from the need to acquaint students with the various makes of typewriters and to provide the vocational typist with experience on electric machines.

Other equipment needed in the classroom will include a demonstration stand and typewriter for the teacher, copyholders, an interval timer, a stop watch, dictionaries, storage cabinets and files, and wastebaskets. A teacher's desk is optional. If the teacher is working with his students as he should be, he will have little time to spend at his desk.

Objectives in Typewriting

Students who enroll in typewriting today do so for one of two reasons. Either they are interested in using typing as a vocational tool, or they wish to master this skill for their personal use. At present increased attention is being given to the personal-use objective in the curriculum, and many junior high schools are now offering one semester of typing for personal use in the seventh, eighth, or ninth grades so that the students may use their typing skill throughout high school and college. At one time business educators expressed considerable concern about these dual objectives; they believed it was impossible to teach students with different objectives in the same class. While today it is generally recognized that at least in the early learning stages the objective of the student has little effect on the teaching procedures or content, some persons still maintain that the content of a one-semester personal-use typing course differs sufficiently from the content of a vocational course to necessitate a personal-use text. Most authorities, however, agree that there should be no difficulty in teaching a class of students having both personal and vocational objectives and that the content in the first course should be much the same regardless of the students' objective. One of the dangers of setting up special personal-use courses is that of lowered standards for such classes. Teachers should remember that, even though a person may have learned to operate a typewriter, he is not likely to use it to any great extent unless he has developed considerable skill in its operation. Consequently, while some persons may be able to develop a satisfactory personal-use skill in a one-semester course, there are probably many other persons who will need a full year of typing to acquire a usable typing skill. In advanced typing the course content naturally is focused on the development of vocational typing skill and the typing of office-production jobs. A person with a personal-use objective does not need these advanced skills and knowledges. If he does choose to enroll in the advanced typing course, he should be expected to meet the same standards and master the same subject matter as those taking the course for vocational purposes.

The course content of a personal-use typing course will be largely dependent upon the length of the course. If most students with personal-use objectives enroll for only one semester, then special care should be taken to include all the skills and knowledges such persons will need in their typing applications. The one-semester course emphasizes the fundamentals which include mastery of the keyboard through correct typing techniques and a knowledge of machine parts, special keys, and characters. Skills taught include composition of simple letters, addressing envelopes, erasing, horizontal and vertical centering, and easy tabulations. If a full year of personal-use typing is offered, then drill is provided in the second semester to develop higher typing rates. In addition the students are given instruction in composition at the typewriter, typing more difficult letters, manuscripts, outlines, and other personal-use projects.

The Psychology of Typewriting

Every typing teacher needs a thorough understanding of the basic principles upon which typing skill is built. These fundamental principles of skill learning have been developed over the years by Bryan, Harter, Book, and many others. All authorities in the teaching of typewriting agree that typing skill is a constantly changing phenomenon. When a student first attempts to type, his motions are diffused, awkward, and wasteful. As he gradually develops skill, his motions become fluent and sure, and waste movements are eliminated. The principles which follow represent a composite of the thinking of typing authorities regarding the psychology of learning.

Typewriting is a skill which is controlled more by the mind than by the hands. When a student is first learning to type, he is slow in his responses, not because he cannot move his fingers quickly enough, but because the mental stimulus required to activate the correct finger has not yet been established. With correct, purposeful practice, these stimuli which bring about the correct responses and typing sequences become so firmly established that the typist no longer struggles to recall which key is controlled by each finger but reacts automatically to the letters which he sees in the copy.

Typing skill can best be learned when the student is highly motivated. The student who is enrolled in typing because he wants to be able to type his own assignments or because he wants to have some means of earning a livelihood is ordinarily highly motivated. He will direct his full attention to mastering the keyboard and to building speed and accuracy in typing. The student who elects typing because he believes it is an easy course or because someone else has insisted that he learn to type is frequently poorly motivated and will not put forth the intensity of effort required for rapid skill development.

The development of typing skill is often accompanied by excessive fatigue. The student may concentrate with such intensity upon the locations of the keys and the manipulation of the parts of the typewriter that he is tense and nervous. He is afraid he will strike the wrong keys. Consequently he pushes the keys hesitantly rather than hitting them quickly with a firm stroke. The teacher should study each student in the class carefully to determine those students who are working too hard and those who are not putting forth enough effort to make maximum progress. Students who complain of tired muscles and strain in their hands and arms are working too hard with incorrect techniques. The teacher should help the student learn how to apply maximum effort without becoming emotionally upset or unduly fatigued.

The development of skill requires the elimination of waste motions and poor techniques. Too many teachers seem to believe that their function in the classroom is to build speed and accuracy in typewriting. This is certainly one function of the teacher, but speed and accuracy must be built upon correct techniques. The student should be given enough practice on the right kind of materials to enable him to gain confidence in his skill through the development of proper techniques.

Students should be given the opportunity to progress at their own learning rates at all times. In typewriting some students are able to master the keyboard in two weeks, some in three weeks, and some require a far longer period of time. Drill material should be of such a nature that the learner may progress according to his ability. It should be remembered that some students are still typing on the letter-association level when other students in the class have progressed to the syllable and word-association level. Students should be encouraged to progress as rapidly as possible. However, they should *never* be pushed for speed and accuracy development at the sacrifice of correct techniques.

Since individuals do differ in their learning rates, one of the responsibilities of the teacher is to provide a learning situation in which each student has the type of practice that is best for him. Requiring all students to type the text material the same number of times, maintaining too rigid a classroom routine, requiring too much group activity, and giving too little attention to individual learners will interfere with the progress of some members in the class. Typing is a course that is readily adaptable to meeting individual differences of the students, and the teacher should see that these differences are properly met.

Practice on any single phase of the learning process should be given in a natural rather than an artificial situation. For instance, teaching the parts of the machine before they are actually used in typing results in little learning. Whenever a machine part is taught, it should be used immediately in the typing practice.

The repetition necessary to acquire typing skill should be discontinued as soon as it ceases to be effective. To get the most from any practice, the student must keep his mind focused on what he is doing. When his mind is no longer fixed on his practice or begins to wander, the typing practice soon loses its effectiveness. For instance, the expert rhythm drill can be an exceedingly effective warm-up at the beginning of the period. However, the drill should be discontinued and some other warm-up substituted when students no longer concentrate upon the purposes of the drill but begin to let their hands and wrists "bounce" as they type.

Opportunity should always be provided for relearning in a successive practice period what has been forgotten since the previous practice period. In the early learning stages in typewriting, the warm-up practice should be immediately followed by the relearning process. The warm-up is designed to limber-up the muscles used in typing. The relearning practice is designed to recall the letter locations learned from the previous periods. Some teachers are so eager to present the entire keyboard rapidly that they do not allow sufficient time for relearning of letters presented earlier. As a consequence the students become discouraged or develop poor stroking techniques due to uncertainty regarding letter locations.

Practice of a skill is often ineffective when the learner is discouraged with the results of his practice. Teachers need to realize that not every student needs to be typing the same drills at the same time. When a teacher sees that a student is discouraged in his efforts to complete a particular drill or exercise, he should suggest that the student try some other exercise which he may be able to type better than the one on which he is working. It is quite probable that repeated failure on the exercise has set up a "mental block" which the student cannot overcome. Once he has successfully completed the new exercise, he may return to the one on which he was working previously and be able to complete it without further difficulty.

Practice of a skill does not necessarily lead to perfection. Practice is not effective unless the learner is concentrating upon the work, knows the purpose of the drill, and is able to evaluate his own progress. Students should never be asked to type a drill unless they know what the practice is supposed to accomplish. All too often students in the typing classroom are not developing better typing skill when they practice the drills in the text because they are not concentrating upon their work. Their minds are elsewhere. Students should be taught "how" to practice and the purpose of each practice period. Only correct practice can lead to perfection.

One phase of a skill should not be built at the sacrifice of another. In the past many teachers have become so dazzled by "high-speed" drills that they have pushed their students for high typing rates ignoring the detrimental effects such drills may have had upon accuracy in typing. Students need both speed and accuracy in typing. In addition they need the control necessary to apply these raw skills to typing problems and production jobs. Today's typing teacher must provide for the development of skill in all three of these areas.

Short learning periods are more effective in developing skill than longer ones. Whether a period is of "short" or "long" duration depends upon the stage of learning in typing. When the student is learning the keyboard locations, a fifteen-minute period will seem extremely long to him. But later in typing applied problems this period will seem very short. The elements of both interest and fatigue must be considered in determining the length of the practice period that will be most effective.

The learner should be working toward a goal that will be reasonably easy for him to attain. As soon as he reaches this goal, a new goal should be set up which will provide him with the incentive to continue working to increase his skill. The teacher should always avoid setting unreasonable standards such as perfect copies, and she should adjust the assignments to the varying abilities of the individual students. A student will quickly become discouraged if he is constantly given goals that he is unable to attain. When the goals are within his reach, progress is apt to be steady and he becomes convinced that he can reach the standards expected of him. Once he nears his objective, he may begin to lose interest or to practice carelessly unless a new goal is set. When the learner constantly has a definite series of goals to be attained, his interest is maintained at a high level and the practice patterns remain effective.

Plateaus in typing are not necessarily a sign that no learning is taking place. Nearly every typing student sooner or later reaches a plateau in his skill development. He may seem to be unable to build further skill. He may be having difficulty reducing the number of typing errors on his timed writings. Such plateaus are not unusual. The learner may have built his typing speed very rapidly at the beginning. He then needs a period of time to "fixate" the skill at that level before he can proceed to a higher level. A student may be making too many typing errors because he is afraid he is going to make errors; he may be practicing on the wrong kinds of material; he may be practicing using incorrect techniques; or he may simply need additional drill and practice before he can reach a higher level of accuracy. While a student may see little signs of progress when he is on a learning plateau, if he is doing the right kind of practice on the right kinds of material, then skill is actually being developed each day which will make it possible for him to eventually move on to a higher level of typing skill.

The development of a skill proceeds at a slower rate as higher levels of skill are attained. Most students are able to reach a typing rate of thirty to thirty-five words a minute quite easily and quickly. The student should understand, however, that he should not expect to continue to build his skill at the same rate. A longer period is required to build a typing speed from sixty to seventy words a minute than is required to increase one's speed from thirty to forty words a minute. In the same way, a longer period of time is required to attain a typing skill of ninety to a hundred words a minute than was required to move from sixty to seventy words a minute. If students are made to understand that higher levels of skill do require more time and more intensive practice than the lower levels, they are less apt to become discouraged with their progress.

Most learners can increase their skill with correct practice. Students often claim that they cannot increase their skill because they have reached their maximum potential. In reality few persons ever attain the maximum typing skill of which they are capable. Even very rapid, accurate typists will admit that with intensive practice, using drill material selected to meet their individual needs, they could increase their typing skill. The expert typist who is typing 100 words a minute might not find it feasible, however, because a great deal of time and intensive effort would be necessary to increase skill at these high levels. Probably the average typing student does not begin to attain the level of skill of which he is capable.

Length of the Typewriting Course

The number of semesters of typing offered in the high schools in the different states varies widely. Some schools offer two years of typing, some offer three semesters, and many schools offer only one year. Recently with the emphasis upon an academic curriculum in the high school many schools have transferred the typing program to the junior high school. A survey by Lloyd [2] of seventeen cities in 1961 revealed that approximately 27 per cent of the typing enrollment was in junior-high-school classes; 44 per cent was in senior-high-school first-year typing; 15 per cent was in senior-high-school second-year typing; and 15 per cent was in other courses involving typing. Of the seventeen cities, seven had no junior-high-school course while the other ten had heavy enrollments in junior-high-school typing. Four cities had no second-year course in typewriting but included much of the second-year course work in office practice. Probably between one-fourth and one-third of the students enrolling in typewriting in the secondary schools continue through the vocational level. In an analysis of the typing programs of the fifty states, Lloyd concluded that the four-semester program now being followed by thirty states would continue in only twenty-one of these states; that a three-semester program would be the pattern in seven states; and a two-semester program the pattern in twenty-two states.

[2] Alan C. Lloyd, "The Changing Pattern of Typewriting Courses," *Business Education Forum* (November 1961), pp. 16-18.

He predicted a three-level sequence of courses in the future—a one-semester course on the eighth-grade level for personal use; a one-year general-typewriting course on the tenth-grade level; and an additional year for vocational students which would combine office practice and typewriting.

Where typing is offered in junior high school, the usual practice appears to be that of offering only one semester for personal use at this level and deferring further training in typing until the tenth or eleventh year in high school. The question immediately arises whether students completing a one-semester typing course in junior high school do develop sufficient skill for personal-use purposes. As yet no satisfactory follow-up study has been made to determine the effectiveness of the one-semester program. Certainly persons can learn to type in one semester, but the extent to which the skill so acquired is used is not known. Some cities such as Los Angeles recommend that the personal-use typing course in junior high school be a two-semester course.

Many high schools which offer primarily an academic curriculum feel that they only can justify one year of typing. Other schools with strong vocational programs include two years of typing in the curriculum. In states such as Pennsylvania, it has been found that basic typing skill, applications, and knowledges can be developed during the first year and that a vocational skill in production typewriting can be developed in the third semester. In Virginia three semesters of typewriting are offered in the vocational program, followed by a one-semester course in Clerical Practice and Vocational Office Training.

The year in which typing is offered will depend somewhat upon the over-all curriculum. In a school offering two years of shorthand, students are usually encouraged to enroll in beginning typing their tenth year. If only one year of shorthand is offered, the students usually defer typing until the eleventh year, so that part of the time in second-year typing may be devoted to transcription.

Course Content in Typewriting

The course objectives and course content in typing are clearly dependent upon the number of semesters offered. However, the objectives may be broadly classified as mastery of the keyboard, development of correct techniques, building speed and accuracy,

teaching typing knowledges, teaching basic typing applications, and
the building of production-level skill.

The course content for a two-semester personal-use typing program recommended by the Los Angeles City Schools is given below:

Personal-Use Typewriting—Junior High School [3]
(Eighth or Ninth Grade)

First Semester

	Weeks
Keyboard control	1-3
Figures and timings	4-5
Symbols and timings	6-7
Timings and review	8-9
Timings and personal typing	10-11
Timings for control and centering	12
Timings and problems	13-15
Typing for control	16
Personal-use typewriting	17-18

Second Semester

	Weeks
Business letters	1-2
Basic skill drive and review	3-4
Letters and memos	5
Simple tabulations	6
Letters, tabulations, memos, and labels	7-8
Business letters	9-10
Review	11
Manuscripts	12-13
Business letters	14-15
Correspondence manual	16-18

The Business Education Service of Virginia suggests a three-
semester program in typewriting to be followed by a semester of
Clerical Practice and Vocational Office Training. The course content
recommended for this three-semester typing program follows:[4]

[3] *Instructional Guide for Typewriting in Junior and Senior High School,* Los
Angeles City Schools, Division of Instructional Services, Publication No.
SC-553, 1958, pp. 5-6.

[4] *Business Education—Part II, Typewriting,* Business Education Service of

First Semester

1. Learning the keyboard
   a. Technique approach
   b. Skill-building drills
2. Parts of the typewriter (each part to be presented only as needed for a particular problem)
3. Techniques
   a. Position at the typewriter
   b. Paper insertion and removal
   c. Stroking
   d. Reaches
   e. Eyes on copy
   f. Use of nonkeyboard parts
      (1) Shift key and shift lock
      (2) Carriage return
      (3) Backspacer
      (4) Margin release
      (5) Space bar
      (6) Tabular mechanism
      (7) Paper-release levers
      (8) Carriage-release levers
      (9) Variable line spacer
      (10) Cylinder knobs
4. Proofreading
5. Centering (simple)
6. Care of the typewriter, daily from this time on
7. Checking the typewriter, daily from this time on
8. Typewriting from arranged copy (sentences and paragraphs)
9. Typewriting from unarranged copy
10. Single envelopes
11. Personal letter writing
12. Folding and inserting letters in envelopes
13. Single carbon copies
14. Centering (advanced)
    a. Menus
    b. Programs
    c. Invitations
15. Outlines

the Division of Vocational Education, State Board of Education, Commonwealth of Virginia, XLIV (March 1962), 29-31.

16. Typewriting from handwritten copy
17. Composition at the typewriter

Second Semester

1. Daily skill-building drills
2. Daily cleaning of the typewriter
3. Daily checking of the typewriter
4. Dictation at the typewriter
5. Composition at the typewriter
6. Postal cards
7. Index cards
8. Labels
9. Changing the ribbon
10. Manuscripts, footnotes, bibliography (optional)
11. Advanced letter writing
    a. Two-page letters
    b. Subject line
    c. Attention line
    d. Postscripts
    e. Enclosures
    f. Judgment placement
    g. Interoffice memoranda
12. Tabulation
    a. Mathematical placement
    b. Judgment placement
    c. Ruling
13. Making corrections
14. Filling in forms (two samples only)
    a. Application forms
    b. Income tax forms
15. Duplication (one sample for personal use of preparing a stencil or master only—no machine operation)
16. Typewriting from rough drafts

Third Semester

1. Daily drills
2. Daily cleaning of the typewriter
3. Daily checking of the typewriter
4. Composition
5. Dictation
6. Filling in forms (advanced)
7. Multiple carbons including use of red carbon

8. Financial statements
9. Legal documents (only two documents required)
   a. One-party document
   b. Two-party document
   c. Filling in legal forms
10. Preparing duplication stencils and masters (advanced)
    a. Drawing on duplication media
    b. Filling in duplicated form letters
11. Production typewriting
    a. Letter writing
    b. Addressing envelopes in quantity
    c. Addressing cards
    d. Typewriting cards
    e. Filling in forms
    f. Filling in form letters
    g. Tabulation

The four-semester program in typewriting recommended by the Los Angeles Public Schools follows:[5]

First Semester

	Weeks
Basic techniques and keyboard control	1-3
Continuity typing	4
Figures and symbols	5-6
Speed emphasis	7
Personal-use typing	8
Building typing power	9
Centering and tabulation	10
Business letters, envelopes, carbon copies, rough drafts	11-13
Improvement of basic skills	14-15
Manuscripts and outlines	16
Typing for personal use	17
Typing for control	18

Second Semester

	Weeks
Reconstruction of basic skills	1-2
Business letters	3
Form letters, envelopes, rough draft	4

[5] Publication No. SC-553, *op. cit.,* pp. 15-18.

Form letters, production typing	5
Carbon copies, production typing	6
Technique improvement	7
Tabulations, judgment placement	8
Tabulations, two-page letters	9
Manuscripts, footnotes	10
Typing for personal use	11-12
Typing for club activities	13
Speed and control emphasis	14
Business-letter variations, erasing	15
Special problems in office procedures	16
Interoffice, carbon copies	17
Production-comparison typing	18

Third Semester

	Weeks
Reconstruction of basic skills	1
Technique improvement	2
Speed emphasis	3
Control building	4
Office forms, telegrams	5
Invoices and credit memoranda	6
Invoices, purchase orders	7
Shipping forms	8
Form paragraphs, postal cards	9
Letters with tabulated reports	10
Tabulated reports	11
Production comparison	12
Production measurements	13
Speed emphasis, control building	14
Preparation of masters, filling in items	15
NOMA Letters, chain feeding	16
Production-measurement review	17
Measurement comparison	18

Fourth Semester

	Weeks
Production-measurement review	1
Production-measurement comparison	2
Building sustained typing power	3
Sampling letter problems	4
Production measurement	5

Stenciling and form fill-in	6
Production measurement comparison	7
Taking an employment test	8
Production unit	9
Form letters with fill-ins	10
Production practice jobs	11
Production measurement comparison	12
Legal typing	13-14
A day in the office	15
Speed emphasis	16
Typing for control	17
Production measurement	18

Introducing the Keyboard

A number of different approaches have been recommended for introducing the students to the keyboard. However, to date no research indicates conclusively that one approach is any more effective than another. The approaches most often used in the high-school and college typing texts today are the homerow approach, the skip-around or word-pattern approach, the vertical finger approach, and the whole-keyboard approach.

Homerow Approach. Teachers using the homerow approach first teach the locations of the fingers on the homerow and then present extensive drills using these keys. Since the homerow is the base from which all typing reaches are made, this is an easy way in which to introduce the keyboard. However, only one vowel is included in the homerow locations, which means that much of the drill material consists of nonsense typing rather than word or phrase typing.

Vertical Approach. In texts following the vertical plan, all keys struck by one finger are presented at one time. For example, the reaches to *j, u, m, n, h,* and *y* are presented as a group. Usually the next group of reaches presented is the group controlled by the *f* finger—*f, g, v, b, r,* and *t.* Since *j* and *f* are the two strongest fingers, these reaches are taught first. Then the reaches for the *k* and *d* fingers are located, for the *l* and *s* fingers, and for the *;* and *a* fingers. This approach, like the homerow approach, usually results in the use of considerable nonsense-drill material.

Skip-Around or Word-Pattern Approach. Most texts using this approach present those key locations first which are needed to prepare meaningful copy. In some instances special effort is made during the first two or three days to concentrate on reaches controlled by the stronger fingers of the left and right hands. Practically no nonsense-drill material is used in texts using the skip-around approach. Attention is directed to mastering key locations through the typing of short, simple words in which the letters may appear at the beginning, in the middle, or at the end of the words. Often particular emphasis is given to words containing doubled letters as these are the easiest letter combinations for the beginning typist and help him master these reaches quickly. Because they give him a feeling of confidence, he tends to strike the keys with a sharp, staccato touch.

Whole-Keyboard Approach. Teachers using this plan present the entire alphabetic keyboard during the first day of typing. Although the entire keyboard is presented the first day, presentation is not the same as mastery, and additional drill must be provided on succeeding days to enable the students to learn the key locations.

Regardless of the approach used in presenting the keyboard, most authorities today agree that the student should carefully observe the location of the new key and make the reach several times, watching as his finger moves to the new location. This procedure gives him confidence that he is making the correct reach to the new location and enables him to get the feel of the reach even before the key is struck. After the student has observed his finger make this reach a number of times, he should be ready to practice the drill material in the text, keeping his eyes focused on the copy.

A survey of the typing texts now on the market reveals that authors today present the alphabetic keyboard locations in one to two weeks, with most texts requiring approximately seven days to complete these locations. Thus the letters are all presented in a relatively short period so that the student may quickly master them. Authors believe that students should master the alphabetic keyboard as soon as possible and should strike the keys rapidly from the very first day. This is possible if the drill material in the early lessons in the text is based solely on simple words, phrases, and short sentences. Key locations may be learned quickly through carefully constructed drills such as the following:

Repetition of words	if if if if if	if if if if if	if if if if if
Lesson 1, first	it it it it it	it it it it it	it it it it it
reaches	is is is is is	is is is is is	is is is is is
	if it is if it is	if it is if it is	if it is
	if it is if it is	if it is if it is	if it is

Changing one letter *in typing pattern*	hit lit fit sit sin tin fin din did hid lid hire hire fire fire dire dire tire tire sire sire
Doubled letters	need need seed seed heed heed deed deed feed feed toot toot foot foot root root soot soot loot loot
Presentation of letters *g and y in beginning,* *middle, and end of* *word*	gas gas get get got got ego ego egg egg leg leg lay lay hay hay dye dye rye rye yet yet yes yes

Teachers should remember that not all students learn at the same rate. Some of the students may master the keyboard locations rapidly while others appear to be very slow in learning them. The Educational Developmental Laboratories points out that the difficulty experienced by some students in learning to type may well be caused by forcing them to attempt new key locations before they have mastered the locations presented previously.

Teaching Machine Parts

In discussing the psychology of teaching typing, it was pointed out that the parts of the machine should be taught when they are to be used in typing. Beginning teachers sometimes make the mistake of presenting twelve or fifteen machine parts the first day the students are in class, even though the students are not interested in machine parts and will be using only a few of them that period. The cylinder knobs should not be presented until the students need to insert paper into the machine. The paper release should not be mentioned until paper is to be removed from the typewriter. The margin release should not be taught until the students need to use this key. On the other hand, when students need to use special parts of the machine, they should know where they are located and their purpose. Many students complete two years of typewriting without understanding the use of the various scales on the typewriter or knowing the difference between the line-space disengaging lever and the variable line spacer.

Developing Correct Techniques in Typewriting

Whether the student becomes an expert typist depends in large measure upon the techniques that he develops during the first six to eight weeks he is in the typing class. The teacher who attempts to build speed and accuracy in his class without proper attention to technique will soon find that he is attempting the impossible. Fast and accurate typing depends upon correct typing techniques. Therefore, during the first few weeks the primary concern of both the teacher and the student should be to develop correct techniques and then build typing skill upon those techniques.

It has been stated by many speed typists that the difference between the amateur and the champion is largely one of waste motion. The expert typist has learned how to type with the least possible waste motion. His movements are rapid and accurate because they are efficient. The novice is still struggling with the manipulation of the machine. He has not yet learned how to reduce his motions to the minimum, and consequently many of his motions are wasteful and inefficient. Certainly the teacher should not expect the student to perform in the same manner as the expert when he first begins to type. However, he should try to help that student eliminate useless motions and learn the typing patterns of the experts as soon as possible. To do this, emphasis during the early stages of typing should be placed almost entirely on correct techniques.

Stroking. When practicing the drills on new keyboard letter locations, correct stroking patterns are far more important than accurate copy. The teacher should demonstrate to the students as a group the correct stroking techniques. Following the demonstration the teacher may have the students type the drill with her, again emphasizing correct stroking. After the drill has been typed once or twice in this manner, the students may type the drill at their own individual rates with the teacher observing each person to be sure he is using a quick, fast stroke. It is now generally recognized that one way to develop correct stroking is through building rapid stroking patterns. Students who hit the keys hesitantly tend to push the keys. Students who are taught to strike the keys quickly usually strike and release the key in the proper manner. Although little attention should be given to the accuracy of the copy, the teacher can determine from looking at the students' practice work those students having serious stroking problems. Skips in the copy and blurred letters are an indication that a student is not stroking the keys correctly and needs individual help.

Eyes Fixed on the Copy. The student who begins to look back and forth from the text to the keyboard or the copy that he is typing is setting up a handicap to the building of fast and accurate typing skills later in the course. Many teachers have found that students who are told to watch their fingers make the reaches to new letter locations before any drills are typed have the confidence they need later to type the drills in the text without looking back and forth from the copy to the keys. Other teachers have found it helpful to place drills on the board and have the students type the copy from the board. Years ago it was thought that using blank keyboards would automatically force the students to keep their eyes on the copy, but experience has proved this to be a poor teaching device. Those students who want to look at their keyboards will do so regardless. Today typing authorities agree it is far better to have lettered keyboards in the classroom. The importance of keeping "eyes on copy" cannot be overemphasized. Many times one of the major differences between the good typist and the poor typist is one of concentration on the copy.

Correct Reading Habits. Many students develop incorrect typing techniques because they have never learned how to read copy correctly while typing. Their typing errors may be traced to this problem. Most students attempt to read too far ahead of the word that they are typing. Research has shown that slow and careful reading should be required in typing. Students should not attempt to read too far ahead in the copy as this results in constant eye regressions and typing errors. However, to some extent, looking back in the line is normal. It has been found that typewriting requires about 3.6 times more fixations and regressions than ordinary reading and that the eye span in ordinary reading is 3.4 times as long as in typing. The amount of the word absorbed at one time appears to be dependent on the speed of the typist. The eye span of the champion typist will include .67 to .70 of the word at a glance while the ordinary typist absorbs only .32 of a word at one glance.[6]

A few students develop incorrect techniques because they have not learned to concentrate on the copy. The slightest distraction causes them to lose their place, to look up, and to break their stroking rhythm. The problem is, of course, tied in closely with failure to keep their eyes on the copy.

Machine Manipulations. For years typing teachers seemed to believe that correct typing techniques applied solely to correct stroking. Today it is recognized that many persons who have correct stroking patterns will never become expert typists because they are

---

[6] Donald C. Fuller, *Reading Factors in Typewriting* (Doctoral Dissertation, Pennsylvania State College, published by Oklahoma A. & M. College, 1945).

unable to manipulate the parts of the machine with dexterity. These machine parts require special drill because, in most instances, even though they are used frequently, they are not employed as often as are the letters of the alphabet. Today most typing texts include special drills on the use of the backspace key, the margin release, the tabulator set and clear keys, the tabulator key or bar, the shift key and shift lock, and the space bar. The stroking of these keys is not the same as the stroking of the alphabet keys and, because they are not used as frequently, all too often students do not learn to use them by touch. Special attention to the development of skill in the use of the manipulative parts of the machine will do much to build increased speed and accuracy in typing.

If teachers gave more attention to correct technique in first-semester typing and less to grading, undoubtedly students would also consider typing technique of greater importance than they now do. In order to stress the importance of technique, some typing teachers use technique-error charts such as the one shown in Exhibit 5.1. The teacher may rate the student each six weeks, showing the student those areas in which he needs improvement.

EXHIBIT 5.1

Technique-Error Chart

1. Position
   a. Body not directly in front of typewriter
   b. Body too close or too far from typewriter
   c. Feet not on the floor in correct position
   d. Spine not straight
   e. Head bent
   f. Elbows out too far from body
   g. Elbows too close to body
   h. Wrists too high
   i. Wrists resting or sagging
   j. Fingers not curved
   k. All fingers not on homerow
2. Handling Paper
   a. Paper held incorrectly
   b. Wrong technique for straightening
   c. Incorrect removal
3. Reach Errors
   a. Uses right finger but wrong hand

     b. Uses wrong finger and wrong hand

     c. Uses wrong finger but right hand

4. Stroking and Touch Errors
    a. Strike-overs
    b. Crowding
    c. Piling
    d. Ghost letters
    e. Touch too heavy
    f. Touch too light
    g. Uneven touch

5. Spacing Errors
    a. Failure to space
    b. Not enough space
    c. Too many spaces

6. Manipulation of Special Machine Parts
    a. Shift key
        (1) Failure to keep fingers on homerow while operating shift keys
        (2) Uses shift lock instead of shift key
        (3) Capitals too high or too low
        (4) Letter following capital too high or too low
        (5) Capitalizes letter following a capital
    b. Tabular bar or key
        (1) Failure to use tabular bar or key
        (2) Uses wrong finger on tab bar or key
        (3) Uses wrong stroke on tab bar or key
        (4) Uneven indenting
    c. Uses wrong finger and stroke on back space key
    d. Carriage return
        (1) Failure to return carriage at right time
        (2) Returns carriage with incorrect position of hand
        (3) Hand follows lever all the way across
        (4) Looks to get fingers back on home keys
        (5) Pause after returning carriage before beginning to write
    e. Incorrect use of margin release

7. Reading Copy
    a. Omissions
    b. Additions
    c. Transpositions
    d. Substitutions

8. Centering Errors
    a. Failure to have the material correctly centered

        (1) Horizontal
        (2) Vertical
     b. Too much time spent on centering

The teacher may also have the student rate himself and then compare the two ratings. Remedial drills are selected to correct those techniques which need improvement.

Technique charts are not as widely used as formerly because many teachers feel that they are too time-consuming for the benefits derived from their use. While the experienced teacher may not need a chart to help him analyze technique errors, the beginning teacher may find such a chart helpful in analyzing the typing techniques of his students. All too many beginning teachers fail to observe incorrect techniques until after these techniques have become firmly established patterns. The charts also serve to impress upon the students the importance of technique in the development of typing skill.

Speed and Accuracy in Typewriting

Speed and accuracy in typewriting are basic to the development of a vocational skill. The typist must possess both qualities. He will not be successful if he is a fast but inaccurate typist; neither will he be successful if he is an accurate but slow typist. The typing teacher must provide for the building of both these skills in his classroom.

There has been much discussion in the past as to whether speed should be built before accuracy, accuracy before speed, or whether the two skills should be built concurrently. Years ago teachers believed that accuracy should precede speed and they required their students to type perfect copies of all drills and typing problems. Later typing authorities began to question this technique and advocated building speed first, then dropping back for control at regular intervals. Thus a student typing thirty words a minute might strive to reach forty words a minute in a speed drive. After he had reached forty words on speed-building drives, he was instructed to drop back to approximately thirty-five words a minute typing for control. Once his control level had been established he might push his speed to forty-five words a minute and so on. Many teachers used this plan of building speed and accuracy in their typing classes. Recently typing authorities have been advocating a "middle-of-the-road" course, building accuracy with speed. Teachers following this procedure place initial emphasis upon correct techniques. The technique approach enables students to develop the neuromuscular control essential for high speed. Once the pattern is developed and controlled, it is relatively easy to attain a high degree of accuracy at high speed. This emphasis on building accuracy with speed is based on the principle that the beginning typing student should be started at a fast pace so he will develop correct stroking patterns and that a high degree of typing skill can be developed fairly easily. Some authorities state that students should be typing at a minimum rate of ten words a minute after the fifth lesson and that after the early lessons most drills should be directed at a minimum rate of fifteen to twenty words a minute. Through repetitive one-half to one-minute timings, it is possible to build the stroking rate of about 75 per cent of the typing students to twenty to twenty-five words a minute on easy drill material.

A student should never be told to type as fast as he can regardless of errors. Such a procedure results in incorrect techniques and often completely destroys the student's ability to type with control even when this is his objective. The student will find when he attempts to type as fast as he can without considering errors that his fingers "become thumbs." He will clash the keys, have light and dark letters in his typing, irregular spacing, and other typing errors that are signs of poor technique.

Typing speed may best be developed through the use of easy copy in the early stages of learning. After the students have had an opportunity to type the material through once, they should be given short, repetitive timings on this same copy. Each student sets a goal toward which he will work, and the timings force him to make a concentrated effort to reach these goals. Repeating the practice under timed conditions enables the students to build their speed rapidly. At first the timings may be only one-half to one minute in length and may be repeated as many as three to five times. Gradually as the students build their typing speed, copy of average difficulty is used and the length of the timings is increased from one to five minutes.

While there is no better way to force speed to higher levels than through the repetition of easy copy, improved techniques will also contribute to the building of higher typing rates. If the student will learn to do each typing operation a little more skillfully than he has been doing it in the past, he will be able to increase his typing speed. If he can learn to throw the carriage a little faster, to return to the keys and start typing a little quicker, to decrease the time required to type capitals, to locate the backspace keys and the margin release, and to develop more rhythmic stroking, he will find that his typing speed will increase even though he may not have increased his stroking rate.

Beginning typists sometimes think that they will never be able to type thirty words a minute—that is so much faster than twenty words a minute. If the teacher will demonstrate typing at twenty, thirty, and forty words a minute, the class will see that these rates are actually very slow, that the difference is largely one of rhythm, not of stroking the keys rapidly. To reach these levels the student does not need to be able to type fast—but he does need to type with continuity and rhythm, which are basic factors in building high typing speeds later.

Many special teaching aids are available today which are designed to help the students build speed and accuracy to high levels. The tachistoscope can be used to encourage more rapid response to visual stimuli. This instrument provides for control of exposure time as well as area exposed. The Controlled Reader automatically presents material at a predetermined, continuous, rhythmic pace measured in lines a minute. It may be used either to force speed or to drive for more accurate typing responses. Recorded lessons on tapes and records free the teacher so he may work individually with students needing assistance. Records can also provide for group-paced writing and direct dictation. In some schools closed-circuit television instruction and team-teaching techniques are being utilized in an effort to reach larger numbers of students and to develop higher levels of skill through enrichment of the learning process. The typing teacher should be familiar with these and the other teaching aids available and determine which ones can be used most effectively in his classes.

Drills in Typewriting

Much of the student's time in typewriting is devoted to typing drills. These drills are designed for many different purposes and may be classified in numerous ways. The particular classification that the teacher uses is unimportant. However, it is imperative that both the teacher and the students understand what each drill in the text is supposed to accomplish. Often drills that the students type are totally ineffective because they do not know the objective of the drill or how it is supposed to change or strengthen their present typing patterns.

In many typing texts, the labels attached to the drills in no way indicate the nature or purpose of the drill. Usually this is carefully explained in the teacher's manual, but unless the manual is read and the purpose interpreted to the students, the drill may not result in the desired learning.

Some of the more common classifications of typing drills are warm-up drills, letter-location drills, technique drills, accuracy drills, speed drills, rhythm drills, facility drills, and concentration drills. Many of the drills in these various classifications overlap or may be used for different purposes, depending upon the directions accompanying the drill.

Warm-Up Drills. The chief purpose of the warm-up drill is to loosen or "flex" finger muscles used in typing. Secondary purposes include concentration on skill building, review of some part of or all of the keyboard, setting the pace for the period, and getting the students to begin work even before the bell rings.

EXHIBIT 5.2

Illustrations of Warm-Up Drills

Expert rhythm drill	a;sldkfjghfjdksla;sldkfjghfjdksla;sldkfjghfjdksla;sldk
Variations	a;qpa;slwosldkeidkfjrufjghtyghfjrufjdkeidkslwosla;qpa; a;z/a;slx.sldkc,dkfjvmfjghbnghfjvmfjdkc,dkslx.sla;z/a; a;qpa;z/a;slwoslx.sldkeidkc,dkfjrufjvmfjghtyghbnghfjru aa;;ssllddkkffjjgghhffjjddkkssllaa;;ssllddkkffjjgghhff a;;slldkkfjjghhfjjdkkslla;;slldkkfjjghhfjjdkkslla;;sll ;aalsskddjffhggjffkddlss;aalsskddjffhggjffkddlss;aalss
Alphabet variations	abcdefghijklmnopqrstuvwxyz abcdefghijklmnopqrstuvwxyz aabbccddeeffgghhiijjkkllmmnnooppqqrrssttuuvvwwxxyyzz zyxwvutsrqponmlkjihgfedcba zyxwvutsrqponmlkjihgfedcba
Alphabetic words	zombie bijou plaza vivid torrid quake cadavers witch fixing
Alphabetic sentence	Al Flick was vexed and predicted the jury verdict.
Fluency	own one oil one robe took look book good goal loan lay lie let low lot lag law log old talk milk silk net not now nor nip new nap man sun mean noun want
High-frequency words	the this that those then you your his her our can was will

Balanced-hand words	down right sign form coal then them clay cork lake girls
Balanced-hand sentence	The bugle corps may go to the lake to do the work.
Speed sentence	Few of us ever try to type as well as we should.
Phrases	if it, to do it, you cannot, he is not, I will be able
Numbers and symbols	$6 $66 $666 8% 88% 888% #4 #44 #444 9¢ 99¢ 3″ 33″
Single-letter concentration on j	judicial jumper adjutant adjust jewel junior judge

The warm-up exercise may consist of a single line embracing all the letter reaches on the keyboard. On the other hand, it may consist of two or three lines, each one having a different purpose. In this case one line may consist of the expert rhythm drill, the second line may be designed as an accuracy drill, and the third line may be designed to build fluency and speed at the beginning of the period.

A one-minute warm-up on the expert rhythm drill is an excellent way to flex the finger muscles and strengthen the fingers *if* correct technique is used in typing the drill. However, if the students use a "punch" stroke coming from the hand, arm, or shoulder, or permit their hands and wrists to "bounce," the drill may actually have a detrimental effect on their typing skill. This one-minute warm-up might be followed by one minute of drill material requiring close concentration such as (*a*) typing the alphabet forward and backward, (*b*) typing an alphabetic sentence, (*c*) typing sentences using numbers and symbols, (*d*) typing numbers from 1 to 100, and (*e*) typing numbers with symbols such as $1, $2; 1¢, 2¢; 1%, 2%; and so forth. The third part of the warm-up might consist of a thirty-second or one-minute speed sentence. This part of the warm-up should result in fluent, fast typing and should set the pace for the rest of the period.

Technique Drills. When a technique drill is used, the student should be told the particular technique that is being emphasized and should not be expected to concentrate on several different techniques at once. For example, a margin-release drill should not be combined with a drill on the backspace key or the tabulator key. The purpose of technique drills may be to improve the manipulation of some part of the machine, to improve the student's typing rhythm, to keep his eyes on the copy, to keep the hands low, to improve the stroking of certain fingers on either hand, or to improve the student's technique in reaching from one bank of keys to another. The student should always be told the purpose of the drill before he is asked to practice it.

Speed Drills. Probably more time is spent in most typing classes on speed and accuracy drills than on all other types of drills combined. Therefore it is most important that the teacher be familiar with the various types of speed drills she may use and the purposes of each.

Balanced-hand words and sentences. Since the letters in the words alternate between the two hands, this copy can be typed faster than any other kind of material.

Easy words, sentences, and paragraphs. Often this material consists of high-frequency words.

Word- and phrase-level typing.

Twelve-second to one-minute repetitive writings; also drills building from one-half to three minutes.

EXHIBIT 5.3

Illustrations of Technique Drills

Carriage throw:

Set the margin stops at 10 and 75 and a tabulator stop at 45. Then practice the carriage return drill below until you can return the carriage quickly and begin typing with no break in your typing rhythm.

	She does not
try to learn.	She does not
try to learn.	

Margin release:

Have the students set their margins for a 60-space line. Then ask them to type line-for-line material in the text using a 70-space line. The students will be forced to use the margin release at the end of each line.

Backspace key:

Ask the students to type a paragraph in which they must backspace and underscore several short words in the paragraph. Drill on the back space key may also be given through an exercise in typing uneven column tabulations such as the one shown below.

721	776	110	921	4,592
1,493	29	1,092	623	3,731
565	583	3,318	545	76
8,190	4,792	766	11,001	890

Shift-key drill:

Have the students type material containing many proper nouns. Another procedure that will force the students to concentrate on the proper use of the shift key is to give them fifteen-second timings on sentences in which the number of words capitalized increases in each sentence. The students are to try to type each sentence at the same rate as the first sentence.

> Many young boys do not know the value of a dollar today.
> Many young Boys do not know the value of a dollar Today.
> Many young Boys do Not know the Value of a dollar Today.
> Many young Boys do Not Know the Value of a Dollar Today.
> Many Young Boys do Not Know the Value of a Dollar Today.

Tabulator-key drill:

Tabulator-key drills should be designed to fit the typing level of the class. A beginning class should be given a simple drill in which the students are required to type only short words. Later they may be given a drill in which words and figures are combined. An advanced class may be given a drill composed entirely of columns of figures in which the length of the figures in each column is the same; eventually the drill may be increased in difficulty until the columns include figures of varying lengths, which will require the students to backspace or space forward from the point at which the machine stops when the tabulator key is depressed. If the stroke count is given for these drills, the students may be given thirty-seconds and one-minute timings on them.

Words:				Strokes
now	too	for	was	16
you	any	the	are	32
got	say	all	can	48
him	for	men	lie	64

Words and Figures:				
use	421	one	123	16
too	897	now	989	32
has	603	not	766	48
her	510	dog	405	64

Figures:				
2233	9988	5566	2277	20
2345	9876	2389	4354	40
6789	9753	4567	7645	60
8901	8642	1023	9889	80

Type the foregoing drill dropping the first number in each column of the second and fourth lines of figures (spacing forward from the tabulator set).

Type the foregoing drill adding a 5 before each column in the second line and a 6 before each column in the fourth line (backspacing from the tabulator set).

Eyes on the copy:

Any material that is unusually difficult may be used to force students to keep their eyes on the copy. Material containing extremely long words or unfamiliar or foreign terms will accomplish this purpose. Concentra-tration drills may also be used to force students to watch the copy.

Stroking drills:

Almost any copy may be used to improve the students' stroking. However, the material should not be unusually difficult or some of the students will not be able to maintain an even stroking rate. The teacher may call the strokes and type with the students in order to get them to type evenly. Once they are typing rhythmically with good stroking, she may then have them continue this practice individually at their own rates.

Left-hand and right-hand words and words drilling on particular fingers:

These drills are ordinarily designed to develop additional strength and power in the fingers.

Reaches from the third to the first bank of keys; reaches from the first to the third bank:

These drills may be designed to increase the accuracy of the typist, but many times they will serve equally well to improve the students' technique in reaching from the first to the third or from the third to the first bank of keys. When attention is focused on such drills, it is often possible to eliminate waste motions and thereby increase the speed with which these reaches are made.

Flash words, starting with two-letter words and building to five- or six-letter words.

Syllable drills. Long words are first broken into syllables. After the syllables can be typed fluently, the word is typed several times.

Preview drills. Words and phrases are selected for practice before the paragraph is typed. By practicing these words in advance, the student is able to type the paragraph rapidly and yet maintain an unbroken rhythm.

Goal writings. The copy is marked in five- or ten-word intervals.

The student selects a speed goal five to ten words beyond his present typing rate. When he is able to reach this goal, he increases his goal another five to ten words. In some cases, as soon as the student reaches his first goal for one minute, he tries to build that speed to two minutes and finally three minutes before he goes on to a new speed goal.

Call-the-throw drill. The student selects a sentence slightly beyond his present typing rate. His objective is to finish typing the sentence before the carriage throw is called. If he is unable to complete the sentence, the next time he tries to type more strokes than he did the first time and continues in this manner until he is able to complete the sentence in the time allowed.

Sometimes the student is told to keep moving on to the next sentence each time the carriage throw is called as long as he is able to finish the sentence. When he is unable to complete a sentence, he remains on that sentence until he completes it before the carriage throw is called.

Rhythm drills. The teacher sets the tempo for the class, and gradually keeps increasing it until the rhythm of the class breaks. This type of rhythm drill is especially good for a beginning typing class. Later it may not be particularly helpful since the speed range is so great that only a part of the class benefits from the drill.

EXHIBIT 5.4

Illustrations of Speed Drills

Flash Words	of it to go do so it is of me be by on at as an no if it is
	the man say can day too for not lie lay for got his big put
	this that then them they been here ours good gave play laid
	these month right typed their there shall those paper taken
Syllable Drills	con di tion pro ces sion tran scrip tion con fi den tial
	re spon si bil ity ste nog raph er rea son able de ter mine
Repetition of Similar Sentence	The new teacher was late to her typing class the next period.
	The young teacher was late to her typing class the next period.
	The young teacher will be late to my typing class in the morning.
	The young teacher must not be late to her typing class another time.
	The young teacher must not be late to her typing class in the morning.
Previewed Drill	practice If you will practice each day, you will soon know
	quickly your keyboard well. Once you have learned to strike
	sharply the keys quickly and sharply, you should be able to
	keyboard build your typing speed.

techniques   You should always try to type as well as you can.
master   Now is the time to master those techniques upon which
power   you will build your future typing skill. Good tech-
              niques lead to future typing power.

Speed   Power Drive
Building
Drive

Directions: You will be timed for one-half minute on the
sentence below. Type the sentence as many times as you can
at your control rate.

                          Rate Indicator

                                                      Words
Type each line as many times as you can.   8

Directions: Determine your score on the rate indicator as
follows: Figure the total number of words typed in 30
seconds; multiply by 2; subtract one word for each error.
Now, using your final score on the rate indicator, locate your
speed (or the speed nearest your rate) in the right-hand
columns of the Power Drive. This will indicate where you
will start on your Power Drive.

| Number of times you complete the line | A | B | C |
Your speed in words a minute.	2	3	4
1. The men took the boats to the lake.	28	42	
2. The rain did not stop the ball game.	29	43	
3. She paid the boy for the paper today.	30	44	
4. Mary is planning to have a party soon.	30	46	61
5. That jet plane has been lost two weeks.	31	47	62
6. John did not find anyone to do the work.	32	48	64
7. Be sure to put the pens back on the desk.	33	49	66
8. They will build a house there on that lot.	34	50	67
9. She tries hard to do the best work she can.	34	52	69
10. I will meet the boy at the train in an hour.	35	53	70
11. The track team will run in the meet tomorrow.	36	54	72
12. This power drive should help build your speed.	37	55	74
13. It is true the early riser often gets his worm.	38	56	75
14. Few of us ever try to type as well as we should.	38	58	77
15. Do not stop typing until you hear the bells ring.	39	59	78
16. Please come to this typing class on time each day.	40	60	80

Repetitive three-three-three plan. Actually this is a special type of preview practice. The student practices in groups of three specific words and phrases which appear in the material to be typed. For instance, if he is previewing a letter, he might type this phrase: on on on the the the date date date on the date on the date on the date.

Repetition of similar sentences. The copy in each sentence is the same as the copy in the preceding sentence with the exception of two or three words. Two or three strokes are added to each sentence. The objective of the student is to be able to complete each sentence as rapidly as he typed the first one, thereby increasing his typing speed two or three words during the one-minute drill.

Accuracy Drills. Teachers now know that telling a student to type more accurately does not produce accurate typing. The student would certainly type more accurately if he could. He has no desire to make errors. His trouble is that he does not know what to do to reduce his errors. It is the function of the teacher to teach him what drills he should use to develop accurate typing, not simply to tell him to relax and type more accurately. It is true that usually relaxation and accurate typing go together. But the teacher must set a relaxed atmosphere for learning so the students will be able to type with the desired degree of accuracy. Excessive interruptions during the practice period, an unusual amount of noise outside the classroom, and too much criticism on the part of the teacher during the period—all create tension. Setting goals that the students cannot attain leads to discouragement and increases errors. All these factors the teacher can and should control. Once the unnecessary tensions have been removed from the classroom situation, the teacher may then introduce the accuracy drills that the students need to improve their typing skill.

Alphabet drills—words, sentences, and paragraphs. Alphabet drills may focus attention on one letter of the alphabet that causes the student trouble, or they may include all the letters of the alphabet for the purpose of increasing student mastery of the keyboard locations. A student making the same typing error consistently should be assigned a drill on words emphasizing the particular reach giving him difficulty. The alphabet sentences and paragraphs are excellent practice material for the entire class. Being slightly more difficult than most contextual material, they force the student to type a little slower than usual and help him find his control level of typing.

Extremely difficult material. For those students who are typing much too rapidly to be accurate and who seem unable to distinguish between speed-spurt typing and control typing, exercises based on extremely difficult material are often helpful. In order to type the material, the student must slow down.

Call-the-throw drill for control. Call-the-throw drills may be used for the development of either speed or accuracy. Both the teacher and the student must understand the objective for which the drill is being used. The drills may be used in a number of ways. Occasionally the teacher may tell the student to select a sentence that represents his control level of typing, to type it through once, wait for the carriage throw which will be called by the teacher, and then repeat the sentence. The drill may be continued in this manner for thirty seconds or one minute. At other times the teacher, after telling the student to select a sentence as before, may have the student type through the sentence, throw the carriage when the throw is called, and then go on to the next sentence. He will continue moving on to the next sentence as long as he is able to type it without an error and complete the sentence. At any time that he makes an error he will repeat the sentence until he types it accurately. If he does not complete the sentence, he will repeat it until he is able to finish it before the carriage throw is called.

Drills on figures and symbols. These drills may be in the form of conditioning exercises, sentences, paragraphs, or even call-the-throw drills.

Repetition of thirty-second to one-minute drills on sentences and paragraphs with a limited number of errors permitted. In some of these drills the student progresses to the next paragraph as soon as he completes the preceding paragraph without an error. In other cases he selects a goal that he will try to reach in the one-half minute. As soon as he is able to type to that point in the paragraph without an error, he increases his rate objective five words a minute. When he reaches this goal, he increases his rate another five words a minute. In this case an attempt is made to build speed and accuracy concurrently. These thirty-second to one-minute repetitions should not be continued until the students become exhausted and their errors begin to increase. Some teachers keep a chart on the board showing the number of students completing each timing without an error. When the number begins to decrease, they immediately go on to some other typing activity.

Still another way in which straight-copy paragraphs may be used

EXHIBIT 5.5

Illustrations of Accuracy Drills

Alphabetic:

One letter—h   reach should hatch churches thoughts healthy hearth

Sentence   Zeb just explained quickly the dangerous tax bill.

Paragraph   Every typing student should master the parts of his ma-
(j and z   chine thoroughly. He should be as skillful in the use of the
omitted)   shift key and the tabulator key or bar as he is in the
stroking of the keys and the carriage return. He should
understand the difference between the line space disengaging lever and the variable line spacer. The purpose of the
various scales on the typewriter should be clear to him. Unless he knows how to use every device on his machine
quickly and efficiently, he cannot hope to become an expert typist.

Difficult   The commission has examined a number of the amend-
material   ments demanded by the community. They plan to recommend the elimination of some commitments and have appointed a committee to implement economy measures. The
manner in which the commission has eliminated numerous
wastes has impressed the men and women of this community.

One-hand   sedate retract estate deceased exaggerate regressed secret
words   afterwards referred decreased crafts caged grease dreads

Double-letter   moon mass pill fuss roll comment referred succession jiggle
words   dazzle accommodate parallel bookkeeping committed looking

Adjacent-finger   motion choice billion boil religious foil opinion stoic
letters   conscious choir station noise solution coiled contagious

Letters controlled   forfeit relieve conceit field eighteen lien deceive
by same finger,   science their wield beige wierd deign friend seige
opposite hands

Difficult reaches: any monogamy penny enemy rainy stormy sunny many ali-
1st to 3d bank   mony
3d to 1st bank   under plunder asunder drunk dump stump trump untold unless

Drills on fingers   Type the numbers 98 and 65 and 54 and 32 and 10 and 234
and symbols   and 567 and 890 and 167 and 545 and 678 and 231 and 80.
12345 6789 9876 5432 1010 0918 8023 7359 4824 9235
2389 9541 4009 6822 7667 6756 5522 3101 5296 6426
1010 2020 3030 4040 5050 9911 8812 7713 6614 5515

Is it correct to say "7 and 4 are 12" or "7 and 4 is 12"?
Of course you have noted that 7 and 4 are 11, not 12. It

is correct to type fractions with the / symbol. Two common fractions written with this symbol are 2/3 and 3/4. In writing mixed numbers, the whole number and the fraction are separated by one space (10 2/3). If the space is omitted, the mixed number appears to be an improper fraction (102/3).

to increase accuracy is to start with one-half minute timings and increase them by one-half minute each time. The student's objective is to type without an error for a longer period each day than he had been able to type previously. For instance, a student who typed for one and one-half minutes on Monday without an error would start Tuesday with the one-half-minute drill and try to build the length of time during which he types without an error to two minutes. If a student is unable to type some of the paragraphs without an error after repeated tries, the teacher may suggest that he go on to the next paragraph. Continued failure on the same material may set up blocks which the student cannot overcome regardless of the effort he puts forth. Some teachers allow one error on each timing.

Drills on difficult reaches. Many students hesitate or make errors whenever they encounter difficult reaches in the copy. For example, the reach from *e* to *x* often causes trouble. Many of the reaches from the third to the first or from the first to the third bank of keys are troublesome. Words and sentences drilling on these reaches will develop accuracy in typing them.

One-hand words. Obviously one-hand words are much more difficult to type than balanced-hand words. Most typing texts today contain a number of drills on one-hand words to build both speed and accuracy in typing these letter combinations.

Double-letter words. Although double-letter words represent one of the easier stroking drills for the beginning typist, they represent one of the most difficult for the advanced typist. Frequently the doubled letter upsets his typing rhythm, causes him to omit one of the letters or to crowd the letters too closely together. A double-letter word is a slow word to type and therefore needs special drill.

Adjacent-finger drills. Occasionally some typing students confuse the location of letters controlled by adjacent fingers. This is particularly true of the reaches to *o* and *i, r* and *t, n* and *m,* and *v* and *b.* When a student is consistently having difficulty with one of these reaches, he should be assigned an adjacent-finger drill on the letters causing the trouble.

Opposite fingers, same reach. A letter-location error similar to the adjacent-finger error is that caused by confusing the keys controlled by the same fingers on the left and right hands. Probably the reach most often confused here is *e* and *i*.

Unison typing in class. One of the most important functions of the typing teacher is to help his students know the difference between typing for speed and typing for control. Many students are tense when they type because they always type at their top rate of speed. They have not learned when to type for speed and when to type for control. Unless the student learns how and when to type for control, he cannot hope to become an accurate typist. If a class seems to have difficulty relaxing after a speed drive or is not dropping back to the control level at the proper times, the teacher may find it helpful occasionally to do a unison typing drill with the class. The drill should be paced at a rate at which everyone in the class can type it easily, without any strain. Occasionally a drill such as this, just before beginning a timed writing, will help the students find their control level so that they will not start typing at too fast a speed.

Concentration Drills. Concentration drills are actually a special type of accuracy drill. A student may find that he is making typing errors because he is unable to concentrate upon his typing. Telling the student to concentrate on the copy may only further distract him

EXHIBIT 5.6

Illustrations of Concentration Drills

Drill to omit repetition of words

The girl girl in my typing class who who always typed at a high high speed with almost no no errors said that she she attributed her her skill to to practicing a short, easy sentence or or paragraph over and over and over. She said that that she also typed material which was filled with filled with left-hand words words containing difficult reaches reaches and words with with doubled letters. She said she said that such copy copy was always difficult for for her until she had had practiced it it many many many times and was was able to to type such material in in a rhythmic pattern without without uneven stroking or or hesitations. She emphasized that it is it is the way you type and the kind of of material you you practice which often makes the the difference between the expert and the and the ordinary typist.

Drill on correcting copy	Thank you for your letter of Nov. 16th. They found the reference in Vol. 4, Section 2, Page 101. I gave him $1.00 to purchase 20 five-cent stamps.
Drill on supplying omitted vowels	D--r M-d-m: Th-nk y-- f-r y--r l-tt-r -f M-y 15 -n wh-ch y-- s-y y-- w-ll b- -bl- t- s-ttl- y--r b-ll by th- f-rst -f n-xt m-nth. W- f-lt c-nf-d-nt s-m- -n-xp-ct-d d-ff-c-lty w-s r-sp-ns-bl- f-r th- d-l-y -nd -ppr-c--t- y--r pr-mpt r-ply t- --r -nq--ry. W- sh-ll l--k f-rw-rd t- r-c--v-ng y--r ch-ck -n f-ll p-ym-nt -f y--r -cc--nt w-th -s by th- f-rst -f n-xt m-nth.
Drill on correcting punctuation and capitalization	We appreciate your order for 30 copies of teaching business subjects by douglas blandford and anderson since our dallas office is temporarily out of stock of this book we have forwarded your order to our new york office i am sure it will be processed promptly by our new york office and that you will receive these books within a week if you do not receive your order promptly please let us know and we shall be glad to check into the matter for you here in dallas it is a pleasure to be of service to you and we shall look forward to serving you again in the near future.
Drill on following directions	Center the following heading: Business Letters. Triple space and indent five spaces for the following sentences: Business letters represent big business. Today it is estimated that the average business letter costs over $2.50. High salaries and clerical costs are a major part of the expense of producing a business letter. Underscore the first word in the following sentence: Today every businessman should know how to dictate business letters rapidly and accurately. Correct the misspelled word in the next sentence: Every secretary should know the principals of effective letter writing.
	Place quotation marks around the following quotation: A New York businessman recently said, I consider the art of written communication one of the most important skills which any young executive can possess. Place dashes where they should occur in the next sentence: Every business letter you write whether it is to John Doe or to the president of an important company should be a goodwill ambassador for your firm.

and make it impossible for him to do so. Instead he will be worrying lest he is not concentrating. He may be distracted by someone who is typing next him. Students often say that they are disturbed because their neighbor types faster than they do. In some instances if the student is only slightly faster, it may spur the slower typist on to greater efforts. But if the range is too great between the two, it may very well make it difficult for him to concentrate on his work. The student may be so concerned about some faulty technique in his typing that he cannot concentrate on anything else. A typist who has used the first finger on the backspace key for ten years will have difficulty concentrating on anything else if he decides to break the habit. It may have a very detrimental effect upon his over-all typing skill. Listening intently for a weak bell may make it impossible to pay proper attention to the copy. Making too much effort to complete a certain amount of typing within a given period or trying to finish a job without making an error may distract the typist and make it difficult for him to concentrate on his work.

Every student should be urged to keep his eyes fixed on the copy. If he has developed a rhythmic, continuous pattern of stroking, he will find it relatively easy to focus on the copy since he will have little trouble with clashing keys. If he is having difficulty in typing for control, the suggestion that he concentrate upon the meaning of the material being typed may be helpful. Any condition which causes unnecessary tension is apt to interfere with the typist's powers of concentration. Frequently teachers themselves are responsible for such problems through setting goals which are unattainable, demanding perfect copies, or hovering over the students as they type. All these practices should be avoided.

The ingenious typing teacher will find that there are many different types of drills that may be used to increase the student's concentration while typing.

Eyes on copy. The teacher may time the students as they type a paragraph to see how long they can type without raising their eyes from the copy.

Difficult contextual material. Difficult material is helpful because it serves to establish correct reading rates.

Copy that includes instructions. The students must concentrate on the material they are typing since they must follow the directions given in the copy.

Omission of vowels or words. The students are to insert the missing vowels or words as they type the copy.

Drills containing spelling and punctuation errors. The drill may either contain spelling and punctuation errors that are to be corrected as the students type, or it may be a problem paragraph that is not punctuated at all.

Rhythm Drills and Facility Drills. While many typing authorities classify rhythm and facility drills as warm-up drills, speed or accuracy drills, or concentration drills, they are considered sufficiently important here to be discussed in a separate classification. A common type of rhythm drill is one in which the class types together, with the tempo gradually being increased. The drill material should be composed of words and phrases to be automatized and should be practiced before the class attempts to type it in rhythm. Other rhythm drills are those in which each student types at his own pace, attempting to type at an even rate, balanced-hand drills, and drills on words of various lengths. Facility drills are usually designed to develop fluency in typing difficult reaches—such as long reaches from one bank of keys to another—difficult words and phrases, and one-hand words.

Records and tapes are used by some typing teachers to assist their students in developing a smooth typing rhythm. The records or tapes may be typed at varying rates, starting with a fairly slow rate and gradually increasing in speed. The students are instructed to type with the record or tape, maintaining the same rhythm and pushing for increases in speed. Records or tapes in which the students are instructed to type to the music serve much the same purpose. Such materials may highly motivate the students, but ordinarily they should not be used for more than five to ten minutes of any one class period.

Teaching Figures and Symbols

At one time teachers did not consider it necessary for typing students to develop skill in the typing of numbers and symbols. Today with high-speed computers playing an increasingly important role in the business world, it is imperative that typists be able to type numbers and symbols rapidly and accurately. More and more information is being coded into figures rather than words, from seven-digit telephone numbers to zip codes. The use of punched cards and magnetic tapes emphasizes the importance of accuracy in the typing of figures. An error in the typing of a figure on a punched card or magnetic tape does not represent one error, but a multiplicity of errors, since the error is repeated each time the card or tape is processed. The typing teacher should have a definite procedure for building skill on the top row of keys. The following methods represent tested ways to build such skill.

1. Do not introduce the top row of keys until the student has first mastered the alphabetic reaches. Many typing texts defer the teaching of this row for at least two weeks after the alphabet keyboard has been presented. By this time the students should be typing fifteen to twenty words a minute for one minute.

2. Present the figures in a manner that will result in good stroking techniques. If the student is having to concentrate too much upon the location of the key, he may type it with a hesitant, push stroke rather than with the quick, sharp stroke that he uses on the alphabet keys. Some such pattern as this might be followed to get the students to use the correct stroking while learning these reaches:

1 11 111 2 22 222 12 21 121 212 112 221 7 77 777 17 71
171 717 771 117 27 72 227 722 272 727 271 721 217

3. Do not have the students type the intervening keys between the homerow and the figures. The student may practice in this manner once or twice before making the reach from the homerow to the top row. But continuing this type of practice results in hesitation when the student needs to make a direct reach from the homerow to the top row as he will in typing contextual material. For example, the teacher might use a drill such as this to present the top row:

f fr4 f4 44 444 k ki8 k8 88 888 48 84 848 448 488 884

4. Do not present too many figures and symbols in one period. Not more than two figures or symbols should be presented in any one period. All too often these keys are presented but are not thoroughly taught. Sufficient time should be allowed for thorough mastery of each key immediately after it is presented.

5. Dictate some of the number drills. This procedure helps the students think of the numbers as a group rather than as individual digits.

6. After the top row has been introduced, provide some practice in typing these figures and symbols every day. Sometimes the teacher assumes that once the top row has been taught, no further special drill is needed except at irregular intervals throughout the course. Actually special drill is needed on this row every day if it is no more than one or two minutes during the warm-up period.

7. Use many different types of drills to build skill on the top row. For example, here are some of the variations that may be used:

1. Typing from 1 to 100
2. Typing by 2's, 3's, 4's, or 5's
3. Drills using the various symbols such as
   $1, $2, $3, $4; 2%, 3%, 4%, 5%; 5¢, 6¢, 7¢, 8¢, 9¢.
   (Review only one or two symbols each day.)
4. Drills in which the last figure becomes the first figure in the next combination:
   12, 23, 34, 45, 56, 67, 78, 89, 90
5. Drills using opposite fingers:
   20, 39, 48, 57, 12, 93, 84, 75
6. Dictation of sentences containing numbers:
   The room was 18′ x 22′.
   His telephone number is 382-5786.
   The book costs $1, but she reduced the price to 89 cents.
7. Speed drills on typing groups of figures. (The figures should be stroke counted so that the students can compute their typing rate. With practice on such drills, the students should be able to type them at 25 to 40 per cent of their straight-copy rate. In the exercise below the last two digits in each row of figures indicate the number of groups of five strokes each that the student has typed. Thus in the first line, the student has typed the equivalent of twelve words):

7201 8902 6403 8904 5605 6906 4407 5508 6609 7710 3411 5412
7613 4314 8715 4016 3217 4818 9819 5720 3421 5622 8723 3424
1234 7890 6712 8934 5606 4818 9327 4813 3590 9067 5832 1136

8. When typing copy containing nothing but figures, teach the students to move to the top row. This is sometimes called the *pipe-organ method* of typing numbers. The fourth finger of the left hand is placed on 2, the third finger on 3, the second finger on 4, and the first finger controls 5 and 6. If the typewriter has a "1" key in the top row, then the fourth finger would be placed on the 1, the third finger on 2, the second finger on 3, and the fourth finger would control 4 and 5. Students are usually taught to keep the right hand on the home keys since they will have to be in this position to strike a 1 and to reach the comma, which will be required in typing numbers of more than three digits. Most students can type figures much faster when

they move their left hand to the top-row location. However, they should not be permitted to type all drills in this position since much copy contains both figures and words.

9. Include drills containing both figures and words.

1. The warm-up drills on figures might be: 1 and 2 and 3 and 4 and 5, and so on.

2. Another device is to have the students type for one minute a sentence of average difficulty and compute their typing rate. Then have the students take a number of thirty-second drills on a sentence containing figures and symbols, the objective being to reach the same typing rate as they attained on the first sentence.

Analysis of Typewriting Errors

At one time most typewriting teachers believed in a detailed analysis of typewriting errors which were recorded on error-analysis charts. These charts might show the errors each student made most frequently, but they did not show why the student made the errors. Also some teachers began to suspect that too much time was being devoted to such analysis to the detriment of their classroom teaching. A few teachers today still keep error-analysis charts or have their students keep them. However, it has been found that such charts are of most value during the first semester of typewriting after the key locations have been presented. At that point they will show errors that students may be making consistently, and remedial drills may be assigned to correct these errors. The keys most commonly struck in error are *m* for *n*, *r* for *t*, *t* for *r*, *o* for *i*, *n* for *l*, *s* for *d*, *r* for *e*, *e* for *i*, and *a* for *s*. In the more advanced stages of learning, studies of students' errors have shown that at this stage there is little pattern in the errors. The students do not consistently make the same errors, and authorities are inclined to believe that the typing errors of advanced typists are chance errors dependent sometimes upon the nature of the copy, sometimes on the physical condition of the student, sometimes upon noise and other distractions making concentration difficult. Obviously it is impossible to assign remedial drills for such chance errors.

Today rather than using error-analysis charts most teachers study the drill papers of each student, note any errors occurring consistently, and make notations on the paper suggesting the proper drills for each person. If certain errors occur in many of the papers, the teacher may then select some remedial drills to be practiced by the class as a group under her direction. Errors in technique that result in slow, faulty motions in the operation of the typewriter must be observed by the teacher during the class period. Many such errors cannot be found through an analysis of the paper alone. Errors should not be analyzed when the purpose of the practice is to force the students' typing speed to new levels. However, when the student is typing at his control rate and is not forcing for speed, errors may be analyzed effectively.

The beginning teacher needs to be alert to the common causes of typing errors. She should watch for these errors in her classes and know how to correct them. Most typing errors are due to the following causes:

1. Incorrect techniques in stroking and machine manipulation
   a. Faulty key stroking
   b. Irregular typing rhythm
   c. Fingers not held close to the keys
   d. Excessive arm and wrist motion
   e. Improper use of the shift key
   f. Faulty carriage return
   g. Incorrect stroking of the space bar
   h. Failure to operate machine parts by touch
2. Incorrect procedures in reading the copy
   a. Reading ahead of the word being typed
   b. Failure to keep eyes focused on the copy
   c. Looking up at the end of each line
   d. Looking to see what has been typed or if an error has been made
   e. Poor spelling which interferes with typing the copy correctly
3. Errors in typing knowledges
   a. Incorrect syllabication
   b. Incorrect application of typing usage rules
   c. Wrong form in typing problems

Blurred letters, skips in spacing, too-light or too-heavy letters indicate that the student is using incorrect stroking techniques. Blurred letters are the result of pushing the keys instead of hitting them. The student should be shown how to strike the keys with a strong finger motion and to release the key immediately.

Students who jam the keys often do so because they are not certain of the reach to the proper letter. Instead of striking the key in the center, they strike between two keys, thus depressing both of these keys together. Jammed keys may also be the result of irregular, unrhythmic stroking. Crowding of letters is also a sign of irregular stroking and weak fingers. Rhythm drills, finger-manipulation drills, and drills on alphabet letters or on lines of two-, three-, four-, and five-letter words are often helpful.

Errors in which students confuse adjacent keys, strike the wrong vowels, or strike a key controlled by the same finger but on the opposite hand are frequently caused by uncertainty regarding the location of the letter. In these cases the students need further drills on these letters and should think each letter as it is typed. Transposition of letters may also be due to uncertainty about the letter location. In the case of advanced students, transpositions are probably the result of reading too far ahead in the copy. The student needs to type at a slower rate or on the letter level, keeping his eyes on the word that he is typing until this error has been corrected.

Some students make frequent errors because they let their fingers "fly" away from the homerow keys and thus lose their homerow position. These students should be taught the importance of well-curved fingers held close to the home keys. At the same time the importance of quiet hands and arms should be emphasized. Excessive motions not only cause errors but may interfere with the development of typing speed.

Many students pile letters at the end of the line of typing. This is the result of speeding up in an effort to crowd in extra strokes before the margin locks. The students need to listen for the bell and should type somewhat slower with even stroking. When necessary, they should syllabicate rather than try to crowd the letters before the machine locks.

The omission and addition of letters are common typing errors. The omission of letters may be caused by too-light stroking with the result that the key makes no imprint on the page. In some cases it is caused by reading too far ahead. The students should practice even, rhythmic stroking on the letter level. The addition of letters may also be caused by reading too far ahead of the point at which the student is typing. It may also be due to poor concentration with the result that the student types some familiar sequence on the root word which is not part of the sequence in the copy—for example, *importance* instead of *important,* or *perfection* instead of *perfecting.*

Here again the students need to concentrate on the copy, making a definite effort to keep their eyes focused on the syllable or word they are typing. Other errors due to poor concentration are caused by looking up at the end of each line of typing, looking at the typed copy after an error has been made, or being distracted by the bells on other typewriters. A person who is a poor speller may misspell words which are correct in the copy because he is not concentrating closely enough on the letters and words he is typing.

In two surveys of typing errors, it has been reported that over 20 per cent of the total errors made by students were due to incorrect use of the nonletter keys—errors in machine manipulation. A common error in this classification is raised or lowered capitals caused by failure to depress the shift key far enough or failure to hold the shift key long enough. Many students have irregular left-hand margins, the result of incorrect techniques in returning the carriage. Failure to space between words or extra spacing between words may result from poor control of the space bar. Lingering on the space bar may cause the machine to skip, or resting the thumb on the space bar may result in the omission of spaces between words. Another common error caused by faulty machine manipulation is unevenly tabulated columns. In this case the student has failed to hold the tabular key or bar until the carriage stopped moving.

Excessive pushing for speed, incorrect posture at the typewriter, tenseness and lack of confidence, long fingernails, and fatigue may also contribute to inaccurate typing.

Because so many typing errors seem to be "hit-and-miss" errors, it is sometimes difficult to determine what type of drill will be most effective in increasing the students' accuracy. If these errors seem to be the result of poor concentration, then concentration drills may be used. However, in many cases the reason for the error is not apparent. The teacher needs to realize that the letter that was struck incorrectly may be of no importance at all. For instance, it has been found that many typing errors occur because a student sees a difficult typing combination approaching. He tenses and makes an error in some simple word, but then types the difficult word correctly. The reverse can also happen. The student may manage to type the difficult word accurately but immediately thereafter makes an error in an easy typing combination, not because he cannot type that word, but because his rhythm has been broken by the difficult typing combination. Many typing authorities recommend that a student be given directions similar to the following when he is typing to improve his accuracy. Suppose the student is practicing paragraph material. He types through the paragraph once, preferably previewing the paragraph before typing it. Then he checks for errors. When he finds an error, he should type the word once or twice slowly and then somewhat more rapidly. Then he should type the word in its normal setting, typing one or two words that appear before and after the word in which he made the error. Thus if some other word caused him to make the error, he will be practicing that word also.

Proofreading

Proofreading is a skill that should be taught. When the student tells his teacher that he did read his work carefully but simply did not see any errors, he is probably telling the truth. The eye tends to see what the student knows should be in the typed copy, not what has been typed. Then, too, proofreading is often hastily done, which results in many of the errors being overlooked. Because students feel that time spent proofreading is time that could be devoted to producing typed copy, they rush through the job much too quickly.

As offices install automated equipment, more and more typewriters will produce punched paper tape as well as the typed copy. Errors captured on this common language media are repeated each time they are handled automatically by other machines. Consequently high-level proofreading ability is essential. Students need to realize that while proofreading is time consuming and costly, the error which is overlooked on the punched tape or card is usually much more costly.

Probably teachers have many times contributed to the careless manner in which their students proofread their work. Teachers have frequently been guilty of spending long hours grading typing problems and production work, marking every error which the students have overlooked. Thus the students never fully accept the responsibility of locating their own errors. On problem typing or production work, a better procedure might be to check the problem until an error is found. Then if the teacher would simply mark the problem unacceptable and return it to the student, the student would still be responsible for locating the error or errors which he has overlooked. The teacher would save many hours by not continuing to grade papers which are already unacceptable, and the student would have to proofread his work carefully to make sure he did find all the errors he had previously missed. If the teacher requires all problem and production typing containing errors to be retyped correctly, the students soon learn to take time to check their work carefully before removing it from the machine.

Lloyd [7] points out that one reason students fail to find their errors is that they are penalized when they do. He suggests that a better basis for grading would be to set a minimum number of errors allowed on a designated quantity of work or to grade the students on their improvement in proofreading. In other words, he would reward students for finding their errors, rather than penalize them for locating the errors. In proofreading typographical errors are the easiest to detect and include all errors due to stroking incorrect keys or poor machine manipulation. Content errors are the most difficult to locate since they include such errors as incorrect dates, amounts of money, and other errors in the context.

Methods of Proofreading. Because proofreading is such an essential part of the typist's work, many procedures have been developed and used successfully by typing teachers in aiding the student to improve their proofreading habits.

Proofreading by the paper-bail method. By turning the cylinder until the paper bail is just below each line of writing, the copy may be checked carefully before it is removed from the machine.

Proofreading material by comparing copy. For instance, the same paragraph may be duplicated twice on a sheet of paper. The student is told that the copy in the first paragraph is correct. He is to compare the copy in the second paragraph with the first paragraph and circle any errors that he finds. The teacher may time the students on such drills if he chooses.

Proofreading by two students. When students are typing complicated tabulations and reports, there is no reason why one student should not read the copy aloud to another student to check for errors. In business it is common practice to require that all tabulated reports be proofread by two persons working in this fashion. Why should we not permit our students to do this in the classroom?

Teach the students how to look for typographical, content, and technical errors:

---

[7] Alan C. Lloyd, "Let's Make Proofreading Affirmative," *Business Education World* (March 1950), pp. 335-337.

Check for typing errors.

Check the placement of the material on the page.

Check the accuracy of figures in addresses, dates, amounts of money, and so on.

Check the dates in the copy.

Check the spelling of names in the copy. Be sure names are spelled the same throughout the material.

Check the division of words in the right-hand margin.

Check the punctuation within the copy.

Check for errors in grammar.

Check the spelling of cities, states, and other proper nouns.

Check for errors in typing form.

Check letters for any special lines such as carbon-copy notations, enclosures, and the like.

Students may be given letters to proofread in which the errors become increasingly difficult to locate. For instance, the first letter may contain only typographical errors. The next letter may contain typographical errors and errors in word division. The third letter may have some spelling and grammatical errors. Errors in content should be added last since they represent the most difficult type of error for most students to find. If students are given material containing too many different types of errors when proofreading is first emphasized, they will miss many of the errors. When the material being proofread gradually increases in complexity, they will have become sufficiently skilled in proofreading to find most of the errors without difficulty. Timing the students on these exercises helps to create interest in proofreading.

Many students have never learned to proofread for any kind of error except typographical mistakes. The foregoing drills and instructions will make the students aware of the importance of checking the content of the copy carefully. They will soon realize that errors in content are usually far more serious than most typing errors.

Related Knowledges in Typewriting

At one time typing was classified strictly as a skill subject. Many persons who do not fully appreciate the content of the course would still consider typing merely a skill. Typing *is* basically the development of a skill, but the development of that skill without the related knowledges used in applied typing jobs would be parallel to teaching shorthand without transcription. The student might be able to type accurately and rapidly, but he would not be able to apply that raw skill to an applied typing job. Students often have the idea that typing is only a skill and do not give enough attention to the knowledges they are supposed to master as they proceed through the course. As a consequence, although they may be fast, accurate typists on straight copy, they are not able to produce a satisfactory quantity or quality of work on typing production units.

The typing teacher should place enough emphasis on the importance of typing knowledges to make sure that the students are learning the knowledges that appear in each lesson. One way in which she can do this is to give a five- or ten-minute objective test on these knowledges every two weeks during the first semester. These short, objective tests will enable the teacher to determine whether the students do know the information that has been presented and will make it possible for her to cover much more material than would be covered through the use of typing exercises. It is not recommended that such tests be used extensively, as most of the time in the classroom should be spent in typing; but using short, objective tests occasionally to check the students' mastery of the informational phases of typing will impress upon the students the importance of this part of the work. Examples of such tests are given in Exhibits 5.7 and 5.8.

EXHIBIT 5.7

English and Typing Usage Test

Check in the proper column whether the sentence is typed according to correct English and typing usage. If the sentence is typed incorrectly, underscore the error.

Right Wrong

___	___	1. The state passed a sales tax effective January 15th.
___	___	2. The tea is to be at three o'clock in Faculty Hall.
___	___	3. Helen's train, due at 1:45 p.m., arrived at 3 p.m.
___	___	4. I gave her $1.00 to purchase thirty 5-cent stamps.
___	___	5. The article, "Missles," was in last months MODERN AGE.
___	___	6. "Do not come to class", he said, "if you are not prepared".
___	___	7. The Farmers Union Building is at 109 Peach Street.
___	___	8. He x'd out a paragraph and then o.k.'d the letters.
___	___	9. If Bob drives west, he may find oil in west Texas.
___	___	10. The chairman said that there were 120 men, 72 women, 9 boys, and 7 girls at the picnic.

EXHIBIT 5.8

Test on Centering

Complete the following statements:

1. There are _____ vertical spaces in 2 inches.
2. If 40 is the centering point for pica type, for a 50-space line the left margin should be set at _____ and the right margin at _____.
3. If 50 is the centering point on elite type, for a 50-space line the left margin should be set at _____ and the right margin at _____.
4. A half sheet of paper has _____ vertical line spaces.
5. A standard sheet of paper has _____ vertical line spaces.
6. In a 5-inch line, pica type, there are _____ horizontal spaces.
7. In a 5-inch line, elite type, there are _____ horizontal spaces.
8. On a standard sheet of paper there are _____ horizontal pica spaces.
9. On a standard sheet of paper there are _____ horizontal elite spaces.
10. A pica type machine has _____ spaces to a horizontal inch.
11. An elite type machine has _____ spaces to a horizontal inch.
12. A pica type machine has _____ spaces to a vertical inch.
13. An elite type machine has _____ spaces to a vertical inch.
14. You are to center a problem with twelve lines of typing and a one-line heading, double spaced on a full sheet of paper. You would start typing on line _____.
15. An exercise with nine lines and a one-line heading is to be typed single spaced, centered vertically, on a half sheet of paper. There would be _____ lines in the top margin and _____ lines in the bottom margin.

Composition at the Machine

Typing authorities are becoming increasingly aware of the importance of teaching students to compose at the typewriter. There are two reasons why special emphasis should be given to this skill. First, composition at the machine, starting with simple words and building to phrases, sentences, and paragraphs, may help the students learn to type on the word level since they are thinking not of strokes but of words. Second, students take typing for personal use and probably do much of their typing while they are composing at the machine. It should not be necessary for them to write everything they wish to type in longhand before they type it, yet many students follow this time-consuming practice because they have never been taught to compose at the typewriter. Students should be able to sit down and compose letters, rough drafts, and reports at their machines.

Because many typing experts believe that composition at the machine does help students type on the word level, they recommend that simple exercises be introduced during the second or third week of the course. Others feel that this type of practice should be delayed until the students have thoroughly mastered the keyboard and do not introduce composition at the machine until the middle of the first semester. Regardless of the exact time at which this practice is introduced, most persons agree that it is a skill that must be taught. The following steps represent a simple approach to building this skill.

Dictation to the Machine. It has been found that more persons are "visually minded" than "auditory minded." Up to this time the students have always had a visual image of the copy that they were to type. Learning to type from dictation may be used as a preparatory step to introducing composition at the typewriter.

Dictation of questions that may be answered in only one or two words.

> What is your first name?
> What is your last name?
> In what town do you live?

Dictation of questions that may be answered in short phrases.

> What musical instrument do you like best?
> What are your favorite hobbies?
> What is your home address?

Dictation of familiar expressions which the students must complete.

> An apple a day. . . .
> A bird in the hand. . . .
> Don't cross your bridges. . . .

Questions that must be answered by complete sentences.
Topics about which the students are to compose a paragraph.
The teacher may give the class two or three topics and let them choose the one on which they prefer to write.

Rowe suggests composition at the typewriter can be built to even higher levels through advanced composition projects. He recommends synopsis composition in which the student is asked to read several paragraphs and then condense the material into a few sentences. He also recommends having students compose letters at the machine, type notes to their classmates, and fill in application blanks.

Erasing

Authorities do not agree upon the best time for introducing erasing. Many teachers like to defer the teaching of erasing as long as possible, contending that if students are allowed to erase they will soon clog their machines with erasure dust. Other teachers point out that deferring the teaching of erasing is not the answer—the students will erase whether they have been taught to do so or not. They believe the problem is not in erasing but in failing to teach the students how to erase properly early in the course.

There is little reason to teach erasing before applied typing exercises are introduced. However, when such units as business letters are presented, it is difficult to make the students appreciate the importance of accurate, neat work and careful proofreading if they are not required to correct all their errors. On the other hand, the students should not be required to correct all material that they type since this would result in a serious loss of time which could otherwise be devoted to typing practice. In most typing texts applied typing exercises are introduced soon after all the keyboard locations have been taught. If students are expected to produce accurate, acceptable material, then erasing must be taught early in the course.

Erasing should be carefully taught, not left to chance. Students should know the difference between hard and soft erasers and when to use each. They should be able to make effective use of eraser shields of all kinds. They should be given practice in erasing, crowding, and spreading until they are able to correct their errors neatly and quickly.

Directions: Type the sentence as it first appears. Then make the corrections given in the parentheses.

Corrections	The girl sad at her desk.	(Change sad to sat.)
	The girl set at her desk.	(Change set to sat.)
	The girl gas at her desk.	(Change gas to was)
Crowding	The girl drove up the street.	(Change girl to youth.)
	The girl drove up the street.	(Change the to their.)
Spreading	The child ran to their car.	(Change child to girl.)
	The child ran to their car.	(Change their to his.)

The students should be given a number of these drills frequently and timed on them. Each student should try to decrease the time he requires to make the different types of corrections, with final emphasis always being placed on neat erasures.

The importance of learning to erase neatly and quickly can also be emphasized by occasionally administering timed writings in which students are required to correct all their errors.

Production Typewriting

Although much has been written during the past few years about production work in typewriting, many persons confuse the terms *problem typing* and *production typing*. Problem typing refers to the application of typewriting knowledges and skills to a problem situation. A teacher may present the principles of tabulation to a typing class and then require the students to type a number of tabulation problems. In a true production situation the student types a number of problems in a given period of time so that his production rate may be computed. Included in the production time are all those activities involved in completing the job, from the time the task is assigned until it is finished. Not only the actual typing of the problems but also reading and following the directions, planning the layout, handling materials, preparing carbons, proofreading and correcting errors are all part of the total job on which the production rate is computed.

Typing teachers now realize it is important to build typing skills to production levels—in fact, that it is a necessity for vocational typing students. The objective in production typewriting is to combine basic typing techniques and skillful machine manipulation with the fundamentals of applied typing in such a way as to master the advanced techniques necessary to perform on the high level of an office typist. Production-level typing can be developed only if the student has acquired dexterity in the manipulation of his machine, has built his typing skill on sound basic typing techniques, and has learned the fundamentals of applied typing.

Most students with low straight copy rates are unable to do production typing with any degree of success. The relationship between copy speed and production rate is high, though it may vary somewhat with the complexity of the work involved. It should also be noted that the steady, accurate typist has been found to do better in production work than the faster but less accurate typist. Since progress in production work is highly related to typing accuracy and speed, the typing teacher should recognize the importance of emphasizing basic skill building along with the training in fundamental related knowledges in the beginning typing course.

Formerly it was assumed that the proper time to introduce production typing was in the last semester of the typing program. This may be the ideal time to introduce highly complicated, long production tests requiring several periods to complete. This practice, however, leaves a wide gap between the first course in typing and the final production stage and partially accounts for the inability of the students to attain higher production rates on such tests. Today many typing authorities recommend that the concept of production typing be introduced in the first-semester course, gradually increasing the difficulty and length of the production period as the students improve in speed and accuracy. Under this plan production rates should be built when each new applied typing job is introduced. For instance, if this week the student is to learn to type a medium-length block-style letter, then he should not only master the skills and knowledges involved, but he should build his typing skill to the point where he can produce an acceptable number of modified block letters within a given period of time. Production work then becomes a natural outgrowth of new learnings. It is not a separate skill that is deferred until the third or fourth semester of typing. More and more materials in typing texts are being stroke-counted or word-counted so that students' production rates may be easily calculated. Exhibit 5.9 is an illustration of a drill designed to teach the students to type a modified block letter rapidly and accurately. The drills are all based on the content of the letter. The student builds skill not only in typing the introductory and closing parts of the letter, but also in typing the difficult words, phrases, and figures. Speed and accuracy in typing straight-copy material are provided through short timings on each paragraph of the letter. A five-minute timing is then given for building typing power. With this type of drill, the student should be able to type the letter at a rate that will approach his straight-copy typing rate. This emphasis upon production speed in typing business letters may then be transferred to the typing of unarranged letters.

It should be remembered that the students' straight-copy rate does not give an accurate indication of the production rate he will achieve. Production rates reported in production-typewriting studies have been low. A production rate of twenty-five words a minute on typing production tests from one to two hours long covering various types of typing activities is exceptional even for the very rapid straight-copy typists.[8] Naturally on a ten-minute production test consisting entirely of short business letters, the students' production rates would come much closer to approaching their straight-copy rates than on longer tests covering more complicated material. Most production tests should be at least thirty minutes in length. Recent classroom studies have shown that much more emphasis needs to be given to production work in the areas of tabulation and mixed types of production problems.

Those teachers who believe that production typing is the final stage in the development of vocational typing skill emphasize that production work does not involve new learnings but rather the building of further typing power in applying the learnings that have been taught previously. For example, the teacher may give the students several letter-production jobs. The students have already been taught the various letter styles, the typing of carbons, envelopes, and so forth. Now the student is expected to coordinate all of these knowledges and skills into a letter-production situation similar to one he might encounter in an office. He is given a number of letters to type in a certain period of time. He is expected to follow all instructions accompanying the letters, to type carbons and envelopes just as he would in an office, and to proofread every letter, being sure it is mailable before he submits it to the teacher.

The students should be given definite goals toward which to work. The teacher may require the completion of a specified number of mailable letters for an "A," "B," or "C" grade. Or he may set up his standards in words a minute. On every production job the students should be timed and should know exactly what standards they are expected to meet. Otherwise much of the value of such production jobs is lost. Students who have been typing sixty words a minute sometimes find they are unable to average more than twenty words a minute on letter-production work. For the first time they begin to realize that speed and accuracy on straight-copy typing is not enough, that they must be able to transfer those skills to production jobs if they are to meet the requirements of an office.

---

[8] Production rate in these studies was computed only on mailable typewritten material. Material containing errors should not be included in figuring production rate.

EXHIBIT 5.9

November 2, 1964   17

Mr. William W. Wiley   37
521 Commerce   49
Philadelphia 10, Pennsylvania   78

Dear Bill: 88

Subject: Motor Freight Lines   117
Order #589-197-78 & #589-295-77   148

You will remember our asking you last December not to have stock   212
merchandise shipped to this customer without first clearing the   275
orders through us. Because of the delay in receiving green refer-   341
ence copies on stock orders, it sometimes is not possible for us   405
to stop shipment. We had asked that you not sell this customer   468
any more without clearing through us because of our past experience   535
with them.   545

As you know, you did not apparently feel that our request was justi-   613
fied, for you sent the foregoing two orders through. Now we have a   680
situation of referring $240.72 to our attorney for collection.   742

It is the policy of the department to cooperate to the best of our   808
ability, and we feel justified in requesting cooperation from the   873
field in matters of this sort. We regret that you did not go along   940
with us.   948

In 1963 it was necessary for us to charge off $645.51 to bad debts,   1015
since the customer made a settlement of only 25 per cent. We also   1081
incurred collection costs of $38.72 plus the necessity of advancing   1148
$35 for court costs. In view of this, we fail to understand why any-   1216
one should think our request to properly clear credit or to have terms 1286
in advance would be unreasonable.   1319

Very truly yours,   1336

Marvin Oakes   1348
Im   Credit Department   1369

EXHIBIT 5.10
Building Production Speed

Warm-up:

a;sldkfjghfjdksla;sldkfjghfjdksla;sldkfjghfjdksla;sldkfjghfjdksla;sldkfjgh
a;qpa;slwosldkeidkfjrufjghtyghfjrufjdkeidkslwosla;qpa;slwosldkeidkfjrufjgh
a;z/a;slx.sldkc,dkfjvmfjghbnghfjvmfjdkc,dkslx.sla;z/a;slx.sldkc,dkfjvmfjgh
a;qpa;z/a;slwoslx.sldkeidkc,dkfjrufjvmfjghtyghbnghfjrufjvmfjdkeidkc,dkslwo

Technique Drill:

Mr. William W. Wiley 521 Commerce Philadelphia 10, Pennsylvania
Mr. William W. Wiley 521 Commerce Philadelphia 10, Pennsylvania
Mr. William W. Wiley 521 Commerce Philadelphia 10, Pennsylvania
Very truly yours, Marvin Oakes Credit Department
Very truly yours, Marvin Oakes Credit Department
Very truly yours, Marvin Oakes Credit Department

Word Drill (Unbalanced-hand words and double-letter words):

December shipped first orders because reference possible apparently feel
request referring attorney collection policy cooperate matters regret
necessary charge settlement incurred necessity credit advance

Phrase Drill:

to have to this through us is not for us that you not of our past with them
now we have if it is the to the best and we feel we regret that you did not
with us since the in view of this we fail to understand in advance would be

Rhythm Drill:

It is the policy of this department to cooperate to the best of our ability.
We regret that you did not go along with us.
In view of this, we fail to understand.

Number Drill:

5 10 15 20 25 30 35 40 45 50 55 60 65 70 75 80 85 90 95 100 105 110 115 120
$123.45 $234.57 $345.78 $456.67 $567.89 $678.90 $987.65 $876.54 $765.43
$38.72 $27.61 $39.67 $45.86 $51.03 $32.54 $38.99 $66.54 $71.18 $36.92 $44.50

Sustained, Even Typing:

1. Type through the body of the letter once, smoothly, at a rate well
   within your control.
2. Practice any words in which you made errors or on which you hesitated.

Power Drive:

Thirty-second drives: Two thirty-second timings on Rhythm Drill Sentence.

One-minute timings for speed and accuracy (depending on individual needs):

One-minute timing on each paragraph.

Individual remedial practice.

Repeat one-minute timings on each paragraph.

Five-Minute Production Timing:

Type straight through four paragraphs in body for five minutes.

Instructional Pointers:

1. Backspace centering of subject line.
2. Subject line underscored.
3. Reference initials typed on same line as writer's title.

Production Drive:

1. Type as many copies of the letter as you have time for.
2. Proofread for mailability; correct all errors.
3. Reset tabs for paragraphs and closing lines each time you repeat letter.
4. Figure typing rate.

Production jobs may be set up on all types of applied typing work —centering problems, tabulation exercises, stencils and master sheets, envelopes, letters with fill-ins, form letters, and so on. The most advanced types of production jobs that may be given to the students are those consisting of many different typing applications with specific directions for each. The production job may extend over an entire week. This type of job measures many skills that the typist should have: ability to follow directions; ability to handle materials efficiently; ability to type various kinds of problems; ability to produce under pressure for several consecutive periods; ability to proofread accurately; and ability to produce an acceptable quantity and quality of work.

Standards in Typewriting

The standards that typing teachers require their students to meet vary widely from school to school and in some cases vary according to the objectives of the students. In the past many teachers have insisted that the standards for junior-high-school typing or personal-use typing should be lower than those required in the first year of the senior-high-school typing program. Recent surveys indicate that these assumptions are fallacious.[9] In a West Coast city tests given over a three-year period to 2,000 students in thirteen junior high schools revealed that at the end of a year of typing instruction, junior-high-school students averaged between forty to forty-two gross words a minute with seven errors on a five-minute test. Senior-high-school students averaged forty-two to forty-four words a minute with five to six errors on the tests administered at the end of each year of the three-year period. These results show that the standards for personal-use typing in junior high school can be almost identical with standards for the first year of typing in the senior high school.

In Los Angeles junior high schools four factors are considered in the evaluation of the typing students: (*a*) basic techniques; (*b*) selected problems; (*c*) timed production tests; (*d*) timed writings on straight-copy material. Basic techniques are checked using a technique sheet. Selected problems are graded only after the student has had some practice in typing similar problems. The timed production tests administered on typing problems provide an evaluation of the students' typing ability in terms of speed, accuracy, and knowledge of correct form. The timed production tests include such problems as the typing of personal and business letters, addressing envelopes, and the typing of tabulations and manuscripts. The timed writings in the first semester are three to five minutes in length while in the second semester only five-minute tests are used. The tests are graded on the basis of gross words a minute, with not more than one error a minute permitted. No separate grade is given for accuracy and students must meet the end-of-semester standards shown in Fig. 5.11 on at least three timings.

Standards for vocational typing courses also vary widely, and studies have shown that office-entrance standards and school-achievment standards frequently are not in agreement. Naturally production-typing standards are more difficult to determine accurately than are straight-copy standards, yet even here there are many problems. Some teachers grade on net words a minute, some on gross words a minute, and others on correct words a minute. Some teachers re-

---

[9] Alan C. Lloyd, "The Changing Pattern of Typewriting Courses," *Business Education Forum* (November 1961), pp. 16-18.

EXHIBIT 5.11

End-of-Semester Standards on Timed Writings
Los Angeles Junior High Schools*

Personal Typing 1 (3-5 minute tests)	Grade	Personal Typing 2 (5-minute tests)
37 or more	A	45 or more
30-36	B	40-44
20-29	C	33-39
15-19	D	25-32

* *Instructional Guide for Typewriting in Junior and Senior High School,* Los Angeles City Schools, Division of Instructional Services, Publication No. SC-553, 1958, p. 12.

quire their students to correct all their errors in timed writings. Some teachers allow only a certain number of errors on timed writings; others increase the number of errors as the student increases the number of words typed. Some teachers use five-minute timed writings while others use ten-minute writings. Some teachers use new-matter copy for all tests, others use practiced material, and still others use a combination of these two types of copy.

Straight Copy Standards. The trend today on straight-copy timed writings is to grade the student on correct or gross words a minute in beginning typing. In the vocational typing course, the grading scale is often based on net words a minute to emphasize the importance of accuracy. Gross or correct words in beginning typing will give a much more accurate picture of the rate at which a student is typing than will net words a minute. Suppose a student types 1,000 strokes in five minutes with ten errors. That student has typed forty gross words a minute with ten errors, thirty correct words a minute, and twenty net words a minute. Looking only at the twenty net words a minute, the teacher might conclude that the student is not typing fast enough when the problem may be that he is typing far too fast. If he would type with greater control, his typing rate computed on the basis of net words a minute would rise rapidly. It can be seen that net words a minute tends to distort the picture of what the beginning typist is capable of doing. Also the penalty for errors is much greater accordingly for the slow typist than for the fast typist. Gross words represents the fastest method of computing typing rates for both students and teachers. Little is gained by using correct words a minute as the rate computed in this manner will ordinarily be about the same as when gross words are used.

Though teachers may not agree upon the standards that should be required in each semester of typing, they do agree that the student should be given goals toward which to work throughout the semester. The grading scale for speed and accuracy shown in Exhibit 5.12 gives the student speed and accuracy goals for each six-week period. Although the student may not reach these exact standards each six weeks, the standards do give him a yardstick by which to measure his progress. Throughout the first two six-week periods no test is longer than three minutes. After that time, the tests are increased to five minutes. A separate grade is given for speed and accuracy. Ten-minute tests are not introduced until the fourth semester at which time the students also begin to compute their rate on net words a minute. Because of these two changes, the standards on new material for the fourth grading period in the second year remain the same as for the third period.

The standards for grading typing students in the Los Angeles senior high schools include the same four elements considered in grading typing students in the junior-high-school typing program —basic techniques, selected problems, timed production tests, and timed writings on straight-copy material. In first-semester typing, the final mark is primarily on the student's performance of basic techniques and on timed writings on straight-copy material. In the second semester of typing, the final grade is based equally on all four factors. In second-year typing the typing of problems and the timed production tests are weighed much more heavily than the other two factors in determining the student's final grade. The scale used for timed writings is shown in Exhibit 5.12. No separate grade is given for accuracy but any timed writing containing more than five errors is not considered for grading purposes. Students must type at least three five-minute timings which meet the minimum speed and accuracy requirements.

In some grading scales, the error allowance increases as the number of words typed a minute increases. It seems only logical to allow a student more errors if he is typing more strokes. However, since research has shown that fast typists are ordinarily the most accurate typists, this increase in error allowance may not be so important as it seems.

EXHIBIT 5.12

Grading Scale for Speed and Accuracy on Timed Writings

FIRST YEAR OF TYPEWRITING   USE GROSS WORDS

Period	Practice Material	Time	Grade	Errors	New Material
1	28	3	A	0-1	25
	23	3	B	2	21
	20	3	C	3	18
2	35	3	A	0-1	33
	30	3	B	2	28
	27	3	C	3	24
3	38	5	A	0-1	35
	34	5	B	2-3	30
	30	5	C	4-5	25
4	42	5	A	0-1	39
	38	5	B	2-3	34
	34	5	C	4-5	29
5	46	5	A	0-1	42
	42	5	B	2-3	37
	37	5	C	4-5	32
6	50	5	A	0-1	45
	45	5	B	2-3	40
	40	5	C	4-5	35

SECOND YEAR OF TYPEWRITING   USE GROSS WORDS

Period	Practice Material	Time	Grade	Errors	New Material
1	50	5	A	0-1	45
	45	5	B	2-3	40
	40	5	C	4-5	35
2	54	7	A	0-1	49
	49	7	B	2-3	44
	44	7	C	4-5	39
3	58	7	A	0-1	53
	53	7	B	2-3	48
	48	7	C	4-5	43

Net Words

4	60	10	A	0-1	53
	55	10	B	2-3	48
	50	10	C	4-5	43
5	63	10	A	0-1	57
	58	10	B	2-3	53
	53	10	C	4-5	48
6	65	10	A	0-1	60
	60	10	B	2-3	55
	55	10	C	4-5	50

EXHIBIT 5.13

**End-of-Semester Standards on Timed Writings
Los Angeles Senior High Schools***

Typewriting 1	*Grade*	*Typewriting 2*
40 or more	A	50 or more
35-39	B	45-49
25-34	C	35-44
20-24	D	30-34
Typewriting 3	*Grade*	*Typewriting 4*
60 or more	A	65 or more
55-59	B	60-64
45-54	C	50-59
40-44	D	45-49

* Publication No. SC-553, *op. cit.*, p. 22.

Production Standards. The following standards are suggested for various types of typing production jobs.

1. Typing letters, with carbons and envelopes	½ to ⅔ the basic typing rate (8-10 average length letters an hour)[10]
2. Addressing envelopes	50 per cent of basic rate or minimum of 2 envelopes a minute (120 to 150 an hour)
3. Typing rough drafts	40 to 60 per cent of basic typing rate

---

[10] This standard is the equivalent of a production rate of twenty-five to thirty-five words a minute based on medium-length letters averaging 150 words.

4. Manuscripts with footnotes	40 to 50 per cent of basic typing rate
5. Manuscripts without footnotes	60 to 75 per cent of basic typing rate
6. Tabulations	25 to 50 per cent of basic typing rate
7. Stencils	4 single-spaced stencils an hour
8. Transcription from voice recording machines	25 words a minute
9. Typing form letters with envelopes (medium length)	10 to 12 an hour

The foregoing standards can serve only as a rough guide to the typing teacher. Obviously there are many variables in each of these typing production jobs that cannot be controlled in setting up standards. Some letters are more difficult to type than others, depending on the vocabulary, form, and length. Rough drafts, manuscripts, and tabulations all may vary in difficulty. Some stencils require as much time for planning the layout as for typing. The speed with which records may be transcribed will depend to some extent upon the dictator and his skill in dictating. However, the fact that the standards may be difficult to determine does not justify failure to attempt to set up such standards. The students need these goals to stimulate their interest and effort in production typing. The manuals accompanying the typing texts frequently offer suggestions regarding the standards that should be required in office-production jobs. In the past undoubtedly there has been too much emphasis on straight-copy standards to the detriment of production typing. The present trend toward increasing the emphasis on production standards is a recognition of the need to decrease the gap between the school and the office by making the classroom standards more realistic.

Teaching Electric Typewriting

With the increasing popularity of the electric typewriter in the business office today, many high schools have either purchased some electric machines or plan to do so in the near future. Some schools with vocational office-training programs have equipped entire rooms with electric machines. Most typing teachers in small high schools, though, report that their electric typewriters are installed in the same room with their manual machines. In this situation the problem is one of teaching the students to transfer from manual machines to electrics and from electrics to manuals so that all students will have an opportunity to operate both types.

At one time teachers hesitated to attempt to instruct students on both manual and electric machines in the same class. Today most teachers agree that the teaching procedures for electrics and manuals are so similar that this situation can be handled without difficulty. The students who learn to type on electric machines must have special instructions in setting their margins, adjusting the impression indicator, turning the motor switch on and off, returning the carriage, and stroking. The stroking technique represents the major difference between the operation of the manual and electric typewriters. Although the students on the electric machines will be using a "tapping" stroke rather than a sharp "staccato" stroke, once the teacher has demonstrated the correct stroking techniques for both manual and electric typewriters, the students may be given the same drills for developing correct stroking regardless of the machine on which they are typing. The class may then be taught as a group and need not be divided into two sections. For the most part, the instructions will be the same for both groups.[11]

The First Lessons on the Electric Typewriter. Because stroking does represent the major difference between manual and electric typewriting, special attention needs to be given to it during the first typing periods. One manufacturer of electric typewriters recommends drills such as the following to teach students to "tap" the keys rapidly from the beginning:

With the motors off, ask the students to tap rapidly the homerow keys in this manner: *f* 1 2 3 4 5 6. The students tap *f* six times. Then *j, d, k, s, l, a,* and *;* are practiced the same way.

With motors on the students type this drill:

fffffffjjjjjjddddddkkkkkkffffffjjjjjj

---

[11] Schools equipped with the new *Selectrics* will not need drills on the carriage return since only the "element" moves across the page. The "element" which makes the key impressions on the paper does not allow raised capitals, jammed keys, or overlap of typed letters even though the student may not be typing rhythmically.

To teach the correct stroking of the space bar, have the students repeat the foregoing exercise, spacing between each group of
letters:

fffff jjjjjj dddddd kkkkkk

To teach the students new letter locations, use a similar type of
drill. With the motors off, have the students feel the reach to *r*,
watching as they make the reach. After the students have practiced tapping the keys with the motors off, they practice the
same drill with the motors on. This insures rapid stroking of new
locations from the beginning:

frrrrf frrrrf juuuuuj juuuuuj

Next write short words on the board. Dictate the word and type with
the class. Then combine these short words into easy phrases. At
first dictate slowly, gradually speeding up the dictation:

if it is in, to do so, he fed the hen, it is her red hen, it is too hot,
it is not too soon

Time the students on these short phrases, starting with thirty-second
timings and gradually decreasing to ten seconds. The students'
objective is to type the phrase as many times during the ten-
second timings as they typed originally on the thirty-second
writings.

Changing Electric Operators to Manual Typewriters. Students
who have learned to type on electric machines have little difficulty
transferring to manual typewriters. Here again, special attention
must be given to the difference in stroking on the two types of machines. The students should be told frequently to "strike the keys,"
with the teacher demonstrating the correct technique. Special attention will need to be given also to the carriage return and to the shift
key. At first the students will forget that they must now throw the
carriage manually. Also some of the students may have "raised" capitals, since they are accustomed to touching the shift key lightly rather
than depressing and holding the shift key. Drills on stroking technique, carriage return, and the shift key will enable the electric operators to acquire skill on the manual machines quickly and easily.

Changing Manual Operators to Electric Typewriters. The problem
in transferring students from manual machines to electric is, of

course, the exact opposite of transferring electric operators to manuals. In this case, since the students are used to striking the keys they will tend to continue to do so when they first transfer to electric typewriters. Therefore it is important that the early drills be focused on "tapping" the keys. The same drills that were used for students who first learned to type on electric machines will work equally well here.

Students frequently think that, because they are transferring from manual typewriters to electrics, they should immediately be able to type much faster than they were typing previously. Developing high speed should not be their major consideration when they first transfer to the electric typewriter. Correct techniques should come first. Usually the first two or three periods on the electric machines the students will be inaccurate in their typing. Some of them will tend to let their fingers rest too heavily on the keys, thereby activating those keys. The teacher should emphasize primarily correct techniques. This will enable the students to type rapidly and accurately on the electric machines much sooner than they will if their initial emphasis is on speed. Most teachers tell their students to type at somewhat less than their normal rate when they first transfer to the electric typewriter. Students who follow these instructions have greater control of the machine and will have more confidence in their ability to transfer without difficulty. The teacher should give the students a period of time to adjust to the electric typewriter before grading the problems they type on the electric machines.

Projects and Questions for Discussion

1. Examine the typewriting room at your school. Make a list of the items pertaining to physical facilities which you believe could be improved.

2. Go to the library and look at some books written in the field of behavioristic psychology. Make a summary of any principles found in these books which have an application to the psychology of developing a skill. Indicate any which would have value in the teaching of typewriting.

3. Examine several typewriting textbooks available for use in the secondary school. What differences do you find between these and your college typewriting book? What differences are there among the secondary textbooks?

4. Prepare a list of the advantages and disadvantages of the various keyboard-presentation methods. Which do you prefer and why?

5. There are differences of opinion on when to introduce the skill of erasing in typewriting. Compare these different points of view from your reading articles on the subject in the various business education periodicals.

6. Look at the research bibliographies in your library and see what is listed in the field of teaching typewriting. Obtain one of the studies listed through an interlibrary loan and make a report on what is reported in the study.

7. Miss Hill said to her advanced typing class: "If I were a businessman and had to choose between a fast, inaccurate typist and a slow, accurate typist, I would hire the slower typist." Do you agree or disagree with Miss Hill? Why?

8. Many persons agree that all students are not able to master the keyboard in the same length of time. How would you handle this problem in your beginning typing classes?

9. Miss Jones, a new typing teacher in your school, admits that she is a poor typist but says she does not need to be an expert to teach the subject. What do you think about Miss Jones's statement?

10. Miss Williams gives her typing classes a five-minute timed writing once each class period. Miss Johnson gives timed writings once each two weeks. If you were teaching beginning typing, how often would you give five-minute timed writings?

11. A teacher has said, "I do not believe it necessary for students to learn the numbers and symbols on the typewriter keyboard by touch. Let them look where the numbers and symbols are—they will anyway." What do you think?

12. Mr. Andrews complains that his typing students are too tense when they take timed writings and consequently make far too many errors. He says he keeps telling them to relax, but it doesn't seem to do any good. What suggestions could you make to Mr. Andrews which might help him with this problem?

13. You want a demonstration stand and typewriter in your classroom. Your principal says the room is already crowded and that he does not believe the typewriter would be used enough to justify the expense involved. How would you answer his objections?

14. Miss Wilson is always behind in her paper grading. She says she believes in grading every paper her typing students hand in to her. Would you follow this procedure?

15. Mrs. Larson says she prefers to teach typing to any other subject —that it requires no advance preparation. "After all," she tells you, "all you have to do is have the students type a lesson each day." How would you feel about this statement?

16. What kinds of motivation devices would you consider to be the best ones to use in teaching typewriting?

17. Mr. Jackson, who is in charge of the typewriting program in your school, has issued a memorandum that no teacher is to display any charts giving the names of their typing students and a record of their timed writings. Some of the teachers do not understand why Mr. Jackson objects to this practice. Why do you think he disapproves of such charts?

18. What would you do if your typing students consistently overlooked errors in their timed writings and in their typing problems?

19. Some of your advanced typing students are fast typists but very inaccurate. Others are very slow but seldom make errors. How would you provide for these differences in your daily classroom teaching?

20. Several of the football boys enrolled in your beginning typing class because they thought it would be a "snap" course. At the end of the first twelve weeks, they are still looking at their hands as they type. When you try to correct them, they say they are only taking typing for personal use so what difference does it make. You have tried numerous corrective drills, but they continue to watch their hands. Can you break them of this practice and if so, how?

21. Miss Davis said to her typing class the first day, "Practice makes perfect. Therefore I shall expect each of you to practice at least one hour each day in addition to the time spent in class." Is Miss Davis' statement correct?

22. A typing teacher in your school does not permit her beginning typing students to practice outside of class for the first three weeks. Do you think this is a sound rule? Why?

Case Problems

1. Henry is enrolled in your beginning typing class. You discover the first day that he has been typing on his father's typewriter, using the "hunt-and-peck system," ever since he was in the fourth grade. Now he is having considerable difficulty. He does try to use the touch system, but frequently he forgets and slips back to his hunt-and-peck method. Further, he is discouraged with his progress. When he uses the touch system, he makes a great many errors and is slow. Consequently on timed writings, he frequently reverts to looking at the keys. Whenever he does this, his typing rate and accuracy is much better than it is with the touch method. He has about decided to drop typing. His counselor feels, however, since he is interested in journalism, he will need this skill. Is there any way in which you could help Henry? Would you advise him to drop the course?

2. Mary Jo is a senior in advanced typing. In first-year typing, she usually made excellent grades. She was a rapid typist and always scored high on straight-copy tests. However, in advanced typing Mary Jo is having trouble. She types very well as long as the teacher is conducting short drills or timed writings. But whenever the emphasis is placed on production work and the students are required to produce for an extended period without interruptions, Mary Jo "blows up." She seems to be incapable of sticking to a job for more than ten minutes at a time. Consequently, all of her production grades so far have been unsatisfactory. What can be done to help Mary Jo do better on production typing jobs?

3. This is your first year of teaching at Northwest High School. You find that most of the students in your advanced typing class are very fast typists but highly inaccurate. Upon checking, you find that the beginning typing teacher told the students to type as fast as they could. They were not to worry about their errors—they would take care of themselves.

Although you do not say so, you do not agree with this philosophy since it is quite obvious the errors have not taken care of themselves. You know your students will not be able to do satisfactory work in production typing until they reduce their errors. What steps would you take to try to improve the accuracy of the class? How would you incorporate special drill work in the advanced typing class?

4. Your school system offers a one-semester typing course in the seventh grade of junior high school. No further typing instruction is offered until the tenth grade, where a one-year typing course is offered for students enrolled in either the vocational or academic curriculums. Many of the students who enroll in this course have had the one-semester junior-high-school typing course. You find that they do not have enough skill to permit them to enroll in second-semester typing. However, they are bored in first-semester typing since they already know the keyboard and have some typing skill. The placement of these students has been a problem ever since the junior-high-school course was first introduced. What recommendations would you make to the principal regarding the placement of these students?

5. James Brown is enrolled in your beginning typing course. He is an attractive, popular football player. He has considerable difficulty maintaining passing grades, but he is conscientious about his work, prepares all of his assignments, and studies hard. Although he practices faithfully, he is making little progress. His hands are extremely large, and often he makes many errors because his fingers are not on the correct homerow keys. After many hours of extra practice he has developed a good typing

stroke, but he cannot seem to type more than fifteen words a minute with any degree of accuracy.

Your standard for passing at the end of this six weeks is twenty-five words a minute. The coach tells you if John fails typing this six weeks, he will not be able to play football for the rest of the season. John has come into the typing lab an extra period every day for the past month, but he has shown little improvement. At the end of the six weeks, he is still typing only fifteen words a minute. What would you do in this situation?

6. A local businessman has just talked to your typing classes and has told them that he will not employ any typist in his firm who is not able to type with 100 per cent accuracy. After listening to his talk, you decide your standards have not been high enough. Therefore, you tell the students that in the future they are not to turn in any work which is not perfect. In your advanced typing classes, this procedure is working satisfactorily since the students are permitted to erase and correct their errors. However, in your beginning typing classes the students are not yet permitted to erase. At the end of the second six weeks, you find that a number of the first-semester students have not turned in any work at all, and you give them a failing grade.

The day after the students received their report cards, one of the parents comes to the school to discuss the failing grade which her daughter Jane received in typing. She asks to see some of Jane's typing papers. When you tell her that Jane did not turn in any work all six weeks, she says she cannot understand how you can fail a student if you have never seen any of her work the entire six weeks. You explain your ruling about perfect work and that Jane has never been able to complete any exercise perfectly. Jane's mother says that this is a ridiculous procedure, that you as a teacher cannot possibly know how to help Jane if you do not collect any of her papers.

After the woman leaves, you begin to wonder whether she may be right. Have you used good judgment in requiring that all work turned in by your students be perfect? Why do you suppose your procedures have worked satisfactorily in your advanced classes but not in the beginning classes?

7. Bill is a senior enrolled in second-year typing. He has the ability to do good typing work but lacks initiative and ambition. At the beginning of the semester, you informed the students that in advanced typing all typing problems assigned had to be completed and that any assignments which they were unable to complete during the class period might be completed outside of class.

Bill is dating a girl who is the best typist in the class. Every Monday

Bill brings you all the typing problems assigned the preceding week, completed without error in proper form. You strongly suspect that Bill's girl friend, Marianne, is typing all of his problems for him, but you have no way to prove it. You hesitate to discuss the matter with Bill and Marianne since you have no proof whatever that this is the case.

Bill is meeting your requirements as you set them up at the beginning of the course. You feel, however, that something should be done since you have told the students the classwork would constitute two-thirds of their final grade. You are afraid that if Bill is permitted to "get by" with this practice, the word may get around and other students will try the same thing. What errors have you as a teacher made up to this point? What would you do if you were faced with this problem?

8. Bob Green has been a problem ever since the first day he reported to the first-year typing class. The teachers generally agree that he is a troublemaker in his other classes also. He resents discipline in any form, yet he is always talking, bothering other students, or trying to take his typewriter apart. He shows no interest in learning to type. The class meets at 2:30 in the afternoon, and each day during the first twenty minutes of the period Bob does his best to upset the class routine. Then after repeated warnings, he settles down and you discover a few minutes later that he is asleep. You much prefer to have him sleeping than annoying the class, but you feel since he is in a typing class he should be practicing. You have discussed the matter with Bob, but his behavior has not changed.

Finally you go to the principal and suggest that Bob be transferred to another class in which he might be more interested. The principal tells you that Bob is not interested in school and that he thinks he will gain more from a typing course than any other course he might take. You express considerable doubt and finally point out that he certainly is not developing much skill while he is sleeping and that in spite of numerous warnings from you, he falls asleep nearly every day. The principal asks you if you know that Bob gets up every morning at 4:00 A.M. to handle a paper route, that the money he earns on his paper route goes to help support his sick mother and younger sister. You of course did not know this. When you ask the principal what you should do about Bob, he tells you to use your own judgment and do the best you can. What would you do if Bob were in your class?

9. Mary is capable and attractive with good potentialities. She has one problem—she is extremely nervous. When she knows no one is watching her and she is under no pressure, her work is excellent. But on tests she becomes so upset that her work is somewhat below average in quality although you know she is capable of much better performance. You are

concerned about Mary's future. Since she cannot stand to be rushed or pushed in any manner, you wonder how she will be able to work in a business office. Should you advise her to go into other work or hope that Mary will outgrow her nervousness and develop into a good typist?

10. Your advanced typing class is extremely careless about proofreading, both on their timed writings and their production work. Although you have talked with them over and over about this matter, they still continue to turn in work containing numerous errors. Finally you tell them that they will receive a failing grade on any production work which contains uncorrected errors. Furthermore, you will only check the work until you find an error. If there are other errors, they will not be marked since the work is unacceptable anyway, and it will be their responsibility to check for additional errors. Any work containing errors must be re-typed until it is acceptable.

Some of your students feel that you are being unreasonable. They say that they do not have time to retype their production work. It is true that in some instances students have had to retype a letter five or six times because their work contained several errors which they themselves did not find. Many of the students are getting behind in their class work. You still believe that making the students responsible for finding their own errors in their production work is a good practice. However, it is obvious that many of them are going to be unable to keep up with their assignments. What changes, if any, would you now make in your procedures?

Suggested Readings

Anderson, Ruth I., *et al.*, "Some Typing Authorities Speak," *Business Education Bulletin No. 2.* Englewood Cliffs, N.J.: Prentice-Hall, Inc., 1960.

————, "Motivating the Superior Typing Student," *Business Teaching Aid No. T-11.* Englewood Cliffs, N.J.: Prentice-Hall, Inc., 1962.

Blackstone, E. G., and Sofrona Smith, *Improvement of Instruction in Typewriting.* Englewood Cliffs, N.J.: Prentice-Hall, Inc., 1949.

Blevin, Jr., Bruce, *The Wonderful Writing Machine.* New York: Random House, Inc., 1954.

Business Education Forum, National Business Education Association, November Issues (Typewriting Series), 1947-1964.

Clem, Jane E., *Techniques of Teaching Typewriting.* New York: Gregg Publishing Division, McGraw-Hill Book Company, 1955.

Crawford, James B., *Production Typewriting,* Monograph 97. Cincinnati, Ohio: South-Western Publishing Co., 1960.

Fuller, Donald C., *Reading Factors in Typewriting*. Doctoral dissertation Pennsylvania State College, published by Oklahoma A. and M., 1945.

Lamb, Marion M., *Your First Year of Teaching Typewriting*. Cincinnati, Ohio: South-Western Publishing Co., 1947.

Lessenberry, D. D., *Methods of Teaching Typewriting*. Cincinnati, Ohio: South-Western Publishing Co., 1949.

Odell, William and Esta Ross Stuart, *Principles and Techniques for Directing the Learning of Typewriting*. Boston: D. C. Heath & Company, 1945.

"Psychology Applied to Skill Building," *Business Education World*, Business Education World Service Booklet 23, 1943.

Rowe, John L., "How to Meet Changing Needs in Typewriting," *Business Education World*, September to November, 1963.

Russon, Allien R. and S. J. Wanous, *Philosophy and Psychology of Teaching Typewriting*. Cincinnati, Ohio: South-Western Publishing Co., 1960.

Stolurow, Lawrence M., "The Psychology of Skills—Parts I and II," *Delta Pi Epsilon Journal*, II (April 1959 and June 1959).

Stuart, Esta Ross and Leonard Porter, "Some Fallacies in Teaching Typewriting," *Business Teaching Aid No. T-5*. Englewood Cliffs, N.J.: Prentice-Hall, Inc., 1960.

Tonne, Herbert A., Estelle L. Popham, and M. Herbert Freeman, *Methods of Teaching Business Subjects*, Chaps. 4-6. New York: Gregg Publishing Division, McGraw-Hill Book Company, 1957.

West, Leonard, *What Research Says to the Teacher of Typewriting*, Delta Pi Epsilon Research Bulletin No. 2, 1962.

————, "Some Relationships Between Straight Copy Typing Skill and Performance on Job-type Activities," *Delta Pi Epsilon Journal*, IV (November 1960).

6

Teaching Shorthand and Transcription

Shorthand

The history of shorthand, from the introduction of Tiro's crude system in 63 B.C. to the refined shorthand systems of the twentieth century, is an interesting story which includes the development of hundreds of shorthand systems and covers a period of over two thousand years. It has been estimated that more than fifteen hundred shorthand systems have been invented for use in the English language alone. In the United States today, however, most public schools teach *Gregg* shorthand. *Pitman* is taught in some Eastern cities, including Philadelphia and New York.

In addition to the symbol systems of shorthand, there are several systems based on the longhand alphabet which are especially popular in the business schools in this country. Advocates contend that with an alphabet system it is possible to build sufficient skill for most office jobs in much less time than is ordinarily required to master a symbol shorthand system. One of the best-known alphabet systems is *Speedwriting*. Other alphabet systems are the *ABC* system, *Briefhand,* and *Forkner*. Machine shorthand is also used in some

187

parts of the country. In this case the stenographer operates a machine which records the dictation on a paper tape. The machine is noiseless and easily portable. Since print rather than shorthand symbols is used to record the dictation, persons using this system point out that anyone can transcribe the notes readily. The machine used for this purpose is called the *Stenograph*.

Regardless of the shorthand system that the business teacher-trainee may have learned, the principles for effective teaching of either alphabet or symbol shorthand remain the same.

Objective of Teaching Shorthand

Much has been written about the objectives of teaching shorthand, but today most business educators agree that the primary objective in the teaching of shorthand is that of vocational use. It is now generally recognized that attempts to justify the teaching of shorthand solely for personal use or for its contribution to general education are questionable. Research has shown that those persons who use shorthand personally are the persons who have developed the highest degree of skill in the shorthand classroom—usually about 100 words a minute or more. Persons who are able to take dictation at only sixty to eighty words a minute lack confidence in their ability to read their shorthand notes and consequently are hesitant to use it. They may write shorthand during the shorthand class, but they seldom attempt to take notes in shorthand in other classes.

The recent trend favoring the academic curriculum in the high school has once again caused renewed interest in the possibility of developing either a symbol or alphabet shorthand system which will be practical for personal-use purposes. Many of the alphabet systems now being promoted claim that students learning these systems can develop not only personal-use skill but vocational skill in much less time than is possible with a symbol system. No doubt there are occasionally a few students who do enroll in shorthand for some personal reasons such as helping them take notes in college, but these are unusual cases. With today's crowded high-school curriculum and the increase in number of units in academic subjects required for graduation, most students cannot afford to devote the time necessary to develop skill in shorthand for personal use.

If the beginning teacher realizes that he is teaching a vocational course and must therefore meet the vocational standards of the business office, he will plan his course of study and set up his teaching methods strictly on the basis of this objective.

The Shorthand Teacher

The beginning teacher must possess three very important qualities to be successful in teaching shorthand. First, he should be highly skilled in shorthand. He should not only thoroughly understand the shorthand system that he plans to teach, but he should also be highly skilled in reading and writing that system. It is not enough for the shorthand teacher to tell the students how to write shorthand or even to write isolated outlines on the board. He should be able to demonstrate to his students the art of taking dictation. The teacher who is able to meet the same standards that he expects his students to meet will find his students will both respect and admire him. Moreover, the teacher who has acquired a high degree of shorthand skill—and who makes the effort necessary to keep that skill razor-sharp—will find that he better understands the problems his students encounter in trying to develop a high degree of skill in reading and writing shorthand.

Second, the shorthand teacher needs to know how to teach shorthand. Being skilled in shorthand does not guarantee the ability to teach the subject effectively. The teacher must know what procedures should be followed in presenting shorthand theory, in building reading and writing skill, and in developing correct transcription techniques. Authorities now agree that some procedures are far more effective than others in building shorthand and transcription skill. The shorthand teacher should be familiar with these procedures and know how to use them in his shorthand classes.

Third, the shorthand teacher must have the drive and enthusiasm necessary to motivate his students to their best efforts at all times. A skills teacher soon learns that his classes are quick to respond to his own mental and physical condition. If he enters the classroom tired and despondent, the class senses this atmosphere and the students become sluggish in their reactions that period. If the teacher enters the classroom promptly, full of enthusiasm and energy, the class tends to respond in an alert, vigorous manner. It is, of course, possible for a shorthand teacher to possess so much drive that he pushes his students until they become tense. This seldom happens, however. Many teachers might find their shorthand students would be able to accomplish far more each day if they themselves possessed more drive and vigor in the presentation of the subject.

The Shorthand Student

In many school situations, the shorthand teacher has little say about which students shall be admitted to his shorthand class. Since shorthand is a vocational subject, the customary practice of admitting all students who show an interest in learning shorthand immediately creates problems. Some students possess neither the mental ability nor the English background to be successful in shorthand and transcription. Others lack the necessary interest and will not prepare their homework assignments with any regularity. Such persons are usually unsuccessful in shorthand.

The student who enrolls in shorthand should have the qualifications necessary for success in the subject, namely:

1. At least average mental ability
2. A sound English background
3. Skill in typing
4. A keen interest in learning shorthand
5. The personal qualities needed for office work

Most schools have test records showing the students' mental ability. Some schools also have scores on standardized English tests which show the areas of English in which the students have deficiencies—spelling, vocabulary, reading comprehension, grammar, and so forth. In other schools students are required to have at least a "C" average in their English courses before they may enroll in shorthand. Many schools require a "B" average in English before a student may enroll in transcription.

In school situations where only one year of shorthand is offered, it is essential that the shorthand students have some typing skill before enrolling in shorthand. Machine transcription will have to be introduced sometime during the second semester, and the students will make more rapid progress in transcription if they are able to type at least forty to fifty words a minute accurately on straight-copy material. If shorthand is taught the twelfth year, then the students should enroll in typing the eleventh year. Where two years of shorthand are offered, enrolling in typing and shorthand concurrently is not so serious a problem. However, even in this situation most teachers encourage the students to enroll in typing in their tenth and eleventh years and in shorthand in the eleventh and twelfth years.

The last two qualities necessary for shorthand success are much more intangible than the first three and sometimes cannot be determined until after the student enrolls in the course. In some instances teachers have been successful in arousing the interest of students who were enrolled in shorthand, not because of their own personal choice, but because of outside pressures. In many cases, lack of interest results in poor daily preparation which eventually leads to failure.

Although it is no more the responsibility of the shorthand teacher to attempt to develop the personal qualities that students will need for success in the business office than it is that of any other teacher, it is highly important that attention be given to these essential qualities. Building a high skill in taking dictation and in transcribing shorthand notes is of limited value if the student is unable to secure a job or is unable to keep a job for any length of time because of undesirable personal qualities.

Since in most school situations no provision is made for the selection of those students who enroll in shorthand, the shorthand teacher is immediately faced with this problem: How can he maintain vocational standards with an unselected group, and what is his responsibility for those who are unsuccessful? The problem should be discussed frankly with the administration before a decision is reached. Also the teacher should realize that he must assume considerable responsibility in the way of guidance and counselling with those students who obviously are unfitted for office work.

The Shorthand System

The particular system of shorthand being taught has little effect upon the teaching methods which will be used in the classroom. The principles of skill building are the same whether the student is learning an alphabet or a symbol system. Many shorthand teachers have been unnecessarily disturbed by the recent changes which have been made in Gregg shorthand. They sometimes seem to believe that they will be unable to adapt to new outlines and that they will no longer be effective shorthand teachers. Any person who has learned a shorthand system can certainly relearn a few of the shorthand outlines. As long as the basic alphabet remains the same, the shorthand teacher has nothing to fear. True, he may occasionally write an Anniversary or Simplified outline on the board, but this should not cause him any embarrassment. The students will be impressed because the teacher does know more than one outline for the word involved.

The teacher's primary concern should be to determine whether the revisions of the shorthand system being taught do enable the students to master the system more readily and do develop vocational-level skill in a shorter period of time. The teacher should seek to find the answer to the following questions: Does the decrease in memory load resulting from the reduction in the number of brief forms and an increase in the number of outlines written in full enable students to master the system more quickly? Are students able to write more rapidly and with fewer hesitations due to the reduction in memory load? Are the students developing higher skills in less time than was required formerly? Do longer outlines enable students to transcribe their notes more rapidly and with greater accuracy?

For years it has been assumed that students write shorthand by sound. True, shorthand is supposed to be written according to sound. However, some persons are beginning to question whether many students do write by sound. They believe students often try to write shorthand outlines from memory. If this is the case, the longer shorthand outlines may cause greater hesitation than that which resulted from the learning of long lists of brief forms and abbreviated words. The student who writes outlines from memory may have more difficulty reconstructing long outlines than he would have in memorizing the short forms. It is entirely possible that most students write partially by sound and partially by memory. Much more research is needed before many of these questions can be answered accurately.

The Shorthand Course—One Year or Two?

In the past ten years there has been an increasing emphasis on the importance of general education in the high-school curriculum. There is a definite trend to increase the requirements in English, history, science, and mathematics, thereby decreasing the number of elective hours available for vocational training. As a result, many schools are now offering shorthand for one year instead of two. Elaborate claims have been made by teachers and publishers alike that it is possible to develop shorthand and transcription skill in one year in the high school. Few authorities will question that it may be possible, but many will question whether it is now being done.

Surveys measuring the dictation and transcription ability of students who have completed only one year of shorthand have shown that the majority of these students were unable to produce a single mailable letter dictated at sixty words a minute. Analysis of the test papers revealed that the major weakness was due to insufficient time for teaching transcription.

Since many high schools are including only one year of shorthand in the curriculum, the high-school teacher must try to find a solution to this problem of developing a vocational skill in such a short period of time. The teacher in a school offering two years of shorthand has no problem, but the teacher in the school offering only one year obviously must work out some arrangement whereby her students may have additional time for building transcription skill. With an unselected group of students one year is usually insufficient. If the school offers two years of typewriting, the teacher should work out a plan for providing transcription practice in second-year typing for those students enrolled in shorthand. This procedure is the answer in many schools. In other schools offering a course in secretarial practice or office practice, a part of this course may be devoted to transcription. Regardless of the procedure finally selected, the shorthand teacher should make every effort to see that her students do receive enough practice in shorthand dictation and transcription to enable them to meet the requirements of the business office.

There is little doubt that many rural and small high schools are offering shorthand even though there is small need for it in the community and the time provided for such training is inadequate for students to attain vocational competency. Business teachers and administrators need to consider thoughtfully the place which shorthand should have in the high-school curriculum.

The foregoing statements are not meant to imply that shorthand is not needed today. A few persons have claimed that it will not be necessary to teach shorthand in the near future since dictating machines will take the place of this skill. Nothing could be further from the truth. Granted businesses are using dictating machines much more extensively than they did formerly. In certain areas of work they make possible sizeable cost reductions. Some businessmen find the machines convenient for recording dictation in the evening or on weekends. However, many men prefer to employ secretaries and stenographers who can take shorthand manually as well as transcribe from voice-recording equipment. The want ads in the daily newspapers provide testimony to the serious shortage of persons skilled in the art of taking and transcribing shorthand. The Department of Labor has predicted that this shortage will continue into the 1970's. The person who is proficient in recording and transcribing shorthand is very much in demand. Most people today believe that even if dictation machines should show a tremendous gain in popularity in the future, there will always be a place in the business world for the person who knows shorthand.

Shorthand Methods—Manual or Functional?

Many methods of teaching shorthand have been advocated in the past. Because today almost all teachers use either the functional or the manual (traditional) method or a combination of these two methods, only the manual and functional methods will be described here.

Manual (Traditional) Method. According to the handbook that accompanies the Gregg Shorthand Manual, the manual method of teaching shorthand is characterized by the following features:

1. Use of rules—the rules may be taught in one of two ways. They may be presented first and then followed with words illustrating their application. Or if the teacher prefers, words illustrating the rule may be presented first so that the students may draw their own generalizations about the rules involved in writing these words.

2. Use of word lists—the manual method makes extensive use of word lists throughout the text.

3. Early introduction to writing—many teachers using the manual approach introduce writing the first day of the shorthand course. Other teachers defer writing two or three days.

4. Penmanship drills—much attention is given to penmanship with special drills emphasizing proportion of strokes, size of vowels, and slant and placement of the line of writing.

5. Vocabulary tests—manual teachers emphasize the importance of accurate outlines through frequent testing on shorthand vocabulary.

6. Use of formal reviews—teachers using the manual method provide for formal reviews on shorthand theory at regular intervals.

7. Use of an intensive reading and writing approach—students are instructed to read and write each letter in the text several times but are not required to read as extensively as are students taught by the functional method.

8. Many types of activity from the beginning of the course—from

the first days of the shorthand course students perform many different activities including reading shorthand, copying shorthand plates in the text, recording practiced material from dictation, recording new-matter dictation, and transcribing plate material into longhand.

Teachers using the manual method claim that it is a logical, orderly approach in teaching and learning shorthand and that there is an intelligent emphasis on understanding the "why" in shorthand as well as on "knowing how."

Those opposed to the manual method point out that teaching rules in shorthand frequently results in a hesitant style of writing since students may stop in the middle of an outline in an effort to recall a particular rule applying to the word. They also claim that the manual method focuses attention on the strokes making up each outline rather than on the meaning of the entire sentence, which may result in slow reading habits with little comprehension of what is read.

Functional Method. The functional method of teaching shorthand was introduced by Louis A. Leslie in 1934. The basic features of this method are:

1. The reading approach—approximately the first four weeks of the shorthand course are devoted to reading shorthand with writing being deferred until the students are able to read shorthand plates with considerable fluency.

2. No rules taught—rules as such are never taught in the functional method. Students are discouraged from asking questions regarding shorthand theory since it is felt that the extensive reading and copying of accurate shorthand plates will answer most of their questions more effectively than will class discussion.

3. Use of the key—in functional shorthand texts, a printed key to the plate material is included in the back of the text. The key is provided to assist students in their studying and to enable them to read more extensively and with greater fluency than would be possible otherwise.

4. No word lists—in theory the functional method never makes use of word lists. In actual practice, however, lists of words will be found in functional-method texts though little emphasis is placed on their use.

5. No formal penmanship practice—functional teachers say that penmanship practice is unnecessary since the students are reading and copying correct shorthand-plate material from the text each day.

6. No repetition practice—students are instructed to read and

copy the shorthand plates in the text only once. Consequently, review is automatically provided in each lesson of the shorthand text, making formal review unnecessary.

8. No papers to correct except for occasional tests—functional-method teachers explain that for the most part correcting papers is unnecessary for at least two reasons. First, the students read and copy correct shorthand outlines extensively and should therefore be able to reproduce correct shorthand outlines. Second, as long as the shorthand student writes outlines that he can transcribe correctly, there is no reason to insist that the outline be exactly like the outline in the text. In other words, functional-method teachers believe that any shorthand outline that can be transcribed correctly is a correct shorthand outline.

9. No tests except for administrative purposes—teachers who follow the functional method closely state there is no reason to give shorthand tests at any time except when it is necessary to report grades to the administration.

10. A simplified early-learning situation—in the functional approach, for the first few weeks the students' attention is directed solely to reading. Then writing is introduced, and still later the dictation of new material and the transcription of shorthand notes are added to the learning situation. Advocates of the functional method point out that the introduction of only one learning activity at a time greatly simplifies the beginner's problem of mastering shorthand.

Teachers favoring the functional method emphasize the simplicity of the learning approach with only one element being introduced at a time—first, reading shorthand plates; second, copying shorthand plates; third, taking dictation of new material without a preview. They also claim that it is easier to hold the students' interest in shorthand when a new learning element is added from time to time and that this procedure serves to protect the students from the strain resulting when too many different learning activities are introduced simultaneously. Functional teachers contend that the reading approach eliminates the initial diffuse movements that result when writing is introduced too early, that students have greater confidence and have less tendency to draw their outlines. Functional teachers believe that the reading approach makes it possible to develop unusually high reading rates from the beginning of the shorthand course. Finally, teachers using the functional method say that the early emphasis on the meaning of what is read and written provides excellent basic transcription training.

Teachers who prefer the manual method point out that students using functional texts may become dependent on the key and be unable to read the shorthand plates without it. They believe that, when the first four weeks of the course are devoted solely to the reading of shorthand plates, the students soon lose interest since they are primarily concerned with learning to write shorthand. They believe that the long initial reading period makes it difficult to bridge the gap between reading and writing. Finally, manual-method teachers state that students who are not taught any of the rules or the "why" of shorthand seem to be unable to write shorthand outlines that they have not previously encountered, that they are entirely dependent upon visual images of the correct outlines which they have read and copied from the text.

Differences and Similarities Between the Manual and Functional Methods. Though much has been written about the differences between the manual and functional methods of teaching shorthand, probably today there are more points of similarity than of difference between the two methods. Both methods emphasize the importance of blackboard demonstrations, suggest that at least for the first few days the reading approach be used, recommend extensive reading of shorthand plates and quick prompting of the students when reading plates, the timing of dictation soon after it is introduced, and the previewing of all material except tests. Both methods stress the importance of developing speed and fluency in reading and copying shorthand, emphasize the importance of using contextual material for reading and writing practice and the repetitive use of this material for dictation practice. Both methods suggest that the application of shorthand rules is of greater importance than the mastery of these rules, that automatization of shorthand outlines is essential, and that little time should be devoted to testing.

Interestingly enough, research studies have consistently shown that today there are few shorthand teachers who follow all the suggestions given in the teacher's handbook accompanying the shorthand text they are using. Teachers who say they are following the manual method are using many of the functional-method techniques. Likewise teachers who say they are using the functional method are still employing some of the manual-method techniques. It is recommended that beginning shorthand teachers follow closely the suggestions in the handbook accompanying their shorthand text. With experience they should be able to determine those procedures which prove most effective in their classes and those procedures which they feel need some slight modification to enable them to achieve the best results with their students.

Classroom Procedures

Authorities are in general agreement that any time in the classroom not devoted to reading and writing shorthand is wasted. This is literally correct. The only way to build shorthand skill is through reading and writing shorthand. The inexperienced teacher might think that reading and writing shorthand for forty to sixty minutes five days a week would soon become monotonous and that he would lose the interest of his students. Building shorthand skill is like building any other skill—there must be correct repetitive practice, but it need not result in following a dull routine. For example, consider some of the ways in which it is possible to vary the procedures used in beginning the shorthand class each day.

1. Start with a blackboard review of yesterday's theory.
2. Start with the blackboard presentation of the theory to be assigned for the next day.
3. Have a short blackboard drill on derivatives, words, brief forms, or phrases.
4. Dictate for a warm-up a letter students have practiced the previous day.
5. Start with a warm-up on a phrase letter.
6. Start with a warm-up on a brief form letter.
7. Have the students read from the plates in the text included in the day's assignment.
8. To emphasize the importance of penmanship, have the students read the shorthand notes they have written for homework practice.
9. Use a letter for penmanship practice containing similarly written words, dictated at a rate well within the writing ability of the class.
10. Dictate a letter that is "loaded" with some principle of shorthand theory on which the class needs special practice.
11. Use one-minute progressive speed drills on previously practiced material. Repeat the same letter three or four times at increasingly rapid rates.

12. Use some untimed dictation about current events, announcements, assignments, and the like to get attention quickly at the beginning of the hour.
13. Have the students start taking dictation from a shorthand record or tape as soon as they enter the classroom.
14. Have a line of shorthand on the board which the students are to practice writing until class begins.
15. Occasionally to get the class off to a rapid start, give a brief warm-up and then dictate some material to be transcribed.
16. Occasionally give a short test at the beginning of the period to motivate the students to arrive promptly (reading transcription from current assignment, brief form test).

Shorthand teachers also need to realize that not only should the procedures used to begin the class be varied but the activity within the class period should be changed frequently. Beginning shorthand students soon tire of reading plate material. They will also become fatigued quickly if all the dictation practice is given at one time during the period. The teacher should plan her daily lesson in such a way that no one activity is continued for an undue length of time. The following outline shows one plan for providing for a frequent change of class activity in a beginning shorthand class:

1. Blackboard review of theory in today's lesson	3	min.
2. Reading a letter in today's lesson	1	
3. Preview of the letter on the blackboard	½	
4. Dictation of the letter at 60 w.a.m.	1	
5. Review of the preview on the board	½	
6. Dictation of the same letter at 75 w.a.m.	1	
7. Read back last part of letter from shorthand notes	½	
8. Dictation of the letter at 90 w.a.m.	1	
9. Presentation of part of theory in tomorrow's lesson	5	
10. Repetition of steps 2-8 on second letter in day's lesson	5½	
11. Presentation of rest of theory in tomorrow's lesson	5	
12. Repetition of steps 2-8 on third letter in lesson	5½	
13. Drill on brief-form chart in back of text	3	
14. Repetition of steps 2-8 on fourth letter in lesson	5½	
15. Review of tomorrow's theory on blackboard	3	
16. Sustained dictation of four letters at 80 w.a.m.	5	
	46	min.

Four minutes allowed for taking roll, collecting homework, and other deviations from the foregoing plan.

Use of the Blackboard

The best visual aid that any shorthand teacher can possibly have is plenty of blackboard space. It is impossible to teach shorthand effectively without making extensive use of the blackboard. The business teacher-trainee should not only be familiar with the techniques for making most effective use of the blackboard, but he should be able to write fluently, rapidly, and legibly on the board. Many beginning teachers hesitate to use the board because they lack confidence in their skill in writing on it.

The teacher-trainee will find that the arm motions involved in writing on the board are quite different from those used in writing at a desk, and he should spend considerable time practicing writing on the board before doing his student teaching. On the other hand, knowing that the arm motions and slant are different at the board, he will never have his students write at the board. However, for the inexperienced teacher, there are many ways that the use of the blackboard can be helpful in the shorthand class.

1. Always write the shorthand outlines on the board after the students come to class. The students can see correct shorthand outlines in the textbook usually written with far better penmanship than most classroom teachers can ever hope to achieve. But the book cannot show the student how the outline is constructed. This is one of the few things the teacher can do for the student in the classroom that the author of the text cannot possibly do. Therefore always write the shorthand outlines on the board while the students observe the manner in which the strokes are joined.

2. Write heavily enough so that the shorthand can be seen easily by every student in the room. Beautiful shorthand outlines written so lightly that they cannot be seen beyond the first or second row are of little help to the students. Yellow chalk can be seen most easily in the back of the room, but it is difficult to erase the outlines completely once the board has been used.

3. Write your shorthand outlines fluently and rapidly. Here again the teacher can perform a function in class that the text can never perform. Often the pace at which the teacher writes outlines on the board tends to govern the pace at which the students write shorthand at their desks. A teacher who draws outlines on the board

because by doing so he is able to write better outlines is doing his students a disservice. Those students are apt to draw their outlines at their desks. It is better to write with fluency at the board even if it means sacrificing beauty of the outlines. Of course the outlines must be legible, but the teacher needs to remember they need not be perfect. Just as the teacher learns to read almost any shorthand outline from working with all of his students, he will find that the students will become accustomed to his penmanship and will soon be able to read his outlines easily.

4. Watch the proportion of your strokes. Student teachers in shorthand classes sometimes find that their students have difficulty reading their shorthand because they do not distinguish carefully between the size of the different strokes. Their *p*'s and *b*'s, *r*'s and *l*'s, and *k*'s and *g*'s are often the same length. Their *e*'s and *a*'s may be difficult to distinguish. The student teacher should practice blackboard writing regularly until he is able to write all his strokes with the proper proportion.

5. Write your shorthand outlines across the board rather than in columns. Students are used to reading across the page. They will read shorthand more rapidly if the outlines are written across the board. The teacher may find it well to divide the board in half so that he will not have to reach so far in writing the outlines, can maintain better size and slant, and will not be standing where he obstructs the view of some of the students.

It is a good plan to put the presentation of the next day's theory on a board where it may be left throughout the period. The teacher may then review the presentation at any time without having to re-write the words. It is also well to put the preview of the material to be dictated on the board in an organized manner. If the teacher wishes to drill on derivatives of words appearing in the dictation, these should be placed on a separate board. Outlines should not be scattered here and there without any logical order. When this is done, a student needing to refer to the board for an outline that he is unable to write is usually unable to locate the outline quickly enough to enable him to keep up with the dictation.

6. In drilling on outlines written on the board, the teacher should be careful not to stand in front of the outline to which he is pointing. He should stand aside so that the entire class is able to see the form easily. He should also be careful to stand to one side when writing outlines on the board.

7. The teacher should not assume that one reading of an outline will result in mastery of it. The outlines should be read by the class in random order a number of times, very rapidly. The teacher can determine from the manner in which the class reads how much drill is necessary. He may also check further by having one of the slower members of the class read the outlines alone.

Whether it is necessary to return to the preview on the board after a letter has been dictated depends on the reaction of the students. The teacher should observe the students as he dictates. If he notices that a number of the students have to refer to the board frequently for outlines, it is obvious that additional drill is needed and it should be provided before the dictation is repeated.

Teaching Shorthand Theory

For many years authorities in the teaching of shorthand advocated that little attention be given to the mastery of shorthand principles by the students. It was said that any shorthand outline was a correct outline as long as the student could transcribe it correctly. On the surface this explanation appears satisfactory, and teachers frequently paid little attention to the shorthand outlines of their students. They were also told that tests on shorthand theory, such as word lists, vocabulary, and brief form tests, would hinder the students in the development of their shorthand skill and that they would cause hesitation in writing since the students would be overly conscious of incorrect outlines and would not try to construct an outline if they did not know the proper form. It was claimed that the reason teachers were unable to write shorthand fluently and rapidly was because they were too concerned about correct outlines which interfered with the development of high-level skill.

Today some shorthand authorities are beginning to challenge many of these statements. The shorthand teacher who has a thorough mastery of the shorthand system should be able to recall most shorthand outlines so automatically that there will be few hesitations in his writing. If he is unable to develop a high-level skill, it is far more likely due to insufficient mastery of the outlines rather than due to the insistence on writing correct outlines! Neither teachers nor students can record shorthand with fluency unless they can recall most of the outlines instantly. Several recent research studies have indicated that much more emphasis needs to be given to thorough mastery of shorthand principles as applied to the writing of shorthand. It may well be that those teachers who have insisted upon emphasizing the fundamental shorthand principles and who have continued to give vocabulary tests and brief form tests may not be following a procedure which is detrimental to the learning of shorthand but may actually be utilizing procedures which are exceedingly helpful to the advanced shorthand student. It seems logical that a student should be able to write correct shorthand outlines with less hesitation than he can construct his own outlines. All too often the student who constructs his own outlines writes these outlines somewhat differently each time which causes confusion when he attempts to read back his notes. Incorrect outlines are often difficult for students to transcribe if a period of time elapses between the dictation and the transcription. Further, it does not seem reasonable that students should read one set of outlines in the text and be writing an entirely different set of outlines when taking dictation. Teachers often find when they examine their students' shorthand notes the reason they are unable to read back the dictation is not so much due to the inability to write rapidly as to the number of outlines which have little resemblance to the forms in the text. It has been found that incorrectly written shorthand outlines not only are a frequent cause of errors in transcription, but that they cause hesitation in transcription even though the outline may be transcribed correctly.

The shorthand learning load is far less than that in many other courses, and the shorthand teacher may find that insistence upon thorough mastery of shorthand theory will improve his students' ability to take dictation and to transcribe rapidly and accurately.

Reading Shorthand Plates

According to Brewington[1] the shorthand reader can be identified as a reader, a word caller, a speller, or a symbol decipherer. The student who can recognize only one shorthand stroke at a time is a symbol decipherer and will never be able to read shorthand fluently until his recognition unit increases. For most students, stroke or symbol deciphering is the first step in learning to read shorthand. As the recognition of the shorthand symbols becomes more rapid, the student's recognition unit should increase to words, phrases, and even

[1] Ann Brewington, "Shorthand Reading Processes, *UBEA Forum,* (October 1947), pp. 27-29, 43.

eventually to thought units. The student who does not progress beyond the word-recognition level will never be a skillful stenographer since his reading span will be so short that he will have difficulty in his attempt to transcribe for meaning rather than for isolated words. The transcription of meaningless sentences and phrases is often due to this basic weakness in shorthand reading. The final stage then in the development of reading skill is the ability to grasp thought units rapidly without looking back over the shorthand lines for the meaning.

What are the best ways to develop skill in meaningful reading of shorthand? Most teachers follow the practice of verbatim reading of the shorthand plates. In this case the students first learn to read shorthand by spelling out the shorthand characters letter by letter. To avoid the development of slow, meaningless reading habits, the teacher may ask the students to read each shorthand plate twice, trying to reduce the time required for the second reading. This procedure may also help the student learn to recognize as word-wholes words occurring frequently throughout the exercise. From this stage he progresses to the phrase and the thought level of reading. The dangers of word and symbol reading can be avoided by careful attention to the students' reading habits and by correct use of the shorthand key.

In the first few periods of shorthand, many teachers have the students read both individually and as a group. Group practice is particularly beneficial to the slower students as they receive help from the other students. However, group reading should not be continued for too long a period, or the slow students will become dependent upon the rest of the class. Most of the period should be devoted to reading by individuals. The teacher should analyze the students' difficulties in reading so that he may make constructive suggestions to assist them in their daily preparation. Some students may have trouble learning word signs, while others may be unable to recognize phrases; still others may not easily differentiate the various shorthand characters and symbols.

When a student pauses or hesitates on a word, the teacher should prompt him quickly. This saves valuable class time, keeps the other students from becoming bored while the person reading is trying to decipher the outline, and helps the student retain the meaning of the sentence that he is reading. In the beginning stages of reading, some teachers find it helpful to have the student spell as quickly as possible the outline causing the trouble. In this way the teacher can determine whether the student simply is unable to put the sounds together or whether he is misreading some of the shorthand strokes. Later such a practice should be unnecessary. If, as one research study has shown, shorthand reading habits formed early tend to persist throughout the course, then it is highly important that the student form correct reading habits from the beginning.

One way to encourage students to develop rapid reading rates in shorthand is to set up reading goals that the students are expected to meet throughout the course. Most authorities believe that students should be able to read shorthand plates at 150 words a minute by the end of the first semester. Others state that students should be able to read shorthand plates at two-thirds of their reading rate on printed material by the end of the year. Leslie has pointed out that requiring high reading rates is unnecessary as students will never need these rates in transcribing their shorthand notes. Although Leslie's contention is correct, it is also true that setting up reading-rate goals and timing the students on their reading rates in class provides excellent motivation for the student. Since there seems to be a fairly close relationship between the ability to read shorthand rapidly and the ability to write shorthand, any procedure that will encourage students to develop rapid reading rates may be considered highly desirable.

Homework Assignments

Students should be given specific instructions as to the procedures to be followed in doing their homework. Otherwise they may derive very little benefit from the time devoted to such practice. Though the instructions may be changed from time to time, if the teacher is careful to tell the students exactly how to prepare their homework at the beginning of the course, it should not be necessary to give further instructions until some additional activity is to be added.

Theory. Students should be told to study their theory in the·lesson before attempting to read and write the letters in the assignment. Although the theory has already been presented in class, this was merely a presentation and was not meant to result in thorough mastery. The students can complete their assignment in much less time if they will always study the new theory and words before reading and writing the contextual material. Students should be told whether they are to read the words only or whether they are to write them, and how many times they should do each or both.

Reading. If the teacher is using a shorthand manual without a key, he should show the students how to spell out their shorthand outlines in the lesson and what to do in case they are unable to read some of the words. These words should be carefully marked so that they can be checked quickly the next day in class. The students should be encouraged to read the letter through rapidly after they have read it through spelling the outlines, as this will help them get the meaning of what they have read.

If the teacher is using a functional-method text, he should show the students how to use the key in reading their lessons. The students should be encouraged to spell out the strokes in any word with which they are unfamiliar but should be told not to linger over the outline. Use of the key will enable them to read more extensively and will help them grasp the meaning of what they are reading. Some teachers instruct their students to read the letters in the lesson only once while other teachers believe that reading the letters twice will result in more rapid, fluent reading habits.

Writing Practice. The teacher should be particularly careful to give the students specific instructions regarding homework writing practice. Many students write page after page of shorthand notes each evening but derive little benefit from such practice. They may think they are doing exactly what they are supposed to do, but it is apparent by their work the next day in class that no learning took place while they were writing their homework. The students should be instructed to read every letter through carefully before attempting to write it. After they have read the first letter, they should copy the letter in thought units. Copying shorthand plates, outline by outline, does not necessarily mean the student will know how to write these outlines the next day in class. Often he will find he is able to write few of the outlines correctly from dictation. If the student will read a phrase and then write it in his shorthand notebook, he will be more aware of the meaning of what he is writing and alert to those shorthand outlines he does not know or that cause him executional difficulty. Such outlines should either be practiced several times at the point where they are encountered or they should be marked in the text and practiced several times after the letter has been written. A student who conscientiously practices writing from the shorthand plates in this manner will be much better prepared to write this same material from dictation the next day in class than is the student who simply copied the plates without giving any thought to what he was copying.

Amount of Homework Practice. The individual teacher must decide for himself how much homework he will require of his students. Years ago it was customary to require students to write a certain number of pages of homework each night. Such a plan does not allow for differences in the size of students' shorthand notes and may encourage poor penmanship practices. Students quickly learn the larger they write the sooner they will finish their homework. The teacher should encourage his students to practice according to their individual needs. The best students in the class often do not need as much writing practice as the slower students. Usually the student who is unable to get the dictation in class the following day is either not spending sufficient time in practicing the shorthand plates at home or is not doing his homework in the prescribed manner. Many teachers ask their students to practice writing all the shorthand plates in the assignment at least once but not more than twice. An assignment usually consists of one lesson a day.

While the teacher must collect the homework to see that it has been done, he does not need to correct or grade it. If he has the students occasionally read in class from the notes written for homework, he will know whether students are writing legible outlines with proper proportion. When the students first begin to write their homework, the teacher should check the papers for the correct proportion of outlines and for outlines which have been drawn rather than written fluently. At these times the homework should be returned to the students so that they may read any comments regarding their notes. At times the teacher should check to see that the entire assignment is being written according to his instructions. Most of the time all that is necessary is a check to see that the homework is done each day.

The teacher should encourage the students to obtain additional practice through taking dictation from the radio or television or taking notes in their other classes. The teacher should urge the students to use their shorthand for personal use at every opportunity. When a student begins to use his shorthand for taking notes at the library, when composing term papers or reports, for taking minutes at club meetings, and in general substitutes shorthand for longhand whenever possible, he is learning to "think" in shorthand. The student who uses his skill to this extent will undoubtedly prove to be superior in shorthand.

Penmanship Practice

Most shorthand authorities today are of the opinion that penmanship drills are of limited value. They believe that with the right kind of dictation practice in the classroom and the right kind of homework practice at night most penmanship problems will soon disappear. However, there are a number of points regarding penmanship that beginning teachers should understand.

First, their students' shorthand writing will usually look very much like their longhand writing. It will have the same distinctive characteristics. Furthermore, the students will usually carry over to their shorthand writing the same weaknesses that are found in their longhand writing. Students who write illegible longhand often write illegible shorthand. Students who write in longhand with a backhand slant will write their shorthand in the same manner. Students who write longhand in a cramped style will write shorthand similarly. When these characteristics interfere with the student's shorthand progress, it is often necessary to do remedial work with him in his longhand writing before any improvement will be seen in his shorthand writing. The wise teacher will not attempt to change the size or slant of a student's shorthand notes as long as the student can write shorthand fluently and transcribe his notes accurately.

Second, the dictation practice in the classroom may at times cause penmanship problems for some students. Students whose shorthand writing speed is below that of most of the class frequently must make a great effort to get the dictation when the teacher increases the speed. A few students may find that the dictation is so far beyond their writing ability that the legibility of their shorthand breaks down completely. If much of the dictation practice in class is beyond their writing ability, eventually they may acquire sloppy, careless writing habits in an effort to get some outline written for every word dictated. Unless special attention is given to these students, they may soon form the habit of writing all their shorthand in this manner regardless of the dictation rate. These students should practice their homework carefully and make sure that every outline is legible. They should also exercise the same care when the dictation is given at low rates in class.

Third, pushing the entire class for the high speeds in dictation may result in illegible notes. It is true that if the students are to develop fast writing speeds, they must be pushed beyond their present shorthand writing ability. On the other hand, pushing too hard for high speeds may have a detrimental effect on the students' shorthand skill. When most of the period is spent in forcing the students' shorthand speed, it is a good practice to dictate some fairly easy material at a comparatively slow rate both at the beginning and the end of the hour. This practice helps to insure that the students begin the period writing legible notes and that they drop back to a point at the end of the period where they are again writing clear, legible outlines. It also has an excellent psychological effect upon the students as most of them will find that they are able to get all the dictation just before they leave the classroom.

Good Dictation Practices

It has been mentioned previously that, for best learning results, the time in the shorthand classroom should be devoted solely to the reading and writing of shorthand. Since it is impossible for the students to build their shorthand writing skill without proper dictation practice, the teacher should be especially careful to employ only those dictation practices which will give the best results. Also, the students should have clearly in mind the purpose of the dictation. Otherwise they will be unable to give proper attention to the points that the teacher wishes to emphasize. Perhaps teachers themselves do not fully appreciate the many purposes of and benefits to be derived from class dictation. Davenport and Murphy list fifteen possible reasons for giving dictation:

1. To learn to hear accurately
2. To develop fluency of writing and improve shorthand penmanship
3. To develop speed
4. To emphasize particular shorthand principles
5. To consider application of punctuation rules
6. To emphasize phrasing
7. To emphasize brief forms
8. To add words to shorthand and English vocabulary

9. To develop word carrying capacity
10. To learn to construct new forms and outlines
11. To develop comprehension and memory of context of material
12. To give ideas to be used composing letters
13. To give material for transcription
14. To develop ability to take dictation directly at the typewriter
15. To give practice in writing in unusual situations[2]

Many experienced teachers have found that certain methods are helpful to them in their shorthand teaching.

1. *Time the dictation.* The first few days that writing is introduced, only a small portion of the period will be devoted to writing, and the teacher may wish to defer timing the dictation until the second or third week. Other teachers may wish to start timing the dictation after the first two or three days. The class period when timing is begun is not too important, but it is important that the dictation be timed soon after writing is introduced. The teacher cannot control the writing speed of the class unless he does time his dictation with a stop watch or timer. When the teacher does not have a watch, the tendency is to dictate at a "sympathetic" rate. If a student in the first row is not getting the dictation, the natural inclination of the teacher is to dictate slower for him. Yet slowing down for this student may mean that the rest of the class receive practically no benefit from the dictation if they were all able to write at a much faster rate. Many teachers believe that they can estimate their shorthand dictation speed, but experiments with experienced teachers have shown that in estimating the speed of the dictation, they miss the actual rate by ten to forty words a minute. Shorthand writing skill is built by a carefully controlled dictation speed, and this control is impossible without correct timing.

2. *When introducing dictation, dictate at fifty to sixty words a minute with frequent pauses.* When writing is first introduced, most students cannot write at this rate for any sustained period, but they can write at fifty to sixty words a minute for short intervals. Introducing dictation at this rate accomplishes two purposes. It makes it impossible for the students to draw their outlines—they must strive for fluent writing; and second, it gives the students practice from the beginning in remembering the dictation.

---

[2] Elizabeth Davenport and Glen Murphy, "Classroom Procedures to Teach Writing of Shorthand," *Business Education Forum* (October 1948), pp. 33-35.

Dictation at thirty to forty words a minute results all too often in the drawing of outlines. Today most teachers recognize that, if necessary, when writing is first introduced, it is better to sacrifice beauty of outlines than to endanger the students' ability to write shorthand fluently later on.

When dictation is introduced at fifty or sixty words a minute, the teacher may find it necessary at first to dictate for only twenty seconds, giving a ten-second pause; then to dictate for another twenty seconds. Next the length of the dictation period is increased to thirty seconds followed by a five-second pause, and then gradually to one minute with no pause. In this manner the student learns to write outlines fluently and becomes accustomed to hearing one word while writing another, an important skill in recording shorthand dictation. The student who is not able to record the first part of a sentence while listening to the last part will often be confused when the dictation rate increases. Every shorthand student should learn to carry one group of words mentally while writing another group.

3. *Use easy material to introduce dictation.* If a teacher is following the functional approach, writing will not be introduced until the eighteenth to the twenty-first period. In that case the teacher may wish to go back to the first lessons in the text in which contextual material is presented. The students have been reading the outlines included in these early lessons for at least three weeks, and they will find this material much easier for their first writing practice than the material in the current assignments. It is almost impossible to use too easy material for introducing shorthand writing. Easy material encourages the students and convinces them that they will be able to master the art of writing shorthand skillfully.

4. *Insist that the students use pens.* The shorthand student often tells his teacher that he cannot write with a pen. Actually he cannot afford not to write with a pen. At the lower writing speeds, it may not appear to make much difference whether the students use pen or pencil, but when they begin to push for speed, the importance of using a pen quickly becomes apparent. As the tension increases with the strain of pushing for higher writing speeds, the natural tendency is to cramp the fingers tightly around the pencil and to bear down heavily on the paper. This cramped style of writ'ng and unnecessary pressure is impossible without ruining the pen point, and the students' energy may be used to move the pen forward rapidly across the paper rather than to push the pen point down through the paper.

Further, most people find it possible to write for much longer periods of time without fatigue by using a pen.

5. *Preview the dictation on the blackboard.* Before going to class, the shorthand teacher should pick out the words, brief forms, and phrases on which he feels his students may need special drill. Beginning teachers often ask how they can determine which words to include in the preview and how many should be included. The beginning teacher usually can remember those words or phrases which he found difficult when he was learning shorthand. The students in his classes will probably find many of these same words difficult for them. The number of words to be included in the preview will of course depend upon the difficulty of the material to be dictated. In general, however, a preview of 7 to 10 per cent of the material is ample.

The preview should be written on the board rapidly and fluently. During the first semester of shorthand, the students should spell and read each word as it is written on the board. The words should be read several times until the class seems to know them thoroughly. Frequently the mistake is made of placing a preview on the board, reading it once or twice before dictating the letter, and then never referring to the preview again—the assumption being that no additional practice is needed. If the teacher finds, while he is dictating the letter, a number of the students are still referring to the board for outlines, then it is clear that the preview "has not taken" and that additional drill is needed.

6. *Occasionally use a postview.* Recently some teachers have been recommending the use of a postview. In this case the material is dictated before any outlines are placed on the board. Then the teacher places on the board those outlines which the students were unable to write fluently or which they could not recall. Authorities are not in agreement about the value of the postview, but some use of this procedure should prove helpful to the students before new-matter dictation tests are introduced.

7. *Avoid dictating isolated words except for previews.* Isolated words are never as good for writing practice as is contextual material. Whether blackboard previews should ever be dictated is largely a matter of individual preference. The teacher may occasionally find that words causing executional difficulty are written more fluently in context if they have been practiced in advance. But in many instances, better use of class time can be achieved by hav-

ing the students read the preview rather than by writing it. For the most part, dictating isolated words is a poor teaching procedure. Students do not fail to attain high shorthand speeds because they cannot write individual words fast enough. Research has shown that most of the students who are slow shorthand writers are slow because they lose too much time in passing from one outline to the next. They cannot automatically recall the shorthand outlines needed. Their problem is mental, not physical. Contextual dictation is, therefore, the right kind of dictation for these students.

8. *Do not permit students to acquire the habit of merely copying from the text while dictation is being given.* Permitting the students to have their textbooks open and to refer to them when necessary may be a good teaching practice when writing is first introduced. But permitting the students to copy the shorthand from the text indefinitely without regard to the dictation is a poor teaching procedure. Students who become too dependent on the text often will write several sentences behind the teacher's dictation. In this case they might just as well be at home copying the shorthand plates. Further, the student who becomes too dependent upon the shorthand text while taking dictation is certain to encounter serious difficulties when new-matter dictation is introduced.

The teacher who introduces dictation at fifty to sixty words a minute will have little trouble with students continuing to copy their shorthand from the text. He may permit his students to have their texts open and to refer to them when they need to do so, but the students will find that they cannot keep up with the teacher's dictation if they must refer constantly to the text for outlines. The open textbook need never be an issue in the shorthand classroom. Correct teaching procedures will provide for thorough previews of difficult words and will also encourage the students to follow good study habits so that they will be prepared to take dictation on the material practiced in the homework.

9. *Use short dictation spurts of one minute and build up to three minutes of sustained dictation as soon as possible. Gradually increase the period of sustained dictation to five minutes.* The principle of building shorthand speed through the use of one-minute dictation spurts has been accepted as a sound teaching procedure for many years. The improvement of shorthand speed in taking dictation comes from briefer pauses between outlines and within outlines. The briefer pauses result from a quicker mental response, not from

greater manual speed or dexterity. Repetitive dictation of one-minute spurts helps to develop the quick mental response necessary for building shorthand speed. Using this procedure, it is possible to build the student's writing skill to a rate thirty to forty words a minute above his recording speed on new-matter material. After a number of letters have been practiced according to the one-minute repetitive speed-building plan, these letters can be used for three minutes of sustained dictation at ten to twenty words a minute below the highest speed at which the one-minute spurts were dictated. By the second semester of shorthand, the teacher should be able to increase the period of sustained dictation to five minutes.

Suppose the objective of the majority of the class is to record three minutes of new material at eighty words a minute. Most of the class is now able to write material for three minutes at seventy words a minute with not more than 5 per cent error. In this situation, the teacher might dictate the first letter practiced by the students in their homework at seventy words a minute for one minute. This rate will make it possible for everyone in the class to get the dictation easily and accurately. The letter might then be dictated a second time at ninety words a minute and a third time at 110 words a minute. After several letters have been practiced in this manner, three minutes of sustained dictation should be given at 90 to 100 words a minute. The exact rate at which letters are dictated should be determined by the ability of the class, but in any case the one-minute speed-building plan should be followed in forcing the class to new levels of shorthand writing skill.

Occasionally the one-minute speed-building plan may be varied to sustain class interest and to encourage the students to push toward new speed levels. For example, assume that the students can take new-matter dictation at sixty words a minute. The teacher previews a short letter and dictates the first sentence at 120 words a minute. Then he dictates the second sentence at 120 words a minute. Then the first two sentences are dictated at 120. The third sentence is dictated at 120 words a minute, and the first three sentences are then dictated at this rate. This procedure is continued until the students have taken the whole letter at 120. The entire letter is then dictated at 100 words a minute. A variation of this plan is to dictate the first sentence at 120; then the first and second sentence at 120; the first, second, and third sentences at 120; and so on until the letter is completed. The letter is then dictated at 100 words a minute and most of the class will be able to record every word of the dictation.

Grubbs[3] describes two types of dictation for relieving the monotony of evenly spaced dictation. One is *spurt dictation*. This type of material, like the preceding plan, is excellent for "breakthroughs" of plateaus in skill development. Instead of dictating in twenty-standard-word groups, it is suggested that the teacher dictate by the line, using a six-second dictation interval per line. Thus, dictating each line in six seconds, a line of twenty-five strokes or five words would be dictated at the rate of fifty words a minute, a line of thirty strokes or six words at sixty words a minute, and so on. Each additional five strokes will increase the rate of dictation by ten words a minute since six seconds is one-tenth of a minute. Exhibits 6.1 and 6.2 are illustrations of letters arranged for spurt dictation.

The other plan recommended by Grubbs for occasional use is *progressive dictation*. Here the dictation rate gradually increases throughout the letter. The material is arranged in the same way as the spurt-dictation material except that in this case the lines steadily increase in length. Each line is dictated in six seconds and the student is forced to write at ever-increasing speeds as the dictation progresses. Exhibit 6.3 illustrates a letter arranged for progressive dictation.[4]

The three plans which have been described here should be used infrequently and primarily for motivational purposes. The one-minute speed-building plan or some slight modification of it should ordinarily be used for increasing students' dictation rates.

10. *In building shorthand speed, push the dictation speed to the limit of the students' recording ability. All students should get all of the dictation some of the time, but all students should not get all of the dictation all the time.* Speed-building dictation should start at a rate at which almost all of the students can record the dictation and should gradually be increased until the best students in the class are having to make a real effort to get the dictation. In this way all the students benefit from the time devoted to dictation. If dictation is given at a rate at which all the class is able to record it all the time, it is clear that no speed building is taking place. Students are simply

---

[3] Robert L. Grubbs, "Rx for Effective Shorthand Teaching," *Business Education World* (New York: Gregg Division, McGraw-Hill Book Company, 1960-1961).

[4] *Ibid.*

EXHIBIT 6.1

Spurt Dictation

If you dictate in six seconds a line of	*Your dictation rate is*
25 strokes— 5 words	50 wam
30 strokes— 6 words	60 wam
35 strokes— 7 words	70 wam
40 strokes— 8 words	80 wam
45 strokes— 9 words	90 wam
50 strokes—10 words	100 wam
55 strokes—11 words	110 wam
60 strokes—12 words	120 wam
65 strokes—13 words	130 wam
70 strokes—14 words	140 wam

Letter for Spurt Dictation

Dear Mrs. Smith: Miss Frances White has	80
requested that I write you a letter of	80
recommendation in relation to her appli-	80
cation for the scholarship offered by your	80
organization. Miss White has completed a number	90
of courses with me, and I found her to be an	90
excellent student. She is very much interested in	100
her work and is highly cooperative with her instruc-	100
tors and her fellow classmates. Miss White has considerable	120
ability and applies herself well to any job assigned to	110
her. In addition to her excellent qualities as	90
a student, I would say that Miss White is	80
of the highest character and has high standards of	100
ethics. She has a pleasing personality and works well with	120
others. She has made a great many favorable contributions to educa-	130
tion in this state and has always shown a willingness to do far more	140
than might be expected on an assignment.	80
It gives me great pleasure to recommend Miss	90
White to you. I can assure you that the quality of	100
her work would be a credit to you. Cordially yours,	100

EXHIBIT 6.2

Spurt Dictation

If you dictate in ten seconds a line of	*Your dictation rate is*
40 strokes— 8 words	48 wam
45 strokes— 9 words	54 wam
50 strokes—10 words	60 wam
55 strokes—11 words	66 wam
60 strokes—12 words	72 wam
65 strokes—13 words	78 wam
70 strokes—14 words	84 wam
75 strokes—15 words	90 wam
80 strokes—16 words	96 wam
85 strokes—17 words	102 wam
90 strokes—18 words	108 wam
95 strokes—19 words	114 wam
100 strokes—20 words	120 wam
105 strokes—21 words	126 wam
110 strokes—22 words	132 wam
115 strokes—23 words	138 wam
120 strokes—24 words	144 wam

Letter for Spurt Dictation

Dear Mrs. Gregg: I am enclosing a letter which came in re- 72

cently. You will be particularly interested in the third paragaph. 78

We are delighted that you will serve as our delegate to the council 78

meeting next month. Incidentally, a news reporter was by and requested that 90

I ask you to send a brief summary to me of pertinent news items immediately after 96

the meeting so that he could include them in a story. I doubt if it will be
the type of infor- 114

mation I can use, but I told him we would cooperate in sending some
information. Mrs. Jennings will also be at 132

the council meeting, and this might be an excellent opportunity to
determine 90

her opinion concerning the special project which we have discussed at
length. 90

If we can be of any assistance to you in preparing for the council meeting, be 96

sure to let us know. Very sincerely yours, 54

EXHIBIT 6.3

Progressive Dictation

		Approximate wam per line
Dictate each line in six seconds.		
Dear Mr. Ford: We do not expect students		80
to complete all the material included in		80
the tests, but we must have enough copies to		90
take care of everyone in the class. You may		90
wish to indicate to your students that they should		100
not be disturbed if they complete only a portion of		100
the letters. We have not indicated whether errors are to		110
be corrected or not since practices vary on this in schools		110
during the first semster. If you are having students correct		120
errors, then we would prefer they do so on the test. If your		120
students are not making corrections or typing carbons and envelopes,		130
simply do not include this as part of the test but have them indi-		130
cate their proofreading ability by circling errors. Since the study		140
is being conducted through all four semesters of typewriting, may we sug-		140
gest that you keep the materials that were sent earlier and administer them		150
some time during the second semester. We will appreciate any help you		
can give.		150

Sincerely yours,

getting practice in taking dictation at a rate they have already established.

11. *Use dictation tapes and records for a part of the students' homework practice, if possible.* If the teacher makes his own records, he can dictate them according to the one-minute speed-building plan which he will use in class the next day, dictating a preview for each letter. Or the teacher may prefer to dictate all the letters in the lesson at a rate that best meets the needs of the majority of the class and have them practice writing through the letters once. The students should copy the shorthand plates from the text before attempting to write the letters from tapes or records.

The dictation tapes may either be purchased commercially or prepared by the teacher. The plastic records are somewhat more adaptable to the needs of most students than tapes since some voice-recording machines record at 33 rpm. These records can be checked out by the students and used on their record players at home.

12. *Recognize individual differences in your students by making special assignments to those few who are having difficulty in class.*

In every class there are usually two or three students who are unable to complete the entire assignment. Frequently they are slow shorthand readers and are not ready to write shorthand as soon as the rest of the class. Therefore, when writing is introduced, it too causes them difficulty. If the teacher will shorten the assignment for these two or three students for a few weeks, they will usually begin to show considerable improvement. These students may learn to read more fluently if they are told to read half of the assignment through two or three times rather than reading the entire assignment through once. In the same way, if the teacher will tell these students in advance which letters she plans to use for dictation in class the following day and asks them to write them through several times instead of writing the entire assignment, they will be able to get much more of the dictation in class than they could otherwise. Of course they should be required to complete the entire assignment just as soon as they begin to show improvement.

The student who records anything for the dictation, mostly illegible forms which cannot be read back, is probably a poor student. He is not ready for new-matter dictation. This is the type of student who can benefit from extra reading and copying of each assignment and from additional study of the brief forms and charts at the back of the text.

The student who misses a large portion of the dictation is not ready for the speed being dictated. He should take dictation from records and tapes outside of class. If the shorthand lessons in the text are recorded on tapes, practicing these tapes before the material is dictated in class will enable such a student to record much more of the class dictation the following day than he has been able to record previously.

The capable student who misses large sections of the dictation may be hesitating too long over unfamiliar or difficult words. He is unwilling to write an outline incorrectly. He should be encouraged to write such words according to sound even though the outline may not be perfect. Once he begins to write the difficult words by sound, he will be able to record the rest of the dictation easily.

The student who complains that his hand becomes tired may be pinching his pen either because the dictation is too fast for him or too high a degree of accuracy is required. Pen-pinching is the result of mental tension and ordinarily disappears when the dictation is given at a slower rate.

13. *Introduce some new-matter dictation the first semester, especially in schools where only one year of shorthand is offered.* Many teachers find that, when only one year of shorthand is taught, better results are secured if new-matter dictation is introduced the latter part of the first semester. This type of dictation can be introduced fairly early through the use of the blackboard preview. After the students have practiced the letters on which the blackboard preview is based, the teacher may dictate some very simple material that is "loaded" with the same preview. As this dictation will be composed largely of the same vocabulary that the students have been practicing, many times they do not even realize that they are being introduced to new-matter dictation. Teachers who are hesitant about composing their own material may prefer some of the graded materials that are available for use with the shorthand manual.

14. *Avoid talking about new-matter dictation in class.* When new-matter dictation is first introduced, it should consist only of words that students have written over and over again but that are rearranged in a new setting. If new-matter dictation is introduced during the first semester, the teacher may wish to delete any words that students have not previously encountered. Teachers who introduce new matter through the use of the blackboard preview will find that their students will be able to write such dictation easily. The first-semester students should be told that, though their dictation tests will not be on practiced material, they will not include any word they have not yet had in class. Thus there is no such thing as new-matter dictation. It merely consists of words already mastered, arranged in a new setting.

15. *If you introduce new-matter dictation the first semester, do not use much new material in any one class period.* A little new-matter dictation the first semester will go a long way. Usually one short letter, occasionally two, should be enough in any one class period.

16. *Increase the amount of new-matter dictation for speed building during the second semester.* Some authorities recommend the use of the text the second semester for homework practice only, with all dictation in class consisting of new material. Others believe that their students are able to attain higher speeds when they use the text material for speed-building purposes in class. Still others feel that a combination of these two procedures will give the best results. However, most teachers indicate that, if they do use the text ma-

terial for class dictation, they gradually increase the amount of new-matter dictation used for speed building throughout the semester.

17. *Check your teaching procedures regularly to see how much class time is being devoted to reading and writing shorthand.* Many teachers think that they are spending the entire period in shorthand reading and writing. Actually they may lose several minutes at the beginning of the period, spend too much time having students read back their shorthand notes, fail to make the best possible use of the time spent at the board, and as a consequence have little time left for dictation and speed building. If someone were to time them with a stop watch to see how many minutes in the period were spent reading and writing shorthand, they would be amazed to find how much class time they were losing each day. After the initial learning stages in the first semester, most of the class period should be devoted to dictation practice. The students can read the shorthand plates at home. They can even check their reading rates. But they cannot get a controlled dictation-practice situation without the shorthand teacher. Therefore the teacher should devote most of the period to giving the students the type of speed-building practice essential for fast shorthand writing.

18. *Do not give dictation tests too frequently.* Surveys show that most shorthand teachers give dictation tests once a week, beginning with the second semester. This is one fifth of the available teaching time. Time spent testing does not build skill—it only tests to determine how much skill has been attained already. Usually dictation tests every two weeks should be sufficient to determine this. Rather than scheduling a dictation test at specific intervals, the teacher may decide to give a test whenever most of the students in the class seem to have acquired sufficient skill to pass one. When tests are given too frequently, students become discouraged because they are unable to pass them. Sufficient time must be allowed between tests to permit students to build additional skill.

19. *Start with three-minute dictation tests and gradually increase to five-minute tests.* In many schools, three-minute dictation tests are given the first semester, and five-minute tests are introduced the second semester.

20. *Give dictation tests at ten-word-a-minute increases rather than at twenty.* Teachers who give dictation tests at ten-word intervals find that their students progress with greater regularity and do not

become discouraged as sometimes is the case when they are attempting to build an increase of twenty words a minute.

21. *Allow every student to proceed as far and as fast as he can.* Teachers who permit their students to progress as rapidly and as far as they can seldom have any trouble with motivation or student interest in their shorthand classes. This procedure means each student is given an opportunity to work toward an individual goal. If a third of the class has passed a dictation test at sixty words a minute, a third at seventy, and a third at eighty, then the teacher will need to dictate tests at seventy, eighty, and ninety the next time a test is given. In other words, a test should be dictated to meet the needs of each student in the class. Under this plan many students will continue to work for higher speed levels even after they have attained the requirements for an "A" on shorthand dictation speed.

22. *Require the students to pass at least two tests at each dictation rate before proceeding to the next rate.* Some teachers require their students to pass three tests at each level. This plan helps prevent plateaus in shorthand progress. Every shorthand teacher knows that dictation tests vary in difficulty regardless of the standard word count.[5] Therefore, by requiring students to pass two or thee tests at each rate, the teacher is sure that the student actually has the skill necessary to pass a test at that rate of speed before he goes on to the next level. When students are permitted to try the next speed as soon as they pass one test, they may have considerable difficulty passing the next speed level. Often the trouble is the result of going on to the next level before they had sufficient skill to do so.

23. *Learn to dictate skillfully.* The manner in which the teacher dictates will have a most important effect upon the ability of the students to get the dictation. Dictation should be given in a natural tone. Material dictated in a high, loud voice increases the tension in the class. Likewise if the students must strain to hear the dictation, they cannot give their full attention to their shorthand writing. The teacher needs to learn to enunciate distinctly so that the dictation may be understood easily in all parts of the room.

The dictation material in most shorthand texts and teachers' manuals is marked in twenty-word intervals. Table 6.1 gives the number of seconds to be allowed for the dictation of each group of words

---

[5] The "standard-word" method of counting dictation was devised by Louis A. Leslie in 1931. A word is considered to consist of 1.40 syllables rather than the actual word. The actual number of words in the material dictated may be either greater or smaller than the number of 1.40-syllable words.

Conversion Table for Dictation Speeds*

Words per Minute

Groups of													
35	70	87.5	105	122.5	140	157.5	175	192.5	210				
30	60	75.0	90	105.0	120	135.0	150	165.0	180	195.0	210		
25	50	62.5	75	87.5	100	112.5	125	137.5	150	162.5	175	187.5	200
20	40	50.0	60	70.0	80	90.0	100	110.0	120	130.0	140	150.0	160
15	30	37.5	45	52.5	60	67.5	75	82.5	90	97.5	105	112.5	120

Time Intervals in Seconds

30	24	20	17	15	13	12	11	10	9	8	8	7
60	48	40	34	30	26	24	22	20	18	17	16	15
30	12	60	51	45	40	36	33	30	27	25	24	22
60	36	20	08	60	53	48	44	40	37	34	32	30
	60	40	25	15	06	60	55	50	46	42	40	37
		60	42	30	20	12	06	60	55	51	48	45
			60	45	33	24	17	10	04	60	56	52
				60	47	36	28	20	14	08	04	60
					60	48	39	30	23	17	12	07
						60	50	40	32	25	20	15
							60	50	41	34	28	22
								60	51	42	36	30
									60	51	44	37
										60	52	45
											60	52
												60

Example: To dictate at 70 words a minute material counted in groups of 20, place your finger on the line that reads "Groups of 20." Run your finger along that line until you reach 70. Drop down to the first figure below the rule, which is 17. To dictate at 70 words a minute material counted in groups of 20 standard words, dictate each group in 17 seconds. The figures below 17 indicate the point on the watch where the second hand should be at the end of each group of 20 words. These time indications have been carried through the first two minutes.

---

* Charles E. Zoubek, *Dictation for Transcription* (The Gregg Publishing Company, 1937), p. xi.

for shorthand speeds from 30 to 210 words a minute. For material that is to be used as a test at a given speed, probably the most satisfactory procedure is to divide the material into quarter minutes, using a diagonal bar to indicate the end of each quarter minute and the number of the minute to indicate the end of each minute.

At first the beginning teacher may find it somewhat difficult to dictate smoothly and quietly from the printed page while timing the material and also observing the students. He may experience some difficulty in gauging a dictation rate or in changing from one speed level to another. With a little practice, however, he will become proficient not only in dictating evenly with a stop watch but in judging the speed at which he is dictating. Should the teacher fall a few words a minute behind in the dictation, he should make them up over a period of several word groups and not try to make them up in one group. If he finds he is dictating too rapidly, he should drop a few words over a period of several groups. In this manner the students are not bothered by noticeable speeding up or slowing down of the dictation. If the teacher finds he has fallen very much behind in the dictation, he should not try to make it up. As soon as he discovers that he is considerably behind the point where he should be, he should make every effort to dictate the remainder of the material evenly at the desired speed.

24. *Base the student's dictation grade in the course upon his final achievement at the end of the semester.* The student's rate of progress throughout the semester is not nearly so important as the final outcome. The dictation rate that the student can take at the end of the semester is the important factor, not how many tests he took to reach that level. Such a procedure greatly stimulates the student, for in most instances he has never before been enrolled in a course where his failures were not averaged with his successes.

Shorthand Dictation Equipment

Many schools today are considering the feasibility of installing some type of dictation equipment in the shorthand classroom. These installations range from a single tape recorder to elaborate multiple-listening units. Some require special wiring and represent a considerable investment of funds while others are relatively inexpensive and simple in plan and operation.

The simplest equipment consists of a single tape recorder or record player which is used to supplement the teacher's dictation. The teacher may prepare his own tapes or records or may purchase commercial dictation materials. When only one recorder is available, all students must take dictation at the same rate of speed. The principal advantage of using tapes and records under these circumstances is that the teacher is free to observe the students and work with them individually. The equipment may also be available to students for practice when no classes are scheduled in the shorthand room.

Small schools have found that it is possible to utilize dictation equipment even with a limited budget through the use of jacks and earphones. A single tape recorder may be installed with attachments permitting up to six students with earphones to listen to dictation given at one speed while the teacher dictates at another speed to other members of the class. The tape recorder is the only costly item as the jacks and earphones are inexpensive. As money becomes available, additional tape recorders may be purchased. Each recorder added to the installation increases the number of dictation speeds which can be given to the students simultaneously. Thus if a room were equipped with four tape recorders with outlet boxes serving up to six students each, placed at intervals around the room or with the outlets at each desk, students would be able to select for their practice from ony one of four dictation speeds. For instance, the tapes on Recorder A might be at the rates of sixty to eighty words a minute; on Recorder B, from seventy to ninety; on Recorder C, from eighty to one hundred; and on Recorder D, from ninety to one hundred and ten. This arrangement can be set up wherever it is needed and is especially suitable for schools which cannot afford permanently installed listening units.

Some of the new high schools have installed shorthand dictation laboratories. These rooms are equipped with a battery of tape recorders or dictating machines with each desk wired for individual reception. Each student selects the dictation speed which he wishes to practice by "listening in" on the proper channel. These laboratories may be equipped with machines using only tapes, with machines using only records, or with a combination type of equipment using both tapes and records. Since this is a costly installation, it should be noted that the dictating machines making up the console arrangement may also be used for machine transcription in office practice or for dictation at the typewriter in typing classes. Obviously the most efficient equipment is that which allows the teacher to control the console and the students to select the desired speeds at their desks.

The shorthand teacher who has this equipment available should know how to use it effectively. The teacher should *never* use the equipment as a substitute for his own teaching but rather as a means of improving his classroom instruction. It is doubtful whether any shorthand teacher should use tapes and records during the entire shorthand period. Any audio equipment loses part of its effectiveness if it is used excessively. Then too, student interest and attention may begin to lag before the end of the period. The teacher can inject enthusiasm into the class in a manner impossible for any machine installation to duplicate. In a speed-building lesson the teacher may vary the amount of time devoted to machine dictation from period to period, but some time should always be allowed for teacher dictation, drill, and theory review.

The dictation tapes or records used each day should be carefully selected. All the lessons in the *Gregg Manual* and some abbreviated longhand systems may be secured on commercial tapes. Shorthand dictation records may be secured from a number of companies. On the tapes accompanying the *Gregg Manual* a spiral pattern of speed development is followed. It is recommended that, if the teacher is making his own tapes or records, he follow a similar pattern. Thus, utilizing the one-minute speed-building plan, he may first dictate words the students should practice, then dictate for one minute at sixty words a minute from one of the letters in the day's assignment, then repeat this same dictation at seventy-five, and then at ninety. This procedure would be continued until the entire letter has been dictated. The teacher might then dictate the entire letter at seventy-five words a minute, instructing the students to write with control. If the teacher's objective is speed development, then obviously he should not dictate the material in the assignment through once at a single speed, since this procedure will not help the students build their shorthand rates to higher levels.

While the foregoing plan is the one most frequently used by teachers in preparing their own tapes and records, it is possible to follow a different procedure in those schools having the console installation with each student selecting his dictation rate at his own desk. In this case, if four channels are available, the lesson may be dictated at sixty words a minute for Recorder A; the same material at seventy-five words a minute for Recorder B; at ninety words a minute for Recorder C; and at 100 words a minute for Recorder D. As soon as a student is able to take the dictation at sixty words a minute, he switches to the next channel and from there to the third channel. Students must understand the importance of switching from one channel to another if they are to build their dictation skill. The chief disadvantage of this approach is the possibility that some students will select one channel and remain with it throughout the period.

Van Derveer[6] points out that such a machine installation may be used for purposes other than speed building. If students are asked to read the shorthand plates while listening to the same material on records or tapes, they may be forced to develop more rapid reading rates than they would otherwise do. Also listening to the records as they read their shorthand plates emphasizes the necessity of listening, an important aspect of skill development. The student can also check his recording ability by listening to the tapes or recorder while he checks his notes. If he is required to fill in all words and phrases missed when he was taking the dictation, he will know exactly how much of the dictation he was able to record.

What should the shorthand teacher do while the students are taking dictation from the machines? He will, of course, need to watch the records to see that tapes are changed and rewound when necessary. He should make sure each student is working at speeds which will force his skill development to higher levels. He should assist individual students with outlines which they are unable to write and with other writing problems. If some students are weak in vocabulary or theory, he may work with these students as a group while the rest of the class works from the machines. He is free to give special assistance to students who have been absent or who are having difficulty keeping up with the class. If two or three students are slower than the others in developing their dictation rate or if two or three show unusual ability, he may dictate to these students at rates meeting their individual needs. The teacher who properly utilizes shorthand dictation equipment should be able to achieve better results in less time, but to do this he must carefully select the dictation material he will use, make sure the material follows sound principles

---

[6] Elizabeth T. Van Derveer, "The Multiple-Listening Station in Shorthand Speed Building," *Business Education Forum* (October 1963), pp. 13-14.

of skill development, and plan how he may most effectively use his own time during each class period.

Testing in Shorthand

As was mentioned earlier, time devoted to testing in shorthand is time that cannot be spent in building reading and writing skill. The testing program in shorthand should be limited in the amount of time required and should include only those types of tests which will yield maximum benefits for the time so used. The following types of tests are the most commonly used tests in shorthand.

Word Tests. Of all the types of tests used by shorthand teachers, probably word tests have been subject to more criticism than any other type. Yet teachers continue to use them. The word test usually consists of ten to twenty-five words or more selected at random from the lesson. The words are dictated to the students who are instructed to write the correct shorthand outline and in some cases, after the entire list has been written in shorthand, to transcribe the words in longhand. Teachers who use such tests believe that students should learn to write shorthand outlines as they appear in the book. Teachers opposed to these tests point out that they have little practical value and that they encourage a hesitant style of writing by placing undue emphasis on accuracy of shorthand notes. Probably the chief advantage of such tests is one seldom mentioned. When a teacher makes a practice of giving such tests unannounced, the students may be motivated to prepare their daily lessons more carefully and with greater regularity than they might otherwise.

Longhand Transcription Tests. Longhand transcription tests designed to measure the students' reading skill are especially helpful to teachers using the reading approach. The student is told to transcribe for three to five minutes whatever plate material the teacher may select from the text. The material may be from the day's lesson, or it may be chosen from any material that has been assigned during the week. The student is graded on the number of correct words he is able to transcribe in this length of time. Such tests are not generally continued long after writing has been introduced and the students are able to take shorthand dictation. In using longhand transcription tests, teachers should remember that many persons do not write more than thirty to thirty-five words a minute in longhand; and consequently, no matter how fast they may be able to read the shorthand plates, they will never be able to transcribe more than thirty to thirty-five words a minute in longhand.

Shorthand Dictation Tests. The shorthand dictation test is considered the best type of shorthand test that can be used, since it gives a true picture of the student's ability to record dictation. Such tests may be introduced as soon as the students are able to take practice dictation at sixty words a minute. Since these are progress tests rather than occupational proficiency tests, a 5 per cent error allowance is ordinarily permitted. This error allowance includes both shorthand and nonshorthand errors.

Some teachers will prefer to give two grades to the shorthand transcript, one for transcription and one for English. The English grade would include such errors as misspelled words, punctuation errors, and errors in paragraphing. In the transcription grade any deviation from the material dictated would be considered an error.

Pretranscription Training

Pretranscription training should be introduced during the first semester of shorthand. This training should not be deferred until typed transcripts are required because such a procedure will seriously impede the progress of the students. Many shorthand teachers administer English, typing, and spelling tests to their shorthand students early in the course so that they can determine the kinds of remedial work that should be included in the first semester. Other teachers include in the shorthand program assignments in such phases of English as punctuation and capitalization, drills on correct typing usage, and lists of spelling words.

The shorthand texts now emphasize the English problems found in the shorthand plates through the use of marginal reminders. As soon as marginal reminders are introduced in the text, the students should be instructed to encircle in their notes the punctuation as they copy it, to look at the reminder in the margin to check the reason for the punctuation, and to study any spelling words in the margin. When the students read in class, the teacher should require words listed in the margin to be spelled as they read and punctuation marks read and briefly explained. For example, the student should read, "Although our rates are most reasonable (comma, if clause), you will find our accommodations (a-c-c-o-m-m-o-d-a-t-i-o-n-s) excellent." Occasionally the teacher should give a short spelling test on the words in the marginal reminders and other words in the lessons which may need special attention. Early emphasis on these factors frequently pays rich dividends when transcription is introduced the second semester.

Shorthand Standards

Probably shorthand teachers will never agree upon the standards that should be required. They argue, and rightly so, that some allowance must be made for different school situations and differences in student backgrounds. Teachers in schools offering two years of shorthand may feel that it is not necessary for them to "push" their students so rapidly as do teachers in schools offering only one year of shorthand. A recent survey showed that the standards most often required by shorthand teachers were sixty words a minute at the end of the first year, eighty words a minute at the end of the third semester, and 100 words a minute at the end of the fourth semester. For most jobs that would be open to high-school graduates, 100 words a minute should be sufficient. However, a writing speed of 120 words a minute is often a requirement for higher-level jobs.

The teacher in the school offering only one year of shorthand has a difficult problem in arrving at satisfactory standards. He knows that sixty words a minute is not sufficient for most office jobs—that eighty words a minute represents the minimum level his students should reach if they are to secure employment. And not only must his students be able to record dictation at eighty words a minute, but they must also be able to transcribe mailable letters. Many teachers say it is impossible to reach these standards in one year. Other teachers have accepted the challenge and are meeting these standards year after year. If students are not reaching the minimum standards in the one-year shorthand program (and evidence shows frequently they are not), perhaps the teacher should consider whether it is advisable to continue offering the subject. This decision should be based on a follow-up of the students to see whether they are attending a business school or college for additional training before entering office work.

In first-semester shorthand, the grading plan may include such factors as shorthand reading rates, transcription of practiced material dictated at seventy to ninety words a minute, and new-matter material dictated at sixty to eighty words a minute, knowledge of spelling and English fundamentals, and scores on brief form and vocabulary tests. The ability to transcribe accurately practiced or new-matter dictation should constitute at least 50 per cent of the student's grade; in some schools this factor is weighted even more heavily. Another plan is to require that a student meet the minimum for a "C" grade in dictation and transcription before he is permitted to enroll in second-semester shorthand. Teachers who place an unusually heavy weighting on the ability to take practiced or new-matter dictation at a minimum rate of speed and transcribe it accurately contend that this is one of the best indicators of a student's probable success in the second-semester shorthand course.

While it is not recommended that all schools should attempt to train stenographers in a one-year shorthand program, it is recognized that this situation exists in a large number of schools in many states. In these schools the standards suggested by the teacher's manuals accompanying the shorthand texts are often inadequate since machine transcription is not ordinarily included as a part of the grading scale. Therefore the following standards are included simply to indicate the minimum standards students should be expected to meet in schools offering a one-year program.

First Semester

First Six Weeks:

a. Longhand transcription for three minutes from text. Students 30% should be told what is required of them, and they should be given a set of standards so they can determine their progress. Grading scale (minimums):

4th week	A	20 up	B	15-19	C	10-14 *
6th week	A	22 up	B	17-21	C	12-16

b. Reading rates—record at least three reading rates for every 40% student within each grading period. Grading scale:

4th week	60 up	(minimums)
6th week	80 up	

c. Word lists—a vocabulary test of fifty words and a brief form 30% test of fifty words to be given during the six weeks with a minimum of 90 per cent accuracy required.

d. No grade is given the first six weeks on transcription of dictated material. However, some dictation of two to three minutes in length should be given.

e. The teacher must watch for any weaknesses in a given class and give remedial work accordingly. Spelling is one of the areas needing special attention.

Second Six Weeks:

a. Transcription from text. Grading scale (minimums):   20%

8th week	A	24 up	B	20-23	C	12-16 *
10th week	A	27 up	B	23-26	C	17-22
12th week	A	30 up	B	25-29	C	20-24

b. Reading rates—continue to record at least three reading rates   40%
for every student within the six-weeks' grading period. Grading scale (minimums):

8th week	90 up
10th week	100 up
12th week	110 up

c. Word lists—a vocabulary test of fifty words and a brief form   20%
test of fifty words to be given during the six weeks with a minimum of 95 per cent accuracy required.

d. Dictation—three minutes over practiced material from home-   20%
work to be transcribed in longhand, with 95 per cent accuracy required. Grading scale:

12th week   A   70 wam   B   60 wam   C   50 wam*

Third Six Weeks:

(Transcription from text is no longer part of grading scale.)

a. Reading rates—continue to record at least three reading rates   30%
for every student within the grading period. Grading scale (minimums):

14th week	120 up
16th week	130 up
18th week	140 up

b. Word lists—a vocabulary test of fifty words and a brief form   20%
test of fifty words to be given during the six weeks with a minimum of 95 per cent accuracy required.

c. Dictation tests (minimum requirements—two tests passed):   50%
three minutes' dictation of previewed, practiced material dictated at seventy words a minute and transcribed with 97 per cent accuracy, or five minutes' dictation of previewed, practiced material dictated at sixty words a minute and transcribed with 95 per cent accuracy.

---

* Minimum standards are based on a grade of "C." In schools where a grade "D" is given, the scale may be lowered ten words a minute, but with the understanding that the student will not continue shorthand the second semester.

Second Semester

Fourth Six Weeks:

a. Reading rates—record at least three reading rates for every   10%
student within each grading period. Grading scale:

    A   150 up   B   140 up   C   130 up

b. Word lists—a vocabulary test of fifty words dictated within   30%
five or six minutes and a brief form test of 100 words to be
dictated at the rate of one every three seconds with 95 per
cent accuracy required in the transcription of these outlines.

c. New-material dictation tests, 95 per cent accuracy required   60%
with two tests passed and at least three minutes of dictation
on each test. Grading scale:

    A   80 wam   B   70 wam   C   60 wam*

Fifth Sixth Weeks:

a. Reading rates—record at least three reading rates for every   10%
student within each grading period. Grading scale:

    A   170 up   B   160 up   C   150 up*

b. Word lists—a vocabulary test of fifty words dictated within   20%
five or six minutes and a brief form test of 100 words to be
dictated at the rate of one every three seconds with 95 per
cent accuracy required in the transcription of the shorthand
outlines.

c. New-material dictation tests—95 per cent accuracy required   70%
with two tests passed and not more than twenty minutes allowed for transcription (three or five minutes of dictation on
each test). Grading scale:

    A   90 wam   B   80 wam   C   70 wam*

Sixth Six Weeks: **

a. Reading rate—190 up
b. Word lists—a vocabulary test of fifty words dictated within   10%
five or six minutes and a brief form test of 100 words to be
dictated at the rate of one every three seconds with 95 per
cent accuracy required in the transcription of the shorthand
outlines.

c. Dictation tests—minimum requirements, two tests passed: 80%
three minutes' dictation of new, nonpreviewed material dictated at eighty words a minute and transcribed with 97 per cent accuracy, or
five minutes' dictation of new, nonpreviewed material dictated at seventy words a minute and transcribed with 95 per cent accuracy. Grading scale:

    A 100 wam   B   90 wam   C   80 wam*

d. Transcription of mailable letters**   10%

Transcription

No matter how skillful the shorthand student may be in recording dictation, he is not properly fitted for work in an office unless he can transcribe his notes quickly and accurately. For many years teachers assumed that, if a student could take dictation rapidly, knew how to type, and was well grounded in English, he would be a successful stenographer. However, experience has shown this is not the case. A student may possess skill in each of these three areas but still not be successful in transcription. The coordination of these three skills into effective transcription patterns requires correct training and practice. Most authorities believe that machine transcription should be deferred at least until the second semester of shorthand.

Transcription of plate material that has been assigned previously for homework reading and writing practice is the first stage through which the student can be introduced to machine transcription. Shorthand plates are excellent material for the first *few* days of transcription practice since they can be read easily, and the student can concentrate on good transcription techniques. During this period emphasis should be placed on reading in thought units, keeping the

---

* Minimum standards are based on a grade of "C." In schools where a grade of "D" is given, the scale may be lowered ten words a minute, but with the understanding that the student cannot enroll for second-year shorthand.

** In schools offering only one year of shorthand, the weight given to the various factors included in the grading the last six weeks may differ from the foregoing scale. For example, in such schools the transcription of mailable letters may constitute as much as 30 per cent of the grade.[7]

[7] "Course Guide for First-Year Shorthand," developed by Texas Committee on Course Guides for First-Year Shorthand, Ruth I. Anderson, Consultant.

eyes on the shorthand notes, and typing smoothly and evenly as the shorthand notes are being read.

EXHIBIT 6.4

First Day's Lesson in Transcription*

a. Read a short letter from a shorthand plate in the text.

b. Review letter style (pure block)

 2 in. top margin for letterhead

 Dateline double spaced below, balanced with letterhead; current date

 8-10 spaces from date to inside address

c. Placement of letters

Length		Line Length		Date to
		Pica	Elite	Inside Address
Short letter	4 in. line	20-60	26-74	8-10
Medium letter	5 in. line	15-65	20-80	6- 8
Long letter	6 in. line	10-70	14-86	4- 6

    (Centering point at 40)

d. Place on board inside address and closing lines:

 Miss Janet L. Jackson, 4021 Oak Street, Danville, Illinois

 American Travel Bureau, Henry B. Henderson, General Manager

e. Demonstrate to students correct transcribing technique:

 Eyes on copy

 Carriage moving rhythmically. Combination of English, typing, shorthand

 Erasing when necessary, carriage moved to right or left

 Proofread before removing from machine

 Call attention to proper placement of materials while transcribing

f. Preview on the board difficult shorthand words appearing in the letter read in Step 1.

g. Write on the board in shorthand fluent typing phrases or words difficult to type. Have students type these words and phrases for ten seconds each.

h. Have students type letter from homework notes, observing amount of space notes took in notebook. Explain to students how to judge the letter length from their shorthand notes.

i. Dictate words in shorthand preview and have students write.

j. Dictate the same letter students have read and typed once from

---

* Plan designed for a one-year shorthand class in which only a limited amount of time may be devoted to transcription.

homework notes. Use the inside address and closing lines written on the board.

k. Note amount of space notes took when letter was dictated (short letter).

l. Have students read notes back, inserting correct punctuation.

m. Have students transcribe the letter from the dictated notes.

n. Dictate a new-matter letter containing approximately 100 words and having little or no internal punctuation. Dictate the letter to Mr. A. B. Brown, 5026 N. Walnut Street, Wichita, Kansas. From: American Can Company, F. L. Wilson, General Manager.

o. Shorthand preview for letter: closely, concludes, damaged, preliminary, investigation, have, had, meantime, I am sending you.
Typing preview: must have been, I have made, I am sending you, of the matter, particular, as yet, in the meantime, immediately, damaged

p. Have students read the letter aloud, giving any internal punctuation and spelling difficult words.

q. Have students transcribe letter. If time have them repeat the letter, trying to improve their transcription techniques and reduce their transcription time.

Transcription of notes written for homework practice is the second stage by which the student can be introduced to machine transcription. Since the students have copied these notes from their shorthand texts, the notes should be accurate and easily read. This is extremely important in the early stages of transcription practice as it helps to insure that the student will continue to use the transcription techniques emphasized in the first stage.

The third stage of introducing machine transcription is the transcription of practiced dictation material. This material has been practiced by the student as part of his homework. It is then dictated in class for transcription. Emphasis continues to be on correct transcription techniques.

The fourth stage of introducing machine transcription is the transcription of new-matter dictation consisting of short business letters. By this time the student should be able to transcribe simple material without difficulty.

Transcription of new-matter dictation consisting of medium-length business letters is the fifth stage that can be used, while transcription problems gradually increasing in complexity is the final stage.

In the one-year shorthand course it will be necessary for the teacher to move through these transcription stages very quickly. In fact, some teachers prefer to omit the introductory stages so that more time can be devoted to transcription of the students' notes.

Rate of Dictation. Dictation for transcription should always be given at ten to twenty words a minute below the student's shorthand dictation rate. It should be remembered that on dictation tests, the student is ordinarily given an error allowance of 5 per cent; but, in transcription the student is expected to produce mailable copy. If he is to do so, material dictated for transcription must be dictated at a rate somewhat below the top shorthand recording speed. A student who can pass a shorthand dictation test at 100 words a minute with 5 per cent error cannot transcribe mailable letters dictated at this same rate. The dictation speed must be lowered to eighty or ninety words a minute.

The necessity for reducing the dictation rate for mailable transcription work makes it all the more important that typing and shorthand speeds be built to the highest possible level before mailable-letter transcription is introduced. Few teachers believe that material dictated for machine transcription should ever be dictated at less than sixty words a minute. Thus a student would need to be able to record shorthand at seventy or eighty words a minute before he would be ready to transcribe letter material dictated at sixty words a minute.

Coordination of Teaching with Material Dictated for Transcription. Just as it is almost impossible to dictate material that is too easy when the students first start to write shorthand, in the same way it is almost impossible to dictate material that is too simple when machine transcription is introduced. The letters should be carefully checked in advance to be sure that they contain no unusual English problems. In fact, many teachers find that the students build their transcription skill more quickly if the letters are carefully selected and contain only one or two types of punctuation. One of the most serious weaknesses in our transcription teaching is the attempt to test the students on transcription problems that the teacher has not yet taught in the transcription class. If, during the first week of transcription, the teacher reviews two comma rules such as the use of the comma in a series and the use of the comma following an introductory adverbial clause, then the letters dictated for transcription that week should contain no internal punctuation other than these two comma applications. Ordinarily, however, no effort is made to coordinate what has been taught with the material to be transcribed.

Students are supposed to be able to solve complicated punctuation problems before they are reviewed in class.

Exhibit 6.5 is an illustration of the punctuation rules as they might be presented in an introductory lesson in transcription. After the

EXHIBIT 6.5

Illustration of an Introductory Lesson in Punctuation in Transcription

Rule 1. Use a comma to separate the main clauses in a sentence when they are of equal importance and are joined by a coordinating conjunction—and, but, or, for, neither, nor, and so on.

Examples   His secretary took dictation all morning, and she will transcribe the letters this afternoon.

The custodian cleaned the floors last night, but he has not yet had time to wax and polish them.

Note   Do not use a comma to separate a compound predicate.

The custodian cleaned the floors last night but did not wax and polish them.

Rule 2. Use a comma to set off an introductory clause when it is immediately followed by an independent clause.

Examples   If you need any further information regarding this program, please do not hesitate to write me.

Although the market dropped a few points yesterday, he does not think this is the time to purchase additional shares.

Problem   Punctuate the following letter:

Dear Mr. Wilson:

Our firm is interested in your janitorial service and we would like to receive full information concerning it. Although we may not decide to use your service at this time we do want to know just what this service includes and the charges on a yearly basis.

As I interpret your brochure it is possible to select the service we desire from a number of different plans. In our building we would need nightly janitorial service and we would require additional services every three months. If the cost is not too expensive we would like to sign a contract for one year. I have used similar janitorial services in other cities and have always found them most efficient.

When you are free to go through our building I shall be glad to discuss this subject with you further.

Very truly yours,

rules have been presented on the board and discussed and the students have been asked to punctuate the letter illustrating the application of these two comma rules, the teacher should dictate the letters that the student is to transcribe. These letters should contain no punctuation other than the application of these two comma rules and the punctuation required at the end of each sentence. Exhibit 6.6 is an illustration of an advanced lesson in punctuation in the

EXHIBIT 6.6

Illustration of an Advanced Lesson in Punctuation in Transcription

The students have now studied the following punctuation rules:

a. Comma between two independent clauses joined by a coordinate conjunction
b. Comma to set off words used in direct address
c. Comma to set off words used in apposition
d. Comma after an introductory dependent clause
e. Comma to set off long introductory clauses and phrases
f. Comma to set off words in a series
g. Comma to set off parenthetical words and phrases
h. Semicolon between two independent clauses connected by a conjunction when either clause has a comma within it

Today's rules:

Rule 1. A comma is used to indicate the omission of "and" between two adjectives.

Examples 　This is a large, cheerful office.
　　　　He needs an efficient, personable secretary.

Note 　The comma is not used if the first adjective modifies the second adjective and the noun as a unit.

　　　　The material was shipped in a heavy corrugated box.
　　　　He selected a light green paint for the office walls.

Rule 2. A clause or phrase that may be omitted from the sentence without changing the meaning should be set off with commas.

Examples   Our publishing company, which is in the heart of the downtown district, is near the railway express and freight offices.

Mrs. Mary Willis, who is secretary to the president of the company, is writing a manual for executive secretaries.

Note   A comma is not used to set off a clause or phrase that is necessary to the meaning of the sentence.

The land that I have selected for our building site is in a new industrial area.

The man who wants to succeed in business must be willing to work hard.

Problem   Punctuate the following letter:

Dear Mr. Lawton:

As an important business executive you need a comfortable cheerful office in which to work. However if you are like many businessmen you are too busy handling the mail and making decisions to be concerned with the selection of office furniture modern equipment carpeting and other furnishings.

We know Mr. Lawton many business executives in this community and we hear their comments about the crowded schedules with which they are faced daily when they arrive at their offices. That is why we are writing you about our outstanding interior decorating service. We are sure you will agree when you talk with one of our decorators that we can do much to make your office more enjoyable and pleasant.

The personnel of Contemporary Interior Decorators is especially trained in planning modern offices which are functional in design yet beautiful in appearance. Any office planned by one of our talented young designers will be a joy in which to work. In addition you will find that our new color tones our efficient office layout and our contemporary furniture styles will create a peaceful relaxed atmosphere conducive to creative effort.

May we call and discuss with you a plan for giving your office a fresh new look?

Very truly yours,

transcription class. Since the students have now studied seven comma rules and one rule for the semicolon, the letters dictated for transcription may include these eight rules plus several applications of the two rules presented in this lesson. This procedure of coordinating what is taught in the transcription class with the material dictated for transcription represents an orderly, logical approach to the development of a complicated skill. The usual procedure of dictating any letter in the book is neither logical nor justifiable. Teachers do not expect shorthand students to know the theory that has not yet been presented, but they often make the mistake of expecting the student to apply principles of English before they are reviewed. It is true that at some previous time the students have studied the principles of English that they need to apply in transcription. But transfer of learning does not take place automatically. The students are so engrossed in the problem of integrating three separate skills that many of them will not be able to apply principles previously studied without additional review. However, once certain rules of punctuation, capitalization, typing usage, and so forth have been reviewed, the student should be expected to apply them correctly in all his transcription practice.

Occasionally students complain that the teacher is much more particular in judging whether a letter is mailable than any businessman will ever be. That should be true. Many businessmen do not know the fine points of punctuation and typing usage—that is not their concern. They expect their stenographer to know them. Furthermore, if a student should work for a businessman who is more concerned with rapid transcription than he is with correct English and typing usage, the student will soon learn that he need not be too particular in transcribing his letters.

The problems involved in transcription should gradually increase in difficulty. At first, when emphasis is solely on the development of correct transcription techniques, every effort should be made to see that the material being transcribed contains few transcription problems. Some teachers have the students transcribe in paragraph form the first few days so that they are not confronted with the problem of letter style. When the students can transcribe paragraph material with facility, they are then introduced to short business letters. After a few days' practice, they may be required to correct all errors. Next they may be asked to make one carbon copy of each letter. By the end of the course the students should be able to transcribe material containing fairly difficult vocabulary, long, two-page letters, material with multiple carbons, office memoranda, business reports, different letter styles, and so on. This procedure is merely the application of the long-accepted principle in education—always go from the simple to the complex.

In a one-year course the teacher will find that to build transcription speed and accuracy, she will need to concentrate on just a few of these transcription problems. The students should be able to transcribe short, medium, and long letters; but little time should be devoted to transcription of long letters. There is no time for involved problems such as two-page letters, multiple carbons, and so on. The development of basic transcription skill should not be sacrificed for these advanced learnings. Even though the transcription time may be limited, the transcription teacher must emphasize letter placement, erasures, use of carbon paper, proofreading, spelling, word division, commonly confused words, and punctuation.

Build transcription speed with accuracy. Transcription speed without accuracy is worthless. Accuracy without transcription speed may not be totally worthless, but it can be expensive and annoying. Though most teachers agree that accuracy in transcription is more important than speed, they also agree that transcription speed is essential for success in most stenographic jobs today. Slow transcribers are not usually the most accurate transcribers. It has been found that pupils with the highest production rate have the highest percentage of mailable letters.

Transcription drills. Although most of the time in transcription should be devoted to transcribing the students' own shorthand notes written from dictation, special transcription drills are especially valuable when transcription is introduced. They may also be used from time to time to increase transcription speed and accuracy.

1. Comparison of typing and transcription rate—the first day in transcription the students may be given a five-minute timed writing on some straight-copy material to determine their typing rates. They may next be given a five-minute timing on the same material written in shorthand. The transcription rate on straight copy is then compared with the typing rate.

2. A drill emphasizing the importance of accurate typing—the teacher may use a straight-copy drill to compare the typing and

transcription rate of the students when they are required to correct all their errors.

3. Comparison of typing and transcription rate on letter copy

4. Transcription of the same letter from shorthand notes two or three times in order to increase the students' transcription rate

5. Drill on typing from shorthand outlines written on the board words and phrases appearing in the letters to be transcribed

6. A preview of the difficult shorthand outlines in the letters to be dictated for transcription

7. Transcription power drive (See page 244.)

8. Transcribing in thought units—the material to be transcribed is marked in thought units with dotted or colored lines, and the students are instructed to read and transcribe in thought units, keeping the carriage moving at all times.

Check but do not grade the first letters transcribed. The first letters the students transcribe should be checked to determine the type of remedial work necessary. However, these letters should never be graded. Grading too early in transcription will result in incorrect transcription techniques.

Grade all letters on the basis of mailability. When letters are graded, they should be graded on the basis of mailability. More and more teachers are insisting that all letters transcribed must be mailable if the student is to receive any credit for his work. A few teachers give partial credit for letters that are unmailable but in which all errors are correctible. Even this is a questionable procedure, since the student should learn to locate his errors before submitting the letters to the teacher. In an office the boss can scarcely afford to spend his time proofreading for his stenographer or secretary. Most teachers consider a letter mailable if they would be willing to sign it. Wanous has defined a mailable letter as one that closely follows the thought of the dictation, contains no uncorrected errors, appears neat with clean erasures, has even margins, is well balanced, and contains no omissions.

Analyze the types of transcription errors students make and provide remedial work on these errors. Some transcription teachers like to keep transcription-error-analysis charts for their students or ask the students to keep them. Although such charts will show the teacher the types of errors occurring most frequently, many teachers

EXHIBIT 6.7

Transcription Power Drive

Directions: Type each sentence as many times as you can in one-half minute.
Your teacher will call "throw" at the end of a half minute, and you should start
transcribing the next sentence, trying to transcribe as many words on each
succeeding sentence as you did on the first sentence.

	Number of times you complete this		
	2	3	4
	Your speed in words a minute		
1.	32	48	
2.	33	49	
3.	34	50	
4.	35	52	
5.	35	53	
6.	36	54	72
7.	37	55	74
8.	38	56	75
9.	38	58	77
10.	39	59	78
11.	40	60	80
12.	41	61	82
13.	42	62	83
14.	42	64	85
15.	43	65	86
16.	44	66	88
17.	45	67	90
18.	46	68	91
19.	46	70	93
20.	47	71	94

Adapted from E. R. Stuart, V. V. Payne, and R. I. Anderson, Complete College Typing (Englewood Cliffs. N. J.: Prentice-Hall, Inc., 1959).

prefer a less formal method of analysis. For instance, a teacher may
simply jot down the types of errors that appear in a set of transcripts
as she corrects them. She can then select her material and illustrations for class discussion and remedial work on the basis of this list.

How the error analysis is made is relatively unimportant. The follow-up of the errors occurring most frequently is of prime importance.

English errors account for over 50 per cent of most students' transcription errors; content errors, over 25 per cent; typographical errors, 10 per cent; and letter mechanics, under 10 per cent. The most frequent English errors are errors in punctuation owing to the omission of commas, omission of apostrophes, incorrect use of the hyphen, incorrect compounding and division of words, and unnecessary punctuation. Students most often fail to use commas to set off introductory adverbial clauses, nonrestrictive clauses, appositives, parenthetical elements, and independent participial phrases.

By the end of the last semester of shorthand, all types of dictation situations should be included in the transcription program. Though the early transcription practice should be based on easy material containing few transcription problems, additional problems should be introduced gradually until the student is able to handle any transcription situation he might encounter in the business office. Students should be given practice in such varied procedures as the following:

1. Transcription of letters—there is no need for a student to be confused by a dozen different letter styles, but he should know two or three of the letter styles most commonly used in the business office. Bulletin-board illustrations can be used to show him that any basic letter style may be adapted to the needs of a particular office. Teaching too many letter styles puts a ceiling on the student's transcription rate. Instead of setting up his letters automatically in correct form, he must constantly check to see what particular style he is supposed to use that week.

2. Enclosures—students often have the attitude that the omission of the enclosure notation is a minor error—that it can always be added to an otherwise mailable letter. However, the omission of the enclosure notation may result in the omission of the enclosure, thereby doubling the cost of the correspondence for both companies involved.

3. Carbon-copy notations—some companies include only the names of the persons receiving carbon copies, others include the addresses, and still others will often use blind carbon-copy notations. Students should know how to handle each of these situations.

4. Special mailing instructions such as air mail, special delivery,

registered—some companies will not require these notations to be typed on the letter, but other companies believe that these notations are necessary for later reference should there be any delay in the handling of important correspondence. Students should be taught where to type these notations.

5. Postscripts—students frequently are confused by the proper arrangement of reference initials, enclosure notations, and post-scripts. They should know too that postscripts should never be typed alone on a second sheet unless that sheet is stapled to the letterhead. Important messages may be overlooked when postscripts are not attached to the rest of the letter.

6. Two-page letters—although some companies staple the sheets of letters that are more than one page and do not use a second-page heading, many companies require a formal heading on these sheets. Students should be familiar with two or three of the most common styles of headings for two-page letters.

7. Multiple carbons—in offices multiple carbons are the commonplace rather than the exception. Transcription of multiple carbons serves to emphasize the importance of accuracy in transcription. The inaccurate transcriber will find that his transcription rate drops rapidly when he must correct four or five carbon copies each time he makes an error.

8. Envelopes—after the initial stages of transcription students should be required to type envelopes, both business and legal size.

9. Letter placement—students should learn how to adjust the placement of a letter on a page. If a letter is slightly longer than they had originally estimated, they should know how to make adjustments in the closing lines such as allowing only three spaces for the signature, placing the reference initials on the same line as the signature, single spacing before typing the enclosure notation, and so on. Likewise if the letter is shorter than anticipated, the closing lines may be spread out to make any adjustments needed.

10. Transcription of varied types of dictation material such as office memoranda, articles, business reports, and telegrams should be learned by students.

The outline for a transcription program incorporating all of the foregoing elements is shown in Exhibit 6.8. In this case three periods a week were used for transcription. Two periods a week were devoted to drill on transcription problems, dictation, and transcription. The third period was devoted to transcription production, with the

EXHIBIT 6.8

Transcription Program in Advanced Shorthand

Week 1	Drill on basic transcription techniques Students' typing and English skills and knowledges are determined Typing and transcription rates on straight copy; compared on letters
Weeks 2-5	Comma rules. All letters dictated will be loaded with comma rule being studied that period.

      Week 2: Comma before coordinate conjunction
                  Comma following introductory clause
      Week 3: Comma in series
                  Comma to set off parenthetical expressions
      Week 4: Comma to set off appositive
                  Comma to set off introductory phrase containing verbal form
      Week 5: Comma showing omission of *and* between adjectives
                  Comma with nonrestrictive clauses

    Drill on spelling demons and word division
    Pure block-letter style, open punctuation
    Carbon copies and envelopes

Week 6	Use of the semicolon; letters illustrating use of semicolon Drill on spelling words; remedial drill on English problems Enclosure notations
Week 7	Use of the dash, apostrophe, and quotation marks Introduce the attention line Large business envelopes Modified block style letter, block paragraphs
Week 8	Rules on the use of the hyphen Introduction of the subject line Compound words, words written as one word, words written as two words
Week 9	Capitalization rules Carbon-copy notations
Weeks 10-11	Drill on correct usage of figures Postscripts
Week 12	Blind carbon copies, special notations (air mail, special delivery) Proper names frequently misspelled

Week 13   Office memoranda
               Multiple carbons
Week 14   Letters with tabulations
Weeks 15-16   Simulated office-style dictation projects
               Composition of letters and telegrams
Note: All letters must be transcribed mailably.

students transcribing all period without interruption or assistance from the teacher.

Exhibit 6.9 is a suggested program for teaching transcription in

EXHIBIT 6.9

A Six Weeks' Transcription Program

Week 1: Period 1   Dictation and speed building
        Period 2   Dictation and speed building
        Period 3   Dictation and speed building
        Period 4   Drill on transcription techniques, with emphasis on "eyes on copy" and "transcribing in thought units" (demonstrate)
                    Notes read from a letter written for homework; punctuate it
                    Letter placement and style discussed (block with open punctuation)
                    Letter written for homework, which has been read in class, transcribed
                    Short letter of new material dictated; students read it back, and punctuate it
                    Letter transcribed
        Period 5   Introduce comma rules; comma after introductory clause; before coordinate conjunction
                    Have students punctuate illustrations
                    Dictate two or three short letters, including only the foregoing punctuation rules (block style with open punctuation)
Week 2: Period 1   Dictation and speed building
        Period 2   Dictation and speed building
        Period 3   Dictation and speed building
        Period 4   Introduce comma rules: comma in a series and parenthetical expressions
                    Dictate two medium-length letters, including applications of four punctuation rules

Note: Call attention to differences in length of short- and medium-length letters and placement on page.

Introduce erasing

Period 5   Introduce comma rules: appositives; introductory phrases containing verbal forms

Enclosure notations

Dictate two or three medium-length letters, including only the rules that have thus far been presented

Week 3: Period 1   Dictation and speed building

Period 2   Dictation and speed building

Period 3   Dictation and speed building

Period 4   Introduce comma rule: restrictive and nonrestrictive clauses; review word-division rules

Dictate one short- and one medium-length letter for transcription (modified block, mixed punctuation)

Period 5   Distribute spelling "demons" to be studied

Dictate short- and medium-length letters for transcription

Week 4: Period 1   Dictation and speed building

Period 2   Dictation and speed building

Period 3   Introduce comma rule: comma showing omission of conjunction between adjectives

Introduce carbon copies

Dictate short- and medium-length letters for transcription (modified block, mixed punctuation)

Period 4   Introduce comma rule: use of the semicolon

Dictate short- and medium-length letters for transcription

Period 5   Introduce postscripts

Carbon copies

Dictate short- and medium-length letters for transcription

Week 5: Period 1   Dictation and speed building

Period 2   Dictation and speed building

Period 3   Brief review of capitalization rules

Introduce envelopes

Period 4   Introduce attention line

Dictate short- and medium-length letters for transcription, with carbons and envelopes

Period 5   Introduce subject line

Dictate short- and medium-length letters for transcription, with carbons and envelopes

Include carbon-copy notations

Week 6: Period 1   Dictation and speed building
        Period 2   Dictation and speed building
        Period 3   Review of rules of use of hyphen; compound words written as one word and those written as two words
        Period 4   Introduce long letter; discuss placement
                Dictate long letter for transcription
        Period 5   Production period: dictate short-, medium-, and long-length letters for transcription, including carbons and envelopes. (Teacher may elect to use only short- and medium-length letters for production period.)

schools offering only one year of shorthand. Transcription is introduced the last six weeks of the year in the following manner: during the first three weeks three days are devoted to dictation and speed building and two days, to transcription; during the second three weeks two days are devoted to dictation and speed building and three days, to transcription.

Build skill in the use of transcription materials. Although in most classrooms it is not possible to duplicate the quality of the materials used in the business office, all too often insufficient attention is given to the provision of proper materials and to their use. In some instances students have never been required to make carbon copies, have never typed letters on letterheads, and have never prepared envelopes. As a result they are confused when they are confronted with these tasks in the business office. Today there is little excuse for not providing these materials in transcription. Inexpensive letterhead pads are now available. If it is not possible to purchase these pads, letterheads may be duplicated on the school's duplicating machine. Local printers and business firms often have supplies of letterheads that are no longer being used. If envelopes cannot be purchased, paper may be cut to the correct size. Many businesses will save their used carbon paper for the business teacher.

Students should know the various types of eraser shields now on the market and should be familiar with the kinds of paper used for carbon copies, interoffice correspondence, branch-office letters, and so on. This type of knowledge should be a part of the training of every student in the transcription class.

Teach the students how to use their stenographic notebooks in transcription. Students should be given specific instructions on ways to use their shorthand notebooks efficiently in transcription. The following suggestions should prove helpful to them in learning to make effective use of their notebooks:

1. Keep your notebooks in a definite place on your desk. Then you will be ready to take dictation at a moment's notice, assuming, of course, that you keep a pen and pencils with your your notebook at all times.

2. Keep a rubber band around the used portion of your notebook.

3. Place the date at the bottom of the first page of the day's dictation.

4. Draw a line through each letter as soon as you transcribe it.

5. When you are interrupted in transcribing a letter, mark your place with a colored pencil.

6. Leave a space at the beginning of every letter for special instructions such as mailing directions, multiple carbons, and so on.

7. Use a code or letter system for corrections or insertions in the dictation. Then write the correction or insertion at the end of the page; mark both the dictation and the point at which it is to be inserted with the same letter.

8. Write out unfamiliar names in longhand.

9. Indicate beside each letter any items to be checked such as amounts of money, dates, and the like. Indicate by an "X," check mark, or wavy line.

10. Before transcribing, rewrite any incomplete sentences or ambiguous statements.

11. When the boss is interrupted during dictation, use the time to read your shorthand notes, improving outlines and inserting punctuation.

12. Indicate the end of each item in some way such as by a wavy line.

13. Indicate rush items to be transcribed first with a colored pencil.

14. When it is necessary to take dictation on loose paper, fasten the notes in the proper place in the notebook for later reference.

15. Learn to turn pages in your notebook while taking rapid dictation.

16. File your notebooks; the name of the secretary, the dictator, and the inclusive dates of the dictation should appear on the cover.

Set up definite standards for transcription. Students should be given definite transcription goals toward which to work throughout the semester. Unfortunately there has been little agreement among teachers as to what constitutes reasonable objectives in transcription. Part of the difficulty has been due to the differences in time available for transcription. Part of the problem lies in the wide differences in difficulty of various transcription materials. Then again some teachers have their students transcribe for sixty minutes while others use only thirty minutes of the period for transcription. Some never have their students transcribe more than two letters during a period.

Perhaps a conservative estimate of what should be expected of the student by the end of the transcription course would be the transcription of five or six average-length letters mailably in a forty- to fifty-minute period. If the student transcribes six mailable letters of 150 words each in fifty minutes, he is actually transcribing at the rate of eighteen words a minute. If an allowance of fifty words a letter is made for typing the inside address and closing lines, carbon copies, and envelopes, the rate would increase to approximately twenty-four words a minute. A transcription rate of twenty to twenty-five words a minute is generally considered an acceptable minimum production standard in transcription.

Some teachers base their transcription standards on words a minute since they have used these standards in typing and shorthand. Others base their standards on the number of mailable letters a student can produce in a given period. Actually the net result will be the same. In either case the student should not be given credit for any letters transcribed that are unmailable. Such transcription time is completely lost so far as the businessman is concerned. The amount of material dictated for transcription should be gradually increased throughout the semester as should the transcription standards.

Give the students practice in transcribing for extended periods of time. When transcription is first introduced, the teacher may wish to give the students only two or three letters to transcribe. However, the period allowed for transcription should be increased as soon as possible. Otherwise the students will never be able to attain a high degree of speed and accuracy in transcription for extended periods. In an office a businessman usually will think nothing of dictating fifteen to twenty letters at one time. In the classroom the teacher may not be able to duplicate this situation, but she can dictate to her students a number of letters and have them transcribe for the entire period. If the letters must be dictated in the same period, usually not more than thirty minutes will remain for transcription. If the teacher has one period for shorthand and one for transcription, then the letters may be dictated in the shorthand period and the entire forty or fifty minutes of the transcription period used to build sustained transcription power. Transcription standards should be based on the transcription period of at least thirty minutes, not on the transcription of only one or two letters.

During the last few weeks, give the students practice in office-style dictation in which all types of problems are encountered. Many office-style dictation projects have been published in the business-education periodicals within recent years. Or the business teacher may wish to build her own file of office-style dictation projects which will vary in length and difficulty. These projects may be based on actual business letters or letters composed by the teacher. An office-style project may include such varied transcription activities as corrections and deletions in business dictation, typing original copies of the same letter to be sent to two or three persons, changing only one paragraph of a letter, inserting paragraphs, checking the spelling of names referred to in the letter, checking addresses in the current card files, totaling columns of figures, special letter notations, special directions regarding mailing instructions and carbon copies, composition of short letters based on the information dictated or a letter that has been received, composition of telegrams, and so forth.

On the first office-style project attempted, students often have considerable difficulty, and it is well to check the project but not grade it. Thereafter, however, the student should realize that his work in an office may include many problems similar to those in the office-style project, and his work should be graded carefully.

Time available for transcription. Of all the problems of the tran-

scription teacher, perhaps none is more pressing than that of insufficient time to develop transcription skill. If a teacher is teaching
shorthand and transcription in a school offering only one year of
shorthand, obviously she cannot possibly include all the advanced
transcription techniques and projects that have been recommended
in this chapter. She would be foolish to try. In a one-year program,
she will do well to build her students' shorthand skill to seventy or
eighty words a minute and then concentrate for the last six weeks on
simple transcription techniques. By the end of the semester, her
students should be able to transcribe short- and medium-length
letters in acceptable form. It is doubtful whether the teacher should
attempt to include any advanced transcription problems such as
two-page letters, multiple carbons, and business reports. Usually the
best plan is to provide as much practice as possible in transcribing
short- and medium-length letters so that the students can concentrate
on correct transcription techniques and build the basis for developing further transcription speed with practice in an office. Some
schools offering only one year of shorthand offer two years of typing
and additional transcription practice may be secured in the second
year of typing.

In schools offering two years of shorthand or a year of shorthand
and a year of secretarial practice, the teacher will have little difficulty
in attaining acceptable office standards in transcription. In this case
the problem is to decide how the time shall be divided between
further skill development in shorthand and production practice in
transcription. Some authorities recommend that two periods be
devoted to shorthand and transcription the second year. In this
situation one period is used for building higher skill in shorthand
dictation practice. All materials that the student is to transcribe are
ordinarily dictated in this period also. Then the second period is
devoted entirely to transcription practice. This may be an ideal
teaching situation, but with the present crowded curriculum it is
one that is seldom considered practicable.

The second-year shorthand and transcription program should be
carefully outlined before the fall semester begins. After a summer's
vacation, the students' shorthand skill may have become somewhat
"rusty." In that case the first month or six weeks of the second year
might be devoted entirely to speed building in shorthand.

As soon as the students are again writing eighty or more words a
minute, transcription may be introduced. One point often overlooked

in teaching transcription is this—the greater the shorthand skill, the greater the transcription skill. Students who can barely write sixty words a minute in shorthand usually are the students who are the poorest transcribers. Those who can write 100 to 120 words a minute can often transcribe a 100-word-a-minute dictation test containing 500 words as quickly as the student who is writing only sixty words a minute can transcribe a 300-word test dictated at sixty. This clearly indicates that in many instances the problem in transcription is insufficient shorthand skill.

The student who is writing shorthand at slow speeds is still having trouble in recording the shorthand, in writing accurate notes and notes that are legible. He lacks confidence because he lacks skill. The student who can write more rapidly is beyond this point—he knows his shorthand outlines and can take the dictation without undue pressure. Thus the greater the shorthand skill, the easier it is to transcribe the shorthand notes. The weaker the shorthand skill, the more difficulty the student has in reading his notes. Many times teachers assume the problem in transcription is one of typing rate when actually the problem is one of basic shorthand skill.

Each teacher must decide in what manner she will divide her time between building further shorthand skill and teaching transcription. Since transcription authorities have usually recommended a double period, which most teachers do not have, the teacher must work out her own teaching procedures. To be sure that sufficient time will be devoted to both shorthand and transcription skills, the teaching program for the entire year should be worked out in advance. Some teachers use a 2-3 plan in the first semester of second-year shorthand and a 3-2 plan the second semester. In other words, they may devote every Monday, Wednesday, and Friday of the first semester to shorthand dictation practice and Tuesdays and Thursdays to transcription practice. Then during the second semester Mondays, Wednesdays, and Fridays are used for transcription practice and Tuesdays and Thursdays for shorthand practice.

Another variation of this same plan is to use the first three days of the week the first semester for shorthand practice and the last two days for transcription practice. Then the second semester the first two days of the week are devoted to shorthand speed building and the last three days to transcription.

Still other teachers maintain that better results can be secured in less time by devoting the entire first semester of the second year to speed building and the last semester to transcription. Teachers advocating this plan point out that it makes possible the development of the highest possible shorthand skill before transcription is introduced. Therefore, shorthand is not a problem when transcription is emphasized the last semester. Other teachers feel that under this plan the students will lose considerable speed in recording dictation the last semester and that they will not be as skilled in taking dictation at the end of the fourth semester as they were before transcription was introduced.

Some teachers follow none of these plans but spend the first part of each period in building shorthand skill and the last part in transcription. Unless the teacher has an unusually long shorthand period, this plan does not give the best results. Too much time is lost each day getting ready for transcription and in putting away materials at the end of the period. Consequently if the school has a forty- or fifty-minute period, the students may spend only approximately twenty minutes in dictation practice and fifteen to twenty minutes in transcription. This procedure does not provide for an extended transcription period which is an essential part of the students' training in transcription.

Projects and Questions for Discussion

1. Examine at least three different systems of shorthand. Make a list of those principles in the systems which are similar and a list of those principles which are different.

2. Obtain some old letters which have been written to a business firm. Working with a fellow shorthand student practice giving dictation to each other using as the basis for the dictation an answer to the business letters you have obtained.

3. Contact some office-machine-equipment firms in your locality and develop a file of literature which describes the various components of shorthand laboratory equipment.

4. Write a short paper in which you describe some of the research findings in the teaching of shorthand.

5. Make a list of what you believe some of the more common errors a student learning shorthand and transcription would tend to make.

6. Your school offers one year of shorthand. You are not permitted to select your shorthand students. Consequently no matter how hard you work, most of the students in your classes are not able to take dictation at rates over sixty words a minute on new material by the end of the

year. You know they are not receiving enough transcription practice, but you find it impossible to develop much transcription skill in a one-year course. Assuming that only one year of shorthand can be offered, what suggestions can you make for improving this situation?

7. Helen has just transferred into your first-year shorthand class from another school. Her teacher never dictated faster than forty words a minute and as a result Helen draws all her shorthand outlines. You know she will never be able to take rapid shorthand dictation unless she learns to write her outlines with fluency. How would you try to help Helen?

8. Your principal wishes to introduce a cooperative office program in which the students would take first-year shorthand in their junior year and then work afternoons in local business offices their senior year. Would you favor such a plan? Why or why not?

9. Miss Franks and Miss Blair are both teaching beginning shorthand. Only one year of shorthand is offered in this school. Miss Franks wants to introduce typed transcription by the end of the first six weeks. Miss Blair insists that this is too early and wants to defer typed transcription until the latter part of the second semester. Which procedure do you think would give best results?

10. In a one-year shorthand program what provisions would you make for checking the English and spelling proficiency of your students? If you found students with glaring weaknesses, how would you attempt to correct them? Indicate the materials you would use, when you would use them, and the amount of time you would devote to such remedial work.

11. Mr. Haynes never previews any of the dictation in second-semester shorthand. Miss Boynton always previews all dictation, whether it is practiced material, new material, or dictation tests. Would you follow Mr. Haynes' procedures or those of Miss Boynton? Why?

12. Sally Sanders is the weakest student in your advanced shorthand class. Her father is a prominent local businessman with considerable influence in the community. In May Sally comes to class and announces that she is to be secretary to the president of the new bank as soon as she graduates in June. Naturally you are disturbed since Sally's transcripts are seldom mailable. You dislike the idea that your ability as a shorthand teacher will in all probability be judged by Sally's performance. What would you do?

13. Last year Judy King took beginning shorthand in a high school in the East. During the summer her family moved to Texas, and Judy is now enrolled in your advanced shorthand class. The first day of class you discover that Judy is unable to take dictation no matter how slowly you dictate. All of the other students in the class are taking dictation be-

tween sixty to eighty words a minute since this was a requirement for passing the first-year course. Judy says her teacher last year never had the students do anything but read shorthand plates. Should Judy drop the course? If not, what suggestions would you make to her?

14. You are chairman of the business department in your school. This fall for the first time your school has adopted the *Gregg Jubilee* shorthand books. One of the older shorthand teachers comes to you in tears. She says that she has had to master anniversary shorthand, simplified shorthand, and now this! She insists she will be too confused by the new outlines to teach shorthand any longer and asks to have her schedule changed. This is impossible. What would you say to this teacher? How would you help her?

15. Several of your students come in late to shorthand class each day. Others come to class promptly but never get out their pens or notebooks until you start to dictate. You believe it is important that students develop desirable work habits while they are still in school. In what ways can you help these students improve their attitudes and work habits in your shorthand class?

16. A recent research study reported that during the period that persons typed in the transcription process, they typed at only half their usual typing speed. What procedures would you follow in teaching transcription to encourage your students to type more rapidly during transcription? What other factors should be considered in developing higher transcription rates?

17. In your transcription class you do not allow credit for letters which are unmailable. Mrs. Hendricks also teaches transcription in your school, and she uses a point-deduction system according to the seriousness of the errors. Thus students may have several errors in a letter and yet receive a passing grade. Your students are complaining about your unfair grading practices. Mrs. Hendricks insists your grading system discourages the students and impedes their progress. Is she right? If Mrs. Hendricks will not change her grading methods, what should you do?

18. Mrs. Jackson says it is foolish to insist that students continue to spell shorthand outlines from the board after the first three or four weeks of instruction since they are able to read the words by then without spelling the outlines. How would you explain to Mrs. Jackson the need for spelling outlines at least until all the principles have been introduced in the first-semester course?

19. Your principal has said that you may spend $50 for supplementary teaching materials in shorthand this coming year. What materials would you order?

20. Two years of shorthand are included in the curriculum at Bopeep High School. You find that many of your second-year students should never have been passed in the first-year course. They read shorthand poorly and cannot take dictation at any rate of speed. Apparently the teacher who preceded you was not overly concerned with standards. You feel the students are not responsible for their weaknesses yet, on the other hand, you do not see how you can pass them in the second-year course. What would you do?

Case Problems

1. Your principal has asked you to consider the advisability of offering an alphabet system of shorthand for students who are planning to attend college. Investigation shows that approximately 60 per cent of the students graduating from your school do attend college while the other 40 per cent go to work directly out of high school. There is a demand for stenographers in the community, and in the past frequently you have been unable to fill many of the positions available because you did not have enough qualified persons completing the stenographic program.

Do you believe an alphabet system should be introduced for the college-bound students? Do you think an alphabet system would make it possible for you to train more stenographers for the local business firms?

2. You are a teacher in Bean Blossom High School. One of the courses which you teach is a two-unit course in shorthand and secretarial practice offered in two consecutive periods. Most of the students enrolling in the course are seniors, although occasionally a junior is permitted to take the subject. The principal has just approached you about the possibility of deleting this course from the curriculum and substituting two one-unit courses, one in shorthand to be offered during the junior year and one in secretarial practice to be offered in the senior year. He feels that better skills might be developed over a longer period of time and that students who prove to be unqualified for the work would lose only one unit instead of two.

Would you agree with the principal? What advantages and disadvantages do you see in the present arrangement? What would be the strengths and weaknesses of the type of program suggested by the principal?

5. You require your students to take dictation at 120 words a minute by the end of the second year of shorthand. One of your students tells you that she read a magazine article recently in which it was reported a person who could take dictation at eighty words a minute could take the dictation of half of the businessmen in today's business offices and that

a person with a skill of 100 words a minute could meet the needs of two-thirds of the business dictators. It was also stated that many businessmen did not dictate at an average rate of more than sixty words a minute.

The student says that on the basis of this study your standards are unrealistic. How would you justify your standards to this student?

4. The language department in your school has recently installed an expensive language laboratory. However, it is located much closer to the business department than to the language department because no room was available in their area. As a result it is used only a few hours each week. You have checked the equipment and discussed its operation with the company which installed it. The company assures you that it would be possible to use this same equipment for a dictation laboratory in shorthand. When you suggest to your principal that you be permitted to use the laboratory part of the time, he says that it is to be reserved solely for the teaching of foreign languages since mastery of a foreign language is most important to those students planning to attend college. He points out that this equipment will enable the language students to pass advanced-standing examinations which will save them time in completing their college program.

What is your reaction to the principal's statements? How would you attempt to convince him that the laboratory should be available both to business students and college-preparatory students?

5. Last summer Miss Cox, head of the business department of Crowell High School, requested a new tape recorder and a complete set of shorthand dictation tapes for use in the shorthand program. At the beginning of the fall term Miss Cox met with all the shorthand teachers and presented a demonstration lesson showing how these tapes could be effectively used to supplement the classroom teacher. Now, however, she finds that instead of using the tapes to supplement their instruction, the shorthand teachers are depending upon the tapes to do their teaching for them. When she passes a shorthand classroom, she frequently notices that the teachers are sitting at their desks grading papers while the students are taking dictation from the tapes. She does not believe that this is the proper way to teach a shorthand class and is concerned about the situation.

If you were Miss Cox, what would you do?

6. Miss Hilton is the only business teacher at French Valley High School. The school offers a limited curriculum in business including one year of shorthand. Because the typing room is in use every period of the day, it is not possible to include any machine transcription during the shorthand period. Although this is her first year to teach shorthand, Miss Hilton is convinced that a one-year course in shorthand which does not include any machine transcription is of little value. On the other hand,

she finds that there are many stenographic jobs available in nearby cities. Should Miss Hilton recommend that the course be dropped from the curriculum? If not, what suggestions could you make to her which might help her solve this problem?

7. Wilma always makes 100 on her word tests, brief form tests, and longhand transcription tests. She reads shorthand rapidly and prepares her assignments conscientiously. She was an "A" student until you introduced three-minute shorthand dictation tests. At that point her grades began to drop rapidly. You soon discover that Wilma can read the shorthand plates rapidly and accurately, but she seems to be incapable of recording shorthand from dictation. You have concluded that Wilma is trying to learn every shorthand outline in the text rather than to write the outlines by sound. In fact, when you ask her to give you the sounds in a word like "win," she will say, "w-ī-n." Unless you find a way to help Wilma, it looks as though your "A" student might soon become a failure. What should be done to help her?

8. Betty is an excellent shorthand student. She can record new-matter dictation at 100 words a minute without an error. Her teacher thought she would be one of her most outstanding students. However, when transcription was introduced during the latter part of the second semester, it became immediately apparent that Betty was going to have serious difficulties. She had no trouble recording the dictation; she could read her notes fluently. But she could not type a mailable letter. She seemed to have no "English sense" at all. She would transcribe "too" for "two," "advice" for "advise," "accede" for "exceed," "principal" for "principle." Punctuation was inserted without any particular reason, and sentence fragments were not uncommon. In addition to all this, Betty could not spell.

Betty had excellent grades in shorthand before typed transcription was introduced. The teacher does not feel that it would be fair to Betty to fail her in the course. On the other hand, it is quite impossible in the few remaining weeks to teach Betty all the English she needs to know, and Betty certainly is not going to be qualified for a stenographic position of any kind. Since only one year of shorthand is offered and Betty is a senior, there is little possibility of giving Betty much help with her English. What do you think Betty's teacher should do?

Suggested Readings

Anderson, Ruth I., "Shorthand and Transcription," *American Business Education Yearbook,* United Business Education Association, XVIII (1961), 125-38.

————, "Significant Implications of Research in Shorthand and Transcription," *American Business Education Yearbook,* United Business Education Association, XIX (1962), 49-64.

Balsley, Irol Whitmore, *Current Transcription Practices in Business Firms,* Monograph 86. Cincinnati, Ohio: South-Western Publishing Company, 1954.

Blanchard, Clyde I, *Twenty Shortcuts to Shorthand Speed* (2nd ed.). New York: The Gregg Publishing Company, McGraw-Hill Publishing Company, 1947.

Business Education Forum, National Business Education Association, October, 1947-1964. Shorthand issues.

Day, Samuel W. and Nellie E. Day, *Teaching Gregg Shorthand and Transcription,* J. Weston Walch, 1962.

Grubbs, Robert L., "Rx for Effective Shorthand Teaching," *Business Education World.* New York: Gregg Publishing Division, McGraw-Hill Book Company, 1960-61. Reprinted.

Frink, Inez, "Implications of Research in Shorthand Transcription," *National Business Education Quarterly,* March, 1961.

Gregg, John Robert, Louis A. Leslie, and Charles E. Zoubek, *Gregg Shorthand, Diamond Jubilee Series, A Presentation of System Changes.* New York: Gregg Publishing Division, McGraw-Hill Book Company, 1963.

————, *Instructor's Handbook for Gregg Shorthand, Diamond Jubilee Series.* New York: Gregg Publishing Division, McGraw-Hill Book Company, 1963.

Jester, Don, *The Shorthand Transcription Process and Its Teaching Implications,* Monograph 108. Cincinnati, Ohio: South-Western Publishing Co., 1950.

Lamb, Marion, *Your First Year of Teaching Shorthand and Transcription* (2nd ed.). Cincinnati, Ohio: South-Western Publishing Co., 1950.

Leslie, Louis A., *Methods of Teaching Gregg Shorthand.* New York: Gregg Publishing Division, McGraw-Hill Book Company, 1953.

Leslie, Louis A. and Charles E. Zoubek, *Instructor's Handbook for Gregg Shorthand, Functional Method, Diamond Jubilee Series.* New York: Gregg Publishing Division, McGraw-Hill Book Company, 1963.

————, *Instructor's Handbook for Gregg Transcription, Diamond Jubilees Series.* New York: Gregg Publishing Division, McGraw-Hill Book Company, 1963.

Leslie, Louis A., Charles E. Zoubek, and Madeline S. Strony, *Instructor's Handbook for Gregg Dictation, Diamond Jubilee Series.* New York: Gregg Publishing Division, McGraw-Hill Book Company, 1963.

————, *Methods of Teaching Transcription.* New York: Gregg Publishing Division, McGraw-Hill Book Company, 1953.

Thomas, Archie C., *The Development of a Criterion for the Measurement of Shorthand-Transcription Production.* Cincinnati, Ohio: South-Western Publishing Company, 1952.

Tonne, Herbert A., Estelle L. Popham, and M. Herbert Freeman, *Methods of Teaching Vocational Business Subjects* (2nd ed.), IX, Chaps. 7, 8, 9. New York: The Gregg Publishing Company, 1957. Gregg Business Education Series.

Whitmore, Irol A. and Samuel J. Wanous, *Effective Transcription Procedures,* Monograph 57. Cincinnati, Ohio: South-Western Publishing Company, 1942.

7

Teaching
Clerical Practice
and
Stenographic Practice

Today office practice is offered in many schools throughout the country, yet the term is often used to apply to courses which vary widely both in objectives and in content. In subjects such as typewriting, shorthand, or general business, the course content has been clearly defined, and the subject matter usually is similar whether the course is taught in a large city school or in a small rural community. However, in office practice the course content is not necessarily the same in various schools where the subject is offered. The objectives are not always the same. The equipment and supplies with which the students and teachers work are not the same. It is small wonder that, with these variations in objectives and course content, confusion exists regarding the nature of the course.

The office-practice course has always been set up to meet the needs of the individual school, but not until fairly recently has any effort been made to designate clearly the difference in objectives of the office-practice courses that are being offered. *Office practice*, as the term implies, is an attempt to bridge the gap between the school and the office. Some educators have defined office practice as simulated office experience for high-school students. Part of the jobs performed in the office-practice course might be considered to be simulated office experience, but in most instances this definition is too narrow. The course also includes the teaching of many new skills and knowledges, and students cannot complete simulated office jobs until they have acquired the skills necessary to perform those jobs. Consequently, many business teachers believe that the purpose of office practice is to teach new office skills and knowledges and to provide simulated office experience in those areas where the students have developed the skills necessary to perform such jobs. The simulated office experience usually includes production-type jobs in which students are expected to meet the standards for initial office employment. In no case should office practice be taught as a second year of typewriting, bookkeeping, or shorthand. Neither should the course be used solely for the purpose of performing clerical and office jobs for the community to promote good public relations. A few projects of this nature performed in the classroom and supervised by the teacher may be valuable, but only when a learning situation is involved. The size of the class is ordinarily limited to not more than twenty-five students since most schools must use the rotation plan for teaching the machine units. The course, if properly organized, may be of benefit to the prospective clerical worker, stenographer, bookkeeper, or even to the owner of a small business.

Before a discussion of the methods of teaching office practice may be introduced, a distinction must be made among the various kinds of office-practice courses now being offered and the objectives of these courses. *Office practice* or *general office practice* is a course that is usually designed for prospective stenographers, bookkeepers, and general office workers. Because of the nature of the course content, knowledge of shorthand and/or bookkeeping are often prerequisites, and persons who have not completed these courses may not enroll. For many years this was the only type of office-practice course offered in most high schools, and it is still today probably the most widely offered. The course fulfills a real need since it gives students an opportunity to develop new skills in such areas as filing and office machines and at the same time provides practice in doing office jobs such as they will be expected to perform in the business office. On the other hand, the course does have serious limitations in that only those students who have previously studied shorthand and bookkeeping may enroll. Many students in high school who do not wish to take shorthand and bookkeeping may be interested in and have the ability to do general office or clerical work, yet their needs are not considered.

The course entitled *clerical practice* or *clerical office practice* was introduced into the high-school curriculum to meet the needs of the high-school students interested in office work but who lacked either the interest or the capacities for stenographic and bookkeeping work. Many teachers who have had experience teaching the course agree that it is especially valuable for students of average or slightly less-than-average ability. Because many of the general clerical duties performed in the office are routine in nature, clerical work often does not appeal to the superior student. In most schools students desiring to enroll in clerical practice must have completed at least one year of typewriting. Shorthand should never be a prerequisite. Bookkeeping or record keeping may or may not be required depending upon the content of the clerical-practice course.

A third type of office-practice course is the course designated *stenographic office practice, secretarial office practice,* or *secretarial practice.* Although the term *secretarial practice* frequently is used on the high-school level, this designation is misleading. Actually the course should be called *stenographic practice* or *stenographic office practice.* Since the course is designed for stenographic majors, short-hand and typewriting are prerequisites. The course is primarily intended to develop further accuracy in transcription. Units in other areas such as filing and duplicating may or may not be included, depending upon the individual school situation and the objectives of the course. In some schools stenographic practice is in reality the second year of shorthand. In other schools where only one year of shorthand is offered, one semester of second-year typewriting is devoted to stenographic practice for those students who have completed one year of shorthand. In still other schools, stenographic practice is the "finishing course" for the students who have completed two years of shorthand. In the latter case the course usually includes units in such areas as personality development, grooming, reception-ist duties, and so forth.

Secretarial office practice or secretarial practice usually includes the elements found in stenographic office practice plus thorough training in top-level secretarial duties such as the composition of letters, preparation of minutes and business reports, handling business callers, preparing the employer's itinerary, making travel arrangements, and so on. Obviously many of these duties would only be performed by a highly trained and experienced secretary. Therefore the term should be restricted to courses offered on the college level.

Another course occasionally found in large city schools is entitled *office machines.* In this course the students are taught to operate such office machines as the full-keyboard adding machine, the ten-key adding machine, the key-driven calculator, bookkeeping and posting machines, and so on. The instruction given in this course is entirely dependent upon the machines available in the school. Combination textbooks and workbooks for such office machines as the key-driven calculator, the rotary calculator, the ten-key adding-listing machine, and the full-keyboard adding-listing machine may be secured from publishing companies specializing in business-education materials. The discussion in this chapter will be limited to clerical office practice and stenographic office practice.

Clerical Practice

In 1900 one worker out of every forty was employed in clerical work. By 1940 one out of every ten employed persons was a clerical worker. Early in 1963 the United States Office of Education reported that 10 million persons in the United States were employed as "clerical and kindred workers." Of these 2½ million were classified as stenographers, typists, and secretaries. The other 7½ million were employed as clerical and kindred workers. In 1963 about one out of every six workers was working in the clerical field, and it is estimated by 1970 the business office will need 27 per cent more office workers than at present. It is anticipated that approximately 600,000 of these workers will be employed as office-machine operators and that by 1980 over 1 million persons will be employed in this capacity. This very sizable increase in clerical workers is a result of such influences as the continuing growth of large business enterprises and the rapid expansion of the service industries, emphasis upon specialization, and the impact of government regulations requiring additional records and reports. It should be noted that, while the number of specialized clerks employed in business offices continues to increase each year, the number of general clerks is declining. Since far more persons today are employed in clerical positions than are employed in stenographic or bookkeeping positions, business teachers and administrators are beginning to realize the advisability of including clerical practice in their curriculums.

Clerical practice is designed for those students whose high-school program has not included shorthand. The skills and knowledges included in the course are varied and range from the development of dexterity in handling routine office jobs to higher-level operations, such as machine transcription and filing. Many persons believe that clerical practice is designed only for the low-ability student. Actually a clerical-practice course that is properly organized and taught will be beneficial to any student who enrolls in it, provided the student has the mental and manual ability required to successfully complete the units of work. In 1961 Tonne estimated, based on information received from thirty-two states, that 231,640 students were enrolled in general clerical practice.

According to the United States census, a much higher percentage of men workers are classified as clerks than are women workers. Therefore the course should be so designed that it will appeal to both boys and girls. Since shorthand is not a prerequisite, there is no reason why the course should not be attractive to high-school boys planning to enter business.

Automation and Clerical Work

Recently much has been written about the effect of automation on office workers. Some persons have indicated that the continuing practice of training clerical workers in large numbers cannot be justified now that so many offices are making plans for using automated machine operations whenever possible. However, these writers overlook the fact that for many years the schools have not been able to train enough specialized clerical workers. The schools train only a small percentage of those entering nonspecialized types of clerical work. Though it is true that automation will create many new jobs on the technical and highly skilled levels, it is doubtful that automation will have much effect upon such specialized clerical workers as stenographers, bookkeepers, and typists. Automation is rapidly taking over routine, repetitive jobs, but not those clerical jobs requiring training and skill. Further, automation cannot be satisfactorily applied to nonrepetitive tasks. Because of the cost involved it is obvious that information which will be used only once should be handled according to traditional procedures. Thus, while automation is being utilized for the performance of repetitive duties, many clerical jobs will never be automatized.

At present instruction on key-punch machines, collators, tabulators, and other data-processing equipment is limited primarily to large technical high schools, business schools, and colleges. The teacher in the small high school which cannot afford the cost of leasing or purchasing this equipment should note that typewriting skill is needed in the operation of many electronic communication systems. Also many persons believe a skilled typist can be trained as a key-punch operator in a short period of time and that some companies expect to train their own operators. Every teacher of clerical practice should, however, attempt to give her students an understanding of the principles of automated data processing. Students should have some knowledge of the tabulated and electronic data-processing systems found in offices today. They should be introduced to the basic terminology of data processing, the language systems which the machines are able to understand, and the media used by these machines—punched cards, punched tapes, magnetic tape, and forms printed with magnetic ink. The clerical-practice teacher should include in the course illustrations of the various types of business forms and reports which can be prepared with automated data-processing equipment. Of primary importance to these students is the understanding of the processes involved and the systems to which these processes can be applied, not the actual operation of the machines themselves. Clerical students should realize that the offices in which many of them will be working will be automated to a large extent.

The Data Processing Management Association has developed teaching materials for the purpose of acquainting high-school students with automation in office work, and in many areas of the country the Association has arranged for courses in the principles of data processing to be made available to local high-school students. The course is designed to give the students an understanding of data processing and its application to office work rather than to develop specialized skills in the operation of the equipment. Classes are taught without charge by members of the Data Processing Management Association.

Duties Performed by Clerical Workers

A study of some of the surveys that have been made of the duties performed by clerical workers will prove helpful to the business teacher in organizing the units to be included in the clerical-practice

TABLE 7.1

Duties Performed by Clerical Workers

	Rank	Frequency
Use filing system or systems	1	393
Use telephone	2	379
Use adding machine	3	329
Type addresses on envelopes	4	245
Make carbon copies	5	242
Use calculating machine	6	237
Copy data from one record to another on typewriter	7	205
Verify and/or list information from business papers	8	198
Prepare material for filing	9	193
Use stapler	10.5	192
Copy from rough draft or corrected copy on typewriter	10.5	192
Figure extensions on bills, invoices, statements	12	182
Type letters	13	180
Fold, insert letters and seal envelopes	14	179
Type cards	15	173
Fill in printed forms on typewriter	16	170
Use follow-up files	17	162
Prepare trial balances	18	153
Examine and/or sort business papers	19	149
Prepare operating and/or financial statements	20	147
Keep inventory records	21	146
Make journal entries	22	145
Figure discounts	23	143
Compose and type letters with or without instructions as to content	24	129
Make cross references	26	125
Prepare stencil for use on duplicating machine	26	125
Receive business callers	26	125
Type bills, invoices, statements	28.5	115
Make entries in ledger accounts	28.5	115
Open, sort, and distribute mail	30	112

course. Satlow[1] classifies the activities in which clerical workers engage into seven categories: (*a*) typewriting and preparation for duplication; (*b*) filing; (*c*) record keeping; (*d*) handling the telephone; (*e*) operating adding-calculating machines; (*f*) operating miscellaneous office machines; and (*g*) nonspecialized activities. Activities classified as nonspecialized include those of classifying and sorting, checking for accuracy, filling in forms by hand, stuffing and sealing envelopes, collating and stapling, addressing envelopes by hand, operating a folding machine, acting as messenger, ordering supplies, and relieving other workers.

In Pittsburgh[2] a survey was made of the clerical duties performed by 442 general clerks. Table 7.1 gives the activities performed by 75 per cent of these clerks, together with the rank and frequency.

Analysis of Table 7.1 shows that those duties which were performed most frequently by the general clerks required no special skill other than the ability to operate the adding machine, the calculating machine, and the typewriter. A knowledge of record keeping or bookkeeping and filing would be necessary to perform some of those duties having a lower rank and frequency.

Van Derveer[3] has grouped clerical office duties into seven classifications:

1. Mailing
2. Filing and sorting
3. Typewriting
4. Duplicating
5. Adding-machine operation (calculators)
6. Nonspecialized skills
7. Telephoning

A 1959 survey in New York City[4] of the work clerical high-school graduates were performing revealed the following:

[1] I. David Satlow, "Routine and Nonspecialized Skills," *The American Business Education Yearbook*, XVI (1959), 107-108.

[2] Survey of Office Duties and Employer Recommendations for Improving High School Training," *Pittsburgh Schools*, XXIII (September-October 1948), 21-22.

[3] Elizabeth T. Van Derveer, "Patterns of Performance for the Most Frequent Duties of Beginning Clerical Employees." Thesis Abstracts, New York University, 1952 (Second Series, No. 1, Alpha Chapter, Delta Pi Epsilon).

[4] Emma K. Felter, "How the Clerical Program Helps the Student, the School, and the Community," *The National Business Education Quarterly*, XXVIII (1959), 3.

Type of work	Number of Graduates Performing
Typewriting	67
Filing	53
Answering the telephone	51
Handling the mail	42
Operating adding and calculating machines	26
Receptionist	21
Recordkeeping and bookkeeping	19
Operating other office machines	17
Transcribing from dictation discs or cylinders	16
Mimeographing	15
Operating the switchboard	10
Messenger	9
Operating bookkeeping machines	4

A study completed in 1962 in Fargo, North Dakota[5] of 106 high-school graduates employed in office work revealed that the positions most frequently held by these persons were general office worker and general typist. Other positions in order of frequency were file clerk, receptionist, secretary, bookkeeper, switchboard operator, stenographer, and mail-department worker. Typing and filing were the skills the respondents had found most helpful to them. The duties performed daily by the greatest number of graduates were answering the phone, filing, and typing letters.

Analysis of the foregoing studies reveals that many of the skills needed by clerical workers are similar whether the workers are employed in large metropolitan cities or smaller communities.

In addition to the skills required to perform these clerical duties, the clerical worker needs to develop desirable work habits, attitudes, and personality traits. Liles ranks the factors that constitute success in clerical work in this order:[6]

1. Accuracy in clerical operations
2. Dependability
3. Speed in clerical operations—amount of acceptable work produced
4. Ability to follow instructions accurately and without repetition

---

[5] Sister Mary Antonine Foy, "A Design for a Functional Office Practice Course at Hanley High School, Fargo, North Dakota." Unpublished master's thesis, The University of North Dakota (Grand Forks), 1962.

[6] Alton B. Parker Liles, "Some Factors in the Training of Clerical Workers." Thesis Abstract, Oklahoma A. and M. College, 1947 (Delta Pi Epsilon Research Award). Summary of Dissertation completed at the University of Kentucky, 1947.

5. Ability to maintain harmonious working relations with others
6. Industry
7. Capacity for remembering necessary details, figures, instructions, and so on
8. Initiative and/or resourcefulness
9. Ability to work under pressure or abnormal conditions, such as meeting deadlines, multiple assignments, extra work
10. Ability to make judgments or decisions quickly and accurately
11. Natural ability and aptitude for clerical work
12. Presentability of work—appropriateness of arrangement and appearance of work
13. Ability to organize work
14. Attendance, tardiness, and strict observance of recess or lunch periods
15. Does not lose excessive time in personal telephone calls, talking with fellow workers, going to rest room, and the like
16. Personal appearance—appropriate dress and grooming
17. Personality—cheerfulness and/or charm
18. Physical fitness for work
19. Neatness and orderliness in maintenance and arrangement of physical surroundings, such as desk, files, floor, and the like
20. Ability to suggest improvements in clerical techniques and operations

Objectives of the Course

Clerical practice, like many office-practice courses in which emphasis is placed upon the integration of office skills, attempts to bridge the gap between the classroom and the office. Though the objectives of the course will naturally vary from school to school, most clerical courses are based on the following objectives:

1. To improve and coordinate the office skills learned in other courses

2. To improve, when necessary, previously acquired skills in the fundamental processes such as handwriting, English, spelling, and arithmetic

3. To understand the organization and flow of work of the business office

4. To become familiar with those reference books frequently used in the business office

5. To gain an understanding of the techniques for work simplification in the office

6. To become acquainted with the principles and procedures of data processing, the equipment, and the systems to which it can be applied

7. To become familiar with the latest office equipment, machines, and supplies

8. To become familiar with commonly used filing systems and to develop skill in filing and finding business papers

9. To develop skill in the typing of business papers and forms

10. To develop employable skill in machine transcription

11. To develop proofreading skill

12. To develop skill in the use of machines commonly found in the business office

13. To develop skill in the use of duplicating equipment

14. To develop skill in mailing routines and techniques

15. To develop skill in the composition of business communications

16. To develop skill in correct telephone techniques

17. To develop in students a sense of responsibility for the completion of office jobs without close supervision

18. To develop those personal traits and work habits needed in the business office

19. To acquaint students with proper techniques in applying for a job

Prerequisites for Enrollment

Since many of the units in clerical practice involve the integration of previously acquired skills, the course should be offered in the twelfth year in high school. The course may be either one or two semesters in length. Some schools offer a year course in clerical practice. In some large schools, a one-semester course is offered for clerical students and a one-semester course for stenographic students. Still other schools include a one-semester course in advanced typewriting or clerical typing and one semester in clerical practice. Students are frequently selected for clerical practice because the number wishing to enroll so far exceeds the facilities available. Although selection of students is certainly to be recommended, it is unfortunate that the schools are unable to provide training for many students who are interested in clerical work and who could be trained to be proficient clerical workers.

One of the most common prerequisites for enrollment in clerical practice is typewriting. It is true that some clerical jobs do not require typing skill, but an analysis of the duties most often performed by clerical workers indicates that many of these duties do require typing skill. It should also be remembered that many of the nonskilled clerical duties are gradually disappearing as more and more business offices become automated. Certainly clerical students who type will have much greater job and promotional opportunities than those who do not. A typing skill of at least forty to fifty words a minute is highly desirable. Other desirable course prerequisites include general business and business math. The students should have previously acquired basic skills in the fundamental processes such as handwriting, arithmetic, English, and spelling.

Units to Be Included in Clerical Practice

Because the length of the clerical practice course and the objectives vary from school to school, it is difficult to set up a list of the units that should be included in the course. However, on the basis of the duties most often performed by clerical workers, the following units should be included if the necessary equipment, machines, and supplies are available.

Unit I.   Office Organization and Routine
    Job relationships
    Operational charts and flow of work
    Clerical routines; motion-mindedness

Unit II.   The Personality of the Clerical Worker
    Clerical aptitude tests and personality tests
    Personal appearance—dress, hair, make-up, cleanliness, neatness, health, voice, posture
    Personality—initiative, courtesy (manners), enthusiasm, sincerity, voice and speech, cooperativeness, tact, social aptitude, sense of humor, office etiquette
    Mental skills—learning to follow directions, learning from previous mistakes, using initiative to solve a problem, openmindedness to new ideas, suggestions, or criticisms

Responsibility—promptness, trustworthiness, loyalty, ambition, persistence, dependability

Character

Attitude toward the job—promptness and regularity in attendance, pride in one's work, production of a day's work in a day

Unit III. Clerical Typewriting

Skill on the electric typewriter

Statistical typewriting

Addressing envelopes

Typing of direct-process masters and stencils

Rough draft and manuscript typing

Typing business forms and papers

Letter production techniques

Typing from direct dictation

Composition at the machine

Typing multiple carbons

Unit IV. Machine Transcription

Unit V. Filing

Alphabetic

Numeric

Other filing systems

Filing equipment and supplies

Filing procedures such as sorting, cross referencing, charge-out, follow-up

Preparation of file labels, folders, and guides

Retention and transfer of papers

Unit VI. Office Machines

Adding machine—ten-key and full keyboard

Calculators

Unit VII. Duplicating

Stencil duplicating

Direct-process duplicating

Multilithing (if equipment available)

Photocopy and other processes

Unit VIII. Recordkeeping

Petty cash

Payrolls

Verifying bills, invoices, and statements

Bank deposits, reconciling bank statements

Unit IX. Communications

Telephone problems

Operating the switchboard

Handling incoming and outgoing mail
Composing sample letters
Telegraph communications
Selecting and typing form letters and letters with fill-ins
Interoffice and intracompany communications

Unit X.   Automation in the Office
Principles of automation
Procedures followed in utilizing automated data-processing techniques
Terminology of automation
Common language used by automated data-processing equipment
Systems to which data processing may be applied

Unit XI.   Seeking Employment
Personal interview and follow-up
Application letters and data sheets
Application blanks

Equipment and Supplies Needed

Although the equipment and supplies needed to teach clerical practice will vary according to the course content in each school, the teacher should be sure that she will have the minimum materials needed to teach the course effectively. The following equipment and supplies should be found in most clerical practice rooms if the training is to be realistic:

1. Typewriters of various makes—manual and electric, pica and elite type
*2. One long-carriage typewriter
*3. One executive typewriter
4. Miniature filing outfits or practice sets
5. Filing cabinets
6. Key-driven calculators
7. Crank-driven calculators
8. Ten-key adding machines
9. Full-keyboard listing machines
10. Stencil duplicating machines
11. Direct-process duplicating machines
12. Mimeoscope

---

* Desirable equipment but may be omitted if the money available for the purchase of equipment is limited.

13. Styli
14. Transcribing machines
15. Paper cutter
16. Letter opener
17. Stencils and masters
18. Carbon
19. Typing paper
20. Duplicating paper
21. Stationery and envelopes
22. Correction fluid
23. Practice telephone
24. Copy holders
25. Staples and staple remover
26. Dictionary and other reference books
27. Small office supplies such as paper clips, pins, scotch tape, package labels, paste, rubber bands, shears, and so forth

Teachers sometimes find it difficult to determine which office machines should be included in the clerical-practice course. Obviously teachers would be ill-advised to select expensive, complicated machines, machines whose operation is extremely simple and can be learned quickly, machines which will soon become obsolete, or machines which are highly specialized and should usually be learned on the job. Any equipment selected should be similar to the machines found in today's business offices and should teach basic operating techniques. Low-cost, hand-operated models can be used to teach basic techniques, but teachers agree that the unit in office machines should include some electric models. In the business office the students are much more likely to encounter the fully automatic models of the rotary calculator than the semiautomatic or manual models. If only one type of adding machine is to be purchased, the ten-key adding machine should be selected in preference to the full keyboard. Because of the frequency with which both the ten-key adding-listing machine and the calculator are found in the business office, instruction on both of these types of machines should be considered an essential part of the office machines unit. Transcribing machines should also be included in the course. If at all possible, there should be a typewriter for each student. If the business department has no duplicating equipment, the instructor may be able to utilize the duplicating machines in the school office when teaching this unit. Probably a great deal of time should not be devoted to instruction on the stencil or gelatin duplicators as they are rapidly being replaced by the spirit and offset duplicators.

The equipment should have a reputation for dependability and low-cost maintenance service which is readily available. Most teachers prefer machines for which instructional materials are already available. If it is impossible to purchase those office machines needed for the clerical-practice course, the school may wish to consider renting these machines until such time as funds are available for their purchase.

Methods of Teaching Clerical Practice

Clerical practice may be taught by one of four methods—the battery plan, the rotation plan, the integrated or model office plan, and the cooperative plan. In the battery plan, sufficient machines, equipment, and supplies are available to enable all students to work on the same unit at one time. The battery plan makes more economical use of the teacher's time in the classroom than do most other methods. Since all the students are working on the same unit, the teacher can give instruction on a group basis rather than on an individual basis. It is also possible that students may progress more rapidly because class time is utilized effectively. However, very few schools are able to teach the course by the battery plan as it necessitates a considerable investment in machines and other equipment. A few of the technical high schools in some of the large cities do offer comptometer courses and calculating-machines courses under the battery plan.

The rotation plan provides for individual instruction on each unit. The class is divided into small groups with each group working on a different unit. Therefore the teacher must instruct each group individually. When the students in one group complete the work on that particular machine, they rotate to the next machine or the next unit of work. This system calls for very careful advance planning on the part of the teacher so that the groups are set up according to a workable rotation plan. Because so many different types of learning activity are taking place at once, job instruction sheets are frequently used to save time.

Under the rotation plan office and machines training may be offered with a relatively low investment in equipment. It is also more economical than the battery plan in that all equipment is constantly in use throughout the course. Since instruction is given on an individual rather than a group basis, the plan allows for greater flexibility in providing for individual differences. However, many teachers feel that the rotation plan does not often result in the development of a high degree of skill on any one machine. Also, much more teaching skill is required to handle the classroom situation because of the number of different activities taking place at one time. Frequently the teacher finds it impossible to give instruction to all those students who need help with their problems and has to resort to such methods as requesting the more capable students to work with those who need assistance. From the teacher's point of view this procedure may be satisfactory, but it is questionable whether the plan is beneficial to the superior student. The rotation plan is undoubtedly the most widely used method of teaching clerical practice today.

Beginning teachers sometimes encounter difficulty in setting up rotation plans for their clerical- or office-practice course. The steps involved in developing a rotation plan are as follows:

1. Determine the pieces of equipment and instructional units in the course, the number of students who can be assigned to each simultaneously, the estimated number of students who will be enrolled, and the total instructional periods. Any periods which are to be used for class discussion, guest speakers, films or field trips should be subtracted from the total number of periods available for rotation.

2. Determine the number of instructional periods possible for each student. Multiply the number of pieces of any one kind of equipment by the number of students assigned to each piece of equipment. The resulting figure is then multiplied by the number of rotation periods. The total rotation periods divided by the number of students will give the number of rotation periods for each student for each unit.

3. Since one or two students more than the number specified by the teacher as the maximum may be assigned to the course, it is wise to make an allowance for this possibility when first setting up the rotation schedule.

4. Total the periods for each unit and make any adjustments necessary for ease of operating the rotation schedule.

5. Keep related activities in the same block of instruction. For instance, typing production jobs on business forms, papers and letters, and duplicating all involve the use of the typewriter. If not all stu-

dents have typewriters, then better results may be secured by putting all activities involving typewriting into one block in the schedule.

An illustration of a rotation schedule following these steps is shown in Exhibit 7.1.

EXHIBIT 7.1

Developing the Rotation Schedule

Step 1: Six units—5 calculators, 5 ten-key adding machines, 5 transcribing machines, 3 electric typewriters, 5 filing sets, 5 practice sets in record keeping, 1 stencil duplicator, 1 spirit duplicator

Estimated number of students—30
Periods available for rotation (two-semester course)—120

Note: In this course 160 periods are available for instruction. Twenty periods a semester have been reserved for class discussion of units in personality development, telephone manners, office etiquette, grooming, films and filmstrips, demonstrations, speakers, and field trips.

Equipment	Students Assigned Simultaneously	Total Students Assigned
5 calculators	1	5
5 ten-key adding machines	1	5
5 transcribing machines	1	5
3 electric typewriters	1	3
5 filing sets	1	5
5 recordkeeping practice sets	1	5
1 stencil duplicator	1	1
1 spirit duplicator	1	1
		30

Step 2: Pieces of one kind of equipment × students assigned simultaneously × number of rotation periods = total rotation periods ÷ by number of students = rotation periods for each student on each unit

Calculators	$5 \times 1 \times 120 = 600 \div 30 = 20$
Ten-key adding machines	$5 \times 1 \times 120 = 600 \div 30 = 20$
Transcribing machines	$5 \times 1 \times 120 = 600 \div 30 = 20$
Electric typewriters	$3 \times 1 \times 120 = 360 \div 30 = 12$
Filing sets	$5 \times 1 \times 120 = 600 \div 30 = 20$
Recordkeeping	$5 \times 1 \times 120 = 600 \div 30 = 20$
Stencil duplicator	$1 \times 1 \times 120 = 120 \div 30 = \ 4$
Spirit duplicator	$1 \times 1 \times 120 = 120 \div 30 = \ 4$

Step 3: Total periods—make any necessary adjustments at this time

Unit	Total periods
Calculators	20
Ten-key adding machines	20
Transcribing machines	20
Electric typewriters	12
Filing sets	20
Recordkeeping	20
Stencil duplicator	4
Spirit duplicator	4

Step 4: Arrange the units into related instructional blocks.

Instructional Block	Periods
A. Calculators	20
B. Ten-key adding machines	20
C. Transcribing machines	20
D. Filing sets	20
E. Recordkeeping	20
F. Electric typewriters ⎫	
F. Stencil duplicator ⎬	20
F. Spirit duplicator ⎭	

Step 5: Prepare a rotation schedule showing the number of each instructional block and the students assigned to the instructional block. Each student is assigned a number and can determine by looking at the schedule the unit to which he is assigned each week. The first two weeks and the last two weeks of each semester are not included in the rotation plan as these are the periods which will be devoted to special group activities and class discussions.

INSTRUCTIONAL BLOCK	FIRST SEMESTER			SECOND SEMESTER		
Weeks:	3-6	7-10	11-14	3-6	7-10	11-14
Calculators	A 1- 5	B 6-10	C 11-15	D 16-20	E 21-25	F 26-30
Ten-key adding machine	B 6-10	C 11-15	D 16-20	E 21-25	F 26-30	A 1- 5
Transcribing machine	C 11-15	D 16-20	E 21-25	F 26-30	A 1- 5	B 6-10
Recordkeeping	D 16-20	E 21-25	F 26-30	A 1- 5	B 6-10	C 11-15
Filing	E 21-25	F 26-30	A 1- 5	B 6-10	C 11-15	D 16-20
Electric typewriter						
Stencil duplicator	F 26-30	A 1- 5	B 6-10	C 11-15	D 16-20	E 21-25
Spirit duplicator						

Note: Electric typewriting, stencil duplicating and spirit duplicating will be included in the same unit.

The letters refer to the instructional unit; the numbers following, to the students assigned to that unit. Thus during weeks 3-6 in the first semester, students 1, 2, 3, 4, and 5 are assigned to instructional unit A, calculators, etc.

A master plan should be prepared indicating the rotation periods, the students assigned to each period, and the activities which they will be performing. The plan should be prepared just as soon as the teacher knows the equipment available and the number of students which are to be assigned to the course. Then there is no confusion later when the students rotate from one instructional block to the next. With the schedule prepared for the entire semester, students can readily see the importance of keeping up to date with their work. In such a system, it is obviously impossible to permit a student to remain on any one instruction block beyond the designated period as the equipment will be needed by the next student assigned to it.

The integrated or model office plan attempts to simulate office conditions in the classroom by integrating knowledges and skills already acquired. Students are given job assignments similar to those they would encounter on the job. Teachers who use the integrated or model office plan point out that this teaching procedure emphasizes the importance of production of work that meets office standards, provides an opportunity for students to work cooperatively in completing these job assignments, and makes it possible to teach students to apply good work habits in the production of these jobs. Under such a plan it is obvious that the students must have had training on all the office machines included in the course before they can participate successfully in an integrated program. A student cannot produce work that meets acceptable office standards unless he has been trained to operate the machine prior to undertaking a simulated office job.

The integrated office plan frequently creates many instructional problems. It is difficult to determine just how long students will take to complete the various activities assigned to them. Some jobs that involve very little learning may take a disproportionate amount of the class time which should be spent on jobs that would be more meaningful to the students. Because much of the work may consist of jobs that are to be used either by the school or by the community, the quality of the work may be stressed at the expense of correct techniques. It is sometimes difficult to provide for the lower-ability students. Everyone wants his work done by the most capable students. Consequently, the students who least need extra practice in the production of office jobs are often the persons who must devote the most time to such work. Thus it is clear that, no matter how carefully the teacher plans the work, the integrated or model office plan still represents an artificial situation. Office conditions may be simulated, but they can seldom be duplicated.

Most clerical-practice teachers use the rotation plan of teaching clerical or office practice. A careful study of their teaching procedures might reveal that they are using a combination of teaching methods. For instance, the unit in filing may be taught to the entire class as a group. In this case the teacher is employing the battery plan of instruction. The work on office machines may be taught by the rotation plan. Finally when typing, duplicating, or mailing jobs are turned over to the clerical-practice class for completion, the teacher will probably use the integrated plan. The various teaching procedures may be combined effectively within one course if the work is carefully planned.

The cooperative plan of teaching clerical or office practice is most often found in city schools. In this situation, one semester is ordinarily devoted to instruction in clerical-practice jobs such as filing, machine operations, duplicating, and machine transcription. The second semester the students are assigned to work in business offices in the community. The plan operates much like the cooperative training program in distributive education described in Chapter Twelve and the same principles apply. In cities where business firms are willing to cooperate, a highly satisfactory training program can be developed. During the first semester, students are taught how to do the clerical jobs they are expected to perform in the business office. The second semester they are given an opportunity to apply the skills and knowledges that they have learned in an actual business setting. The situation is realistic and, if the students are rotated through various types of clerical jobs in the business office, the learning can be very meaningful.

State and City Programs
in Office and Clerical Practice

A comparison of the objectives and course content of clerical practice and office practice as given in the various state courses of study reveals a wide range of subject matter and teaching procedures. In the state of Pennsylvania, clerical practice is a one-semester course. The *Business Education Manual* for Pennsylvania recommends that clerical students be given instruction in the function of, and drill in performing, the clerical work of the different departments which might be found in a large business organization. Rather than presenting the course content in broad units such as filing, business machines, record keeping, and the like, the content is based upon the clerical duties performed in the various departments. The general content of the course includes:

1. Instruction concerning the function of, and drill in performing, the clerical work of:

   a. The purchasing department

      (1) Handling purchase requisitions
      (2) Keeping files of catalogs, price lists, and card files
      (3) Writing requests for quotations
      (4) Writing and placing purchase orders
      (5) Handling acknowledgments of orders
      (6) Using follow-up devices
      (7) Recording in the purchase-order register
      (8) Making requests for credit
      (9) Filing reports of damaged goods
      (10) Filing reports of over and under quantities received

   b. The receiving department

      (1) Handling freight arrival notices
      (2) Checking content slips
      (3) Using the vendor's invoices
      (4) Using bills of lading
      (5) Using notifications of goods received
      (6) Filing requests for a tracer of overdue goods
      (7) Handling freight bills
      (8) Recording incoming shipments

   c. The stock and stores department

      (1) Using bin tickets
      (2) Writing stock requisitions
      (3) Writing *Condition of Stock* notices
      (4) Writing *Rejection of Purchased Goods* slips
      (5) Handling material requisitions
      (6) Writing inventory sheets

   d. The shipping department

      (1) Duties and qualities of the good shipping clerk
      (2) Packing goods to be shipped
      (3) Marking packages to be shipped

(4) Advantages and disadvantages of shipping by:
    (a) freight
    (b) express
    (c) parcel post
    (d) airmail
    (e) truck
(5) Studying and using shipping rate books
(6) Making C.O.D. shipments by the various services

f. The billing department

(1) Writing, computing, copying bills
(2) Mailing out bills
(3) Verifying or checking the accuracy of bills

g. The cash-handling department

(1) Identifying legitimate money
(2) Detecting counterfeit money
(3) Techniques of making change
(4) Care of cash and cash statements
(5) Writing bank-deposit records
(6) Handling and recording vouchers
(7) Recording in the cash-receipts journal
(8) Recording in the cash received by mail record

h. The posting department

(1) Posting systems and machines
(2) Preparation of ledger cards and debit or credit media
(3) Recording in the sales journal
(4) Recording in the accounts-receivable journal
(5) Recording on ledger and statement cards
(6) Filing accounts-receivable records

i. The time and payroll departments

(1) Recording and filing wage-rate records
(2) Writing individual time cards
(3) Writing and using job tickets
(4) Writing and using payroll exception reports
(5) Writing and using piecework reports
(6) Compiling and writing the payroll
(7) Writing payroll checks
(8) Writing individual payroll records
(9) Planning the cash payroll
(10) Preparing a currency break-up sheet
(11) Writing the memorandum of cash for payroll sheet

j. The accounts-payable department

    (1) Receiving and checking incoming invoices

    (2) Computing discounts

    (3) Writing the accounts-payable voucher

    (4) Recording in the voucher and check registers

    (5) Filing vouchers and checks until the due date

    (6) Obtaining signatures and mailing checks

k. The credit and collection department

    (1) Learning credit policies

    (2) Using credit reports

    (3) Using salesman's credit reports

    (4) Making credit inquiries

    (5) Using commercial credit-agency reports

    (6) Using *Credit Granted* forms

l. The mailing department

    (1) Learning the use of machines in the mailing department

    (2) Keeping the *enclosure missing* register

    (3) Keeping the *mail expected under separate cover* register

    (4) Learning and using postal rates and services

    (5) Preparing the outgoing mail

m. The personnel department

    (1) Learning the policies and functions of a personnel department

    (2) Handling applicants

    (3) Filing the employment applications

    (4) Using and filing the medical-examination records

    (5) Using and filing reference request forms

    (6) Using transfer records

    (7) Using *Left Our Service* forms

n. The filing department

    (1) Indexing

    (2) Filing

    (3) Using filing forms and equipment

o. The cost department

    (1) Using the cost-data envelope

    (2) Collecting and filing cost data

p. The statistical department

    (1) Learning what are statistics

    (2) Making statistical summaries

(3) Preparing graphical representation of statistics

(4) Using machines and devices common to the statistical department

q. Messenger service

(1) Learning the qualities of an efficient messenger

(2) Learning city geography and locations

2. Special drills in handwriting

These drills should be based on improvement needed. At frequent intervals pupils should write specimens of their handwriting and teachers should point out illegible letters and figures. Pupils should then practice, out of class, writing exercises. English, history, and other notes may be graded by the clerical-practice teacher for quality of handwriting.

3. Special drills in the mathematical calculations

Stress the fundamental processes, fractions, decimals, aliquot parts, percentage, and discounts.

The state of Virginia has prepared a *Guide for Vocational Office Training* to be used by the teachers of that state. It recommends that the vocational office course include units in the ten-key and full-keyboard-type adding machines; rotary, key-driven, and printing calculators; posting machine; machine transcription; filing; office duplicating; and special typing problems. The *Guide* outlines both a vocational office-training program which includes cooperative office-work experience and a clerical office-practice course which is offered solely on a prevocational basis.

The Virginia *Guide* suggests that thirteen, sixteen, or nineteen students constitute a desirable class size in either vocational office training or clerical office practice as this number of students may be accommodated easily with a limited number of machines when the rotation plan is used. The *Guide* presents two illustrations of rotation schedules, one for a 100-hour course accommodating fifteen students and the other, a 120-hour course for twelve students. These two rotation schedules are shown in Tables 7.2 and 7.3.

In Washington, D.C., office practice is described as a course "for teaching the knowledges and routine procedures that generally characterize clerical duties, and to familiarize students with specific procedures in office work." The underlying aim is the development of

TABLE 7.2

MASTER ROTATION SCHEDULE—100 hrs.   5 Rotation Intervals
(15 Students)   20 Hours Each

Interval	Student Numbers and Rotation Sequence by Intervals				
1	1- 2- 3	13-14-15	13-14-15	4- 5- 6	7- 8- 9
2	4- 5- 6	1- 2- 3	1- 2- 3	7- 8- 9	10-11-12
3	7- 8- 9	4- 5- 6	4- 5- 6	10-11-12	13-14-15
4	10-11-12	7- 8- 9	7- 8- 9	13-14-15	1- 2- 3
5	13-14-15	10-11-12	10-11-12	1- 2- 3	4- 5- 6

INSTRUCTIONAL UNITS

A Adding Machine	B Duplication	C Rotary Calculator	D Transcribing Machine	E Typewriting Problems
(1) 10-Key, 10 hrs. (2) Full-Key, 10 hrs.	(1) Stencil, 15 hrs. (2) Spirit, 5 hrs.	20 hrs.	20 hrs.	20 hrs.

TABLE 7.3

MASTER ROTATION SCHEDULE—120 hrs.   6 Rotation Intervals
(12 Students)   20 Hours Each

Intervals	Students Numbers and Rotation Sequence					
1	1- 2	3- 4	5- 6	7- 8	9-10	11-12
2	11-12	1- 2	3- 4	5- 6	7- 8	9-10
3	9-10	11-12	1- 2	3- 4	5- 6	7- 8
4	7- 8	9-10	11-12	1- 2	3- 4	5- 6
5	5- 6	7- 8	9-10	11-12	1- 2	3- 4
6	3- 4	5- 6	7- 8	9-10	11-12	1- 2

INSTRUCTIONAL UNITS

A Adding Machine	B Duplication	C Rotary Calculator	D Transcribing Machine	E Typewriting Problems	F Posting Machine
(1) 10-Key, 10 hrs. (2) Full-Key, 10 hrs.	(1) Stencil, 15 hrs. (2) Spirit, 5 hrs.	20 hrs.	20 hrs.	20 hrs.	20 hrs.

Source: Part III, Teaching Guide for Vocational Office Training, Suggested Content, Instructional Procedures, and Achievement goals for Virginia High Schools, Business Education Service, Division of Vocational Education, State Department of Education, Richmond, Virginia, 1963.

good work habits, cooperative attitudes, and good personal traits. The objectives of the course are:

1. To give information useful in handling problems encountered in office work

2. To increase knowledges of office organization and clerical procedures

3. To initiate and improve specific clerical skills

4. To provide a practical foundation for later vocational use by office workers

5. To give practice in meeting clerical production standards

6. To promote job interchange and to build an appreciation for standards of efficiency and business ethics

The units of study with their suggested time allotments are:

I.	Office Organization	1 week
II.	Techniques of Handling and Receiving Callers	2 weeks
III.	Procedures in Handling of Mail	2-3 weeks
IV.	Statistical Reports	2-3 weeks
V.	Office Use of Telegraph Services	1-2 weeks
VI.	Banking Facilities for the Office	1-2 weeks
VII.	Planning Itineraries	1-2 weeks
VIII.	Office Reference Books	1-2 weeks
IX.	Integrated Office Problems	3-4 weeks

In the Dallas schools, office practice and clerical practice are considered the "finishing or polishing-off" courses in the vocational training program. The rotation plan used in Dallas consists of six work cycles, containing six work-station blocks and two units for the class as a group. The plan was designed for a ninety-day semester and a class of twenty-four students. The six work cycles are divided into six work-station blocks of twelve days' duration, each running concurrently. The students are divided into six groups with four students in each group. The six instructional blocks include:

Block I (4 students)	Days
Ten-key adding machine	3
Full-keyboard adding machine	3
Key-driven calculator	3
Crank-driven calculator	3

Block II (4 students)

Mimeograph and mimeoscope	3
Gelatin or fluid duplicator	3
Dictating machine	3
Transcription machine	3

Block III (4 students)

Electric typewriter	6
Manual typewriter	6

Block IV (entire class)

Financial transactions and mailing services	12

Block V (entire class)

Composition of business letters	12

Block VI (4 students)

Work in school offices	12

The rotation plan used in Dallas is shown in Table 7.4.

TABLE 7.4

Dallas Rotation Plan—Office Practice

Duration		*Learning Experiences*					
5 Days		Entire Class—Registration and Orientation Program					
		Block I	Block II	Block III	Block IV	Block V	Block VI
72 Days	Cycle 1	Group A	Group B	Group C	Group D	Group E	Group F
(for 6 work	Cycle 2	Group B	Group C	Group D	Group E	Group F	Group A
cycles	Cycle 3	Group C	Group D	Group E	Group F	Group A	Group B
of 12 days	Cycle 4	Group D	Group E	Group F	Group A	Group B	Group C
each)	Cycle 5	Group E	Group F	Group A	Group B	Group C	Group D
	Cycle 6	Group F	Group A	Group B	Group C	Group D	Group E
9 Days	Entire Class——Discussions, Films, Field Trips, and Remedial Work						
4 Days		Final Examination Period					

Source: Business Education for Secondary Schools (Dallas, Texas: Dallas Independent School District, 1955), p. 120.

In Florida the clerical office-practice course includes units in essential traits and knowledges, typewriting activities, filing, office machines, and other nontyping skills. Nontyping skills include projects designed to improve the fundamental skills and knowledges of arithmetic, penmanship, English, punctuation, and spelling; techniques of handling the mail, using the telephone, sending telegrams, receiving visitors, arranging transportation, performing banking activities; and instruction in the "periphery" skills of collating, arrangement of materials, and the development of efficient work habits.

From the foregoing illustrations it is clear that a rotation plan works best when the same amount of time is allotted to each block of instruction, so that each group of students is ready to rotate at the same time. Some teachers accomplish this result by combining units that they feel do not require so much time as some of the more extensive units. For instance, if a school had very limited facilities, the teacher might set up some simple plan in which all the material to be covered would be included in three major areas with six weeks devoted to each area. Electric typewriting, statistical typing, and machine transcription might be combined in one area; duplicating and filing in another; and such topics as telephone usage, reference books, mail services, and record keeping in another. If eighteen persons were enrolled in the course, six students would be assigned to each area and each group would rotate every six weeks.

Specific Teaching Suggestions

No course is more challenging to the business teacher than is clerical, secretarial, or office practice. Not only is the content of the course widely varied, but much of the instruction must be highly individualized to meet the needs of each student in the class. Since there may be as many as four or five types of learning activities taking place at one time, it is important that the teacher develop as many time-saving instructional devices as possible. The following teaching suggestions are designed to make most effective use of the students' and teacher's time:

1. Have the students assist in administrative details of the class. They will be required to handle these details in an office. Assign students to such tasks as:

   a. Distributing materials

   b. Collecting materials

   c. Keeping attendance records

   d. Making requisitions for additional supplies

   e. Filing finished assignments

f. Serving as time-keeper

g. Serving as payroll clerk

h. Serving as office manager for the week

i. Serving as receptionist—receiving visitors, answering inquiries

2. Have specific jobs that the students are to complete for each unit. The students should know exactly what they are expected to do, how to do it, and when it is to be completed.

3. Do not require all students to complete all the units in the course. Many authorities believe students who show unusual skill in some areas should be allowed to specialize in those areas and thus develop a high degree of skill in them. Though all students should be expected to complete a certain minimum number of units —and they should know exactly what those units are—extra credit should be given to those students who are able to complete additional units and who put forth the effort to do so. However, these units should include additional learnings and should not represent simply more practice at the same level of difficulty as the basic units all students must complete.

4. Use job instruction sheets in those units where they are practical. Many of the jobs in clerical practice can be taught through the use of job instruction sheets. These sheets free the teacher to move about the class and work with any individual needing her help. No time is lost starting work at the beginning of the period. The job instruction sheet is particularly valuable in office-learning activities. The job sheets should identify the machine or unit to which it applies, the texts or manuals students are to use, and the supplies needed. In addition, it should indicate the jobs or assignments to be completed together with a step-by-step breakdown of the procedures to be followed. It may also call attention to special points needing emphasis and list review questions at the end. A job instruction sheet for performing the card punch operation is given in Exhibit 7.2. The job sheets may be typed and duplicated by the students in the duplicating units and filed for use as needed.

5. Demonstrate the operation of each of the office machines. The teacher should be careful to follow the same step-by-step presentation given in the job instruction sheets.

6. Use information sheets or handouts to supplement the text. These sheets may cover a wide range of topics such as grooming, work habits, personality traits, office equipment and supplies, trends

EXHIBIT 7.2

Job Instruction Sheet: Card Punching Operation*

Equipment: IBM 26 Printing Card Punch (program drum has card with entire field of 12 punches)

Materials: IBM cards, IBM Keyboard Exercises for IBM Card Punching Machines, IBM Reference Manual for 24 Card Punch— 26 Printing Card Punch

Directions: First read pages 5-11 and 13 in the IBM Reference Manual. Then make two cards for each line in Lesson 1. (The two cards can be put together for checking purposes.)

Steps	*Key Points*
1. Plug in machine.	1. Fan the cards before stacking and placing in hopper.
2. Stack cards at side of machine.	2. Cards are placed in hopper face forward, 9s down, and are fed front card first.
3. Place cards in hopper on right of machine; turn on main-line switch.	
4. Depress release key.	3. The release key is depressed to make sure the star wheels are at one on the program drum.
5. Depress feed key *twice*.	
6. Turn on automatic switches and print cards.	4. The cards are punched at the first station at the right. When the second card is fed to the machine, the first card is "registered" into position for punching.
7. Place first three fingers of right hand on "home keys" 4, 5, 6.	
8. Depress keys in line one.	
9. At the end of the line, reach up with middle finger to depress dash-skip key.	5. Finger "one" controls 1, 4, 7. Finger "two" controls 2, 5, 8. Finger "three" controls 0, 3, 6, and 9.
10. When you are ready to punch the next-to-last card in the lesson, turn the automatic switches off.	6. Do not space between groups of numbers.
11. Punch the last two cards.	7. After the card is punched, it automatically stacks in card stacker at left.
12. Depress the release and register keys alternately to remove cards.	8. Automatic switches should be turned off when you are ready to punch the next-to-last card so no blank cards will be stacked in the stacker.
13. Turn print key off.	
14. Turn mail line switch off.	
15. Remove cards from stacker. Remove cards from hopper. Unplug machine.	

* *Business Education in the Secondary School, Bulletin* D-3 (Illinois Curriculum Program, 1963), p. 137.

in filing and records retention, telephone manners, recent developments in telephone and telegraph services and equipment, office etiquette, and tips to the job applicant. Masters or stencils may be prepared in the duplicating unit. An illustration of an information sheet is shown in Exhibit 7.3.

7. When possible, use practice sets in such units as filing and clerical office typewriting. Use of these practice sets will save the teacher countless hours in the preparation of instructional material and will, at the same time, provide excellent practice activities for the students.

EXHIBIT 7.3
Information Sheet: Your Salary—Where Does It Go?

Many people today actually do not know how much they earn. They can tell you how much their "take-home" pay is, but they do not fully understand all the deductions made from their checks each week or each month. While different companies make deductions for many different items including pension plans, purchase of government bonds, life insurance, and hospitalization, the two biggest items deducted from your salary check will undoubtedly be for federal income tax and for F.I.C.A.

In determining how much to deduct from your salary for income tax, the salary clerk consults a tax table prepared by the federal government. The amounts in the table represent approximately 18 per cent of your salary after allowance for exemptions. You may count yourself as one exemption. A married man supporting a wife and two children would be entitled to four exemptions. Before computing the withholding tax, $13 is deducted from your salary for each of your exemptions. A single person would be entitled to only one exemption or $13 would be deducted from his salary before computing the withholding tax. If you earn $100 a week and are single, then your withholding tax would be computed on the basis of 18 per cent of $87 or $15.66.

An "exemption" is considered to be a person dependent upon the wage earner for his livelihood. If you are working in an office and your husband claims you as one of his exemptions at his place of employment, then you cannot claim yourself as an exemption. You would report no exemptions, and your withholding tax would be computed on the basis of 18 per cent of your entire salary. Thus if you were earning $100 a week, your tax would be $18. The more exemptions a wage earner has, the smaller is his withholding tax. Each exemption reduces the weekly withholding tax by about $2.34 (18 per cent of $13). Over 50 per cent of the amount deducted for income tax is used by the federal government for the national security.

The letters F.I.C.A. stand for Federal Insurance Contributions Act. This deduction provides the worker with insurance in which the pension received upon retirement is only one part of the coverage. The F.I.C.A. tax or, as it is generally known, the social security deduction, is computed at the rate of 3⅝ per cent of your salary. Beginning in 1966 it will be computed at the rate of 4⅛ per cent; and in 1968, at 4⅝ per cent. The social security tax is deducted on the first $4,800 which a person earns in a year. If your salary is more than $4,800, you will be required to pay no social security tax on the amount you earn over $4,800. The federal government provides tables showing the amount to be deducted from your salary for the social security tax. You can check the accuracy of this deduction by computing 3⅝ per cent of your salary. Thus if you earn $100 a week, your social security tax would be $3.63.

The amount you may expect to receive when you reach sixty-five is dependent upon the average monthly salary you earn from age twenty-one until retirement. The salaries of the five years in which you earn the least are deducted. Once the average monthly salary has been determined, your monthly allotment is computed in this manner: (*a*) 55 per cent of the first $110; (*b*) 20 per cent of the amount over $110; (*c*) 7 per cent of the sums of a + b; (*d*) amount received is the sums of a + b + c. Thus with an average monthly salary of $400, your social security allotment would be figured this way: 55 per cent of $110 = $60.50; 20 per cent of $190 = $38; 7 per cent of $98.50 ($60.50 + $38) = $6.90. Your social security allotment would be $105.40 ($60.50 + $38 + $6.90).

If the husband is the person receiving this allotment, his wife would receive half this amount when she reaches sixty-five. If her husband dies, her allotment would be increased to three-fourths of the amount he had been receiving plus an additional 10 per cent. In addition she would be entitled to a death benefit of three times the monthly allotment, but not to exceed $255. Additional benefits are provided if the father dies leaving children under eighteen.

In 1935, just before the Social Security Act was passed, only one out of every ten persons over sixty-five could support himself. By 1975, only one out of every ten persons over sixty-five will not be able to take care of himself financially. This is the protection your F.I.C.A. tax offers you.

8. Rotate the members of the class through the various units. In most clerical- and office-practice courses limitations of equipment and supplies make such a procedure necessary.

9. Provide special drills for the improvement of the fundamentals

whenever necessary. Obviously there is not time in the clerical-practice course to reteach the fundamentals. Furthermore, this should not be necessary. However, since much of the clerical work in the business office does involve handwriting, spelling, and simple computations, it is important that each student master these fundamentals. Many teachers give their students a test on the fundamentals early in the course to determine those areas in which each student needs further drill. Students whose handwriting is illegible may be given homework assignments designed to correct this deficiency. Others may be given assignments emphasizing spelling or arithmetic skills.

10. Teach good work habits. Teach students to analyze the job and determine how to do it with the minimum of time and motion. The students should learn to organize their work and to arrange their materials according to the principles of motion and time study. An illustration of teaching the folding of letters and their insertion in business envelopes according to the principles of motion and time study is given in Fig. 7.4.

11. Give the students practice in developing skill in proofreading. They should have acquired this skill in typewriting, but regardless of any previous training, too much emphasis cannot be placed upon checking one's work carefully in clerical practice.

12. Use pretests at the beginning of those units in which the students have had some previous instruction to determine any deficiencies and points needing particular emphasis. For example, if the course includes a unit on clerical typing, the teacher needs to know at the beginning of the unit the typing skill of each student. A student who can type only forty words a minute may need job assignments quite different from the student typing fifty to sixty words a minute.

13. Give the students practice in the correct use of the telephone. Every classroom should have a practice telephone. Excellent practice equipment and teaching materials may often be secured from the telephone company. Teletraining equipment and the materials developed in conjunction with it are excellent for teaching the correct use of the telephone.

14. Keep assignments flexible to allow for outside rush jobs, but avoid interruptions unless the jobs will contribute to the students' learning.

15. Give the students actual clerical jobs to perform when such jobs are available and meet the needs of the class. For instance, the jobs in the duplicating unit should usually consist of the preparation

EXHIBIT 7.4

Folding and Inserting Letters in Envelopes
(According to principles of motion and time study)

Steps	Procedures
1. Materials	1. No. 6 envelopes
	2. No. 10 envelopes
	3. Window envelopes
	4. Letters for envelopes
	5. Sponge
2. Working conditions	1. Work on a clear desk.
	2. Lay letters face up on flat surface in front of you. Riffle the sheets so they will not lay directly over each other.
3. Folding letters for No. 6 envelopes	1. Grasp lower edge of paper with left hand and bring it to ¼ inch of upper edge of paper.
	2. With right hand crease paper, moving from left to right.
	3. With the right hand fold the right edge about one-third the width of the paper and crease, using the right hand.
	4. With the left hand fold the left edge over slightly less than one-third the width of the paper. Crease with the left hand.
4. Inserting letters in No. 6 envelopes	1. Place envelope to left of the letters, face down with flaps to right.
	2. Grasp envelopes with left hand and insert the letter with the right hand.
	3. Insert the folded edge first, with the top of the letterhead at the left end of the envelope.
	4. Stack envelopes toward upper left in pile with left hand. Leave flaps open, address down.
	5. Expose gummed portion of flap and apply sponge with right hand.
	6. Take right hand and press gummed area. Slide envelope down with left hand. Repeat.
5. Folding letters for No. 10 envelopes	1. Lay letters face up on flat surface in front of you. Riffle the sheets so they will not lie directly over one another.

2. Fold the bottom edge of the letter with the left hand to within one-third of the distance from the top edge. Use right hand to crease fold, creasing from left to right.
3. Bring top edge down with left hand to approximately ¼ inch of first fold. Crease with right hand, from left to right.
4. Place letter vertically to right side with fold to right.
5. Take face-down envelope in left hand.
6. Insert letter with right hand, inserting the folded edge (last fold) first.
7. Seal as directed previously.

6. Folding letters for window envelopes

1. Lay letters face up on flat surface in front of you.
2. Take bottom edge of paper in left hand and fold up to point below inside address (approximately within one-third of distance from top of the paper).
3. Crease with right hand, from left to right.
4. With left hand turn the letter face down.
5. With left hand fold top third back to expose the inside address.
6. Crease with the right hand, from left to right.
7. Place letters to right side with fold to right.

7. Inserting letters in window envelopes

1. Vertically place envelopes face down to left of letters, with flaps open toward right.
2. Hold envelopes with left hand.
3. Turn all letters over with right hand. Be sure letters have been turned so that inside address is facing the desk.
4. Insert the letter with the right hand. Be sure letter is inserted so that inside address shows through window of envelope.

of materials that may be used in the class. A file clerk may be appointed once a week to file students' papers and other materials that have been removed from the files during the period. Other projects may include the duplicating of Christmas cards, programs for school functions, and stationery for the letter-production units.

16. Stress the importance of organizing work and keeping an orderly desk at all times.

17. Arrange for demonstrations of office machines and equipment from local equipment firms.

18. Invite guest speakers occasionally to speak to the class. Students are especially impressed by the comments of prominent local businessmen or women or of former students now employed in office jobs.

19. Use films or filmstrips when they can add to or re-enforce class discussion. Since such a wealth of visual aids is available, they should be previewed and carefully selected.

20. Have the students rate themselves on a personality rating scale both at the beginning and at the end of the semester. The teacher may also rate the students and compare the two ratings. Such charts may also be used in evaluating character traits and attitudes, office grooming, and office etiquette.

21. Keep an up-to-date resource file of reference material such as articles, pamphlets, and the like that are related to office work and that may prove helpful to the students.

22. Remember that clerical practice should be an activity course. Lectures and even class discussion should be kept to a minimum. Much of the information that the teacher may wish the students to know can be presented through the use of study guides or information sheets. Students should understand that they are expected to study these sheets and will be tested on them.

23. Toward the end of the semester have the students come to class dressed as they would dress in the business office. A discussion of good grooming and appropriate office dress is often ineffective unless the students are required sometime during the semester to come to class dressed as they would for the office.

24. Visit a modern, up-to-date office where students may have an opportunity to see the latest office equipment and data-processing installations and observe the types of jobs performed by office workers. The teacher should have made the field trip in advance so that she may give the students a preview of the equipment and activities

they are to observe. The field trip should be followed later by class discussion. Each class member may write a thank-you note to the firm, or the teacher may announce that the best letter will be signed by all the students and mailed to the company.

25. Have each student visit one office worker on the job to analyze his responsibilities and duties. In this assignment the student should compose a letter requesting an interview and prepare an interview sheet listing the questions he intends to ask. The student then either writes a report describing the procedures and jobs he observed in the office, or presents his report orally in class, depending upon the class time available.

26. Emphasize the importance of regular attendance on the job by requiring the students to make up any time lost through absences or tardiness.

27. Make effective use of the bulletin boards. Display illustrations of unusual letter styles, business forms, statistical reports, new equipment, and supplies. Post proofreading drills occasionally. Change the display frequently.

28. Develop in the students pride in their work by displaying outstanding papers on the bulletin board.

29. Assign committees to prepare posters, charts, and other materials for the bulletin board. Each committee should be given a topic for their bulletin-board display.

30. Give the students practice in filling out application blanks. Have two or three local businessmen interview some of the students before the other members of the class. The interviews should be followed with a discussion of the students' strong and weak points during the interview.

31. In some situations, clerical students may type correspondence and other materials for faculty members. This program requires careful supervision by the instructor, since students should only be assigned work which is related to the instructional units in clerical practice. They should not be expected to do an excessive amount of straight-copy typing, and in no case should they be asked to grade papers for other teachers.

Basic Units for a One-Semester Course

Many teachers find that, in a one-semester course, they are unable to cover all the units recommended in the foregoing discussion. The business teacher should always remember that it is far better to teach a few units thoroughly than to attempt to cover too many units without allowing sufficient time for their mastery. One of the frequent criticisms of the clerical-practice course is that it contains too many unrelated units, many of which either contribute little in the way of skills and knowledges the student will need in the office or else could be learned in a short time on the job. If it is necessary for the teacher to limit the clerical-practice course to a relatively small number of units, the units selected should give training in those skills which research has shown are performed with greatest frequency by clerical workers. Most clerical-practice teachers would agree that provision should be made for training in clerical typewriting, electric typewriting, machine transcription, duplicating, adding and calculating machines, filing, and possibly record keeping. The next question is this—what should be included in each of these units.

Clerical Typing. For the unit on clerical typing the teacher will want to select jobs that will develop skill in those typing activities commonly performed in the business office. Little time can be devoted to the further developing of basic typing skill and accuracy. Most of the time in the clerical-typing unit should be spent in production work—typing business forms and papers, form letters, statements, invoices, payrolls, statistical-typing jobs, and typing from rough-draft copy. With the increased use of automation necessitating the treatment of data in numerical terms, special attention should be given to developing accuracy and speed in the typing of numbers and in the production of statistical reports. Many of the publishing companies have excellent clerical-typing-practice sets which may be used in conjunction with this unit of work.

Electric Typewriting. If the students have not had previous practice on the electric typewriter, some time must be allotted for adjusting to the electric machine. The students should be given appropriate drill material and should be assured that they will not be expected to produce acceptable copy until they have had an opportunity to become familiar with the touch and operation of the machine. If only one or two electric typewriters are available, the teacher may wish to reserve these machines primarily for the typing of stencils, masters, and other jobs that are to be used in the school.

Duplicating Machines. Although multilithing is continuing to gain popularity with businessmen, most schools are equipped to teach only stencil and direct-process duplicating. However, the 1956 report of the Office Publications Company entitled *The Office Equipment Industry* indicates that of the total duplicating machines in use at that time in American business offices, spirit duplicating machines outnumbered offset machines 5 to 1 while the stencil machine outnumbered the offset 4 to 1. The jobs assigned in this unit should gradually increase in difficulty and as far as possible should consist of material that will be used by the class or by other departments in the school system. The first job should be a straight typing job such as typing job-instruction sheets, examinations, or form letters. The next job might involve the use of the Mimeoscope. If the teacher has been unable to secure printed forms for the typing unit, the students might prepare invoices, statements, and payroll forms as a part of their work in this unit. The next job might be the typing of a statistical report or financial statement. Many teachers include at least one job on the typing of a stencil for a program. This requires careful layout so that the material appears in the program correctly when the sheets are folded. Other advanced units may include postcard assignments and color mimeographing.

Many times students know how to type a stencil or Ditto master correctly and how to operate the machines, but they do not develop any judgment in the selection of the best duplicating procedures for a given job. Students should know what process is best suited for each job, the importance of using the correct type of duplicating paper, the number of copies that can be obtained by the different processes, how to clean stencils, and the importance of correctly labeling and filing stencils and masters for future use.

Other Office Machines. In order to select wisely the office machines to be included in the clerical-practice course, the teacher needs to know what office machines are being used in the local business offices and in nearby communities. Many surveys have been made of the machines used in different cities, but the results have varied considerably. In St. Louis a survey showed that the office machines most commonly found in the business offices were typewriters, dictating and transcribing machines, adding machines, calculators, bookkeeping machines, and duplicating machines. In a similar survey in Pittsburgh, it was concluded that the most important machines to be taught in the Pittsburgh schools were the key-driven calculators, full-keyboard adding machines, bookkeeping machines, telephone switchboard, ten-key adding machines, check protectors, mimeographing machines, transcribing machines, and adding machines. Many teachers have indicated that they believe students should receive instruction in the following basic office machines: adding machines of the listing type, calculating machines of the nonlisting type, stencil duplicators, direct-process duplicators, and machine-transcribing equipment. In many schools the unit on office machines is limited to instruction on the adding machine, full-keyboard calculator, and ten-key adding machine.

It has been found that at least 50 per cent and in some cases as much as 90 per cent of the figure work in the office is made up of addition, about 40 per cent of multiplication, and only 5 per cent of subtraction and 5 per cent of division. Therefore it is probably safe to conclude that the ability to perform relatively simple operations on these basic machines is all that is necessary in many clerical jobs. It should be remembered that enough instructional time must be allotted to each machine for the development of skill in these basic operations. Thus a teacher is wiser to include several weeks' instruction on two or three kinds of office machines than to attempt to include a few periods of instruction on several different kinds of machines.

Machine Transcription. Students who are good typists will especially benefit from instruction in machine transcription. If possible, the best typists should be assigned to the machine-transcription unit early in the semester. This procedure will give the poorer typists an opportunity to gain additional typing practice before undertaking machine transcription. All too often students dislike machine transcription because they have never been taught the correct techniques in the operation of the machine. It is assumed that, because the student can type, knows English, and can hear, he can coordinate these skills in the production of mailable copy without any specific instruction in the operation of the transcribing machine. Students are no longer expected to develop the ability to transcribe shorthand notes in this fashion; neither should they be expected to develop machine-transcription skill without proper instruction. If it is impossible for the teacher to work with the student when he begins the machine-transcription unit, the teacher should prepare a job sheet instructing the student in the operation of the machine and in the correct transcription techniques. The student should not be expected to type mailable letters immediately. He must first learn to react to an oral stimulus without having a printed copy or shorthand notes to serve as a visual aid. He must learn to listen to one group of words while typing another. He must learn to watch for corrections and to correctly judge the placement of the letters on the page. In addition, he is expected to decrease the length of the listening periods until he is at last able to keep the carriage of his typewriter moving smoothly. Showing the student how to operate the machine or requiring the student to transcribe one record is not teaching machine transcription. The following suggestions are often helpful to the student:

1. Listen to the first record before you start to transcribe. This will help you become accustomed to the dictator's voice, his mannerisms, his method of giving instructions, making corrections, and so forth.

2. Be sure that the transcribing machine is adjusted properly. The volume should be no louder than necessary. Avoid too high a pitch as this may distort the speaker's voice.

3. After you have listened to the record, set your machine for a sixty-space line and begin to transcribe. Listen to a few words, then type. As you continue practicing on the record, try to decrease the length of your pauses. Your goal should be to develop sufficient skill to be able to type constantly even while you are listening to the dictator's voice on the record. Do not correct your errors. (The first record should be straight copy rather than letters.)

4. Transcribe this same record again, trying to improve your technique and to decrease the length of time required to transcribe the record.

5. Transcribe the second record (an article), correcting your errors. Do not make a carbon.

6. Transcribe the third record. This record will consist of a series of short letters. Be careful to observe the length of each letter on the indication slip and set your margins accordingly before starting to type.

Several different persons should dictate the records so that the students will become accustomed to the different voices. After the student has practiced the first record, he should time himself and try to reduce the time required as he continues his practice. If at all possible, the final records to be transcribed should consist of material that is actually to be mailed. This makes a realistic office-job situation and impresses upon the student the importance of building a usable skill in machine transcription. The students should be given a definite objective toward which to work in this unit. In the office the transcription of one record an hour is usually considered an acceptable transcription rate. Although the clerical students may not be able to obtain sufficient practice during the machine-transcription unit to attain this goal, they should be told how many letters they should complete within the period so that they can judge both the quality and quantity of their production.

Filing. A study of the filing activities of general clerical workers has revealed that much of their filing duties consist of sorting, indexing, and coding by the alphabetic and numeric systems. Therefore if the teaching time is limited, the alphabetic and numeric systems of filing should be taught in preference to other filing methods. A number of excellent practice sets are available in filing. In addition to the basic rules of filing alphabetically and numerically, the student should be taught to sort materials properly for filing, to code and index, to charge out materials properly, to follow up material, to cross reference, to type file labels, to prepare folders and guides, and so forth.

Porter[7] states that the most common weaknesses of file clerks reported by employers are that they: (*a*) take too long to adjust; (*b*) have little or no skill; (*c*) cannot handle the problems of subject filing; (*d*) have poor production standards; (*e*) are inconsistent in their filing, resulting in expensive mistakes; (*f*) lack adequate training; (*g*) lack skill in handling any system other than alphabetic; (*h*) have no knowledge of how to look for items which have been misfiled; (*i*) make errors in filing foreign names; (*j*) are inaccurate in filing numbers; and (*k*) feel that their job is unimportant. Teachers can do much to correct these weaknesses.

In teaching filing, special attention should be given to the errors which students most frequently make. Students may have thoroughly learned the rules for alphabetic filing and yet make errors in their filing exercises either due to carelessness or inaccurate reading. Students tend to read names according to the way they are accustomed to seeing them spelled. They must be taught to read carefully and to scrutinize names closely to avoid such careless errors. A common error in numerical filing is caused by the transposition of figures. The teacher should try to determine the cause of filing errors, or much class time may be wasted drilling on rules students have already learned.

Filing practice should not be limited to the sorting and filing of cards. Students should be given production practice in filing letters.

[7] Leonard J. Porter, *Business Teaching Aid No. K-1* (Englewood Cliffs, N.J.: Prentice-Hall, Inc., 1961).

They should be given problems in which they must make decisions regarding the proper indexing and coding of such material. Emphasis should also be placed on finding materials. Production practice (under timed conditions) should include both filing materials and locating materials already filed.

With the present emphasis on records management, it is important that the teacher be familiar with new developments in this area and include this information in the filing unit.

Clerical Record Keeping. Instruction in clerical record keeping is handled in many different ways, largely depending upon the amount of time available for this instruction. In the small school, some teachers, recognizing the importance of this information to the office worker, include a unit on record keeping. The teacher cannot possibly anticipate how much training his students will need in this area because of the different practices followed by large and small businesses. Regardless of these differences, all students need to understand the importance of accuracy in business forms and the purpose of each. Items which may be included in even a short unit in record keeping are the handling of petty cash, keeping cash records, reconciling the bank statement, recording purchases and sales, recording charge transactions, preparing payroll forms, and computing payroll deductions such as withholding tax, F.I.C.A., and insurance. Excellent practice sets are available for clerical record keeping, and the teacher may find that many students who could never successfully master bookkeeping are able to learn the basic principles of record-keeping.

Stenographic or Secretarial Practice

Stenographic or secretarial office practice is designed for those students who have completed one or two years of instruction in shorthand and typewriting. The basic objective is to give the students training in those activities which they will be required to perform as stenographers in a business office. However, the specific objectives vary widely from school to school. Many of the objectives listed for clerical practice would apply equally well to the stenographic practice course. Like the clerical-practice course, stenographic office practice attempts to integrate previously acquired knowledges and skills and to apply them in practical office situations. Considerable attention is usually given to the development of good work habits, attitudes, and personality. A major portion of the time is often devoted to building transcription skill. In an effort to simulate conditions in the office, toward the latter part of the course some dictation may be given in "office style" so that the students will be accustomed to the manner in which they will be given dictation on the job.

It is difficult to draw a distinct line between the course content offered in the different types of office-practice courses. A comparison of high-school textbooks in clerical and stenographic office practice reveals that some of the units included in clerical practice that are omitted in stenographic office practice are handwriting, clerical typewriting, clerical arithmetic, adding and calculating machines, cash records and forms, and payroll activities. The stenographic office-practice text may include these units not found in the clerical practice text: receptionist duties; dictation and transcription; secretarial equipment and supplies; letter writing; composition and typing of minutes, manuscripts, and business reports; business-reference sources; travel and itineraries; the employer's financial and personal records; and banking transactions. Many of the units are identical in both texts, and others are closely related.

Objectives of Stenographic Practice

Many of the objectives of the stenographic practice course will be similar to those given for the clerical-practice course. In addition, however, emphasis will be placed on the development of further skill in transcription and the application of this skill to practical stenographic problems. The objectives given in the *Business Education Manual* for Pennsylvania illustrate the close relationship between these two courses:[8]

1. To attain a proficiency sufficient to meet the demands of the general office worker, and to inculcate a desire for absolute accuracy, neatness, and thoroughness
2. To develop those personal qualities which are essential for success in the business world
3. To develop reasonable skill and facility in the solution of practical business problems
4. To acquaint the pupil with the fundamental principles of various business forms and the application of those principles to practical problems

[8] *Business Education Manual*, Bulletin 271, Commonwealth of Pennsylvania, Department of Public Instruction, 1949, pp. 166-68.

5. To give the student a knowledge of business and office organization from the point of view of the office worker
6. To develop a practical knowledge of the operations of various voice-writing machines
7. To develop a practical skill in the use of listing and nonlisting machines
8. To develop a practical knowledge of and appreciation for the methods of duplicating materials under varying conditions
9. To emphasize the development of proficiency in the commonly used filing systems
10. To help the student develop further skill in production typing
11. To help the student compose business letters
12. To give the student training in applying for a position
13. To increase the ability to transcribe shorthand notes accurately, giving attention to punctuation, spelling, context sense, and arrangement
14. To apply stenographic skill to practical stenographic and secretarial problems through the medium of laboratory assignments

Units in Stenographic Practice

It has already been pointed out that many units taught in clerical practice are also included in stenographic practice. Most teachers, however, devote considerable time to improving their students' transcription skills. The units designed to meet the objectives in stenographic practice as set forth in the Pennsylvania *Business Education Manual* include:

1. Duplicating
   a. Teach the proper use of multiple carbons, erasing, and drawings.
   b. Teach the correct procedure in typing master copies for liquid and gelatin machines, also how to correct errors and make drawings and color work.
   c. Teach stencil typing, drawing and color work, and correction of errors.
   d. Specific organization charts may be planned in the steps of operating the duplicating machines (stencil, liquid, and gelatin).
2. Filing
   a. Teach the basic principles of indexing and filing with aid of the miniature filing sets and cross-reference sheets.
      (1) Alphabetic filing

      (2) Subject filing
      (3) Geographic filing
      (4) Numeric filing
      (5) Card system and follow-up

3. Clerical Information
  a. Teach students how to answer letters without dictation.
  b. Teach students financial duties, negotiable instruments, and bank-reconciliation statements.
  c. Teach students the use of telephone and telegraphic services.
  d. Teach students typewriting techniques.
    (1) Preparation and correction of rough draft
    (2) Summaries, reports, and legal instruments
    (3) Fill-in form letters, billing forms, and cards

4. Secretarial Information
  a. Help students build transcription speed.
    (1) Punctuation review; grasping meaning of sentences; spelling; syllabication; proofreading; drills on thought phrases before transcription.

5. Personal Information
  a. Qualifications—help students develop accuracy, dependability, cooperativeness, acceptance of responsibility, acceptance of criticism intelligently, loyalty, courtesy, initiative, stability, industry, cheerfulness, neatness in work, physical endurance, imagination, good grooming, punctuality.
  b. Office conduct—that is, stress office hours (punctuality), use of working time, personal habits, note taking, meeting of callers, office etiquette, etc.
  c. Office reference books—help students to become familiar with postal guide, shipping guides, credit-rating books, special dictionaries and directories, secretarial handbook, etc.
  d. Discuss securing and holding a position.
  e. Discuss the relationship between employer and employee.
  f. Cover miscellaneous information.
    (1) Mailing procedures (routing and dispatching)
    (2) Assisting in taking inventories
    (3) Proofreading material
    (4) Attending switchboard
    (5) Transportation procedures
    (6) Travel information
    (7) Business organization

6. Business-Machine Study
  a. Adding listing machines
    Full keyboard and ten key (fundamental processes—adding, subtracting, multiplication, and division)

b. Calculating or nonlisting machines
Crank driven and key driven (fundamental processes—adding, subtracting, multiplication, and division)
c. Dictating and transcribing machines
Transcribing and dictating
d. Bookkeeping machines
Posting and billing, using distribution sheet, accounts receivable, accounts payable, general ledger, trial balance
e. Miscellaneous devices
(1) Consecutive numbering machine
(2) Check protector
(3) Electric typewriter
(4) Long-carriage typewriter
(5) VariTyper
(6) Telephones (intercommunication systems)
(7) Paper cutter
(8) Multiple punch
(9) Various paper fasteners

Specific Teaching Suggestions for Stenographic Practice

Many of the teaching suggestions given for clerical practice may be used equally effectively in stenographic practice. Other suggestions that may be helpful to the teacher include the following:

1. If possible, use the workbook that accompanies the text. It will provide business forms as well as excellent problem-solving assignments.

2. Avoid too much class discussion, recitation, and lecture presentation. On the high-school level, stenographic practice should be primarily an activity course in which the students are given an opportunity to build skill in the production of office-type jobs.

3. Use case problems which have occurred in business offices as the basis of class discussion when teaching the importance of correct attitudes, judgment, cooperation, and other related qualities needed by office workers (a number of actual cases are given on pp. 317-321).

4. Try to obtain letterheads now out of date or on which printing errors have been made from local business firms and printers. This quality of paper makes it possible for the teacher to require neat erasures.

5. Do not correct all the students' transcripts. They should be taught to be responsible for locating their own errors. Check production tests carefully.

6. Keep two folders for each student, one containing work which has been corrected and the other, work in process. Students should be responsible for checking their papers in these folders and correcting all errors in their transcripts.

7. Give the students extensive practice in building transcription power. Emphasize the importance of both speed and accuracy in transcription.

8. Give the students definite goals toward which to work. Time the students on their transcription production so that they may determine their rate of progress. Indicate either in words a minute or number of letters what their transcription rate should be throughout the course.

9. Give the students some practice in taking office-style dictation and in transcribing such material.

10. Teach the students how to make the most effective use of their shorthand notebooks.

11. Teach the students good work habits, both in taking dictation and in transcribing.

12. Emphasize the importance of good tools with which to work in transcription—good quality paper and carbon, the right kind of typing erasers, erasing shields, and so on.

13. Stress the cost of wasted supplies caused by careless errors.

14. Emphasize the importance of proper care of all equipment. Students should assume responsibility for cleaning the type on their machines and putting on new ribbons when needed without any reminder from the teacher.

15. Occasionally interrupt students during the transcription period. Office workers are constantly being interrupted in their work and must learn to cope with such interruptions.

16. See that all students have an opportunity to build skill in transcription on electric typewriters.

17. Do not limit the dictation and transcription practice to business letters. Include practice in completing business forms, preparing business reports, typing minutes, and the like.

18. Emphasize spelling. Include drills on commonly misspelled words, proper names, homonyms, and words often confused. Have the students keep a list of their spelling errors and test them on these words occasionally.

19. Review important principles of grammar, punctuation, capitalization, and typing usage.

20. Emphasize the importance of accurate proofreading. Give the students proofreading drills, if necessary.

21. Provide some practice in the composition of letters and telegrams.

22. Teach the students to record all instructions in shorthand in their notebooks. Do not always provide written instructions or permit them to rely upon memory. Avoid repeating instructions.

23. Occasionally dictate letters and other material to be mailed.

24. Review the correct techniques for inserting multiple carbon packs, chain feeding of envelopes, correcting bound manuscripts, and other specialized typing problems.

25. Toward the end of the semester have the students come to class for one week dressed as they would in the office.

26. Assign one student a week to the "model secretarial desk." This student should see that the desk is equipped with all necessary supplies and should be responsible for doing any stenographic or secretarial work that the instructor may assign to her. Insofar as possible, these jobs should consist of actual office work rather than simulated office activities.

27. During the latter part of the course, assign some dictation projects that will integrate many of the skills and knowledges that have been emphasized in the course. A carefully designed office-style dictation project will provide practice not only in transcription of office-style dictation, but also in such skills as typing multiple carbons, making corrections, selecting correct titles in the inside address and salutation, handling all kinds of letter problems such as additions, deletions, postscripts, carbon-copy notations, and in composing letters and telegrams.

28. Occasionally collect the students' notes of material dictated during the class period and have them transcribe these notes several periods later. This procedure is an excellent way to impress upon the students the importance of writing accurate shorthand outlines.

Evaluation

Whether the course offered is office machines, office practice, or clerical practice, grades should be based on the achievement of specified objectives. If personal qualities and attitudes are to be considered in grading, then the margin of improvement should be considered. In evaluating rates of production, the teacher should consider office standards as well as the progress that the individual student has made. Stuart gives the following production standards often used by business offices, especially in metropolitan areas:[9]

Copying	60 to 70 words a minute
Addressing envelopes	216 to 288 an hour
Four-line fill-in	118 to 158 an hour
Stencils (8½ x 11) paragraph typing	3.5 to 4.7 an hour
Transcription from records	128 to 241 lines an hour
Filing or pulling cards	300 an hour
Form letters	12 to 16 an hour
Form letters with carbons	10 to 14 an hour

Other reports, however, indicate that many companies have not adopted specific standards for measuring the performance of clerical workers. The study of seventy-five businesses in the Forth Worth-Dallas area revealed wide variations in the standards reported. Many companies gave spelling and arithmetic tests, but there was little agreement upon the level of performance considered acceptable. Some companies said not more than four or five errors should be made on the spelling test administered to applicants for clerical positions. Others required 90 to 95 per cent accuracy. There was no agreement upon the standards in arithmetic calculations required of clerical applicants. Only twenty-five of the companies reported that they had a system for measuring office production of clerical and stenographic workers.

In this particular survey the areas in which clerical workers were most often reported deficient in order of frequency were spelling, English, typing, knowledge of office routines and basic business information, arithmetic, and shorthand skill. Teachers should consider the findings of such studies both in determining course content and in evaluating students in clerical and stenographic practice.

All too often standards appearing in business publications are not realistic. Because the nature of office practice, clerical practice, and stenographic practice varies from school to school, the teacher of this course must often develop his own production tests and determine the standards students will be required to meet on them. Thus standards will be dependent upon the importance of the particular

---

[9] Esta Ross Stuart, "Relation Between Office Standards and Classroom Standards," *UBEA Forum* (May 1949), p. 29.

unit, the time allotted to it, and the duties students will be expected to perform in the business offices where they will be employed. If the teacher is able to secure minimum employment standards from these companies, he may be able to utilize these standards in arriving at the minimum requirements for some of the units in the course.

Teachers follow widely different practices in grading students in office practice. Many teachers use the point system. In this system each job to be completed is assigned a specified number of points. Students are required to complete a minimum number of points on each unit, and the jobs that must be completed are designated. Each job must be completed satisfactorily for the student to earn the points assigned to it. If the job is unsatisfactory, the teacher may require the student to repeat the job without credit, repeat the job for credit, do another job, or she may deduct a number of points from those assigned the job. Individual grades are assigned on the basis of total accumulated points. For example, 1,000 points might be required for an "A," 800 for a "B," 600 for a "C," and so on. This plan has the advantage of being definite and objective. However, the entire grading plan must be worked out before the beginning of the course.

Other teachers require the students to complete a certain number of jobs for a "C," additional jobs for a "B," and more advanced jobs for an "A." Still others assign grades on the basis of the quality of the work. The problem of grading in office and clerical practice can be greatly simplified if all jobs are set up in advance and the students are told what they must do to meet the requirements of the course.

It is recommended that teachers consider the desirability of administering civil service examinations and the National Business Entrance Tests to their clerical and stenographic students during the final weeks of the course. Teachers using the National Business Entrance Tests can compare the performance of their students with that of other students throughout the country. In addition, students who pass the tests receive a certificate of proficiency which they may show to prospective employers when they are applying for an office position.

Projects and Questions for Discussion

1. You are teaching a clerical practice course for the first time. Your principal seems to think that the main objective of the course is to give the students practice in completing typing and duplicating jobs for his office and for other members of the faculty. You are glad to have the

students get some practice in these areas, but you feel they need to learn other skills such as filing and machine transcription also. How would you handle this situation with your principal?

2. Some of your students in clerical practice can complete their assignments much more rapidly than other members in their group. What would you do with these students when they have completed their work?

3. You have carefully prepared job-instruction sheets for each unit included in your clerical-practice course. The directions are detailed, and a step-by-step breakdown is given of the procedures students are to follow. In checking their work, you find many of the students have failed to follow the directions given on the job-instruction sheets. You have called this matter to their attention several times, but they still continue to disregard the directions. What would you do?

4. If you were teaching a secretarial-practice course, do you think it would be beneficial to assign students to various members of the faculty for dictation and transcription practice? Why or why not? If you did follow this practice, what controls do you think you would need to exercise over the plan?

5. Helen Young is enrolled in your clerical-practice course. During the second week you discover that she has not had the prerequisite of beginning typing, but is now enrolled in the course. Since many of the units involve typing activities, you are afraid Helen will have difficulty with the course. When you discuss the matter with the principal, he is reluctant to approve your request that Helen drop the subject. He feels that, because of the financial situation in Helen's home, she will need the course to help her secure employment upon graduation. What should you do?

6. You are teaching in a small high school with an enrollment of 200 students. The school is located just 10 miles from a large manufacturing city. You are now teaching one year of shorthand and one year of typewriting. Your principal says next year you may add a course either in clerical practice or in secretarial practice. Which would you choose? Why?

7. Miss Wilson, the other business teacher in your school, says that there is no justification for ever failing a student in clerical practice. Do you agree?

8. Your school has no machines available for instructional purposes other than manual typewriters and a mimeograph and Ditto located in the principal's office. Do you believe you could offer a one-semester course in clerical practice that would be beneficial to the students?

9. Miss Wilson is teaching clerical practice in your school. She in-

sists that the students on the calculating- and adding-machine unit must have every problem correct, or she will not accept their work. If a student has an incorrect answer in any problem, he must rework the entire unit. Do you think Miss Wilson is unreasonable to insist on 100 per cent accuracy on the machines units?

10. Because there are only two transcribing machines in the office-practice room, you have been permitting students to work on their assignments in this unit before and after school and during the lunch hour. One day you observe that many of these students are typing rough drafts of the dictation and later retyping the letters in acceptable form. The students know they are not supposed to retype the dictation as you consider this a time-consuming, wasteful habit. When you question them, they say it is the only way they can complete the unit within the time allotted to them. How can you be sure these students will be able to transcribe machine dictation rapidly and accurately without first making a rough draft? What steps would you take to solve this problem?

11. You have been permitting your students to check the answers to the problems on the business-machines unit with the answers in the teacher's key. Students are expected to rework those problems which are incorrect before taking a production test on each of the machines. One student who had all the practice problems on the ten-key adding machine correct missed over half the problems on the test. The other day you noticed that, instead of checking his answers to the problems he had worked on the calculator, this student was copying the answers from the key. Would you discontinue the practice of permitting students to check work with the key? If not, what would you do?

12. What units do you believe should be included in a one-semester clerical-practice course? In a one-semester secretarial-practice course?

13. What additional units would you include in a school in which clerical practice is a one-year course? What additional units would you include in secretarial practice?

14. Your school has no office machines other than typewriters. You are to teach clerical practice next year, and the principal has said you may have $2,000 to purchase equipment. What machines would you select?

15. If you were teaching clerical practice in a small high school with limited equipment, would you use the battery plan, the integrated office plan, the rotation plan, or a combination of these plans? Why?

Office Case Problems

1. You are responsible for supervising the other girls in your office. One of the girls is extremely attractive, dresses well, and is particularly

well liked by all the junior executives in the organization. In fact, you feel she spends so much time chatting with them that she is unable to do her share of the work in the office and is not concerned about it. Her actions and attitudes are causing considerable resentment among the other girls.

You doubt that her services are worth the trouble she is causing. However, you know that if you suggest she be dismissed, the junior executives will all defend her and say that you are jealous of her popularity with them. What should you do?

2. You have been working late in the office in order to meet certain important deadlines. You have a new stenographer in the office who has been most cooperative and has worked with you several evenings in order to help you get the work done. On Friday evening she worked until 11:00 so that an important report could be mailed early Saturday morning. On Saturday you give her a typed copy of a letter and ask her to prepare a stencil of it and have the mimeograph operator run 200 copies on bond letterhead.

Saturday afternoon you go back to the office to get the letters in the mail and find that there is a typographical error in the letter. Since you need to get the letter out at once, you are in a quandary. The letter must be mailed this afternoon. The mimeograph office is closed, and there is no way for you to get the letter rerun. You dislike the idea of having 200 of your most important customers receive a letter with a typographical error. On the other hand, your stationery is costly, and there have been many complaints lately about materials being wasted. You also have the problem of the stenographer. You do not feel you should reprimand her since the error may have been caused by fatigue. What would you do?

3. You like your job very much. However, a year ago you were assigned a new boss. He has been with the company a little over a year. You have tried in every way possible to help him learn the business and to show him how to avoid problems he might have encountered otherwise. Now you find that he depends upon you more and more and is hesitant much of the time to risk his own judgment. In fact, you feel you are having to make many decisions for which you should not be responsible.

You have about decided that your boss does not have the drive and initiative required for his job. You do not know what to do about it. The obvious solution would be to leave the company. However, after some checking you have found that you are making a great deal more money in your present capacity and have a better position than you can duplicate unless you were to leave the city in which you now work. You do not want to do this as you own your home. What would you do in this situation?

4. You are a very good friend of the boss's wife, Mrs. Hill. You have many interests in common and often spend evenings and weekends together when Mr. Hill is out of town. Because you have an unusually close relationship with both your boss and his wife, you are in their home frequently.

Lately you have been disturbed about one of Mrs. Hill's habits which is becoming increasingly worse. More and more when you visit in their home, she criticizes her husband in front of the two of you which you find embarrassing and suspect that your boss does also. In fact, you often make excuses for not accepting invitations to visit them, and they are beginning to notice it. Your boss finally asks if he has offended you in any way. What should you say?

5. You are executive secretary to the president of your company. In this capacity you find that frequently you must work evenings and weekends. You have requested additional help and have been given another girl in the office. Even so, the situation has not improved much. Your boss calls on you at all hours of the evening and weekends to come to his home or the office to help him get out important work. He himself is the type of person who is consumed with his job. He has little family life and does not seem to realize that, as a widow with two children, you might like to be able to spend some time with them. On the other hand, he is always sending them expensive gifts, and they both adore him.

You are considered to have the best secretarial position in the company and have reached that level by hard work and persistence. You have no desire to lose the prestige and financial rewards you have earned. Now, however, you are beginning to question whether it is worth it— you have little family life and no prospects of the situation improving. You have suggested to your boss that he call on the other girl occasionally, but he says frankly he is accustomed to you and prefers your services. He simply cannot understand that others are not always as devoted to the company and their jobs as he is. You think your boss is wonderful, but you feel you yourself have gone way beyond the line of duty. Now you do not know how to put a stop to it. What should you do?

6. Your boss, Dr. Jackson, insists on scheduling appointments every half hour. In spite of your best efforts he is always getting way behind schedule. At 4:30 he has not yet seen his 3:00 appointment. At that point Mrs. Jones, who had an appointment at 3:30, tells you she cannot wait longer since she is to speak at a dinner meeting that evening.

When you suggest that she make another appointment, she says that she has no intention of making any more appointments with Dr. Jackson unless he keeps this one. Her patronage is valuable to your boss as she is influential socially and brings him a great many new patients. You call your boss on the intercom, and he says he will see her at once.

As soon as Mrs. Jones has gone in to see Dr. Jackson, the 3:00 appointment comes over to you and creates quite a scene. After all, she says, she has been sitting for 1½ hours and thinks it most unfair that, just because she is not an influential society woman, she must wait while persons with later appointments get preferential treatment. You try to explain why Mrs. Jones was permitted to see Dr. Jackson out of turn but the woman refuses to listen. What do you do now?

7. You are right out of college and have gone to work with the ABC Company. Miss Miles is in charge of your "indoctrination." After you have been working only a few days, you discover that she is trying to undermine your position, not so much with your employer, as to discourage you to the point of leaving your job.

For example, one day she changed some figures on the ledger after you had copied them onto the cards. Then she told you if you could not be more accurate, she would be forced to report that you were not satisfactory for the job. You consider neatness and accuracy in your work almost a religion; and when you are able to prove her deception, you take the problem to the office manager. He gives you no satisfaction at all. You would have quit at that point, but you need the job desperately and it is a good one.

After several weeks you begin to realize why Miss Miles has been acting as she has. She is insecure in her job. For financial reasons, she was forced to leave business college before completing her training. You appeared on the scene with a college degree, a major in secretarial science, and excellent recommendations. What would you do?

8. You have an assistant in the office who is a whiz in typing and shorthand. You have so much correspondence to get out that you wonder how you ever got along without her. However, occasionally when she is tired she is careless and makes errors. Whenever you call her attention to these errors, she becomes upset, always cries, and is unable to do much the rest of the day. You find this characteristic very upsetting, and it always has a bad effect on the other workers in the office. They like the girl and act as though you have been unreasonable about mentioning the errors in the first place. However, you do not think it wise to ignore them. The girl is a valuable worker but seems unable to control her emotions. What would you do?

9. Your boss likes to smoke cigars. Usually when he is giving you dictation he smokes them all the time you are in his office. You do not

mind cigarettes or even pipes, but cigars are very annoying to you because they irritate your sinuses. Frequently you have a bad sinus headache after you have been in the office with your boss and his cigar. What would you do?

10. Miss Hammond, who is responsible for materials in the files, frequently has a problem with one of the junior executives, Mr. Baldwin, who insists on keeping files in his desk long past the date on which he has promised to return them. He seems to think any material he takes from the files is his own personal property. When Miss Hammond objects, he points out that it is much more convenient for him to keep any files he is using in his desk drawer.

One day Mr. Allen, another junior executive, requests the file which Mr. Baldwin checked out over two weeks ago. When Miss Hammond asks Mr. Baldwin for the file, explaining that Mr. Allen needs it, Mr. Baldwin says he is not through with it and refuses to return it to her. What should Miss Hammond do?

Case Problems

1. You have been teaching a one-semester course in stenographic practice on the senior level for several years. Students enrolled in this course have had one year of shorthand and one year of typing. About half the students take second-year typing concurrently with secretarial practice. Your principal has just decided that he should apply for federal funds for the office-training program which were made available by the passage of the Vocational Education Act of 1963. He tells you that, according to the state plan approved by the U.S. Office of Education, you will need to begin making plans immediately for a cooperative office-training program. This program is to run for two semesters and will be open only to senior students enrolled in the stenographic program. Would the addition of this course require any other changes in your curriculum offerings and the year in which they are offered? What advantages do you see to such a cooperative program in office training? What problems do you anticipate? Specifically, what preparations must you make before the course is offered next fall?

2. This is your first year of teaching. The schedule which your principal mailed you indicated you would have one class in secretarial practice. Accordingly you spent several weeks preparing for the course and outlining the content you would include. The first day that you meet the class you discover that your course outline is not going to be suitable. Approximately half the students enrolled in the class have had no shorthand, although all of them have had one year of typing. Most of the students are now enrolled in second-year typing. Actually the course

is not a secretarial-practice course but a course in office practice. You are uncertain how to proceed. You do not know how to handle a class in which part of the students later hope to obtain stenographic positions while others plan to do clerical work. Develop a course outline showing how you would teach this course which must meet the needs of students with entirely different objectives.

3. You have twenty-five students enrolled in clerical training, all of whom have completed general business and one year of typewriting. The equipment in the clerical-practice room includes five miniature filing sets (alphabetic, geographic, subject, and numeric), four electric typewriters, a mimeograph, a Ditto, a mimeoscope, three ten-key adding-listing machines, three full-keyboard calculators, three transcribing machines, ten manual typewriters, and a large filing cabinet.

    a. Set up the rotation schedule you would use to teach a one-semester clerical-practice course under these conditions.

    b. Indicate the materials you would use to teach each unit.

    c. Indicate the job assignments you would require the students to complete in each unit.

4. Your principal has agreed that you may teach a class in clerical practice during the spring semester on an experimental basis. Since the course has never been offered before, the principal says he cannot approve the purchase of any textbooks until he is convinced there is a need for the course and that it will fulfill a need of the students in the school. Consequently, you are faced with the problem of having to develop your own instructional materials and duplicate copies for the students.

    a. Prepare a job-instruction sheet designed to introduce students to the electric typewriter.

    b. Prepare a job-instruction sheet for students to follow their first day on machine transcription.

    c. Prepare an information or "hand-out" sheet on the topic of good grooming.

    d. Prepare an information or "hand-out" sheet on the topic "Business Etiquette in the Office."

Suggested Readings

Archer, Fred C., "Practical Tips for Better Office Practice," *The Business Teacher*. New York: Gregg Publishing Division, McGraw-Hill Book Company, 1961. Special reprint.

————, *The Clerical Training Program in the Large High School*. New York: Gregg Publishing Division, McGraw-Hill Book Company, 1961. Special service brochure.

————, *Organizing the Office Practice Course*. New York: Gregg Publishing Division, McGraw-Hill Book Company, 1962. Special service brochure.

Collins, Marian Josephine, *Handbook for Office Practice Teachers*, Monograph 91. Cincinnati, Ohio: South-Western Publishing Co., 1954.

Cook, Fred S., "An Effective Office Practice Course for the Small High School," *The National Business Education Quarterly*, May, 1954.

Frisch, V. A., "*The Organization and Operation of a Clerical Practice Laboratory*, Monograph 68. Cincinnati, Ohio: South-Western Publishing Co., 1947.

Huffman, Harry, *Business Education World*, May, 1953 to March, 1954. Series of ten articles on clerical practice.

————, "14 Principles to Follow in Setting Up a Clerical Practice Course," *Business Education World*, September, 1953.

Job Instruction Sheets—Office Practices and Procedures: Filing; Machines (Adding and Calculating); Duplicating; Machine Transcription; Typewriting. University of the State of New York, 1955. Six sets of job-instruction sheets on the acquaintanceship level and the practical-use level of instruction.

Liles, Alton B. Parker, *Some Factors in the Training of Clerical Workers*. Thesis Abstract published by Oklahoma A. and M. College, 1947. Delta Pi Epsilon Research Award, Summary of dissertation completed at the University of Kentucky, 1947.

Miller, Martha L., "Fourth-Semester Secretarial Training," Business Teaching Aid No. Q-1. Englewood Cliffs, N.J.: Prentice-Hall, Inc., 1961.

Nicks, Earl G. and Robert J. Ruegg, *Methods of Planning for Office Practice* (Underwood Corporation, 1956).

Potter, Thelma M., "An Analysis of the Work of General Clerical Employees," *NABTTI Bulletin No. 37*, December, 1945.

Status Study of Cooperative Office Occupations Training Programs in the United States and Territories. Michigan Department of Public Instruction, Office of Vocational Instruction, Research Services.

Suggestions for Programs of Office Practice and Procedures. Cincinnati, Ohio: South-Western Publishing Co.

Tonne, Herbert A., *Principles of Business Education*, (2nd ed.), New York: Gregg Publishing Division, McGraw-Hill Book Company, 1954.

————, Estelle L. Popham, and H. Herbert Freeman, *Methods of Teaching Business Subjects*, Chap. 13, pp. 275-304. New York: Gregg Publishing Division, McGraw-Hill Book Company, 1957.

Training Clerical Employees, Report No. 578 (The Dartnell Corporation, 1963).

United Business Education Association, *Business Education Forum,* February, 1947-1964. Clerical practice issues.

Van Derveer, Elizabeth T., "Patterns of Performance for the Most Frequent Duties of Beginning Clerical Employees." Thesis Abstracts, Second Series, No. 1, New York University, 1952. Alpha Chapter, Delta Pi Epsilon.

White, Jane F. and Thadys I. Dewar, *Successful Devices in Teaching Clerical Practice* (J. Weston Walch, 1959).

III

THE
NONSKILL
SUBJECTS

As already indicated in the *Overview* to Part Two, the subjects considered in Part Three may often require special teaching techniques and procedures specially adapted to developing physical skills and abilities. Thus the teacher will at times continue, in these subjects, to use adaptations of many techniques and procedures already presented.

However, it is the belief of the authors that the subjects presented in Part Three will *best* serve their educational purposes if the teacher considers them *primarily* to require teaching methodology of the nonskill-development type. Thus the teacher should learn judiciously to devote a major portion of his teaching efforts to those techniques and procedures calculated to best achieve the many understandings, attitudes, and other mental developments associated with these subjects.

It should be understood that often the objectives of a given course, a given school, and a given teacher will require and will justify the treatment of a course as being primarily skill-development, whereas under other circumstances it might best be treated otherwise. Unless unusual factors intervene, though, the business teacher will do well to treat the skill-development factor as relatively minor in the teaching of the subjects presented in Part Three.

In one sense this simplifies the teaching of these subjects, since the rather specialized psychology of skill-development is absent or of less importance. Yet it raises another problem for the teacher: the natural interest and motivation that accompanies skill-development will be absent or less noticeable, and thus the teacher must give special attention to the proper planning for adequate motivation.

8

Teaching General Business

The Subject

Definition and Description of General Business. General business may be defined as a course dealing with the activities in which everyone engages either as a consumer of, a worker in, or a manager of a business. Topics such as the use of money and banking services, insurance, investments, business organization, and record keeping may be included in the course at a level of understanding of the high-school students for which it is designed. Also included may be a study of basic fundamentals such as arithmetic, spelling, and writing as applied to business activities, vocational guidance, and economic education. General business is a prevocational course that is of value for all high-school students regardless of their ultimate vocational choice.

Objectives of General Business. The objectives of teaching general business in the high school can be summarized into four principal goals:

1. To develop in the student a knowledge of those business activities which affect everyone regardless of economic status.

Everyone is a participant in business activities in the normal everyday course of living. It is the purpose in a course in general business to analyze these activities and to enable the student to understand, appreciate, and perform them in the best possible manner.

2. To develop in the student an ability to improve his competency as a consumer of business activities.

Everyone is a consumer of products of business. Through an improvement of consumer practices there should result an improvement of the activities of business enterprise and a consequent improvement of the welfare of the individual.

3. To develop in the student an understanding of the economic concepts under which our free-enterprise system works.

In order for an individual to be well educated it is necessary for him to understand those basic economic principles which affect his economic well-being, both as an intelligent citizen of the country and also as a consumer.

4. To develop in the student certain attitudes and appreciations with respect to our free-enterprise economy.

Too often in our schools, teachers have taken for granted certain benefits and advantages of our economic system and have failed to give students an opportunity to discover for themselves the many advantages that result from the economic system under which our country operates. This does not mean that students should be propagandized or indoctrinated. In a study of any economic system, in order to understand it, an analysis should be made of shortcomings as well as superior features. Teachers sometimes have neglected the latter, taking them for granted, and have only pointed out the former with the resulting danger of developing cynical attitudes and appreciations in students.

The Content of a General Business Course. There are several excellent textbooks in general business available for use by the business teacher. One thing common to most texts is the topics that are usually covered. Authors of the textbooks may give different treatment to the various topics or present the material differently but basically the units of subject-matter are as follows:

Subject-Matter Units Typically Taught in a General Business Course

I. The Individual's Relationship to the Business World
II. Money and Banking Services
III. Planning and Budgeting
IV. The Use of Credit Services
V. Savings and Investments
VI. Insurance and Economic Risk
VII. Travel Services
VIII. Transportation and Postal Services
IX. Communication Services
X. Finding and Keeping Business Information
XI. Government, Social, and Economic Relationships in Business
XII. Careers in Business and Occupational Information

Although at first glance the units of subject-matter in the foregoing list may appear to be highly technical for study by a high-school freshman or sophomore, the teacher must remember that the treatment of the several topics is not exhaustive, and that the authors of the textbooks attempt to relate the units to the everyday business activities that a high-school student may find himself experiencing. The objectives are to *familiarize* the student with and introduce him to the many and varied business activities that will have an important effect upon his life.

College Courses That Will Aid the Teacher in Teaching General Business. There are many college courses in which knowledges gained should be of invaluable aid in the teaching of general business in the high school. Such courses as introduction to business, accounting, economics, business organization and management, money and banking, marketing, and principles of investments are a few that should be especially valuable.

Careful preparation of notes taken in college courses in the areas mentioned above, combined with the saving of textbooks used in these courses as a basis for a permanent reference library, will be of great aid in teaching general business.

Instructional Materials

The Extent of Instructional Materials. The extent and availability of instructional materials for the teaching of general business is almost limitless. There are modern textbooks available which are supplemented by workbooks, teacher's manuals, practice sets, and tests. These textbooks are kept up to date through frequent revisions and are well illustrated and extremely teachable.

Another vast source of instructional material lies in films, filmstrips, pamphlets, and graphic illustrations which are made available to teachers and students through trade associations and business firms. Many of these materials are either free or available at a nominal cost so that the business teacher can build up an extensive library of supplementary instructional materials with little or no expense. These materials cover a wide range of topics but can be classified under the general heading of "economic appreciations." Consequently, teachers find these supplementary materials quite valuable for enriching the general business class.

Care should be taken by the teacher to carefully sift the material thus obtained to eliminate that which might be prejudicial or biased. There is such a wealth of material that the teacher can pick and choose only that which has true educational value and thus eliminate material that attempts to distort facts. Bibliographies of free and inexpensive instructional materials are listed at the end of this chapter.

Methods of Using Instructional Materials. There are many methods by which the various instructional materials available for teaching general business may be used to the best advantage. The textbook, of course, should be used as the basic guide for the course. This does not necessarily mean that the textbook material must be followed by the teacher and students in exactly the same order presented by the author. The teacher should feel free to change the order of presentation as he sees fit. The interests and aptitudes of the students in the class should be the determining factors in this matter. No one unit of subject-matter in general business is particularly dependent upon another. Thus, it is not necessary to master one unit before proceeding to another. There may be a logical presentation of subject-matter as indicated by the authors of the text, and it may well be that the teacher should follow the order of presentation as the simplest means of organizing the course. However, the teacher should not feel it mandatory and should experiment with different orders of presentation if it would appear more desirable from the standpoint of appropriateness and expediency. The text, then, should be used as a guide for the course, but not necessarily a rigid one.

Although all of the textbooks written for general business are rich in illustrative and textual material, the teacher will find it advisable to supplement the text with the many types of supplementary material mentioned above. These supplementary materials can be used in a variety of ways.

One highly desirable method is to enrich the teacher's method of presentation. It is stimulating to a class for the teacher to bring in new areas of knowledge that are beyond the scope of the textbook. Not only does it help to motivate and develop interest on the part of the students, but it also aids in developing in the students a respect for the knowledge of the teacher. Students like to have pertinent materials brought into the class discussion for which they see an application of the textual matter.

The use of an opaque or overhead projector to illustrate visually pertinent and up-to-date material related to a topic being studied is very effective.

For example, preparing a transparency for use on the overhead projector of material such as illustrated in Fig. 8.1 can be used effectively in teaching a unit on occupational information.

Another method of using supplementary instructional material is the development of a reference library for individual student and class projects, including displays of pamphlets and charts pertaining to the topic being studied. Reliance on the school library for sources of information for these types of activities is not wise, for often school libraries are woefully inadequate with regard to resource materials for business.

Supplementary instructional materials can also be used to motivate students who are unusually interested in a particular unit, as these students will have an opportunity to develop their interests further. This technique is also an excellent means of providing for individual differences in students.

The material should be made accessible to the student by having it placed in a filing cabinet appropriately filed by subject. If a filing cabinet is not available, it will be up to the teacher to use his ingenuity to provide some means of storing the material so that the

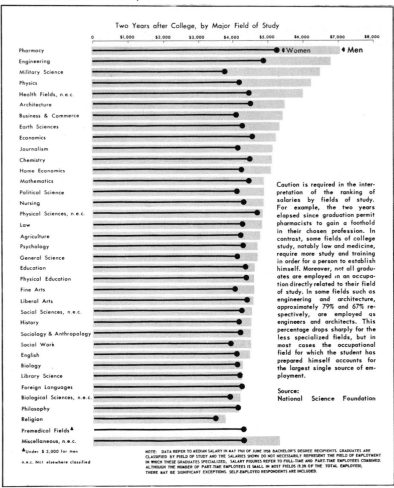

Caution is required in the interpretation of the ranking of salaries by fields of study. For example, the two years elapsed since graduation permit pharmacists to gain a foothold in their chosen profession. In contrast, some fields of college study, notably law and medicine, require more study and training in order for a person to establish himself. Moreover, not all graduates are employed in an occupation directly related to their field of study. In some fields such as engineering and architecture, approximately 79% and 67% respectively, are employed as engineers and architects. This percentage drops sharply for the less specialized fields, but in most cases the occupational field for which the student has prepared himself accounts for the largest single source of employment.

Source:
National Science Foundation

NOTE: DATA REFER TO MEDIAN SALARY IN MAY 1960 OF JUNE 1958 BACHELOR'S DEGREE RECIPIENTS. GRADUATES ARE CLASSIFIED BY FIELD OF STUDY AND THE SALARIES SHOWN DO NOT NECESSARILY REPRESENT THE FIELD OF EMPLOYMENT IN WHICH THESE GRADUATES SPECIALIZED. SALARY FIGURES REFER TO FULL-TIME AND PART-TIME EMPLOYEES COMBINED. ALTHOUGH THE NUMBER OF PART-TIME EMPLOYEES IS SMALL IN MOST FIELDS (8.3% OF THE TOTAL EMPLOYED), THERE MAY BE SIGNIFICANT EXCEPTIONS. SELF-EMPLOYED RESPONDENTS ARE INCLUDED.

Road Maps of Industry, No. 1454. © 1963 by National Industrial Conference Board, Inc. Used by permission.

Figure 8.1

Salaries of College Graduates
Two Years after College, by Major Field of Study

students may have access to it. It may be desirable to have the class aid in collecting material, store it, and file it. This could be an extremely worth-while class project. Care should be taken that the material is stored neatly and is properly replaced when it has been used so as to avoid the appearance of a cluttered and disorderly classroom. Besides the learning of subject-matter, this type of project has several other educational values such as instruction in filing, neatness, and responsibility.

The Community as a Source of Instructional Material. A rich source of instructional material for the teacher of general business is the community in which the school is located. Business activities and the results of business activities can be found everywhere. The local grocery store, telephone exchange, bus depot, drugstore, grain elevator, manufacturing concern are just a few of the many sources in a community to which the teacher may go to obtain supplementary materials for his class. No community is so small that business activity is nonexistent. Too often, teachers overlook the obvious business establishments in their local communities whereby knowledge obtained in the classroom can be seen in action. Look about you to see what is available and then use these sources to enrich your classes.

Methods of Teaching General Business

Problems in Methodology. Before taking up specifically the various methods of teaching that pertain to general business, we should first consider some of the problems that are involved in the methodology. If we can pinpoint these problems perhaps we will then be able to understand some of the difficulties teachers have in teaching this subject and should be able to appreciate better the need for some of the methods that are recommended.

First, it is fairly well established that business teachers in general prefer to teach the skill subjects such as shorthand, typewriting, and bookkeeping rather than the so-called nonskill subjects into which category general business falls. The reasons for this preference are that business teachers are usually better prepared for teaching the skill subjects, the teaching methods are very specific, and the results of instruction are obvious. It can be easily ascertained by a teacher whether a student is improving in his typewriting or shorthand ability. However, in general business where not only subject-matter knowledge is acquired but also where certain attitudes and appreciations are a desired outcome, it is difficult to measure the extent to which these latter disciplines are developed in the student. This situation can be frustrating to a teacher. Also, it is sometimes true that while teachers obtain sound subject-matter training in college courses that have application to the teaching of general business, they obtain little training in the methodology of teaching general business. When taking *skill* courses the prospective teacher can see approved methodology in action. When taking *nonskill* courses the prospective teacher does not get an opportunity to see methodology in action that would be appropriate for use in a secondary-school classroom.

The type of methodology that can best be used in teaching general business, such as informal discussion, is seldom seen in the typical college class. Thus, the prospective teacher has little or no opportunity to observe this type of method because he is not a participant in a discussion but a listener—a "jotter-downer" of notes and too often a "parroter" of the instructor's lecture.

This latter difficulty points to a second problem often experienced by teachers of general business. The emphasis placed upon the mastery of subject-matter knowledge in college courses is often so impressed upon the prospective teacher's mind that he will insist upon the same level of and degree of attainment on the part of his high-school students. There is probably no better way to destroy interest in a high-school general business class than to insist upon detailed mastery of the subject-matter. General business textbooks are full of detail. Too many teachers insist that their students master all of this detail, which in actuality destroys the chances of achieving the major objectives of the course. There is no implication here that knowledge of subject-matter is unimportant. It is important in its proper perspective. That perspective is *how the subject-matter knowledges may be used to understand the broader concepts to which they apply.*

A concept is a mental image or insight one has about an idea or a related group of ideas. The concept results from the knowledge one has about the idea and is reflected in his attitude and point of view toward the idea. Thus, factual knowledge without application of this knowledge in the development of a concept is meaningless.

For example, a teacher of general business in teaching about automobile insurance might be quite satisfied if his students have learned about the various kinds of auto insurance available and the particular function each serves. However, this information is important only to the extent that the student develops a concept of the risks involved in owning property and more important still, the concept of the sharing of economic risks.

To illustrate: Teacher A in presenting a topic on automobile insurance requires that his students memorize the various kinds of insurance available such as liability, comprehensive, collision, and so forth. A student can memorize these satisfactorily and can explain their function without having the slightest idea of the purpose of insurance. On the other hand Teacher B (who is much wiser) will develop with his students the idea of the sharing of economic risk through the medium of insurance and then determine what these various risks are. By this method of developing the concept of risk sharing he will develop mastery of subject-matter in his students as a matter of course.

A third and final problem that causes some business teachers to prefer not to teach general business is that, relatively speaking, this subject is much more difficult to teach than the skill subjects because of the methodology involved. The general business teacher in presenting a lesson must use primarily a class-discussion technique, which involves a great deal more preparation than does the drill and problem techniques typically used in teaching a skill. A teacher can hide inferior ability in the teaching of a skill subject much more easily than can an inferior teacher of general business because of the very nature of the class. In a typewriting class, for example, the teacher can assign work for the students to perform in class individually and the teacher can remain passive with respect to the teaching function. In a general business class the teacher must always be active in performing the teaching function and cannot hide his inadequacies (indefinitely) through class-time assignment.

So much then for the problems in methodology encountered by the teacher of general business. Let us turn to some of the specific methods that can be used.

The Discussion

Many business educators believe that the *best* method of teaching general business in the secondary school is through the use of the discussion technique. Undoubtedly it is one of the best procedures for learning and teaching, because not only does the learner have to acquire the subject-matter of a course, but he also must be able to use it effectively in communicating ideas and facts to others.

There are several different types of discussion techniques that may be appropriate for use in the secondary-school classroom. Some of the procedures are rather informal whereas others are highly formal. Although some of the formal discussion techniques can be used effectively with high-school students, it is probably true that the more informal techniques will be most successful.

Three main types of informal discussion are pertinent for use in the general business classroom. The first of these types can be called simply *classroom discussion.* In this type of discussion the entire class participates in the topic being discussed with the teacher guiding and directing the class. It is this factor of teacher direction and guidance that makes this type of discussion different from the other informal types. More will be said about this in later paragraphs.

A second method of informal discussion is the use of the *committee* or *round-table.* In this method, if it is used properly, a small group of students discusses a problem informally before a class in a conversational manner. The discussion is pointed up by the chairman of the committee; after the conclusion of the discussion by the committee the topic being discussed is referred to the students in class for contributions and questions.

To be effective the committee should meet together several times prior to their scheduled meeting to organize their presentation so that a definite direction and purpose can be achieved. Too often the use of a committee results merely in four or five students giving four or five reports with the use of small-group discussion becoming nonexistent.

In using the committee technique the teacher must assume the responsibility of working with each committee to see that the discussion objective is not lost. The teacher does not have to dominate by any means, but neither can he forego all responsibility for the guidance of learning. Committee techniques will fail unless the teacher properly supervises the group.

Group dynamics is a term used to describe a third method of informal discussion. In this method the discussion is not *directed* but is *guided* by the teacher. The instructor places the responsibility for gathering data, organizing information, making generalizations, and analyzing ideas almost entirely upon the group. It is probably the most challenging method for both student and instructor and is probably the most difficult method to use (and the most abused).

The group dynamics technique works best with a small group. It is highly structured in that there is a discussion leader, a recorder, and an evaluator or observer. The evaluator or observer does not participate in the discussion but sums up his reaction to the discussion at its termination, elaborating on such points as to the effectiveness of ideas brought out, the interaction between members of the group, and so forth. It is doubtful that this technique should be used constantly in a classroom, but it would perhaps be stimulating and interesting if used on occasion.

Teachers should be warned *not* to use this method unless they are thoroughly familiar with it. Too often teachers have attempted to use this technique without thoroughly exploring its proper use. There have been cases of teachers thinking that they were using group dynamics when actually they were using a hodge-podge of disorganized procedures. Consequently the method failed, and for this reason there are teachers and students who condemn the use of group dynamics as an ineffective method. Actually, the difficulty has not been with the method but rather with misconceptions of its proper use. To be used as a learning technique group dynamics must be thoroughly understood by both teacher and students before being used in the classroom.

Classroom Discussion

For a majority of teachers of general business, informal classroom discussion that is both teacher-guided and teacher-directed will be best. It is believed by many educators that discussion cannot be used effectively in large classes. It is the opinion and experience of the authors that the size of classes will not affect materially the degree of discussion. On the contrary, large classes may improve the quality of discussion.

The reasons put forth for the effectiveness of classroom discussion in small classes or groups only is that in this manner everyone will have an opportunity to participate. Also, in small groups the timid person may be willing to participate more often.

These reasons perhaps would be valid if it were considered necessary for everyone to participate every day in the discussion. If the discussion techniques are used the majority of the time in the classroom, then it is logical to assume that sometime during the semester everyone will participate. It does not always hold that in a small group the retiring student will tend to talk more. The retiring person will not be any more willing to speak up in a small group than in a large group. He is the problem of the discussion leader (teacher), and if the proper procedures are used he will assume his share of the participation in the class.

The following elements should be considered for effective participation in the discussion method.

Setting for the Discussion. The physical setting for informal discussion is highly important if the discussion technique is to be used effectively. If the classroom has movable furniture, desks should be arranged so that the participants may see each other. The teacher should define himself with the group so that the psychological barrier of a desk between the teacher and students is removed. Adequate blackboard space should be provided for use in listing discussion points or summarization of the discussion or illustration. Students participating should speak loud enough to be heard by everyone.

Another important factor in an effective discussion is the relationships among the students and the teacher. A friendly atmosphere must prevail with everyone having the feeling that he has something worth-while to report. Each contribution should be accepted as important. Such human characteristics as courtesy, tolerance, and attentiveness should prevail. The discussion should not develop around the theme of argument, but of enlightenment.

Techniques of Informal Discussion. Several major techniques are basic with respect to teacher action in using the discussion methods. In the majority of cases in classroom discussion the teacher should act as discussion leader starting, controlling, and pointing-up the group expression in such a way as to provide a common sense of achievement.

Considerable preparation should be made by the teacher before a topic is discussed in class. Judgment should be made as to the appropriateness and nature of the problem in question. Too many teachers fail in using the discussion techniques because of inadequate planning.

Successful discussion cannot start from scratch. Students cannot discuss intelligently without knowing something or at least having some conception about the topic being discussed—even though these conceptions are erroneous ones.

It is necessary, then, that prior to the discussion the teacher assign for reading the topic that will be discussed the next day. He should point out the particular areas of information that are important to the study. The teacher should then plan with considerable care the means by which he will get the discussion launched. It is easy to say merely "start discussing," but high-school students do not react or always cooperate in this way. *The teacher must develop a way to*

start the discussion that will stimulate and challenge the student.
Discussions seldom arise from direct, specific, or factual questions.
The teacher may think that he can start a discussion by asking the
class to "discuss the functions of commercial banks." Very little if
any discussion would be obtained through the use of this type of
direct question because the question calls for a specific answer rather
than the uses, values, and analysis of the activities of commercial
banks.

In starting a discussion, comparative, analytical, judgment, or
evaluative-type questions should be raised by the discussion leader
or teacher. The following types of questions are illustrative:

1. What economic problems would exist in this country if there
   were no banks?
2. John Jones does not have a checking account in a bank because
   he objects to the service charges he must pay. Therefore, he
   pays all his bills with cash. What difficulties do you see that
   he may encounter?
3. Harold Hughes will never borrow any money from a bank
   because he believes it is improper for a bank to charge interest.
   In addition he believes it is a poor practice to be in debt. What
   do you think about Harold's point of view?

The use of questions such as those listed above would result in the
teacher obtaining answers similar to those received from a direct
question approach. However, additional advantages would accrue.
The student would be stimulated to think through the various problems
involved and by so doing the various interrelationships in the
functions of commercial banks would be developed. In addition, the
students would be encouraged to participate in a discussion in which
their various ideas would be heard and evaluated rather than merely
"parroting" back some points listed in a textbook.

There are many pitfalls that may befall the discussion leader if he
is not aware of them—such dangers as sidetracking or getting off the
subject; monopoly of time by a few people; nonparticipation by
members of the group; and a lack of feeling of accomplishment. This
latter pitfall is probably the most dangerous one for both student
and teacher because in the discussion method intellectual growth
and maturity is difficult to envision.

Discussion pitfalls can be circumvented by good preparation prior
to the discussion. Also, there are certain mechanical techniques that

may be employed to good advantage. Charts or forms developed for the discussion using the chalk board or a flannel board can be used effectively. Typical outlines which might be used are:

Problem

Possible Solutions   *Recommended Solutions*

Issue

Reasons For   *Reasons Against*

Another technique that may be used to advantage is that of "buzz sessions" within the class. In this device the class is subdivided into smaller groups of four or five people with each small group discussing the general topic and then reporting back through a spokesman the results of the small-group discussion. In this way the benefits of smaller groups are achieved and class activity is varied.

To illustrate how classroom-discussion technique might be used in a general business class, let us assume the following fictitious situation:

Situation

For the past several weeks a class in general business has been studying a unit on credit. The topic for the next several days which has been assigned is installment buying and borrowing money for making purchases. The teacher has asked the class to read the chapters in the textbook pertaining to this topic and be ready to discuss the material tomorrow in class.

Procedure

The teacher sets the stage for the discussion of the topic by developing the following case problem. This problem is duplicated and passed out to the class.

Charles Green is a sophomore in high school and is sixteen years old. He has obtained a driver's license and is a capable driver, but his father will seldom let him use the family car. Charles would like to have a car of his own and has found one in a used-car lot that can be purchased for $500. Charles has saved $150 which has been deposited in a building and loan savings association which pays interest at 4 per cent. The owner of the used-car lot is willing to accept this $150 as a down payment on the car if Charles will pay off the balance at the rate of $16 a month for the next twenty-four months. Charles gets an allowance from his parents of $5 a week for performing specified jobs at home.

Charles' father has no objection to his buying the car, but he refuses to assume any responsibility for it. He does insist that Charles buy liability insurance before he gives his consent.

What are some of the factors Charles should consider before buying this car? What are some of the problems he will have if he does buy it?

Points that should be raised from discussion

1. Of what quality is the car and what are the problems which may arise from maintenance costs?
2. How much interest will he have to pay?
3. How much will he lose from taking his savings out of the savings association?
4. What are the operating costs of the car?
5. Are there any nonquantitative factors which should be considered?

The development and use of short case problems such as that illustrated is an excellent means of stimulating thought and discussion on the part of students. Cases can be developed quite easily by the imaginative teacher and they can be related to the experiences which can be understood by the students.

In the illustrated case an emphasis would not be placed upon such specific topics as the advantages or disadvantages of installment buying, or how to compute carrying charges. Actually these things are not important in an isolated state. A person may know or memorize the disadvantages of buying on credit, but if he actually desires something, typically, he will not weigh his desire in terms of whether to purchase or not to purchase. It is much more important that he discover how to solve his problem by thinking of all the difficulties that may be involved. This is what he will or should do as an adult, and if he will use these techniques as he will in solving the case problem, then the student has learned. He has not filled up his mind with abstract facts that will soon be forgotten, but he has seen how he must use these facts to help him solve his problems, which in the last analysis is the process of becoming educated.

Advantages of Informal Discussion. There are several advantages in the use of the discussion techniques in teaching. Some of the more important of these are:

1. Discussion requires both listening and speaking. Consequently it should provide information and stimulate thinking.

2. Discussion requires a student to learn that he must handle the subject-matter of his studies, that he must become competent in using ideas in his thinking and in applying them in solving problems.

3. Discussion speeds up the intellectual activities of the student, for the group sets the pace which is often more rapid than that of most individuals.

4. Discussion stimulates the student to express his ideas and thus they become clearer to him, for as he talks he must arrange the ideas in logical sequence so they can be more easily followed.

5. Discussion provides opportunity for actual practice in learning and teaching how to solve problems.

6. Discussion often adds materially to a participant's stock of ideas.

7. Discussion provides opportunity to correct erroneous ideas and false information.

8. Discussion lends itself easily to the consideration of particular problems that confront students.

9. Discussion affords opportunity for testing, for the student discovers his own strength and weakness. These are revealed to him by the inadequacy of his conceptions, his lack of understanding, and his omissions and neglect of study.

10. Discussion stimulates original thinking as distinguished from imitative thinking.

Disadvantages of Informal Discussion. The discussion technique is by no means a panacea for all of our ills in the teaching of general business. There are several disadvantages to the use of discussion; these should be pointed out. Specifically, some of the disadvantages are:

1. Certain limitations arise from the nature of groups generally— heterogeneousness with respect to abilities, intelligence, interest, and mental alertness.

2. It is slow and time-consuming.

3. It is limited to use with certain types of subject-matter; it cannot be used to determine scientific fact.

4. Often a student is thinking more about what he intends to say

when he has a chance to say it than about what others are saying.

5. It is unsuccessful unless those who participate have considerable knowledge that pertains to the questions to be considered.
6. Sometimes certain traits and characteristics found in teachers are against their use of discussions.

In summary, the following factors are the important ones to consider with respect to the use of the informal discussion method in teaching general business in the secondary school.

1. *The group spirit of the class*—unless the class is willing to cooperate with the teacher in using this method as compared to the traditional question-answer technique, it will not be successful.

2. *The teacher's skill in dealing with certain types of individuals in the group*—

(a) The loquacious members who talk on every possible occasion
(b) The assertive and dogmatic member who talks without evidence
(c) The nonparticipating and shy member
(d) The antagonistic member who is angry with the teacher or with the members of the group

3. *Comprehension of the techniques employed in the discussion method*—too often teachers attempt to use discussion techniques while not fully comprehending the procedures involved. Both class and teacher morale will usually break under this condition with the result that both teacher and class dislike the group approach.

4. *Qualities of the teacher*—the ability of the teacher, as leader of the informal discussion, to be sufficiently flexible mentally so that he can adapt or change method and procedure quickly and adjust immediately to the thinking of the group will be of paramount importance to the success of the group discussion method.

Question-and-Answer Method

The question-and-answer method has often been confused with classroom discussion. Many teachers have erroneously thought they were using discussion when using the question-and-answer method; actually there is little similarity between the two methods.

The question-and-answer is a telling method with the telling being mutual between the teacher and student. The teacher raises a question and asks that either volunteers or a specific student give the answer. The answer is usually in the form of a factual description of the contents of textbook material. Oftentimes the teacher will elaborate on the answer returned by a student before going on to the next question.

Question-and-answer requires factual background on the part of the learners. It appeals to learners who like to get specific, factual knowledge, and it appeals to their feeling of accomplishment when doing so. However, because of this factual element, the use of this method will contribute little to the obtaining of the objectives set out for a course in general business.

There are some advantages to the question-and-answer method as it can be used effectively to spot individual weaknesses, difficulties, and interests, thus enabling the instructor to adapt his instruction to student background. Some valuable uses of the question-and-answer method might be:

1. Check reading assignments.
2. Secure and maintain attention or contact.
3. Explore student background.
4. Develop informational background.
5. Set the stage for discussion.
6. Involve nonresponsive students in class activity.
7. Reveal student difficulties, work habits, interests, and levels of development.
8. Develop factual basis for a principle or generalization.
9. Review work covered.
10. Motivate students to read assignments.
11. Prepare for tests.

Many of the questions to be used in this technique may be written into the lesson plan. The questions should be well phrased, definite, and clear. It is usually more effective to state the question first before the entire group; then direct it to some specific individual. Such a practice tends to keep the group on the alert.

Miscellaneous Techniques

Group and Individual Projects. Written and oral reports, notebooks, accumulations of information about various aspects in general business, posters and displays are some of the projects that can be used effectively in teaching general business. These projects may be used on both an individual and group basis. If at all possible the projects should not be specifically assigned by the teacher to the students but should come as suggestions from the students. Assigned projects lose their appeal to students because they are assigned.

Getting students to suggest or volunteer to work out a project will tax the motivational ability of the teacher to the utmost. However, the successful teacher is one who can accomplish this task without the students being aware that the idea did not stem from themselves.

There will be some student or students who will be overeager in this respect, while others may have a disinterested attitude. The conscientious teacher will attempt to stimulate all of his students to do something in this direction.

There are several ways in which the students may be motivated to work out a project. If a topic that is currently being discussed in class appears to have special interest to the group the teacher may ask the class (or individual in the class) if they know of any means whereby the topic might be explored farther. Through careful questioning the teacher should be able to get some student or group to suggest a specific project.

In one freshman and sophomore class a discussion was being carried on concerning the newer methods of packaging goods. A friendly argument developed as to whether people could tell the difference between a cake baked from a packaged mix and one baked by mixing all of the ingredients by hand. The teacher suggested that the only way one could really tell was by comparison. Students in the class volunteered to bake a cake using both methods and bring both cakes to class to see whether the members of the class could actually determine the difference.

The foregoing example could be severely criticized as a "frill"; it might be objected that a project of this type has no place in the general business class. However, the wise teacher could use this type of project to point out how demands by consumers on manufacturers for more convenient ways of packaging goods oftentimes result in higher prices. A discussion could be developed as to the pros and cons of this sort of thing with resulting learning taking place in important economic concepts.

Sources of information for student projects can be developed by the students with the teacher's help. The teacher must stay in the background, however, and make suggestions only when they are asked for. The teacher's file of supplementary instructional materials will be quite valuable here and he should be constantly building up the file for this purpose.

Field Trips. Tours and visits to business firms are another means of valuable instruction in the general business class. Classroom learning becomes more meaningful if students have the opportunity to see some of the concepts learned in class actually in operation. Plans for the field trip should be made by the students if at all possible—under careful supervision of the teacher. The trip should be planned well in advance and the group should be oriented on what to look for at the place to be visited and also on what is to be accomplished. After the trip is concluded a thorough discussion should be held concerning what has been seen and what has been learned. Specific techniques for conducting a field trip can be obtained from various publications available for the business teacher. It is important here only to point out that this type of technique can be a valuable supplement to the classroom instruction.

Field trips are often considerable trouble and take much planning on the part of the teacher, but the values received are often worth the trouble. Oftentimes the students consider the field trip as a lark and as a means of having a good time. There is nothing wrong with having a good time on a field trip, but the idea should not be lost sight of that primarily the trip is an educational venture. It should be pointed out to the students that they are representatives of the school and that any improper behavior will not only reflect on themselves but on the school as well. Generally, students on a field trip will behave as the ladies and gentlemen they are, but occasionally there will be one or two individuals who will not conduct themselves properly. The teacher, if he knows his class well, will undoubtedly know those individuals who may cause problems and will take steps prior to going on the trip to eliminate any embarrassing situations.

The teacher should also make sure that the administration of the school and other teachers are informed well in advance of the impending trip. It is often necessary for the students to miss other classes. Tact and courtesy should be considered in making sure that other teachers in the school are in accord with the trip and that any disruption in the normal procedure in the school is met with the minimum of inconvenience to others.

Oftentimes teachers in small schools are located in rural areas where visiting opportunities are limited. However, many values can be obtained from visiting the local grocery store, filling station, garage, or mill even though these establishments are not large. The student may be very familiar with the business establishment as a consumer, but visiting the business from the point of view of determining and learning how it operates oftentimes will open his eyes to many things he had not noticed before.

Audio-Visual Aids. Audio-visual devices are commonly employed by many teachers of general business and the technique is found to be quite valuable. Recordings, films, posters, and displays pertaining to business are available from many sources and much of the material is extremely worth-while. The teacher should have some knowledge of what the film contains so that he can judge its appropriateness for the class. Some films, for example, contain propaganda and advertising and have little in the way of concrete information. It is impossible to get away entirely from this sort of thing, but the teacher should watch and choose his films judiciously.

The teacher should also be careful to make sure that the visual aid is an educational device and not one of amusement. Excessive use of films tends to fit this latter pattern to the extent that the class is not aware of the important aspects of knowledge that can be obtained from observation.

Methodology in General. The ability of the teacher to vary his procedure and to adapt his method to fit the abilities and attitudes of the class will be an important factor in his success or failure. The use of only one method to the exclusion of all others will be boring to both students and teacher. Certain units of subject-matter will adapt themselves to the use of particular methods whether it be discussion, question-and-answer, project, or individual instruction. The effective teacher must be flexible enough to determine what method best suits the subject being taught and then use that method. In some instances this may involve changing methods even in the middle of a class period.

Another important consideration will be how the teacher presents his method. Enthusiasm, vitality, and dynamic action on the part of the teacher will determine whether a particular method will succeed or not. The dull, lifeless teacher will have little success regardless of how able he may be in the technicalities of method. The dynamic teacher through such things as gestures, voice, and enthusiasm will accomplish much in maintaining interest and enthusiasm on the part of his students. Motivation accordingly will be less difficult.

Evaluation and Measurement

One of the major problems of the general business teacher is the measurement and evaluation of the abilities of his students. This is a problem with all teachers regardless of ability or experience. It is probably a greater problem with superior teachers because they realize their limitations and inadequacies in this respect more than do the inferior teachers. It is not intended, at this point, to go into the specific details of developing measurement and evaluative devices. These techniques have been taken up in detail in Chapter Four. However, there are some problems in this area that pertain specifically to the teaching of general business, and these should be examined here.

Teachers are faced with the practical problem of assigning letter or percentage grades with respect to student achievement. There are two main methods by which this may be done in the general business class. In the first method the teacher may observe student behavior during class discussions, in the performance of reports or projects, and in the results of class recitation. This type of evaluative technique is necessarily subject to the teacher's opinion as to the value of the student's activity. Although it is possible to assign letter or percentage grades through observation, teachers much prefer to have more tangible evidence of the value of the student's performance in class. This tangible evidence can only be obtained through the use of another type of evaluative device, the examination.

Developing examinations poses some particular problems for the teacher of general business, especially if he subscribes to the idea previously presented—that of teaching for concepts rather than for specific items of subject-matter knowledge. The type of evaluative device used will be different from the traditional type. This does not mean that the so-called objective type of examinations such as true-false, completion, multiple choice, or matching cannot be used. These types can indeed be used, but in the preparation of the questions care must be taken that the evaluation is of concepts rather than of specific items of subject-matter.

Some illustrations of the types of questions that serve this particular objective are given below. These questions were developed by a group of business educators attending a workshop on economic education at New York University.[1]

> *Evaluation by Written Tests*—Although observation is an important means of evaluation, because of the limitations and subjectivity of observation as informal evaluation, this type of evaluation must be supplemented in other ways. Probably the most frequently used means of supplementing evaluation through observation is by written tests. The illustrations which follow are examples of different types of questions which may be constructed for the purpose of measuring achievement of the types of outcomes indicated. In other words, no illustrations of the commonly known true-false, multiple-choice, etc. test are given; rather those types are illustrated which may be used to measure more than mere facts and information, specifically attitudes, understandings, appreciations, and so on.

> 1. *Evaluation of Abilities.* One of the abilities which should be and can be developed in basic business is the *ability to distinguish between statement of fact and statement of opinion.* The type of test questions illustrated here can help in the evaluation of this ability.

> *Directions:* In the list below, some of the sentences are statements of opinion, and others are statements of fact. Indicate to which class you think each statement belongs by placing the proper letter in the space provided for it. Do not try to decide if each statement is true or false, but only whether it should be classified as a statement of *fact* or of *opinion.*

> _____ 1. Insurance may be obtained to provide protection against every type of economic loss.
> _____ 2. Big business leads to monopoly.
> _____ 3. High tariffs increase the prosperity of the country.

[1] The material is taken from part of the workshop report and is titled "Evaluation of Outcomes." This workshop was held under the joint auspices of New York University and the Council on Economic Education.

_____ 4. The economic cost of war is extremely high.

_____ 5. One who buys stock in a company is a part owner of that company.

Another ability that can be evaluated by test as an outcome of the giving of economic emphasis to the teaching of basic business education is the *ability to make wise choices*. The following type of test might give an indication of the extent of this outcome:

Mr. C. E. Lucas has been employed for the past twenty years by the Kollege Korner Kitchen as a waiter, cook, and cashier. His current earnings are $250 a month. He has saved $10,000. The average net earnings of the Kollege Korner Kitchen for the past ten years has been $7,200 per year. The management offers Mr. Lucas:

1. a promotion to general manager with a salary of $300 a month (the promotion will, of course, add to the duties and responsibilities of Mr. Lucas), and
2. an opportunity to buy the entire business including building, equipment, and the present inventory for $20,000.

After some investigation, Mr. Lucas finds that the local banker is willing to accept a mortgage on the property and to lend him the additional cash needed. The loan is to be repaid in monthly installments over a ten-year period. An interest rate of 6 per cent is to be the cost of the loan. He also finds that his brother-in-law, a carpenter by trade, is willing to invest the additional $10,000 provided a general partnership agreement is duly executed. Under the partnership agreement, the duties and responsibilities and the profits or losses are to be shared equally.

Directions:
1. Underline the choice you think best for Mr. Lucas.
   (a) To continue working for the Kollege Korner Kitchen as general manager
   (b) To purchase the business with bank financing
   (c) To form a partnership with his brother-in-law
2. On the following sheet expand on number 1.
   (a) Defend your choice
   (b) Reasons why each of the other two alternatives was not chosen

2. *Evaluation of Understandings.* Evaluation of understandings is one of the most difficult processes of evaluation. Great care must be taken to be sure that the acquisition of mere information

alone is not being measured. Test questions must be so constructed that the student's comprehension of the relation of facts (understandings) is evaluated. This does not mean, however, that students should not be taught basic facts. Information serves as a tool in the solving of problems as they arise and assists in providing understanding.

Questions such as the following may be of assistance in evaluating student understandings:

On the meaning of corporate stock:
1. XYZ Corporation sold $200,000 worth of stock, of which Mr. Wilson purchased ten shares for $100 each. Mr. Wilson therefore (a) becomes a creditor of the company; (b) is an owner of the company; (c) has loaned the company money; (d) is a customer of the company.

_____

On the meaning of index figures:
2. The cost-of-living index figure for 1952 is, let us say, 160 (1940 = 100). In 1940 Mr. Adams earned $4,000 a year. In 1952 he earned, in the same job, $5,000 a year. Is Mr. Adams' real income greater or less than it was in 1940?

_____

The essay question or the completion-of-sentence type of question also may be used to evaluate understanding, thus:
1. Explain how borrowing from a commercial bank, as distinguished from other sources of borrowing, increases the supply of money.
2. Complete the statement: "Inflation exists when _____."

The foregoing examples are excellent illustrations of the types of evaluative devices that can be used in measuring the abilities of students in a general business class. Obviously, it will be difficult for the teacher to develop evaluative devices of his own of the type and nature illustrated. However, the time taken will be very worth-while and the teacher will not be placed in the embarrassing position of teaching for the broad concept and then measuring students' ability by devising examinations that measure specifics. It is this type of teaching that is open to criticism—and in which students lose confidence.

Before leaving this section on evaluation and measurement, mention should be made of one type of evaluative device that is rarely used any more, specifically, the essay-type question. This type of question has great value for use in teaching general business, not only to determine the measurement of concepts, but to provide the student with practice in written communication. Teachers traditionally have complained about the inability of their students to write effectively and have placed the blame on the elementary-school teacher or the teacher of English. Written expression is the responsibility of all teachers, not just of one particular group. The teacher of general business has just as much at stake in the development of this ability as any other teacher.

Of course, there are difficulties in using this type of examination question, such as the time involved in grading the papers and the lack of objectivity. However, both of the objections may be overcome. Better planning of the teacher's time to eliminate waste motions will permit time for grading essays. The argument of lack of objectivity is overruled to some extent by the fact that upon analysis, any examination question is subject to the teacher's wording and selection of the question.

Economic Education

Any discussion of the teaching of general business in the secondary school would not be complete without pinpointing one of the major problems which has confronted educators in general during the past thirty years. This has been the problem of "economic illiteracy" found in a large segment of the American public. Since the major depression of the 1930's there have been many changes and developments in the economic structure of the United States and in the world with a consequent conflict of points of view on the part of many persons.

These conflicting points of view in addition to the increasing complexities of our economic system have resulted in a problem for the American people in comprehending fully economic phenomenon that has a major influence upon their lives.

The data shown in Fig. 8.2 illustrate this problem dramatically with respect to the lack of economic experience of the American population with factors that now and in the future will materially affect its economic well-being.

Both educational and lay organizations have attempted to overcome the economic illiteracy problem through various means. Required courses in economics are quite common on the high-school

Figure 8.2

Economic Experience of the American Population

Road Maps of Industry, No. 1459. © 1963 by National Industrial Conference Board, Inc.   Used by permission.

level. The Joint Council for Economic Education has sponsored workshops for teachers and has distributed educational materials for their use. In addition to these activities business educators have been concerned with this problem and much of the literature in this field has dealt with economic education. The American Business Education Yearbook of 1958 was devoted entirely to educating the youth of America in economic concepts and principles.[2] It is anticipated that major efforts will continue to be made by schools, government agencies, and independent organizations to help overcome this problem.

Many leaders in the field of business education firmly believe that economic concepts can be taught effectively in conjunction with a course in general business. The various units of subject-matter as listed on page 329 have significant economic implications. The teacher of general business can do much in this course to develop attitudes, appreciations, and understandings of our economic system using as a basis for this instruction the content of the general business course.

Elvin S. Eyster of Indiana University has set forth in a complete and concise manner the areas of economic concepts necessary for the general education of every person.[3]

1. The essential characteristics and principles of the American business and labor system, what it is, how it operates, and the role it plays in the economic and occupational lives of all people.
2. An understanding of business practices and procedures, such as consumer credit, installment selling, guarantee of quality, and service agreements that enable consumers to utilize completely and to benefit fully from the economic goods and services offered by business.
3. Principles of management of personal business affairs enabling one to enjoy the highest possible standards of living compatible with his income.
4. The business of government (not the organization and operation of government), with special emphasis upon government business, such as the management and use of public lands, production of power, insurance against possible losses, lending of money, and subsidization of industries.

---

[2] *Educating Youth for Economic Competence,* The American Business Education Yearbook (1958).

[3] *Ibid.,* page 16.

5. Basic economic principles, such as the operation of the law of supply and demand, real wages, prices, and marginal utility.

If an emphasis is placed in the general business course on the development of economic understandings it should be pointed out to the prospective teachers some inherent dangers to this approach.

Many of the concepts in the above list are controversial in nature. Since students often reflect the attitudes of their parents it would be uncommon not to have conflicting ideas on the part of students enrolled in a general business class. This is as it should be because one of the strengths of our American heritage is based upon the freedom of belief with the free expression of these beliefs. *It is not the place of the business teacher to question the beliefs of their students but to enable the students to obtain factual information from which to develop their own points of view and beliefs.*

Inexperienced teachers will often shy away from controversial issues in the classroom or sometimes get into them without giving the problem proper forethought and preparation. The use of the so-called "Socratic" approach in which the teacher "questions" the point of view held by a student under the guise of "making him think" in order to justify his idea has oftentimes had unfortunate results. Students have been known to misjudge a teacher's point of view about a controversial issue merely because the teacher's idea appeared to be in conflict with his own.

The use of discussion techniques and procedures are excellent for use in the presentation and implementation of controversial issues. However, the teacher must insist that rational thinking based upon factual information, not emotional reaction, take place in the discussion. In this way, the teacher of general business can make a significant contribution to the education of our youth and to society in general.

Projects and Questions for Discussion

1. Examine a textbook for use in teaching general business. Describe how the text material can be utilized to achieve the objectives of this course.

2. Most general business textbooks are supplemented by workbooks for use by the student. Examine one of these workbooks and make a list of their advantages and disadvantages for use in instruction.

3. What problems do you see with respect to teaching or not teaching about subjects that may be of a controversial nature.

4. Develop a series of discussion questions which might be used effectively in starting and continuing a class discussion on some topic or topics in general business.

5. What are some specific techniques that you might suggest for teaching a unit on savings and investment in general business? Consider that the class you are teaching is composed of freshmen and sophomores.

6. Do you believe it is possible for a freshman or sophomore student in high school to comprehend some of the major economic concepts that affect our business economy today? Is it important for them to understand certain economic principles that will affect them as adults? Can you cite any student experiences that illustrate the workings of certain economic phenomena?

7. Do you believe that a teacher who is highly proficient in teaching skill subjects such as typewriting and shorthand can also be a proficient teacher of general business? What are the different elements of methodology involved in the teaching of the skills and the "recitation-type" subjects?

8. Develop several case problems which might be used effectively in teaching a topic or topics in general business by use of discussion techniques.

9. Assume that a class in general business is composed of a highly mixed group of students with respect to abilities and interests. What suggestions do you have which would maintain interest and motivate these students?

10. Do you believe it is possible to improve attitudes and appreciations with respect to business activities in a general business class? How might you go about it?

Case Problems

1. Bill Smith is a sophomore student in your general business class. You have been teaching a unit on the buying and selling activities in business. Bill raises his hand and tells you and the class of an experience he had several days ago. It seems that when he placed a dime in a vending machine to get a soft drink he found a way to get his money back and thus get the drink free. Bill cited this experience seemingly to show how clever he was. His classmates seemed to approve of his actions

and several demanded to know where the vending machine was so that they could also take advantage of a "free soft drink."

As the teacher of this class, would you do anything about this situation and attempt to point out to the class that Bill was doing something dishonest, or would you disregard it?

2. While teaching a chapter in general business on governmental controls on business enterprise one of your students asked you to explain the operations of a socialist economy as practiced by Russia. Your class is composed of all freshmen who in your estimation are relatively immature. What would you do?

3. You are a business teacher in a small high school. Your superintendent insists on placing students with low-level ability in your general business class because, as he puts it, "I don't know what else to do with them." As a result you have in your class twenty students, both boys and girls, ranging from the freshman to junior year. You are at a loss as to what to do in the class as some of the students do not seem to understand or even be able to read the textbook. What can you do in a situation such as this?

4. One day while teaching the topic of consumer credit in your general business class one of your students ventures an opinion quite forcibly that it is wrong to ever buy anything on credit. "If you can't pay cash for what you want then you should not buy it, at least that is what my father says." Should you attempt to change the mind of this student? Suppose that you can present good evidence that he is wrong and by so doing imply that his father is wrong—should you do so?

5. Charles Morgan is a teacher of general business and appears to be quite capable. He is a strong advocate of the use of informal classroom discussion as a teaching method and he is quite good at it. At the conclusion of a unit on investments, during which the class had several excellent discussions, Morgan gave an examination and found that the results showed his class to have little knowledge of the principles of the subject-matter. He is quite discouraged and is beginning to wonder whether he is using the proper teaching procedures because he knows that his students have average or better ability. He is considering not using discussion techniques any more and returning to class recitation. What would you suggest he do?

6. Harold Smith is a conscientious teacher of general business and is quite interested in the subject-matter of the course. However, to his dismay he has determined that his students are very poor in the use of correct grammar (both written and oral) and also that their spelling and arithmetic ability is very ragged. He feels that he should do some-

thing about their deficiencies in these areas, yet he does not wish to forego the teaching of the subject-matter of the course. He is convinced that he cannot do both effectively in the time he has. What suggestions do you have for him?

Suggested Readings

Crabbe, Enterline, DeBrum, *Methods of Teaching General Business.* Cincinnati, Ohio: South-Western Publishing Co., 1962.

Educating Youth for Economic Competence, The American Business Education Yearbook, XV (1958).

How to Use Group Discussion, No. 6. Washington, D.C.: National Council for the Social Studies, 1952. 'How to do it" series.

Learning Through Group Discussion. Columbus, Ohio: The Junior Town Meeting League.

Motivation in Teaching General Business, Monograph 107. Cincinnati, Ohio: South-Western Publishing Co.

National Business Education Association, *Business Education Forum,* Washington, D.C. All March issues devoted to Basic Business.

Olson, Milton C., *et al., A Teachers Guide to Economics in the Business Education Curriculum,* Joint Council on Economic Education and the National Business Education Association. Washington, D.C.

Portfolio of Teaching Techniques. New London, Connecticut: Educator's Washington Dispatch.

Toward Better Economic Education, Monograph 104. Cincinnati, Ohio: South-Western Publishing Co.

Bibliographies of Free and Inexpensive Material for Use in Teaching Business Education Subjects

Bibliography of Free and Inexpensive Materials for Economic Education, Joint Council on Economic Education, 2 West 46th Street, New York 36.

Educational Aids For Schools and Colleges, National Association of Manufacturers, 2 East 48th Street, New York 17.

List of Free Materials Available to Professors and Students, The Wall Street Journal, The Educational Service Bureau, 44 Broad Street, New York 4.

Visual Aids for Business and Economic Education, Monograph 92, Cincinnati, Ohio: South-Western Publishing Co.

9 Teaching Bookkeeping

The Subject

The teaching of bookkeeping in the secondary schools of the United States illustrates one of the most traditional aspects of our present-day business education. Bookkeeping instruction was first begun in the private business college and was introduced in the public schools in the early part of the nineteenth century. Today, in terms of enrollment and number of courses offered, bookkeeping is second only to typewriting in the public schools.

In its earliest beginning bookkeeping instruction was strictly vocational in nature, as the sole purpose of teachers of the course was to train bookkeepers. In recent years new objectives have entered the picture—personal-use values and values with respect to certain attitudes and appreciations of our economic structure. The most oft-repeated objectives for teaching bookkeeping in the secondary school are as follows:

1. To develop in students the ability and desire to keep records for personal use

2. To develop in students the ability to interpret and analyze business papers and records in the capacity of a consumer

3. To give students preliminary training for the advanced study of accounting

4. To develop in students traits of neatness, accuracy, and orderliness

5. To develop in students an understanding of some of the problems and characteristics of a business enterprise

6. To provide students with knowledges of record keeping necessary to carry on a small business

7. To train students to become bookkeepers

The reason for straying from the original vocational goal was the questioning by some business educators of the practicability of such an objective. It was pointed out that bookkeepers could be trained on the job in a matter of hours or days in the mechanical methods of keeping a set of books. Why, then, should it be necessary to spend a year or two years in a bookkeeping course in high school for this purpose?

Although this in fact appeared to be the situation, those educators favoring the vocational objective retorted that to train an effective employee in bookkeeping it was necessary that he be versed in all aspects of the bookkeeping process—that the ability to understand the mechanics of keeping a set of books was not the only characteristic of an employable bookkeeper. A truly vocational bookkeeper was one who thoroughly understood what he was doing.

In any event, because of these differences of point of view, two main and general objectives of teaching bookkeeping in the secondary school—the vocational and the nonvocational—are held by most teachers today. It is probable that the vocational objective is considered by bookkeeping teachers to be the most important particularly in light of the increased emphasis upon vocational education. In addition, the development of the electronic computer has resulted in more attention given to mechanical and electronic data-processing techniques in the bookkeeping course. This emphasis is mainly vocational in nature.

There are excellent reasons for teaching bookkeeping regardless of whether the teacher subscribes to the vocational or nonvocational objective or both. The following outline directs attention to some of the specific and general business objectives or items found in almost any good one-year bookkeeping course. If educators, who are now worried about our "economic illiteracy" and our lack of general information about our free-enterprise economy, would make available to all high-school youth a one-year bookkeeping course under a teacher qualified to teach the understandings outlined below, a major share of their worry would disappear.

1. A knowledge of the meaning and significance of ordinary common terms used in the business world today, and an ability to differentiate between them as:

   a. Asset
   b. Liability
   c. Net worth
   d. Expense
   e. Income

   f. Gross profit
   g. Net profit
   h. Depreciation
   i. Bad debts
   j. Accruals

2. Familiarity with many different kinds of transactions common to the business world, and to people who deal with it, and an understanding of the significance of each as:

   a. Cash expenditures
   b. Cash receipts
   c. Credit transactions
   d. Discounting notes
   e. Taking and giving discounts

   f. Exchange of assets
   g. Prepayment of expense
   h. Issuing notes
   i. Returns and allowances
   j. Payment of interest

3. Understanding of the advisability of performing certain functions and of following out certain principles and procedures in order that any given investment may be adequately protected as:

   a. Allowance for depreciation
   b. Proper valuation of inventories
   c. Adequate insurance
   d. Revenue vs. capital expenditures
   e. Protection of working capital

   f. Control of expenses
   g. Interpretation of financial statements
   h. Prompt collection of accounts
   i. Need for conservatism
   j. Accurate records

4. A recognition of those factors which, directly or indirectly, reduce profits, income, and net worth as:

   a. Accrued expenses
   b. Bad debts
   c. Depreciation
   d. Obsolescence
   e. Inefficient labor

   f. Insufficient margins
   g. Seasonal fluctuation
   h. Competition
   i. Unusual losses
   j. Excessive inventory

5. Knowledge of the meaning and purpose of many record-keeping devices commonly in use, such as:

a. Cash books
b. Purchases book
c. Sales book
d. General ledger
e. Subsidiary ledgers

f. Valuation accounts
g. Book inventories
h. Columnar records
i. Account classifications
j. Trial balance

6. A knowledge of various means of estimating the financial worth of a given investment or enterprise as:

a. Examination of two or more balance sheets
b. Examination of two or more profit-and-loss statements
c. Interpretation of comparative statements
d. Per cent of income earned on investment
e. Proportion of earnings left in the business

7. Development of an awareness of common types of "problems" facing a business executive as:

a. The taking of inventory
b. Proper valuation of inventory
c. Selection of profitable items
d. Protection of cash
e. Securing of credit

8. Some knowledge of the possible uses of records, and some ability in their use, as a means of executive control of a going business as:

a. Comparative volume of sales for periods
b. Ratio of net profits to sales
c. Current ratios
d. Turnover of accounts receivable
e. Use of credit records and ratings

9. The development of specific attitudes, concepts, and mental habits as applied to situations arising in business transactions as:

a. The habit of analyzing business transactions and situations in terms of their effects upon the two main financial statements
b. The habit of systematic classification of business information
c. The habit of accurate and complete recording of business information
d. To establish a correct concept of what constitutes profits
e. To develop the concept that business success is fundamentally dependent upon service and efficiency

10. A knowledge of the basic concepts of modern data-processing procedures as:

    a. Manual devices such as pegboard and keysort equipment
    b. Mechanical equipment such as bookkeeping and posting machines
    c. Punch-card equipment such as key punches, sorters, collators, and tabulators
    d. Electronic computer systems

Obviously, technical competence in the knowledges listed above would not be expected of a high-school student. However, close scrutiny will reveal that *familiarity* with and an understanding of the various items is not too much to expect of the economically educated citizen.

Grade Placement and Types of Bookkeeping Courses Offered in the Secondary Curriculum. Typically the bookkeeping courses offered in the secondary school are being offered in the sophomore-junior years of high school or in the junior-senior years. The latter pattern is most usual. A one-year course is most common with a few schools offering a one-semester course and a few of the larger high schools offering four semesters of bookkeeping. The one-semester course has developed in the past few years primarily because administrators were looking for a course of a nonvocational nature that could be incorporated in a personal-use curriculum. Typically, courses of this nature are concerned with personal record keeping. Schools in which four semesters of bookkeeping are offered are usually large city high schools with a strict vocational curriculum.

Course Content. The content of a high-school bookkeeping course has become rather standardized, as can be determined by examining the several available textbooks. This content is usually presented by using a spiral or pyramid technique—going from the simple to the complex—covering the same basic principles several times, but each time adding more comprehensive and difficult material. The first cycle is usually very elementary, taking up the records maintained by a service type of business. After this cycle is completed, a second cycle is begun using a merchandising type of business with its accompanying adjustments for inventories. The third cycle brings in special problems such as payroll records, special journals, depreciation and accruals; and finally the fourth cycle includes partnership and corporation bookkeeping. A list of the units that may be found in the typical bookkeeping textbook is as follows:

Units of Content

1st Cycle (Service Business)
1. Bookkeeping fundamentals
2. The use of accounts
3. Analyzing transactions
4. Journalizing
5. Posting
6. The trial balance and worksheet
7. Financial statements
8. Closing the books

2nd Cycle (Merchandising Business)
9. Purchases
10. Sales
11. Cash receipts and cash payments
12. Worksheet and adjustments

3rd Cycle (Special Problems)
13. Payrolls and taxes
14. Fixed assets and depreciation
15. Notes and interest
16. Accounts receivable and bad debts
17. Accrued and deferred items
18. Bookkeeping systems
19. Partnerships and corporations
20. Data-processing techniques

Instructional Materials

Textbooks. There are many excellent textbooks available for use in teaching bookkeeping. Basically there is little difference in the major texts, as the methods of presenting the material are similar. Common differences lie in the size of type, use of illustrations, problem material, projects, and practice sets that accompany the course. Some texts emphasize the arithmetic of bookkeeping giving specific aids and devices for improving the skill. Other texts emphasize terminology. A teacher's selection of a particular book will in all probability depend upon personal preference. One determinant for selection may be the availability of instructional material that accompanies the text and is provided by the publisher. Such things as teacher's manuals, keys, printed tests, and workbooks are the types of supplementary materials provided.

Workbooks. Every bookkeeping textbook published today is accompanied by a workbook for students' use in working the questions and problems at the ends of the chapters. The use of these workbooks is optional with the instructor. There is some difference of opinion held by teachers with respect to the value of workbooks in teaching. Some teachers believe that students will learn more of the principles of bookkeeping by not using workbooks because they must rule their own journals and ledgers and thus should have a better conception of keeping records. The majority of teachers do use workbooks, for it is doubtful to them that there is much gained educationally by making students rule their own paper. Necessarily, there is much "busy work" involved in working problems in bookkeeping, and if any short cuts can be employed to cut down the amount of busy work it is commendable. The use of a workbook aids in cutting down this busy work and permits the student to spend the major portion of his time in solving problems rather than doing preliminary spade work in developing his own journals and ledgers. In the long run, the use of workbooks will be more economical in savings of both time and paper.

Practice Sets. Another type of instructional material useful in teaching bookkeeping is the practice set. A practice set involves the working of a long problem usually covering a one- or two-month time span of business transactions. The student is provided with a set of journals, ledgers, and working papers specifically designed for use in working the set. It has the twofold purpose of providing the student with practice in working a problem covering the entire bookkeeping cycle and also of motivating the student by providing him with a complete set of books of account. Practice sets may be purchased with or without business papers. Without business papers the set is worked by using a series of printed descriptive transactions found either in the text or accompanying the set. The set with business papers is worked by the use of transactions determined from printed forms such as checks, invoices, and the like. Either type of practice set is valuable in instruction. The set with practice papers probably has greater motivational power as the student works with simulated business papers typifying those found in a business. Thus the working of the set appears to be more realistic.

Other Types of Instructional Materials. There are many other types of instructional materials available for use in the teaching of bookkeeping. These take the form of visual aids and motivating devices which may be either obtained from a publisher or developed by the teacher. Such materials as business forms, financial statements, films and filmstrips are the types commonly used. These types of instructional materials can be quite useful but also can be quite expensive. Teacher-developed instructional materials can be relatively inexpensive. Such items are displays and illustrations of actual bookkeeping records.

Another type of instructional material which has proven to be quite valuable in the instruction of bookkeeping is transparencies for use on an overhead projector. These transparencies can be made by the teacher if the school has a copying machine; if it does not, certain transparencies can be obtained from the firm which publishes the textbook. For example, it is possible to obtain from the publisher the solutions to textbook problems in the form of overhead-projector transparencies. Thus, it is possible for the teacher to illustrate the solutions of problems without the time-consuming factor of writing the solution on the chalk board.

Basic Concepts of Teaching Bookkeeping

One of the most significant decisions which must be made by the teacher of bookkeeping is the degree of effort which will be placed upon the mechanical aspects of the course. The decision which is made will have a material effect upon the methodology used by the teacher in presenting the subject-matter.

Essentially, there are *two* major goals in the teaching of bookkeeping—one is the development in students of mechanical proficiency in the keeping of bookkeeping records. The second goal is the development in students of an understanding of the uses of the information or data resulting from keeping bookkeeping records. Inherent in this latter goal is the development in students of the ability to make use of bookkeeping data for purposes of making decisions about the various problems found in operating a business.

Both goals are important to achieve. It is necessary for a bookkeeping student to be able to master the mechanical aspects of keeping a set of books—this is the job of the bookkeeper. However, equally important is the ability to understand the significance of bookkeeping data and to apply these data to the solutions of specific business problems. In other words, it is important to develop "thinking bookkeepers."

Obviously, the teaching methodology involved in order to achieve each goal is different. To teach mechanics involves the use of drill, memorization, the solving of mechanical problems on the part of students, and a great deal of illustration and explanation on the part of the teacher.

To teach an understanding and application of bookkeeping data to the solutions of business problems involves the use of discussion, problem definition and solving (not mechanical problems but business-decision-type problems), and analytical judgments on the part of students.

It is possible to achieve both goals in a bookkeeping course by varying the methodology used and the techniques employed by the teacher. In the modern bookkeeping course it is important that both goals be achieved and the successful teacher will find ways to vary his presentation to this end.

Specific Methods of Teaching Bookkeeping

A variety of specific methods are sound for use in teaching bookkeeping. Discussion, problem and project, question and answer, and individual instruction are the most commonly used methods. No one method can be said to be the best nor should any one method be used entirely. The effective teacher will vary his method to suit the abilities of his students and the type of subject-matter being studied. In teaching the analysis of financial statements the discussion method might prove to be the most beneficial, while in teaching the trial balance the problem method would be the most effective. In any event it is wise to adapt the method to fit the situation at hand; the good teacher will be able to sense when it is proper to change methods.

Discussion Method. The class discussion method can be used to great advantage in the teaching of bookkeeping, particularly in the teaching of understandings of the uses of bookkeeping data. A teacher can develop many problem situations, of either an actual or imaginary nature, and present them to the class for the purpose of illustrating the various situations when the records of a business are of value to the businessman. For example, the following is an illustration of a case problem which could be developed by a teacher as a basis for discussion in teaching an understanding of the application of bookkeeping data to a specific situation.

During the night of February 19th, thieves broke into the Alexander Jewelry Store and stole some of the merchandise that was on hand. The theft was discovered the next morning when Mr. Alexander, the owner of the store, arrived to open up. He immediately called the police and since he was fully insured against any loss of this type he also called his insurance agent.

Since many small items of jewelry were taken it was not readily apparent how much the thieves took. Both the police and the insurance agent suggested that an inventory be taken immediately. Mr. Alexander did this and after several hours of counting he determined that the inventory of goods on hand after the theft amounted to $30,000 at cost price. However, since Mr. Alexander had purchased and sold merchandise since the last time he had taken an inventory (December 31st of the preceding year) he still was unable to determine exactly the amount of the theft.

What information will Mr. Alexander have to obtain from his records before he can find out how much was stolen?

Assuming that Mr. Alexander's records reflected the following data can you determine the loss?

Sales, January 1 to February 19		$10,000
Purchases, January 1 to February 19		$15,000
Inventory, December 31 previous year		$40,000
Income Statement data from previous year		
Sales	$100,000	
Cost of Goods Sold	60,000	
Gross Profit	$ 40,000	

The development of real or imaginary problem situations by the teacher as a basis for discussion can be an effective device. Using analogies from the teacher's own experience can also be valuable because it often gives an air of realism to the activities of the classroom. The bookkeeping teacher does not necessarily have to have had actual bookkeeping experience (although this experience is highly recommended) to use actual illustrations or analogies drawn from business firms. This information can be readily obtained merely by talking to businessmen about their problems in bookkeeping or it can be obtained through visitations to places of business.

In addition, the modern bookkeeping textbooks include, along with the traditional type of problem, case problems of the type previously illustrated. These, along with teacher-developed cases, should provide a wealth of material for class discussion use.

Problem-and-Project Method. Bookkeeping is a course that is highly adaptable to the problem-or-project method of teaching. The use of the short problems or exercises that are found at the end of chapters in the bookkeeping textbooks is almost mandatory for the successful learning of the theory and mechanics of bookkeeping. Longer problems or projects in the form of practice sets are also highly valuable. Personal projects such as determining the costs and profits of raising a farm animal for future sale or personal budgeting can be very stimulating. In some instances opportunity is provided for bookkeeping students to maintain school or class records. The teacher must always be aware of the availability of projects of these kinds and use them in his teaching as conditions warrant.

When using the problems at the end of chapters as a teaching device, the teacher must be alert to see that this type of activity does not become dull and monotonous. Unavoidably, there is much "busy work" connected with the solving of problems, but through the careful selection and assignment of problems for students to work, unessential material can be kept at a minimum.

There are certain techniques that the teacher must keep in mind in the assignment of problem material. Each problem assigned should be thoroughly discussed and illustrated so that students can determine their errors and thus make any corrections. As indicated earlier in this chapter one of the best devices which can be used for the illustration of the solutions to problems is a transparency of the solution which can be shown on the overhead projector. These can be either copied from the teacher's key or purchased from the publisher. It should not be necessary for the teacher to collect the problems and check them himself, but he should motivate the students to do this for themselves. Bookkeeping teachers often feel that they must collect all problem assignments if only for the purpose of checking on the student to see whether he has completed the assignment. The responsibility for completing assignments should be left with the student.

Some teachers often worry about students copying problem solutions from other students. Students very often copy as the result of the attitude and actions of the teacher. If the teacher insists upon 100 per cent accuracy and criticizes the student who is inaccurate, then that teacher may well expect some of his students to copy work of others. If, on the other hand, the teacher expresses the attitude that errors in bookkeeping are a matter of course and that errors will be eliminated through understanding, then the problem of copying will be minimized. The teacher should encourage students to help each other in solving problems or, if difficulties develop, to come to him for aid.

Teachers must also be careful, in using the problem technique, not to give so much aid to students that they do not have an opportunity to weigh judgments or make decisions for themselves. The inexperienced teacher, in order to be helpful, will often aid his students to the extent that solving the problem becomes a matter of the teacher's judgment rather than of the students'. Teachers will also find it advisable to work out the problems assigned themselves in order to predetermine where students will have difficulty and in order to avoid embarrassment if the teacher does not know the solution.

Individual Instruction. Oftentimes teachers of bookkeeping will find it necessary to give a large amount of individual instruction to members of the class because of the wide range of abilities that are commonly found in the bookkeeping class. This method can be used with special effectiveness in large classes. The procedure is to assign problems for the students to work in class. The teacher then goes about the room giving individual help where needed. When the teacher, as he moves about the class, observes a number of students having the same difficulty, then time is taken out to make the relevant concept clear. After the concept has been taught, then the class returns to working individually. More will be said in the latter part of this chapter concerning the various methods of allowing for individual differences in bookkeeping students.

Teaching General Topics in Bookkeeping

The content of a course in bookkeeping can be generally classified into the areas of (a) getting started, (b) theory of debit and credit, (c) the books of account, (d) the worksheet with and without adjustments, (e) the financial statements, (f) the closing of the books of account, and (g) special problems. It is not the purpose in this textbook to list specific techniques for teaching topics within these general classifications, as the authors believe that teachers must develop these techniques for themselves. The effective teacher will develop his own specific techniques as a result of his own intelligent planning or by obtaining ideas from his professional reading. Suggestions are made in the following pages of general methods of procedure. The teacher should then be able to apply within the framework of this general procedure specific techniques that should result in effective teaching. No one can, or should, take initiative away from a teacher by designating specific techniques to follow.

Getting Started. The start of bookkeeping instruction is very important and should be planned by the teacher with great care. Success in getting the class off to a good start will do much to insure the students' future success in understanding the theory and mechanics of bookkeeping. The use of the discussion method can be valuable at the beginning to bring out the reasons for keeping accurate records both for the individual and for a business. The principle should be developed that bookkeeping is a study of history—the financial history of a business. Analogies can be drawn; for example, the study of the history of our country helps individuals determine and understand future actions, and so can the study of the financial history of a business help a businessman determine the actions to be taken in the future of the business.

The majority of the secondary-school bookkeeping textbooks begin with a presentation of the balance sheet and profit-and-loss statement. This presentation has the psychological objective of showing to the students first the results of keeping records—the financial statements—with the subsequent development of the methods whereby financial statements are determined. This method of presentation can be likened to teaching students how a gasoline engine operates. First, it would be most logical to show the learners what a gasoline engine looks like in its final form. After determining this, then, the proper procedure would be to show how the engine is put together. It would be wise if the teacher helped the students to understand the reasons for this method of presentation because at first glance the method appears to be very illogical.

The next step in getting started is the presentation of the bookkeeping equation: "Assets equal Liabilities plus Proprietorship." Again, students should be made to understand that bookkeeping is the process of gathering historical information about the financial transactions of a business. A financial transaction is either (*a*) a change in the form of property used by a business or (*b*) a change in the ownership of property used in a business. The property used in a business is known as *assets*. The ownership of property is known as *equities*. There are two types of equities in property—*liabilities* and *proprietorship*. Thus, bookkeeping results in the determination of the changes of property and changes of ownership of property used in a business in terms of monetary values.

The foregoing principles are the ones that it will be necessary for students to understand with respect to the bookkeeping equation. However, the teacher should by no means begin by using the terms *assets, liabilities,* and *proprietorship;* nor should the teacher in the beginning use such terms as *equities, financial transactions,* or any other term that will be beyond the comprehension of the student. The principles involved in the bookkeeping equation should be developed gradually through the use of personal illustrations.

For example, in developing the theory of the bookkeeping equation, the teacher might begin by asking students to list the property that they own such as clothes, cash, bicycles, indicating that these items have a money value and that their value can also be expressed in terms of ownership. A simple equation can be developed that the value of the property owned by the students is equal to the value of ownership. From this simple beginning the same ideas can be expressed with respect to the property used in a business. After this concept is well established in the students' minds, the bookkeeping terms *assets* and *proprietorship* can be substituted for property and ownership in illustrating the equation that:

$$\text{Assets} = \text{Proprietorship}$$

The element of liabilities can be introduced next through illustrating the idea that all of the property used in a business may not be paid for, and thus consideration must be given to the creditor type of equity. The theory of the final equation, Assets = Liabilities + Proprietorship, must be introduced slowly, using first simple illustrations and proceeding to the more complex. When it appears evident through discussion and questioning that the students comprehend the concept, then the teacher may substitute specific terms such as *cash* and *equipment* for assets and names of creditors for liabilities to illustrate how changes in the form of assets take place as well as changes in ownership.

The teacher should be cautioned again to proceed slowly during this initial presentation. It may well be that several class hours will be used in developing the foregoing theory. Do not be afraid of going over the equation again and again, using many different kinds of illustrations, and do not make the mistake of presenting unfamiliar terms to the students until they are ready for them. The elements of expenses and income should not be presented until later when the theory of debit and credit is explained.

Theory of Debit and Credit. When the account is introduced in the study of bookkeeping, the theory of debit and credit must also be presented. The use of the account and its particular form should be explained as merely a device peculiar to bookkeeping for keeping a record of the changes in form of property and of ownership in property. A simple "T" account should be illustrated first, with the teacher pointing out that the top of the "T" is a line used for writing the name of the property or equity. The perpendicular line of the "T" is used for dividing the account into halves. The reason for dividing the account into halves is so that on one side we may list (monetary amounts) the additions to property or equity and on the other side we may list subtractions from values of property or equity. The left side of the account is called the *debit* side and the right side is called the *credit* side. No further explanations should be made of the terms debit and credit, other than that debit means *left* and credit means *right*. To explain what accounts are credited for additions and debited for subtractions, and what accounts are debited for additions and credited for subtractions, reference can be made again to the bookkeeping equation, Assets = Liabilities + Proprietorship. Assets are on the left-hand side of the equation and thus should be debited for additions and credited for subtractions. Liabilities and Proprietorship are on the right-hand side or credit side of the equation and thus should be credited for additions and debited for subtractions.

There is no particular logic for this technique other than that custom has decreed that the procedure be followed, just as custom has decreed that we drive on the right-hand side of the road. Accordingly, students should be urged to memorize the theory of debit and credit. Any attempts to show a logical motive behind the theory of debit and credit will only confuse the students in most cases. The idea that debit means left and that credit means right is a very simple concept. By using the equation to recall which accounts should be debited for increases and which to credit, the student should master the theory with little difficulty.

When the items of expense and income are presented again, the bookkeeping equation can be used to good advantage. Income increases proprietorship and expense decreases income. Thus, expense must also decrease proprietorship. The equation can be developed that Assets = Liabilities + Proprietorship + (Income-Expense). The fact that this equation appears complicated can be used to the teacher's advantage. Through the principle of transposition, Expense can be transposed to the left-hand side of the equation and thus eliminate the minus sign so as to make the equation appear like this:

Assets + Expenses = Liabilities + Proprietorship + Income

It should be evident, then, that Expenses are debited for increases (because of being on the left-hand side of the equation) and Income is credited for increases (because of being on the right-hand side of the equation).

The theory of debit and credit is the foundation of double-entry bookkeeping as compared to single-entry bookkeeping. Every transaction is recorded in two parts in double-entry—a debit and a credit with the debits always equaling the credits. In single-entry bookkeeping the theory of debit and credit is not followed; thus the information resulting from this type of bookkeeping is less complete than that resulting from double-entry bookkeeping. Single-entry bookkeeping provides information only for increases or decreases in assets without the corresponding increase or decrease in the equity. Accordingly, single-entry bookkeeping is not as desirable as double-entry because it provides inadequate information for the typical business.

The Books of Account. Little difficulty should be experienced by the teacher in teaching the books of account, the general and special journals, and the general and subsidiary ledgers. The use of the general journal to record transactions prior to posting them to the various accounts can be justified on the basis of convenience. Journals would not necessarily have to be used in bookkeeping. However, it is often necessary for a businessman to refer to a transaction that occurred on a specific day of the month. This commonly occurs where there may be a difference of opinion between the owner of a business and a customer as to whether or not a bill has been paid. Students should be made to understand that the chronological recording of transactions can provide an easy means of reference for a businessman with respect to a given transaction; thus, transactions should be journalized in chronological order. The teacher can provide illustrations of the difficulty encountered in locating specific transactions when a general journal is not used.

The extra work involved in bookkeeping by the use of a general journal can be used as a means of introducing the special journals (sales, purchases, cash receipts, and cash payments). The use of these journals should be justified primarily on the basis of minimizing the work of posting. When transactions of a similar nature occur frequently enough in a business it is most logical to place these similar transactions in a special journal so that the total may be posted in one amount. Illustrations by the teacher showing the extra work involved by not using special journals should appeal to students. Whenever new concepts are introduced in the bookkeeping course they usually can be justified on the basis of either providing more complete information for the businessman or simplifying the record-keeping processes. Students should be made to understand the necessity for the large amount of detail work in keeping a set of books and that whenever it is possible to simplify this detail work, savings are realized both in money and in the work time of the bookkeeper.

The use of controlling accounts with the consequent use of the subsidiary ledgers usually is not presented in bookkeeping textbooks until the final chapters. By this time the concept of simplification should be fairly well developed in the students' minds with consequent little difficulty in comprehension. Difficulty is sometimes encountered concerning the posting to two ledgers, the general ledger and the subsidiary ledger. Students sometimes are confused by the procedure, feeling that double posting is taking place. It should be carefully pointed out that the use of subsidiary ledgers eliminates the use of a large number of accounts in the general ledger, thereby shortening the number of accounts that will be listed on the trial balance. A trial balance of subsidiary ledgers is never taken; the purpose of these ledgers is to provide detailed information for the controlling account in the general ledger.

Many teachers feel that a great deal of time must be spent upon the mechanics of ruling accounts in the ledger, insisting upon neatness and exact procedure. It is the belief of the authors that this technique is inconsequential as compared to the more important principle of understanding the use of books of account. Accordingly, emphasis on the details of this nature should be kept at a minimum.

The Worksheet. Emphasis by teachers of bookkeeping on the worksheet as a device used by bookkeepers has been greatly out of proportion as compared to other important aspects of the course. Understanding of the worksheet is important, but it is often given disproportionate importance because it embodies many important concepts of bookkeeping. Teachers have used the worksheet for examination purposes because it represents a relatively easy problem to develop for examinations. Used out of context in this manner it often is placed in the students' minds as one of the highly important statements for a business. Consequently, there has been much memorizing of the form of the worksheet with little knowledge of the reasons for its use.

The worksheet, as its name implies, is merely a device used by bookkeepers for accumulating the information from the books of account for the purpose of performing the work necessary at the end of a fiscal period. It can be likened to an outline prepared by a student for use in writing a theme in English. Or, it can be compared to the notes used by a speaker in giving an address. In introducing the worksheet for the first time, the teacher could illustrate its value and use by asking students the following: "Let us suppose that I have made an assignment in which I have asked you to keep a record for one month of every receipt and expenditure of money. Let us assume that at the end of the month you had a notebook full of individual transactions listing each receipt and expenditure. I then asked you to type a report in which you would list your receipts under the headings of gifts, earned, and miscellaneous; and you would list your expenditures under the headings of entertainment, clothes, personal, car, and miscellaneous. This report is to be handed in and graded. How would you proceed in writing your report?"

Although the teacher might get a variety of answers as a result of this question, nonetheless through skillful directions he should obtain from the students the procedure that each student would first summarize on scrap paper the classifications of the various receipts and expenditures called for prior to the final typing of the report. The fallacy of attempting to type the report without making this "rough summarization" can easily be pointed out.

Illustrating, then, how this technique is comparable to the techniques of the bookkeeper using a worksheet for the preparation of his reports should fix in the students' minds the necessity and logic of this tool. The mechanics of classifying and adjusting accounts should then be more meaningful if established upon this broad base of understanding.

The first worksheet to be introduced in bookkeeping is the simple six-column type with no adjustments. The purpose of this worksheet is to determine the accuracy of posting through listing the trial balance and to classify the accounts into profit-and-loss-statement accounts and balance-sheet accounts for the purpose of preparing statements. Little difficulty should be encountered in teaching the students the use of this device. Time should be taken to explain the steps to be followed if the trial balance does not balance, such as analyzing the difference to determine where the error might be located. Although many teachers make a fetish of accuracy, it should be pointed out that errors often result from maintaining a set of books. Students should be taught how to analyze errors to determine what steps should be taken to locate them. For example, in the trial-balance errors may arise in transferring numbers from the account in the ledger to the worksheet. An error of this type may be located by dividing the difference of the trial balance by nine. If the difference is equally divisible by nine there is a good likelihood that this type of error has occurred. Another step to be taken is to divide the difference by two. After dividing by two, then the bookkeeper can look to see whether any number in the trial balance is the same as this figure and is incorrectly placed in either the debit or credit column. An error of this nature will double the difference in the trial balance. These are only a few of the checks a student may make to locate errors. Others should be brought to his attention. By this procedure greater understanding is developed.

A second difficulty that may be encountered in using the simple six-column worksheet is the classifying of accounts for statement purposes. The teacher should, at every opportunity, direct the attention of the student to the differences between the temporary and permanent accounts. It may be advantageous to drill the students on the classification of accounts into the major classifications of Assets, Liabilities, Proprietorship, Cost, and Income. Students should also be well versed in classifying accounts into the subclassifications under these major headings. Only through a thorough knowledge of the various classifications into which accounts fall will students be able to prepare financial statements properly.

The worksheet with adjustments poses more difficult problems than does the simple six-column type. This device is usually not introduced into the course until the latter part when a merchandising type of business is being studied. The types of adjustments usually developed at this time are the adjustments for supplies, insurance, and merchandise inventory. The major concept to teach when presenting the adjusting entries is to help the students understand the need for them. Adjusting entries are necessary because of the principle of expediency. Some accounts are not kept up to date because it would be too much trouble for the bookkeeper to do so. Because there are certain accounts that are not kept up to date, adjusting entries are necessary to bring them up to date at the end of the fiscal period.

The teacher can use many different types of illustrations to show why it would be impractical to maintain certain accounts currently. For example, use the account, store supplies. It would appear rather silly for the check-out clerk in a grocery store to run back and inform the bookkeeper every time she uses a paper bag to sack up groceries for a customer. The best way, obviously, would be to count the paper bags on hand at the end of a fiscal period and subtract this number from the paper bags purchased. By making this computation the actual number of paper bags consumed could be easily determined. From this type of illustration it is an easy step to the need for adjustment entries. Similar illustrations can be developed for the prepaid insurance account, salaries, interest, and so forth.

The merchandise-inventory adjustment presents a somewhat similar problem. However, more careful consideration must be given to this entry. The beginning inventory is closed out because it is a part of the cost of goods sold. In a sense, at the close of a fiscal period, a business will not have any of the goods on hand that were on hand at the beginning of the period because theoretically the first goods on hand are the first sold. Thus, the beginning inventory is closed to the income-and-expense summary account since this account is used to summarize cost and expenses and income. The ending inventory, on the other hand, is recorded as a debit to the inventory account because it is the correct amount of inventory at the present time. Since any goods on hand at the end of the fiscal period reduces the cost of goods sold, then the ending inventory should be credited to the income-and-expense summary account to offset the beginning inventory, which was debited to this account.

The teacher should teach this adjustment very carefully, making sure that the students understand the WHY. Again, the use of practical illustrations will be of great benefit.

The Financial Statements. The teaching of financial statements in elementary bookkeeping is not a difficult task. However, the emphasis placed upon these important documents by teachers varies. Teachers who place an undue emphasis upon the mechanics of bookkeeping oftentimes fail to pinpoint the financial statements as the end results of keeping books—without the financial statements, bookkeeping would be meaningless.

A large amount of time should be spent upon the income statement and balance sheet to show how these statements disclose the profit-making ability of the business and its financial condition. Mere preparation of statements is not sufficient—interpretation and understanding must also take place. The teacher should build a file of financial statements from various types of businesses and use these illustrative materials to show how stockholders, lending agencies, and prospective owners of a business can use these data for their various purposes.

Is net worth stated accurately? What are some of the evidences that indicate that a business should adjust its financial procedure? These are among the questions that should be discussed and answered. The forms of the various statements are relatively unimportant as compared with understanding their functions and what they reveal. It is the latter that should be emphasized in teaching bookkeeping.

Closing the Books. The work that must be performed at the close of a fiscal period is known as the periodic summary. Besides the work of taking a trial balance to test the equality of debits and credits, work must be performed that will bring certain accounts up to date (adjustments), and the financial statements must be prepared. The final work to be performed is the closing of those accounts which are temporary so as to clear the books for the succeeding fiscal period. The mechanical work of closing out the temporary or nominal accounts is relatively simple and should not cause the teacher much difficulty in helping students to understand WHY. If students do have difficulty in understanding why certain accounts are closed out at the end of a fiscal period, it is good evidence that students do not understand the nature and characteristics of temporary accounts and thus this concept should be retaught.

By the use of "T" accounts the teacher can illustrate that the cost
and expense and income accounts are merely subdivisions of the
proprietorship account. Actually, there is no need to classify transactions into either income or expense as these transactions could be
entered directly into the proprietorship account. [Refer to the equation, Assets = Liabilities + Proprietorship + (Income-Expenses).]
However, according to the principle of obtaining complete information about a business, certain transactions are classified as either expenses or income so that they may stand out more clearly as either
increasing or decreasing proprietorship. The following diagram could
be used:

Proprietorship

Expense		Income	
−		+	
+	−	−	+

Consequently, after the cost and expense and income accounts
have served their purpose of providing information concerning these
elements to the proprietor for a fiscal period, they are no longer
needed and thus are closed out. The information provided is transferred to the proprietorship account through the closing-out process.

The mechanics of closing the temporary accounts is sometimes
confusing to students because of the many steps involved. This procedure can be clarified to some extent by first showing how the temporary accounts could be closed directly into the proprietorship
account and then giving a contrasting illustration that shows them
being closed into the profit-and-loss summary, thence to the drawing
account and finally to the proprietorship account. The advantages
and disadvantages of the latter method could be discussed as well
as the advantages and disadvantages of the direct method. Through
this type of activity, students will be able to understand the procedure better, as well as learn the mechanics.

Care must be taken not to confuse the students with the closing
process and the ruling and balancing of the permanent accounts.
This latter procedure has no connection with closing accounts, but
is followed for the purpose of setting out the balances of the permanent accounts at the start of the new fiscal period. Careless use of

bookkeeping terminology often leads to confused students. Detailed explanations should be made of such terms as *ruling an account, balancing an account,* the *balance of an account,* and the *closing of an account.* Students may experience difficulty because of lack of understanding of these terms.

Special Problems. Some special problems that oftentimes cause difficulty to bookkeeping students should be carefully considered by the teacher—such topics as payroll and tax procedures, accruals, interest determination, and allowances for depreciation and bad debts.

Payroll procedures and income tax have been given increasing emphasis in the past few years by authors of bookkeeping textbooks —and rightfully so. Payroll bookkeeping is a specialized field in itself and not too much time can be devoted to it in the typical bookkeeping class. In any event, the teacher should be well versed in payroll taxes such as the social security taxes, old age benefits, and unemployment insurance. As there have been several changes in social security taxes in recent years, the teacher should inform himself of the most recent changes in the laws. An excellent device that might be followed (if available) is to visit a business firm that has a large number of employees so that students can see firsthand how payroll procedures are handled. If the teacher can obtain some practical experience in payroll accounting, his presentations of this point will also be materially improved. If a field trip is not feasible, resource persons can be invited to the class for discussion of payroll information. Such persons as businessmen, personnel managers, or the field representatives for the district social security office would be valuable sources of information.

The teaching of income tax in the public schools has also been given increasing emphasis in the past few years. Typically, this instruction has been found in the bookkeeping class, which makes it necessary for the bookkeeping teacher to have up-to-date information about income tax procedure. The Bureau of Internal Revenue has developed an income tax unit which covers a period of approximately two weeks. This income tax teaching kit provided by the Bureau of Internal Revenue consists of teachers' manuals for a general course in income tax and a farm course. Each student is provided with a handbook for use in working both courses; the handbook includes income tax blanks. Also included are large income tax forms for purposes of visual instruction.

The policy of the Bureau of Internal Revenue of providing teaching materials for income tax instruction in high school has been very successful. Consequently, it is highly probable that there will be increases in emphasis on instruction in this area with the teacher of bookkeeping being given the responsibility of seeing that it is carried out.

One other special problem that may be encountered by the teacher of bookkeeping is the teaching of accrual bookkeeping. Such concepts as allowances for bad debts and depreciation, accrued receivables and accrued payables sometimes may be difficult to explain. One method may be to explain and illustrate carefully the differences between cash-basis bookkeeping and accrual basis. Federal income tax regulations may be used as another illustration. Personal illustrations such as a wage that is earned daily but not paid until the end of a week or month can also be used. The idea of income being earned, or costs and expenses being owed, prior to their being paid, should be developed early in the course. When sales or purchases on credit are first taught it is not too early to discuss the principle of accrual bookkeeping. Early introduction of this concept would help to make it easier to teach when it is stressed more in the latter part of the bookkeeping course.

Manual and Machine Bookkeeping

The development of the electronic computer and the subsequent emphasis placed upon electronic data processing has caused more attention being given by authors of bookkeeping textbooks to manual and mechanical devices which are used for bookkeeping purposes. In most bookkeeping textbooks at least one chapter is devoted to computer applications for bookkeeping and it is obvious that greater emphasis will be given in textbooks of the future to machine applications for bookkeeping problems.

Thus, it is necessary that the bookkeeping teacher of the future will have to be well versed in modern data-processing techniques so that he will be able to explain and teach these procedures in the bookkeeping classes. A more complete discussion of data processing in business education is found in Chapter Eleven.

However, in addition to the use of the computer more attention must be given in the bookkeeping course to the application of manual and mechanical devices for keeping records. It is true that except in the smallest type of business the maintenance of bookkeeping records without the use of some kind of manual device or machine is rare. Consequently, the bookkeeping teacher should be familiar with the most common methods of manual bookkeeping devices and bookkeeping machines so that he can illustrate how bookkeeping fundamentals as found in the textbook can be applied in actual practice in business.

The most common methods of manual devices are the pegboards or accounting boards which are commonly referred to as the *one-write systems*. The essential characteristic of these systems is the ability to prepare a receipt, to post to an account, to prepare a customer's statement, and to journalize a transaction all in one operation without the necessity of retranscribing bookkeeping data in several different books of account.

In machine bookkeeping the same characteristics are found, only more of the operations are mechanical rather than manual. The results are the same regardless of the system used—the advantages over "pen-and-ink" bookkeeping are the increased speed in recording bookkeeping data and increased accuracy resulting from the elimination of retranscription errors. Because of the widespread use of these devices bookkeeping students should be made aware of how they are used.

Miscellaneous Problems in Teaching Bookkeeping

There are several other problems in the teaching of bookkeeping which must be faced by the teacher. While these are not all directly related to the methodology of teaching the content of the course because of the nature of these problems they have a significant effect upon the methodology which will be used.

One problem is the wide range of student abilities typically found in a bookkeeping class. This problem is one of the most annoying and frustrating to the bookkeeping teacher because it is so difficult to cope with. In almost every class there will be some students who are unable to comprehend fully the principles involved in bookkeeping and there will be some students who will have little or no difficulty in mastering the concepts of the course.

One solution for teaching the weaker students is individual instruction. This may be accomplished either in or outside of class, but in any event it is a poor solution because of the extra work thrust upon an already overburdened teacher. However, one must either use this type of teaching or else let the poorer students get along as best they can with the teacher giving individual help whenever possible. This is a real problem because of the fact that understanding in bookkeeping is built upon certain fundamental knowledges. Unless these fundamentals are thoroughly understood at the beginning, a student is destined to have difficulty. It is not practical or fair for the teacher to hold back the majority of a class until everyone in the class is thoroughly versed in the fundamentals. Consequently, someone must be left behind.

In the case of better students there are several possible solutions to the problem. The most common "solution" heard mentioned by teachers is to provide the better students with extra work. This is impractical in many cases because it is conceivable that the attitude of the better student might be "the more I study the more work I have to do—so why study?" A much better technique to use in the case of the superior student would be to encourage him to work ahead in the course at his own speed. Do not attempt to keep this type of student with the rest of the class, but stimulate him to proceed as fast as he wishes. Another procedure is to ask the superior student to help the slower students. Oftentimes a student can help another student much better than the teacher because of better understanding of difficulties. Still another procedure might be to give the superior student an advanced textbook, perhaps a college accounting text, which he might study. A personal project might be worked out. In any event, the superior student should be encouraged to work ahead. This should not be mandatory, of course, because then the working ahead might be interpreted as extra assignments. Any technique of this nature must be used with the student's approval or on a volunteer basis. Only then will it be successful.

One development which seems to hold much promise for a solution to the problem of handling individual differences in students is the use of programmed learning materials. On the college level, programmed learning materials for accounting have been used successfully. As yet few programmed learning materials have been developed for use in the teaching of bookkeeping. However, because of the nature of the subject matter found in bookkeeping programmed learning could be used effectively. Some research has been carried out in this area and the results have been promising. It is not unlikely that future developments in the instruction of bookkeeping in the secondary school will find programmed learning materials being used extensively.

Another problem which often confronts bookkeeping teachers is a weakness on the part of students in the fundamental processes of arithmetic. Oftentimes teachers will find that some students have difficulty in addition, subtraction, division, and multiplication, all of which are so often used in bookkeeping. Teachers have to decide, when this condition is apparent, whether or not to take time out from the content of the bookkeeping course to give instruction in these fundamentals. There is no one solution to this problem. It will be up to the individual teacher to make his own decision on whether to teach arithmetic or not, if students are having difficulty. Some of the bookkeeping textbooks provide exercises at the end of chapters that are developed for the purpose of meeting this weakness of students. Some schools provide adding and calculating machines for their bookkeeping classes. It is recommended that whenever machines are available, they should be used by students—as certainly in most businesses they would be available. Interest tables can be provided for students for use in computing interest, and payroll or sales tax tables should be used.

Still another problem found in the teaching of bookkeeping is the paper work with which the teacher may become involved. To what extent should the problems worked by students be checked by the teacher? Should the assignments merely be given a check mark of completion or should they be thoroughly checked? If a teacher is teaching one or more classes in bookkeeping, this paper work can become a tremendous burden. The other extreme is to do no checking at all. This can be accomplished by thoroughly going over in class the problems that have been assigned, each student then checking his own paper. Any errors on the student's paper can be used as a basis for discussion or explanation by the teacher. This method will not determine whether a student has worked the assignment, but if the teacher has instilled the idea that success in bookkeeping to a large degree will be determined by the students' applying the principles of the course in the solving of problems, there should be little difficulty on this score. The teacher should be able to determine by observation those students who are not working the assignments; an individual talk to these students should help to motivate them to perform their homework. The job of the teacher is primarily to teach, not to check papers. Accordingly, paper checking should be kept at a minimum.

Visual Aids and Motivation Devices
for Teaching Bookkeeping

There are many types of visual aids and motivation devices for the teaching of bookkeeping that are very helpful to the teacher. Bookkeeping is a subject that requires the use of a large number of visual devices for thorough comprehension of the instructional material. The subject-matter usually provides motivation in itself, but the course can be greatly enriched by the use of certain techniques that stimulate the student to greater interest in bookkeeping.

Visual Aids. The best type of visual aid that can be used by the teacher is the blackboard. Adequate blackboard space is a must for working all problems that have been assigned, as these problems should be thoroughly illustrated and discussed. It is usually not sufficient merely to go over the problem assignments in class orally. The teacher will find it to his advantage to use the blackboard to visually illustrate how the transactions are recorded, the form of financial statements, the development of worksheets, and any other problem involved in bookkeeping. Any explanation by the teacher of a bookkeeping procedure should be accompanied by visual illustration. The blackboard will provide the easiest means for this.

The use of the overhead projector and transparencies supplements the use of the blackboard effectively. In fact, the overhead projector can be more effective than the use of the blackboard for use in illustrating the solutions to problems. As indicated earlier, most textbook publishing firms will sell at a nominal cost to users of their textbook transparencies which show the solutions to all of the problems given in the text. The projection of these solutions on the screen will save the teacher a tremendous amount of time and will give the students an opportunity to check their work against the correct solution. Also, for those schools fortunate enough to have a copying machine the teacher can prepare his own transparencies with little trouble and at a small cost.

Films and filmstrips are also available for instruction in bookkeeping. The films that are available are not particularly helpful with respect to methodology, but are organized more on the basis of guidance. There are several filmstrips available for instructional purposes that are correlated with specific textbooks. These filmstrips can be extremely valuable, especially in teaching the mechanical aspects of bookkeeping.

The bookkeeping teacher can develop many types of visual aids himself through the preparation of charts, diagrams, bulletin-board displays, and so on. The following are some of the techniques that the teacher may use in developing these materials.

Suggestions for Teacher-Made Visual Aids in Bookkeeping

Use color without fail!
Don't try to put too much on one chart or poster.
Use faint pencil guide-lines (layout!) and then do it *free hand.*

1. Flash cards are easy.   (one side)   (other side)

An entire set is useful on closing and adjusting entries.

Inventory		Entry to record
	Income Sum.	the NEW Inventory

Also, use a set having merely account names—for drill on account classification, recognition of debit or credit balance, in which statement used, whether closed or not, and the like.

2. A series of ledger accounts; use four-colored ball pen for colored lines. Might be: Cash Account with entries only; another showing it "forwarded"; another showing it balanced. Then an account like Sales or Purchases, showing IT open, then forwarded, and finally CLOSED. Use accounts from the text.

3. Copy the first simple P & L Statement or Balance Sheet on a large chart from which to talk to the class! (Use color.)

In a P & L Statement (or Income Statement) you MIGHT write certain important items in RED—as the GROSS profit, the NET profit—or the word *Cost* in "Cost of Goods Sold."

4. A poster—just to hang in the room at the appropriate time or times—relating to any item:

Steps in the bookkeeping cycle
"Closing" the ledger

"Adjusting" the ledger

Showing DAYS responsible for any accrued item

Showing, by lines or arrows, the "Posting" of a journal entry; of the totals of a special journal, and so on (section of original book and then the accounts concerned)

The "discount period" in a note receivable discounted; a "personal" balance sheet—copied from text, perhaps

5. Print up the HEADINGS for all columns in a worksheet—on a cardboard strip that can be placed above the top of your blackboard; perhaps show the BEGINNING of the vertical ruled lines, in colors. Then it is easy to CONTINUE these lines down the board—using colored chalk—and have a MUCH BETTER blackboard worksheet. This might also be done profitably with special journals.

6. For CONTROLLING ACCOUNTS, show a special journal, totaled and ruled, and beside it a book marked SUBSIDIARY LEDGER (Accounts Receivable?) and another marked GENERAL LEDGER—with arrows or colored lines going from the TOTAL to the general ledger, and from the (bracketed) individual items to the subsidiary ledger. Make "ledgers" different colors!

Recommendations: A set of eight Speedball BLICKER pens costs only around $1.00. India ink comes in MANY colors. Use reasonably heavy cardboard or poster board; it CAN be had in color itself! (Use white MOSTLY though.) Clean the pen well after using; temporarily let it set in water when you are not using it. Use art-gum eraser for pencil marks and slight dirt. Learn a simple alphabet to use—printed.

Motivation Techniques. Although for many bookkeeping students the subject-matter of bookkeeping is motivating in itself, nonetheless there are certain techniques that the teacher can use to advantage. Visitations to places of business to observe bookkeeping records has proven to be highly motivating. Prior to visiting places of business, the teacher should warn the students that the records they will see will in all likelihood be dissimilar to the records they have studied in their textbooks. There is a logical explanation to this in that bookkeeping procedures have certain fundamental processes that will be found in any bookkeeping system. However, different types of businesses will adapt the fundamental processes to their own peculiar problems, which results in dissimilar practices. The teacher can take advantage of this situation to ask the students to look for the application of the fundamental processes during the visitation. Another point that should be discussed prior to the visitation is that much bookkeeping today is done on machines. Consequently, the records observed may not appear to be like any the student has studied. Actually it should be pointed out that the records will be similar in many respects but that machine records must be adapted in size and form to be used in a bookkeeping machine.

Visitations by the teacher to places of business to observe bookkeeping procedures will also be helpful to the teacher in enriching class presentation. The teacher's familiarity with actual bookkeeping procedure can be used in class discussion to illustrate how textbook procedures are comparable to actual business practice. Personal experiences of the teacher in actual bookkeeping, either through observation or work experience, can do much to stimulate class discussions. Students will feel that the subject-matter has more life if the teacher can point out actual business problems that are applicable to the topic being studied.

Keeping records of personal projects engaged in by students will also prove of value to stimulate interest in bookkeeping. Farm students who are raising farm animals or produce for sale could have a type of project in which practice using adequate records of income and expenses would be of value. The keeping of records for class projects such as those sponsored by junior or senior classes to raise funds for some purpose can be used. There are many other types of projects, either individual or group, that could be used by the bookkeeping teacher to stimulate interest in bookkeeping. The teacher should be constantly on the lookout for projects and weave these into the course whenever possible.

Evaluation in Bookkeeping

Several problems in evaluation are peculiar to bookkeeping; they revolve around the various bases for assigning grades to students for achievement. The most common bases for assigning grades are examinations, homework assignments, class recitation, and practice sets or projects. Each of these bases is discussed in the succeeding paragraphs.

Examinations. Examinations for determining student achievement in bookkeeping can be placed into two categories, namely, published tests and teacher-prepared tests. Published tests, usually of an objective nature containing questions of the true-false, multiple-choice, and completion type, are very comprehensive. These tests are typically furnished by the publisher of the textbook free to teachers who are using the text. The questions in the test are correlated with the textbook material, and in some cases norms have been developed so that the teacher can compare the achievement of his students with others in terms of the norms. These examinations are quite easy to use since the teacher does not have to prepare the examination and the tests are quite well developed.

Teacher-prepared examinations can be either the objective type similar to the published tests or may be in the form of problems similar to those worked by the students as a result of assignments. It is in this latter category that some difficulties develop.

One of the main difficulties that occurs in the use of problem-type tests is in the grading. If one long problem is used for examination purposes, the teacher is faced with the difficulty of what to do if an error is made by the student in an early part of the test that will cause subsequent errors in the final answer. This difficulty may be eliminated through the procedure of counting off only once for an error that may affect later parts of the problem. Following this procedure will make it necessary for the teacher to follow each error through the problem, which obviously causes much careful analysis of each error and, consequently, takes a great deal of time.

Another problem in using this type of test is that of determining how much to count off for each error made. Some scheme must be developed whereby the test is divided into parts for grading with a proportionate number of points being given to each part. Again the teacher is faced with the problem of determining the weight to be given to each part. For example, let us suppose that the examination is composed of a problem over the worksheet. The student is given a list of accounts with balances plus information for adjustments of account, and with these data he is asked to complete the worksheet. One grading scheme that might be used would be to assign 20 points each to the columns containing the trial balance, the adjustment, profit and loss, and balance sheet with an additional 20 bonus points given if the worksheet is completed in the time allowed without error. Perhaps 2 points could be taken off for each error in a column. Thus, if a student made one error his score would be 78. If he made no errors his score would be 100. However, errors made in the trial balance column should not be penalized again when they are carried over to the remaining columns.

Another problem encountered is the time element. Should students be given a problem that can be completed within the time limit by the poorest student? If so, then the best students are not being challenged. If not, then there may be some students who may say, "I only completed half of the problem, but what I did complete was 100 per cent accurate. I am sure that I would have gotten the problem all right if I had had more time." Whether or not time should play a part in a problem examination is a decision that will have to be made by the individual teacher. It is the belief of the authors that time should play a part, and that the best students are those who can work rapidly as well as accurately.

Many of the difficulties of scoring problem-type tests, as indicated above, can be eliminated by using short problems that test one concept or part of a larger problem. For example, an examination containing short problems such as illustrated below can be used effectively.

> (10 points) John Short, an employee of the ABC Company, has been paid $4,500 in wages from the beginning of the year. His wages earned for the period October 3-17 are $250. His income tax withholding is $19.90. For what amount will Short's paycheck for the period October 3-17 be made? (Use the current F.I.C.A. tax rate)

One type of question that is not used frequently in determining achievement in bookkeeping is the essay type, the reasons being the lack of objectivity and the time required in grading. However, this type of question has great value, especially in determining if students can communicate their ideas to others. Occasional use of this type of question is highly recommended.

Homework Assignments. Another problem in evaluation is to decide to what extent homework assignments should be checked or graded. If the teacher examines carefully every homework assignment, an extremely large amount of time will necessarily have to be spent on the activity with less time available for planning. It is a question of values. Which is more important—preparation for instruction or checking the results of instruction? There is no easy answer to this question. However, if the teacher carefully goes over each assignment in class, discussing the difficulties that have arisen, then there should be little necessity for checking the homework assignments that are turned in. The teacher may wish to determine whether the students have completed the assignment, and this can be done rapidly. Perhaps an occasional spot checking of the papers for accuracy can be made, but as a general procedure it is recommended that the completion of assignments should be a student responsibility and that the students be encouraged to get individual help from the teacher concerning the answers to assignments that are worked incorrectly.

Practice Sets. The grading of practice sets can be another onerous chore for the bookkeeping teacher unless some system is developed whereby this can be done with a minimum of time. Neatness and form of practice sets can be determined by a casual look through the sets, noting these particular characteristics. The age-old debate as to whether or not practice sets should be worked in pen or pencil is unimportant. Those advocating the pen justify their stand by stating that the books of a business are kept in ink and thus the student of bookkeeping may as well keep his set of accounts in the same manner. Teachers holding this belief undoubtedly place a great emphasis on the *How*. On the other hand, those teachers who advocate pencil stress the *Why*. These teachers assume that learning bookkeeping is a practice situation and that a student's assurance should not be marred by being required to use ink and thus being unable to erase a mistake. The latter approach seems to be the more practical. In any event, the choice of pen or pencil is unimportant.

The accuracy of the practice set can be determined by the use of an open-set test over the practice set. The teacher can develop a series of questions which the student may answer by referring to his set. These questions typically can call for the totals of the columns in journals, balances of accounts, net profit, total of selling expenses, and the like. Thus, accuracy of the set can be determined as well as the student's familiarity with the set in knowing where to look for the answers.

Projects and Questions for Discussion

1. Examine and compare two high-school bookkeeping text books. Pay particular attention to the following points:
    a. Order of presentation of the various topics covered in the text

b. Types of study material for students at the end of chapters

c. Illustrations

d. Major differences in presentation of subject matter

e. Supplementary materials available such as teacher's key, workbooks, study guides, tests, and so forth.

2. Develop a case problem or case problems for use in class discussion by a secondary-school bookkeeping class. Adapt the cases to some specific topic covered in a secondary-school textbook.

3. Prepare five short problem-type questions which would be suitable for an examination of a unit in bookkeeping.

4. Prepare a visual aid of some type to illustrate a particular topic in bookkeeping. Select a topic which you think students might have difficulty with and develop the visual aid in such a way that it will help in understanding.

5. Select a specific unit in bookkeeping and prepare a lesson plan for teaching the unit. Include with the plan any visual aids or motivating devices you would use in teaching the unit. Be specific and describe in detail all of the procedures you would follow in presenting the unit.

6. What do you believe should be the purpose of a bookkeeping course—developing mechanical proficiency on the part of students in keeping books or an understanding of the uses of bookkeeping data for the solutions to business problems?

7. How would you go about instructing students in the use of modern data-processing procedures as applied to bookkeeping if you did not have any equipment which to show and demonstrate to students?

8. Do you believe time should be a factor in an examination in bookkeeping or should an examination be such that all students would have plenty of time to complete it?

9. List some procedures you believe would be effective in handling individual differences in your bookkeeping class.

10. In light of the increased emphasis being placed on data-processing procedures in business, what effect do you believe this will have on the form and content of bookkeeping courses in the future in the secondary school?

Case Problems

1. Ed Holmes, who is a student in your first-year bookkeeping class, is the son of a prosperous retail merchant in the city in which you are teaching. Ed is an outstanding student who plans to go to college and major in accounting after graduation from high school. He has been

working in his father's store and in recent weeks has been spending a large amount of time studying his father's bookkeeping system.

On this particular day Ed raises his hand and informs you (and the class) that from all that he can observe books of account as maintained in an actual business do not appear similar in any way to the bookkeeping methods studied in the bookkeeping class. He raises the question that perhaps it is useless to study bookkeeping in high schoool since business practice and theory are so dissimilar.

You as the teacher have never had any experience in keeping the records of an actual business. How would you handle this situation? The class and Ed are all waiting for you to justify your course.

2. You have been teaching in Holman High School for several years. This year in your bookkeeping class you have twenty-eight students with a wide range of ability. After twelve weeks of instruction you have some students who do not understand the theory of debit and credit and you have some who are so proficient and so interested that they have been working problems in the textbook several chapters ahead of where you are now in the text. In between these extremes you have students with average ability.

You realize that it is useless for you to expect the half dozen students who do not even understand the basic elements of bookkeeping to follow your instruction on the current material. You also realize that your more advanced students are becoming bored with studying in class material that they already understand thoroughly. What are some possible solutions for this situation?

3. Mr. Sam Johnson is a first-year bookkeeping teacher. His class has just completed studying the worksheet with adjustments and the subsequent preparation of an income statement and balance sheet. At the conclusion of this unit Mr. Johnson gave an examination which consisted of one long problem in which the students completed a worksheet with adjustments and the financial statements. Mr. Johnson is now grading these papers.

He is finding the grading very difficult and time-consuming. For one thing, he has found that the students have made errors here and there that have an effect on subsequent parts of the test. Johnson believes that a student should not be penalized but once for an error, so he is trying to follow through on the papers any errors made that affect later parts of the test. By doing this it takes him about a half hour to grade each paper. He has thirty students in class. Johnson figures that it will take him about two weeks to get all of the papers graded if he keeps up with his other work. What suggestions do you have to help him cut down on the amount of time spent on grading exam papers in the future?

4. As the bookkeeping teacher in Smithville High School, you find that

your students have difficulty with simple arithmetic. They have difficulty with the fundamentals, and if any problem has the element of percentage in it they are lost. You have never had any experience in the teaching of arithmetic, and besides you believe that the students should acquire these skills for themselves. Consequently, you do nothing about the improvement of the arithmetic ability. Are you right or wrong?

5. As a teacher of bookkeeping as well as typewriting and general business in Attica High School, Jim Simmons found himself swamped with grading papers. He had two sections of bookkeeping with a total of forty-five students; two sections of typewriting and one section of general business. Because of this situation Jim decided not to require his bookkeeping students to hand in their problems that he had assigned. He told his classes that in order to learn bookkeeping it is necessary to work the problems, that he was going to place this responsibility upon them, and that he would not require papers to be handed in for grading. Each student was to corerct his own paper from the solutions developed in class.

After several weeks Jim found that few of his students were working the problems and were waiting until class to complete them. Jim then decided to make the students hand in their papers again, but he told them he would not grade them but merely check them off as being completed. The students complained about this procedure because they felt that if they worked the problems the least the teacher could do would be to check them over for accuracy. Is there any solution to Jim's problem or is he destined to check many papers?

Suggested Readings

Boynton, Lewis D., *Methods of Teaching Bookkeeping*. Cincinnati, Ohio: South-Western Publishing Co., 1955.

Business Education Forum. Washington, D.C.: National Business Education Association, December issues.

Freeman, M. Herbert, and Gilbert Kahn, "Enriching High School Bookkeeping by Relating it to Business Management," *Business Education Forum* XVIII, Nos. 16, 21 (November, 1963).

Forkner, Hamden L., Robert M. Swanson, and Robert J. Thompson, *The Teaching of Bookkeeping*, Monograph 101. Cincinnati, Ohio: South-Western Publishing Co., 1960.

Musselman, Vernon A., and J. Marshall Hanna, *Teaching Bookkeeping and Accounting*. New York: Gregg Publishing Division, McGraw-Hill Book Company, 1960.

10

Teaching the Distributive Subjects

As a natural result of our world-wide economic specialization and of today's large-scale methods of producing goods, the efforts and costs entering into the distribution of those goods to ultimate consumers is great. This means, accordingly, that the opportunities of a vocational nature also are great in the area of distribution, and that there is much specialization within the field.

Techniques and procedures used in getting goods from the hands of the producer and into the hands of the consumer change rapidly. Under our American free, competitive, and profit-motivated economy new and improved ideas are in demand and hence tend to appear rapidly. Thus to a considerable degree the problem of teaching distributive subjects well for vocational objectives becomes a problem of keeping informed about current practices and techniques.

Yet throughout all teaching of distributive subjects runs a common and basic idea, namely, that we are dealing with the needs and likes and desires of people—of human beings. By profession, the teacher already has a superior understanding of the psychology that prompts people to act as they do. Thus the teacher who is interested in distributive subjects is in a position to be of real service to youth who contemplate entering this field vocationally.

The final process of teaching distributive subjects therefore may be said to have three main bases: (*a*) the learning of techniques, procedures, terminology, practices, and policies applicable to the area of distribution under consideration; (*b*) keeping informed about the current practices in the business world; and (*c*) the development of actual facility in the many required relationships with people. The first of these may be achieved largely through regular classroom procedures. The last two usually are best achieved through actual experience at appropriate work in the business world.

Distributive Occupations Defined. Changing times, new developments, and advanced thinking create needs for new terminology. New terminology frequently results in a temporary confusion in the minds of people accustomed to the limitations of terminology formerly used. Today the use of the term *distributive* still results in a degree of confusion in the minds of some people since it is relatively new to the teaching profession.

The United States Office of Education has provided us with a pertinent definition which is quite clear and helpful; it is as follows:

> Distributive occupations are defined as those followed by workers directly engaged in merchandising activities or in contact with buyers and sellers when (*a*) distributing to consumers, retailers, jobbers, wholesalers, and others the products of farm and industry, or (*b*) selling services, managing, operating, or conducting a retail, wholesale, or service business.[1]

It will be noticed that in limiting the distributive occupations to workers engaged in *merchandising activities* (or in contact with buyers and sellers) the above definition removes from consideration those workers engaged in what may be termed the more manual and mechanical trades and occupations even though a necessary part of the distribution of goods; thus it obviously would not include such workers as engineers on trains, mechanics, traffic managers, and similar occupational classifications even though they may be directly associated with the physical distribution (transportation) of goods.

---

[1] *Vocational Education,* Bulletin No. 1, General Series No. 1, Revised (Washington, D.C.: Federal Security Agency, U.S. Office of Education, 1947).

Thus those engaged in distributive occupations are engaged in *merchandising* or are *in contact with buyers and sellers* while assisting in merchandising functions. This specifically does include those managing or operating a retail, wholesale, or service business. In terms of the total number of people employed, this is one of the largest occupational classifications in our nation. It employs both men and women and to very high degree *is* our American business economy. Thus it offers a very real and practical opportunity for successful achievement of the objectives of vocational education.

Distributive Subjects. Names given to the subject-matter taught and to the courses in which it is taught are extremely varied when we examine the entire field of education for the distributive occupations. Some subject-matter and some courses are organized for and taught to regular full-time secondary students; others are intended for college students; still others are intended for employed workers and managers who can attend only a limited number of evening classes. Some courses are intended as basic introductions to the field, others as advanced courses for students already familiar with the field, and still others as short "refresher" courses in various highly specialized areas of the field. The variety of *course titles* used will depend, then, upon the individual school or community, its pertinent objectives, and the students it serves.

Here is a partial list of course titles that have been used at various times and places. Most of these usually have been relatively short courses intended for employed adults.

Receiving and Marking Goods	Store Organization
Stock Control	Store Location
Window Display	Retail Selling
Interior Display	Credits and Collections
Salesmanship	Fashion Selling
Shoe Salesmanship	Store Equipment
Store Arithmetic	Specialty Shop Management
Advertising	Store Services
Newspaper Advertising	Cashiering
Store Layout	Package Wrapping
Retailing	Display Signs
Store Management	Specialty Selling

It will be observed, however, that all of these course titles are indicative of subject-matter centering around the field of selling and retailing. With minor exceptions, this is the case.

When offered for regular full-time high-school students, all of the subject-matter indicated by various specialized courses such as those just mentioned frequently is combined into one or two high-school courses. These high-school courses most frequently are given titles such as Salesmanship, Merchandising, Retailing, Retail Selling, or Distribution. This chapter deals with such courses.

Distributive Education. The term *distributive education* is applied most accurately to a relatively complete program of vocational education for distributive occupations. Thus it includes not only appropriate separate courses such as those already mentioned, but also appropriate laboratory experiences through approved and educationally supervised on-the-job actual work experience. As needed to achieve local educational objectives, it may include pre-employment vocational preparation, vocational education to upgrade those already employed full time, or vocational education appropriate for aiding adults in a guided preparation to change from other occupations into distributive occupations.

The American Vocational Association has defined distributive education as follows:

> A program of education offering training in the selling, marketing, and merchandising of goods and services, for the purpose of improving distribution and upgrading distributive workers, including employees, managers, and owners engaged in distributive occupations.[2]

In the early history of this nation approximately three-fourths of the total economic effort was directed toward production, including manufacturing, with only about one-fourth of it devoted to the work of distribution. Today, however, well over half of our nation's economic efforts are devoted to the work of distribution. It currently is estimated, for instance, that approximately 56 cents out of every dollar the consumer spends goes for costs of distribution.

> Retailing adds up to over 40 per cent of the individual business organizations in this country. Nearly eight million men and women are employed in this field. Retailing is getting even bigger—in the number of persons employed and sales volume. *As the population grows so grows retailing.*[3]

---

[2] *Definitions of Terms in Vocational and Practical Arts Education* (Washington, D.C.: American Vocational Association, 1954), p. 10.

[3] J. Gordon Dakins and Eric Sedwick Stein, *Retailing in Our Economy and Its Implications for Education,* Fifteenth Annual Delta Pi Epsilon Lecture (Cincinnati: South-Western Publishing Company, 1957), p. 11.

Over the years student-enrollment statistics have indicated that the educational profession has been reticent about attacking this problem of improvement of the field of distribution. Yet it is quite widely recognized that better and more efficient workers result in better services at lower cost. Accordingly, in 1936 Congress passed the George-Deen Act providing for federal financial assistance to those states which adopted approved state plans for providing high-quality vocational education for distributive occupations. This was followed in 1947 by the George-Barden Act and in 1963 by the Vocational Education Act, both of which greatly increased the possible available aid for distributive education.

Perhaps largely as a result of the impetus given by these federal Acts, "distributive education" today quite generally refers to a rather specific form of high-quality vocational education conducted under a plan set forth by the individual state and approved by the United States Office of Education. Although each state is free to devise and adopt a plan or plans best suited to its own educational needs, distributive education quite universally includes these common factors as offered to students in secondary education:

1. A regularly certified high-school teacher who also meets special requirements of subject-matter and of actual business experience qualifying him to coordinate the classroom work with the approved part-time on-the-job work program of the student
2. Appropriate designated classroom courses for the student trainees
3. A plan of regular part-time paid work experience for the student on approved types of work in selected work stations and under competent supervision
4. A relatively high degree of attention to the individual students in terms of selection, placement, instruction, and follow-up work

This chapter deals especially with the classroom instruction in such courses as Salesmanship and Retailing. These courses may or may not be a part of a more complete vocational program of distributive education; local factors sometimes make it inadvisable for a community to offer an officially approved distributive education program, including the necessary cooperative part-time supervised work experience at selected work stations.

It should be clearly understood, however, that the *addition* of the other factors necessary for a distributive education program does result in a higher-quality and more complete type of vocational education for distributive occupations. These factors will be discussed in Chapter Twelve, "Cooperative Part-Time Business Education Programs." Related education for adults will be discussed in Chapter Thirteen.

Purpose of the Course. Teachers with limited experience, especially, frequently tend to look upon "objectives" as some nice-sounding professional jargon used as a sort of window dressing. However, the longer one teaches and the more successful one becomes as a member of the teaching profession, the more one tends to realize the futility of attempting to teach a course without having clearly in mind the special knowledges, skills, attitudes, or other results that one plans to achieve through the medium of that particular course. Perhaps this applies especially to the teaching of some of the distributive subjects. Hence, one of the first requisites of planning to teach such a course is the necessity of deciding upon the basic purpose of the course.

Is the course primarily vocational in nature? If so, then its main objective, in broad terms, already is established. Such, for instance, should be true of a course entitled Retail Selling.

On the other hand, a course title such as Salesmanship (which may be perfectly appropriate as a course title, and which often is so used) carries far less specific implication relative to the true purpose of the course. It has been quite truthfully said that we all are salesmen throughout our lives. The tiny baby in the crib uses salesmanship in this broad meaning when it desires and secures attention for its own pleasure. Children at play constantly use salesmanship in attempting to get their small friends to join in the games and activities of their choice. Although used for somewhat different purposes, the waking hours of most adolescents are heavily loaded with salesmanship of the highest type directed toward some member or members of the opposite sex. It has been claimed that courtship is applied salesmanship practiced under the strongest kind of motivation!

To the extent that a course in Salesmanship has as its purpose the understanding of basic principles and practices applicable to everyone throughout life, it really is a course in applied psychology. Possibly it might better be entitled Personal Salesmanship—or even Applied Personal Psychology—if that is intended to be its *major* purpose. Thus we find schools in which Salesmanship is used as a sort of "catch-all" course in which students with varied interests and abilities and plans are found—a "convenience" course available to everyone in selecting a suitable current schedule. Under a skillful teacher it may be pointed out that such a course *may* gain a reputation of being one of the most valuable courses in the school. At the same time, it should be realized that such a course *very frequently* becomes the proverbial "dumping ground" for students who appear to be misfits in many courses with better-established contents and objectives.

Most courses in Salesmanship are considered business courses; they also most frequently are taught by business teachers. Certainly this would seem at least to imply that the learnings in the course are expected to pertain heavily to the use of salesmanship as a worker or employee in some business activity—to be quite largely of a vocational or prevocational nature. It is recommended that advisers and teachers adopt this viewpoint.

However, it must be recognized that a basic vocational or prevocational objective or purpose does not eliminate or negate the use and value of learnings for personal use, consumer information, economic understanding, or other purposes. Rather, it appears quite likely that the purposefulness and motivation provided by the vocational or prevocational viewpoint actually will provide a superior media through which these other (but presumably minor) objectives may be reached.

As already indicated, it seems apparent that distributive subjects offered under the various titles other than that of Salesmanship tend automatically to indicate the major purposes or objectives of such courses.

Measuring Achievement. The proper measurement of achievement always is closely associated with and largely dependent upon the objectives of the course taught. In distributive subjects such as Salesmanship, especially, the teacher must be alert to the dangers of focusing too much evaluative endeavor on some one phase of the course. Success in selling, like success in teaching, is based on principles that have been to at least some extent scientifically established; yet it quite largely is the "art" of applying these principles to specific situations that measures one's success in terms of ability to sell.

Thus the teacher of most distributive subjects must realize he has two main factors to consider in measuring the achievement of his students: (*a*) the knowledge and understanding of principles, of needed terminology, of factual information, and of current business practices, and (*b*) the personal ability of the student to skillfully combine and apply these knowledges to specific practical situations in personally solving practical distributive problems involving only himself and involving desired action on the part of other people.

Illustrative of factual knowledges that might be found in a course such as Retailing are terms like maintained mark-up, retail method of inventory, loss leaders, open-to-buy allowance, merchandising, regenerated cellulose, price line, audit-strip, stock control, resident buyer, Willmark Service System, margin, and many similar terms. No great difficulty is experienced by most teachers in evaluating the extent to which individual students have mastered the meaning of such terms and factual knowledges. It is possible to do this through the use of rather common testing devices.

But measuring the ability of each individual student to skillfully and artfully and accurately combine his personal abilities with his course learnings in solving practical problem situations is not so easily accomplished with valid conclusions. Certainly it cannot be done successfully through the medium of an objective-type written test! It usually can be best done through the medium of an actual work station or through the use of an appropriate make-believe situation or case problem.

It should be observed, also, that the time and effort needed to provide and carry through either an actual experience on a work station or an appropriate make-believe situation are far from negligible. Thus in the distributive subjects such techniques customarily are used *primarily* as learning devices. Yet at the same time they do provide an almost automatic evaluation of the achievement of the individual student. Thus, for instance, in a class in Salesmanship the student may present a sales demonstration before the class. In so doing his preparation for the demonstration and his actual presentation provide excellent learning media. At the same time, the presentation provides the teacher with observable evidence of the extent to which the individual student has achieved his goals.

The remainder of this chapter will be concerned mostly with illustrations of specific techniques and devices that the teacher of various distributive subjects may employ in furthering the objectives of the course. These should be looked upon *primarily* as learning devices, procedures, and techniques. Yet each one often does provide the teacher with an excellent additional opportunity for specific evaluation of achievement of the individual student.

Additional information relative to these and other methods especially applicable to the teaching of distributive subjects will appear in Chapter Twelve, "Cooperative Part-Time Business Education Programs."

Group Discussion. Teachers of the various distributive subjects usually make extensive use of group discussions as an important method of learning. They quite generally rate its effectiveness high. Undoubtedly they are correct in so doing.

It is to be recognized, however, that effective group discussion may take place in many different types of discussion situations, and necessarily must be preceded or accompanied by a very realistic motivation. Thus the discussion may be an informal one, or it may be centered around the report of a committee, or around a debate, or around a panel or a symposium. Similarly it may have been motivated primarily by a preceding demonstration or sales kit, or by a field trip, or by a display or a case problem.

The successful teacher of distributive subjects is likely to fully realize that related discussions are important aspects of nearly every technique, device, or procedure he may be using in his course. Thus the specific suggestions that follow would also provide excellent motivating materials for group discussions.

As is true of all group discussions, in teaching these subjects the teacher also must be constantly alert to quietly help keep the discussion oriented toward worth-while goals. A final summarization is quite essential, accompanied by final conclusions whenever possible.

Demonstration. There are sound psychological reasons why a demonstration always tends to attract and hold the attention. In selling, it is necessary to attract and to hold the attention in order to develop interest and a real desire—all of which ordinarily procedes the closing of the sale. In fact it quite generally is recognized today that such things as getting the attention, holding the attention, demonstrating, developing interest, and making the close are important and basic parts or steps in the entire process of selling. Thus the technique of using a demonstration as a part of the learning process in connection with classroom work is highly appropriate and proper. It not only possesses its own peculiar psychological values, but at the same time tends to duplicate a part of the real-life situation encountered in most sales work; and *skill* in demonstrating can be attained only through a requisite amount of practice, either in the classroom or on the job.

Frequently a demonstration is but a part of a larger skit or sales talk (described next), but it also may be and frequently is used as a separate activity on the part of an individual student. In a true demonstration it is quite customary for the student to have rather full control of the situation, without encountering the additional difficulties occasioned by interruptions and questions and comments from others. This gives the student an opportunity to experience a greater degree of success in learning how to demonstrate than might be encountered were he to launch immediately into a complete sales "skit" in which he, at the same time, must be concerned with all steps in the "sales talk" while reacting to questions, objections, and comments of other parties.

Thus the skillful teacher frequently provides for demonstration practice (either before the class or otherwise) as a separate learning activity *prior to* setting up a demonstration situation embodying other problems and frequently looked upon by the student as a "test" situation.

A demonstration is especially suitable to a situation in which a tangible item, as opposed to an intangible idea, forms the basis of the demonstration—although it may be claimed that a step comparable to demonstration exists in every selling situation. And when there is something that must be actually handled and shown and demonstrated it must be remembered that skillful handling of the tangible item is something that may well be learned separately and distinctly from the entire selling process. The salesman of heavyweight aluminum specialty items, for instance, often is instructed to spend several evenings at home alone *practicing* the unpacking, the setting out for display, and the repacking of his wares; were he to fail to develop skill in doing this his entire sales talk might well be ruined by a clumsy arrangement of utensils scattered about the room —not to mention his embarrassment should he later find it necessary to unpack and repack his cases because he failed to get everything in on his first attempt after completing his demonstration!

Nevertheless, there comes a time when it is necessary for the student to combine the physical demonstration with the mental process that accompanies the entire sales talk, or sales skit. Though it is desirable to "practice" on certain skills separately, it perhaps is even more desirable to gain experience in exercising all of them at the same time!

The Sales Talk. The sales talk is a technique whereby the student organizes into one meaningful whole (a talk) all of the various factors or steps and procedures pertinent to the making of a specific sale. He may present it before the class or a committee of fellow students somewhat as one might present a very purposeful lecture. In this case he has complete control of the organization of the talk, and can present his points and comments in a previously determined sequence believed to be best calculated to produce the results he desires. Or he may present it in a less formal manner with one or more fellow students participating in the role of the prospect, or customer, who presents questions and objections and other unrehearsed comments which influence the character and sequence of items in the talk. Perhaps this procedure might more properly be termed a *sales skit.*

In general, the sales talk includes the introductory greeting or securing of appropriate attention, the holding of the attention as through explanations and demonstrations while an attempt is made to develop a real interest on the part of the "prospect" or customer, the developing of this interest into a desire and a willingness to purchase, and, finally, the closing of the sale followed by appropriate termination of the talk. Thus it can readily be seen that the making of a sales talk presupposes at least some degree of understanding of all "steps" in the making of a sale together with the many psychological influences and reactions accompanying each. To ask the student to give a sales talk before he is ready for this, is likely to result in much waste of time and effort; it is like being asked to practice something before one knows what it is!

A well-prepared sales talk often takes considerable time—time to prepare for it and time to give it. Many teachers make the mistake of using too much of the entire time available for classes in having individual students present such talks before the entire class; it often becomes impracticable to have each student in a class of normal size use the time of the entire class while he presents his talk. Moreover, after hearing the first few talks the class tends to lose interest.

As an alternative, skillful teachers frequently divide the class into small groups and have each individual talk presented before only a small group of fellow students. This group may then follow through with a discussion of the quality of the talk and may even "rate"

(evaluate) the talk on the basis of some predetermined rating scale. Thus the giving of the sales talk may well serve at least three major purposes:

1. It enables the student to actually practice on the information, principles, and ideas he has been learning while also reviewing and further learning them by intelligently combining all of them into one unified whole.

2. It aids in further clarifying and fixing in mind the learnings through discussion in a small group where each student can actively participate in the discussion.

3. It also serves as a basis for an evaluation of the individual student's achievement.

The Sales Skit. All demonstrations and sales talks are, in a sense, a form of dramatization. The sales skit goes a step further, however, and provides a setting in which the dramatization presumably is more realistic. It ordinarily is based on the use of at least two students, one being the salesman and the other being the prospect or prospective customer. It, of course, assumes advance preparation by the student-salesman to such an extent that he will hope to quite largely direct the course of the conversation. Considerably less preparation is assumed on the part of the student-prospect, although he, too, is expected to come prepared with some specific ideas pertinent to his acceptance of the endeavors of the student-salesman. However, the exact conversation and skit is *not* ordinarily rehearsed or talked over in advance. A part of the value to the student-salesman lies in his opportunity to try out his plan and his abilities and knowledges in a situation that to an extent simulates that to be found by the salesman in real life.

All the desirable factors to be found in an ordinary sales talk or demonstration ordinarily are present in the sales skit; in addition the presence of the student-prospect adds a challenge and the excitement of constantly being alert and ready to meet the unknown in the questions, objections, statements, comments, and various reactions of the student-prospect. It really tends to provide about the maximum in the way of truly putting the student-salesman "to the test"; he must be fully prepared in all ways in order to successfully cope with the situation in most instances.

In using sales skits the teacher must take appropriate advance steps to assure on the part of the prospect a seriousness of purpose;

otherwise the natural tendency of exuberant youth is to bring into the skit unusual statements and situations calculated to cause laughter—and on occasion even calculated to embarrass the teacher! Most teachers can find suitable means of avoiding this. Some of the types of precautions sometimes taken by teachers follow:

1. A thorough advance understanding on the part of the student-prospect of the true purpose he is serving
2. Careful selection of dependable students to take the part of the prospect
3. Adopting the policy of having each participant in the skit outline for the teacher in advance the specific items he hopes to include in his part of the skit and requiring that an appropriate endeavor be made to confine remarks to those points
4. Having the teacher act as prospect in the first skit or two in order to help establish the proper attitude, which the prospect is expected to maintain
5. Incorporating into any rating scale used for evaluating the sales talk or sales skit an appropriate evaluation, also, of the part played by the prospect

Of course, it is to be recognized that any impromptu or semi-impromptu skit may legitimately and unintentionally result in humorous or even somewhat embarrassing situations; the teacher who has developed a wholesome interest on the part of his students certainly need have little worry about this. If there is doubt in the mind of the teacher, however, precautions such as those suggested tend to be conducive to the development of a more stable and dependable classroom situation.

Case Studies. A case study actually is a problem situation presented for the purpose of providing a medium for problem-solving based on prior learnings and as a motivation and basis for related class discussion. Thus it becomes an important learning device through (a) requiring the student to call into use and to review and examine his prior learnings, (b) requiring the student to be selective in applying prior learnings to the solution of the problem at hand, (c) giving the student a situation or problem that requires the use of judgment based on prior learnings, and (d) motivating further learning and the development of related abilities through group discussion.

A case study may be, or may be based on, a real situation or it may be entirely hypothetical; it really is immaterial which so long as it is presented to the class in a manner that makes it seem real. Often student-prepared cases are excellent, and in addition provide an extra learning activity through the preparation of an appropriate case.

Due care should be taken to avoid using actual cases in which names or facts are familiar to students and others locally and which might cause embarrassment or undesirable personal connotations. Providing the students with ample hypothetical cases frequently goes far in helping to eliminate the natural tendency of students to turn to actual local cases about which they have some information but which all too frequently involve personalities and touchy local subjects likely to produce some undesirable outcomes in the class.

However, at the same time the teacher should be alert to *use* local real case problems whenever opportunity arises and when it can be done in a manner that will not infringe on good taste or the personal rights of people involved. Certainly real cases within the knowledge of the students or associated with their own community have considerably more interest and meaningfulness to the students than do purely hypothetical cases. It is important, though, that such real cases be introduced in a manner amenable to suitable control of the discussion by the teacher.

Shopping Tours and Shopping Reports. As a means of adding meaningfulness and motivation and of learning through observation, there comes a time in most classes in the distributive subjects when students profit considerably from reporting on purposeful observations made right in their own communities. Occasionally this technique may be valuable as a part of the introduction to the course; however, it usually is more valuable when used after students have completed appropriate major units of the course.

In a shopping report the student discusses his observations and evaluations of actual salespeople at work. The report may be written or it may be given orally and as a basis of class discussion. Again, however, it is most important that the bounds of good taste be observed in respect to the use of names of specific people and businesses. If the evaluation is favorable, no real harm is likely to result from the use of actual names. On the other hand, since the character of the evaluation cannot be known in advance, it simply is "good taste" to omit names when giving the report.

The observations presented in a shopping report customarily are made on a shopping tour. For this purpose it is best if two students go together. It also is best if at least one of the students is an *actual* shopper or prospective purchaser in at least one situation. Similarly, however, it also is desirable that the students observe the salespeople at work with *other* prospective customers, in order that the students may be more free to observe details of the sales presentation. Most frequently, practical reasons limit the report of each student to the observation of but one actual sales presentation.

In preparation for a shopping tour a check sheet of points to observe should be prepared. These should be points that the students already have studied—unless the tour is being used as an introductory motivational device; in that case, the points should be those which are to be studied in the next few units taken up in class work.

As is the case with most other techniques commonly used in distributive courses, the shopping report provides excellent motivation and material for purposeful group discussion; full advantage should be taken of this opportunity in making over-all plans for the course. It provides for the class a number of actual case studies.

Posters and Displays. Everyone today is familiar with the fact that appropriate displays and other types of visual presentations are an important part of selling and of many other phases of the work involved in the distributive occupations. Accordingly, students not only are learning about the subject-matter of their course when they prepare appropriate posters and displays, but they also are becoming familiar with the main characteristics of a technique commonly used in the business world. At the same time such activities create interest, enthusiasm, and pride in their work since they are calculated to bring the endeavors of the students to the attention of others. Attractive displays bring to the business student a personal pride and feeling of being appreciated somewhat comparable to that experienced by the skilled musician or the athlete who gains the applause of his audience.

In preparing displays and posters major attention should be given to these points:

1. Each should have a *single theme.*
2. Each should "tell a story" and tell it simply.
3. Color should be used when possible.
4. Avoid "too much," with the resulting cluttered appearance.

5. An attractive background is important in preparing good displays.
6. Be sure that the final result produces something that is pleasing to the eye.
7. Provide a setting that is appropriately lighted.
8. Provide a new one frequently.

Frequently local merchants and businesses are excellent sources of suggestions and aids when preparing displays or posters. From time to time the local merchant must discard rather attractive displays in favor of a "change" or of newer displays better depicting the current status of his product or customer demand for it. Sometimes these displays have been provided by manufacturers at considerable cost. The time may come quickly for the local merchant when any specific display of this type no longer is of value to him; in most cases he is quite happy to pass it on to a business teacher for classroom use.

Field Trips and Speakers. Although field trips and speakers obviously are separate and distinct types of instructional activity, they are mentioned together here because, actually, often either may be used as a means of bringing the same information to the class; one is a visual method and the other an audio method.

The shopping tour may be considered a type of field trip, too, but it usually does not permit attention to such a wide variety of information as customarily is given consideration in what is termed a field trip.

In using either a field trip or a speaker, much of the effectiveness, as always, depends on the advance planning. Certainly students going on a field trip should know what they are to look for and observe and should be in some appropriate manner prepared to make rational observations; similarly, a visiting speaker should know what it is the teacher currently is interested in teaching to his class so that he will be better able to determine what information is most pertinent to that particular learning.

Field trips, and often speakers, may be used in studying distributive subjects such as these: store arrangement and layout; cashiering; store location; fashion merchandising; window and interior display; credits and collections; store records and merchandise control; customer services; receiving and marking goods; textiles; store organization; and distributive careers. To this list could be added many other ideas, the number and nature depending considerably on the specific distributive subject being taught.

Case Studies of Local Businesses. Since distribution is an area of endeavor so widely spread and so common that it is to be found represented in all communities, both large and small, the distributive subjects provide excellent opportunity for individual students to prepare case studies of local businesses. At times it may be best for two or more students, or for an entire class, to work on the same case study.

When properly approached such case studies also provide the teacher, the school, and education with one of the most effective means of public relations and of building goodwill. Usually everyone likes to receive the compliment of having others interested in his work. Also, we each usually like to give information that others may seek. Thus when a class in a secondary school decides it wishes to prepare a manual or scrapbook or history of a local business, it is indeed a most unusual business management that is not eager to cooperate fully! And after having given this cooperation, it also is an unusual business management that does not feel increased goodwill for that teacher, that school, and education in general.

Many, many different types of items might well be considered in writing up the case study of a local business. Certainly appropriate space would need to be devoted to the people who founded and manage it, to its early start and history, to the services it renders, to the goods it handles, and to the people it employs. But in addition such a study may well become the medium through which the students in the class gain illustrative and meaningful information about those particular phases of business the class is studying. Thus merchandising and customer-service policies may be included; the chief media of advertising and the main lines of merchandise handled may be described; pictures may be taken and details included about any new equipment or desirable store layout or arrangement; in fact, it is unlikely that any single item of information will be studied in class that cannot be illustrated in a case study or store manual or scrapbook devoted to some local business.

Case studies of local businesses, then, provide a most practical and meaningful method of learning in the distributive subjects. At the same time the accumulation of such materials in school, associated as it must be with many and constant pleasant school-community contacts, can result in tremendous values through good public relations.

Other Instructional Aids. A few suggestions have now been given pointing out some of the effective instructional methods especially well fitted for use in the various distributive subjects. However, this by no means exhausts the possibilities available to the alert teacher. Subjects such as salesmanship and retailing are both broad and flexible in their contents, and thus provide opportunities for the use of almost any teaching technique or aid that is available to teachers.

There are many films and filmstrips available for the use of the teacher, most of them at little or no cost. Larger businesses in the field of distribution frequently have their own in-service training programs for which they have prepared special teaching aids; at times they will lend them to teachers for classroom use. In addition many businesses are quite anxious to make these and similar films available as a means of promoting goodwill. It is true that all such aids should be previewed and those rejected which may contain undesirable advertising, misleading statements, or too much material not of value to the particular class in which it is to be used. This still leaves many more desirable ones available than any one teacher needs or can effectively use.

In addition, many teacher education colleges and universities and many state departments of business and distributive education have prepared special films and filmstrips which are available on loan. The teacher usually may obtain some of them through the assistance of personnel in his own state department of public instruction.

Cooperative Part-Time Programs. Although not confined to the distributive subjects, it is well to remember that much of the most effective teaching of distributive subjects for vocational purposes comes about through the use of a good, well-supervised, cooperative part-time program. Many of the techniques already mentioned are most readily and effectively used when such a program is correlated with the classroom study; in addition it provides opportunity for additional instructional techniques which may be used in a planned and purposeful situation.

Since Chapter Twelve is devoted entirely to a consideration of such programs, the reader is referred to that chapter for additional suggestions of effective methods of teaching the distributive subjects.

Projects and Questions for Discussion

1. Secure from the vocational division of your state department of public instruction a copy of the state plan for distributive education. Determine and report on the qualifications for (*a*) a teacher-coordinator and for (*b*) an approved program in distributive education.

2. Investigate available textbooks in Salesmanship (or courses of study in Salesmanship) and determine whether stated objectives appear to be primarily vocational or primarily of a personal-use nature.

3. Interview the personnel director or manager for a large retail store and determine whether or not any endeavor is made to help salespeople improve their salesmanship ability.

4. Have each member of the class keep a "shopping report" for a week for the purpose of discovering either the presence of or the lack of good salesmanship on the part of retail-store employees (identification of stores should be avoided).

5. What conclusions might one tentatively draw from the fact that the distributive subjects are relatively neglected in most schools and the fact that the consumer typically spends over half his money for costs of distribution? What other factors may enter in?

6. It often is pointed out that beginning pay in retail stores is relatively low. Do you think better education of youth in retailing and the distributive subjects would tend to alter this situation any?

7. If you could arrange for but a very limited number of field trips for students in your retailing class, would you give preference to visiting a relatively large store or a relatively small one?

8. What special advantages can you see in having students prepare and give sales talks and sales skits? What possible problems or difficulties might you encounter as the teacher?

9. Why is it that so many schools offer courses (such as typewriting and shorthand) that prepare for office work while comparatively few offer courses preparing for store work? Does this appear to be sound educational planning?

Case Problems

1. Harry Jamison has been D. E. coordinator and teacher two years at the Wapsie Lake High School and seems to have had a successful program. His students take Distributive Practices and have their co-operative program during their senior year. Prior to that year many of

them, but not all, have had General Business, Typewriting, and Book-keeping. Harry now asks his principal to start a course in Salesmanship in the junior year in which all students planning to take the D. E. work will have to register; the course thus definitely would be basically for his D. E. students. But his principal objects, and states that since salesmanship is something every person has to use all his life the course should be a purely elective one open to all students who wish to take it. He believes D. E. students should not be required to take it, since failure to do so might prevent some students from taking D. E. in the senior year should they decide to do so. What do you think should be done?

2. Joan Roberts teaches a class in Salesmanship. As a means of adding interest and motivation to the class, she invited a successful local businessman to talk to her class on "How to Be Successful in Selling." His talk consisted mostly of a lecture on why theoretical "book learning" is useless in learning to sell and why the only way to learn how to sell is to "go get yourself a job and learn from experience." This now has created a skepticism on the part of her students toward their textbook and their classroom work. Discuss the situation.

3. In having his students present sales talks toward the end of his course in Salesmanship, Floyd Walker instructed each to have a class-mate act as the prospect or customer. He also asked that anyone acting as a prospect do his best to seriously represent a typical customer who at first is unconvinced and who asks many questions. One student, Harry Unzer, had access to materials and information from the local Ladies Lingerie Shoppe which his mother owns and operates. Accordingly, with his pal Wallace acting as the customer, Harry prepared a sales talk based on a nationally advertised line of fine lingerie. Both boys handled the situation well and with tact and good taste; however, other boys in class occasionally tried to insert improper humor and a few of the girls in class obviously were somewhat embarrassed, as was Mr. Walker. Discuss the entire situation.

4. The retailing class at Huron High School was about to start a unit on window display and as a part of their preparation for the unit the students were assigned in pairs to observe and be prepared to describe the window displays downtown. Each pair of students was assigned to one side of a specific block of business houses. In reporting on one display, Jane and Virginia criticized it severely since it obviously had not been changed for a long time; there were spider webs and dead flies in the window, and an open container of candy had melted from the sun and had dust on the candy. Unknown to them one of their classmates was closely related to the proprietor of this particular business, and naturally felt embarrassed. Discuss the entire situation and suggest what

you would do as the teacher (*a*) to avoid such a situation and (*b*) to handle it in case it should inadvertently arise.

Suggested Readings

Bernard, Edwin J., "Teach Retail Selling Through Role-Playing," *The Journal of Business Education,* November, 1963, p. 61.

Business Education Forum, Distributive Education issues, April of each year.

Haines, Peter G., "Post-High School Preparatory Education for Careers in Distribution," *Business Education Forum,* April, 1964, p. 13.

Huegy, H. W., *et al.,* "Distribution (Advertising, Marketing, and Retailing)," *American Business Education Yearbook,* XIV (1957), Chap. 16, 191-206.

Jacobs, Lloyd, *et al.,* "The Fundamental Processes in Merchandising Subjects," *American Business Education Yearbook,* XII (1955), Chap. 16, 296-316.

Meyer, Warren G., "New Era in Distributive Occupations," *Business Education Forum,* April, 1964, p. 6. An editorial.

———— and Wayne G. Little, "Distributive Education Facilities," *American Vocational Journal,* January, 1964, pp. 19-21.

———— and Harold O. Topin, "A Career in the Distributive Occupations," *Business Education Forum,* January, 1964, p. 12.

Scolnick, Arnold H., "Distributive Education 1970," *Business Education World,* December, 1963, pp. 28-30.

Turse, Paul L., "What Do You Mean by Distributive Education?" *Journal of Business Education,* October, 1955, pp. 27-28.

Willis, Doris E. *et al.,* "Levels and Competencies in Distribution," *American Business Education Yearbook,* XIII (1956), Chap. 14, 141-51.

11

Teaching Other Business Education Subjects

Traditionally, the business education subjects that have been taught most often in the secondary school have been typewriting, bookkeeping, and shorthand. However, other courses also have been incorporated into many secondary-school business curriculums including business law, consumer business, and business arithmetic. Other courses sometimes taught, but not quite so frequently, are business organization and management, business English, and economic geography. All of these courses, with the exception perhaps of business arithmetic and business English, can be commonly classified as part of the *basic business courses*. Business arithmetic and business English might more properly be classified as part of the "skill" courses.

In this chapter will be discussed some specific problems pertinent to these courses. The techniques already suggested for teaching general business, bookkeeping, and the distributive subjects can also be applied to the subjects discussed here. The various discussion techniques outlined in Chapter Eight are also applicable to business law, consumer business, and economic geography; the various methods of developing skill discussed in Chapter Three can be applied to the teaching of business arithmetic and business English.

However, before discussing some of the pertinent points relevant to the instruction of these courses let us consider one of the most significant and major developments in recent years in the business education curriculum, namely, the inclusion of data-processing procedures and techniques.

Data Processing in the Business Education Curriculum

Until recently, the development of punched card and electronic data-processing courses in the secondary-school business curriculum has been somewhat limited because of several factors. One factor was that the cost of the equipment involved was prohibitive; the other factor was a shortage of trained teachers in the field.

However, in the last several years rapid advances in the development of electronic data-processing equipment (computers) coupled with a shortage of trained workers for business and industry has caused the need to devise ways and means of incorporating instruction in data-processing procedures in the secondary schools. Through the passage of federal legislation, funds have been provided with which schools can purchase data-processing equipment. This, combined with the policy of equipment manufacturers to assist schools in obtaining equipment by allowing educational discounts, has made the acquisition of data-processing equipment by schools economically feasible.

Although equipment is now more readily available to schools for instructional purposes a major problem which still exists is the short supply of qualified secondary-school teachers in the field. Colleges and universities have been slow in providing curriculums for the training of teachers in order to prepare them to teach data-processing in courses in the secondary schools. Consequently, those secondary schools which have incorporated data-processing courses in their curriculums have had to provide in-service training for their currently employed teachers or else to employ personnel who were technically qualified but yet who were not trained as teachers.

Some colleges and universities, recognizing the need to provide opportunities for teachers to become trained in this field, have organized summer workshops and institutes. The necessity to limit enrollments in these workshops, however, has provided a training opportunity for only a small number of teachers.

There is little question in the minds of business-teacher educators that it will become increasingly important for *all* business teachers to become knowledgeable in the field of data processing. Many leaders believe that data-processing procedures will become a significant part of courses in bookkeeping, typewriting, office and secretarial practice—in fact in almost all secondary business education courses—making it necessary that all business teachers including those in training be thoroughly familiar with this field. Even at the present time recent revisions of business education textbooks for the secondary schools have incorporated in them units on electronic data processing.

Thus, for many business teachers now in service or in training who do not have an opportunity to become informed in this field either through college courses or summer workshops the only solution appears to be that of self-instruction. This will not be an easy solution. While there is a great deal of literature in the field much of it is technical in nature, and for the inexperienced person, difficult to understand.

Listed below is a selected bibliography of data-processing information which should prove to be helpful to the prospective business education teacher or experienced teacher in developing a knowledge of the basic concepts in the field of data-processing procedures through a self-study program.

Selected Bibliography of Data-Processing Information

General Information Manual, An Introduction to IBM Punched Card Data Processing, International Business Machines Co., Technical Publications Department, 112 East Post Road, White Plains, New York.

This very excellent pamphlet contains information in easily understood language about the punched card; coding principles; principles of punched card machine data processing; and a discussion of the basic punched-card machines—the card punch, the sorter, and the accounting machine.

(Copies of this and other IBM publications listed below can be obtained through IBM Branch Offices.)

General Information Manual, Introduction to IBM Data Processing Sys-

tems, International Business Machines Co., Technical Publications Department, 112 East Post Road, White Plains, New York.

This pamphlet is similar to the one listed above. It is somewhat more technical in nature but is easily understandable if the *Introduction to IBM Punched Card Data Processing Manual* is read first. Basic computer concepts are discussed with some excellent illustrations. In addition some simple applications of data-processing problems to computers are illustrated.

Punched-Card Data-Processing Procedures—IBM Personal Study Program, International Business Machines Co., Technical Publications Department, 112 East Post Road, White Plains, New York.

This self-study program contains seven booklets which go into some depth on the major punched-card machines. After the text material has been presented self-checking exercises are provided the student in order to help him determine his understanding of the concepts presented. (A similar self-study set of booklets have been developed entitled *Principles of Programming* which deals with computers. These booklets contain too much technical information for the student with little background in computers.)

Saxon, James A. and William S. Plette, *Programming the IBM 1401,* Prentice-Hall, Inc., Englewood Cliffs, New Jersey.

This book containing 208 pages is a self-instructional programmed manual. It is extremely well written and although it is adapted to a specific computer, the IBM 1401, the student can obtain an excellent background for the processing of data on any computer. By only going through the first two units (40 pages) one can obtain an excellent idea of a computer and how it works.

The development of separate curriculums in data processing is generally found only in larger high schools in the United States. Technical High School of Des Moines, Iowa, was one of the pioneers in this development and its various curriculums in this area are given below.

KEY PUNCH OPERATOR

Students who have a typing rate of 40 wpm and pass the qualifying examination may elect to take the Key Punch Operator Course. Enrollment will be limited by the number of machines available for training purposes. While any student may enroll, preference will be given to upper classmen. Students from East,

Lincoln, Roosevelt, and North may enroll first or seventh period and commute to Tech for this single class.

Key Punch Operator	*Credit*
KP Key Punch	½

TAB EQUIPMENT OPERATOR

Students in this program must have a grade average of three and pass a qualifying examination. The course may be taken by eleventh and twelfth grade students.

Tab Equipment Operator	*Credit*
TE1 Tab Equipment 1	½
TE2 Tab Equipment 2	½
*TE3 Tab Equipment 3	½

* Can be taken as general elective

COMPUTER PROGRAMMER

Because of the complexity of the study in this six-semester program, only students who have maintained a grade average of two and pass the qualifying examination will be eligible to enroll. They must have had algebra one and two. The one year science requirement must either be met in ninth grade, summer school, or as an elective during high school.

Computer Programmer	*Credit*
10B English 3	½
Social Science 3	½
Computer Programmer 1	1
Accounting 1	
Business Organization	
Electro Mechanical Machines and	
Typing	
Elective	½
10A English 4	½
Social Science 4	½
Computer Programmer 2	1
Basic Computing Machines	
Accounting 2	
Electro Mechanical	
Machines (Continued)	
Elective	½

11B	English 5	½
	Social Science 5	½
	Computer Programmer 3	1
	System Development and Design 1	
	Computer Programming 1	
	Elective	½
11A	English 6	½
	Social Science 6	½
	Computer Programmer 4	1
	System Development and Design 2	
	Computer Programming 2	
	*Human Relations	
	Elective	½
12B	Social Science 7	½
	Computer Programmer 5	1
	Management Accounting	
	Advanced Computing and	
	Programming Systems	
	Communication Skills	
	Elective	1
12A	Social Science 8	½
	Computer Programmer 6	1
	Business Simulation	
	Elective	1

*Can be taken as general elective

General Electives

Three courses in the business data processing program are being made available as general elective courses. These may be selected by any Tech student upon the recommendation of his counselor.

URE—*Introduction to Unit Record Equipment*

This is a survey course. Experience and instruction is given on all unit record equipment. This course will be of particular interest to bookkeeping, clerical, and stenographic majors. Not available to Key Punch or Tab Equipment students. (¼ unit credit)

TAB EQUIPMENT 3—*Introduction to Computers*

Introduction to Computers provides information as to types and functions of computers. Science, math, and business students will be interested in electing this course. (½ unit credit)

COMPUTER PROGRAMMER—Human Relations

> The Human Relations course provides instruction in the solution of personal problems, employer-employee relations, and the principles of human relations. Students from all of the vocational subject areas will want to consider taking this course. (¼ unit credit)

Similar curriculums can be found in area vocational schools and technical institutes. The data-processing programs developed in these latter schools are generally for post-high-school students and funds are supplied for their operation under the Manpower Retraining Act or the Vocational Education Act of 1963. These curriculums are strictly vocational in nature.

In the typical high school, however, where data-processing equipment is not available, data-processing procedures and information should be provided to students through incorporation in the traditional business education courses. It is not necessary to have equipment available in order to provide students with some familiarity with data-processing procedures. Listed below are some techniques which the teacher may use regardless of the business course he may be teaching:

1. Field trips to firms using punched-card equipment or electronic computers can be highly enlightening to students.

2. Punched cards are relatively inexpensive (as little as $1 per thousand). Teachers can obtain some unpunched punch cards and have students manually draw fields on the cards, code data on them by making pencil marks and manually simulate the uses of the basic punched-card machines such as the card punch, the sorter, and the accounting machine. A simple but effective application which might be used is a payroll process.

3. Manual data-processing devices such as the pegboard are commonly used even in the small business. It is possible to obtain a pegboard being used by a business and have its use demonstrated.

4. The block diagramming of simple data-processing problems for application in an electronic computer system could be effectively utilized. Block diagramming is the first step in writing a program for a computer.

5. Publishing firms are now publishing data-processing practice sets which can be used in an office practice class but which

could also be used effectively in any other business education class.

There are undoubtedly many other techniques which can be used by the creative and imaginative teacher. An organization known as SABE—the Society for Automation in Business Education publishes a journal known as the *Data Processor*. In this journal can be found ideas and suggestions for teaching data processing in business education courses in the secondary schools. Information can be obtained about this organization by writing to E. Dana Gibson, San Diego State College, San Diego, California.

Business Law

Business law in the secondary school is commonly taught in either the junior or senior year. Although the subject-matter is technical in nature, by no means is it the purpose of instruction to make business law, in the secondary school at least, a technical, legal course. Some of the more commonly stated objectives for teaching business law are:

1. To familiarize students with basic principles of business law and their applications common to daily life as an aid in avoiding legal difficulties
2. To train students in the use of common legal documents
3. To develop in students an awareness of the organization of our local, state, and federal court system
4. To help students realize when they should consult competent legal authority in legal matters
5. To develop in students a respect for law and constituted authority

In order to achieve these objectives most business law textbooks are developed around the following items of content:

1. Nature and background of law
2. Contracts
3. Negotiable instruments
4. Agency
5. Sales

6. Bailments
7. Real property
8. Personal property
9. Suretyship and guaranty
10. Court structure

The foregoing list of topics of content appears to be an imposing one for high-school students to study, or for that matter even for adults. The technical aspects of the subject-matter impose one of the major problems of teaching business law. Too often business law courses are taught from the viewpoint of requiring strict mastery of subject-matter detail. The fallacies of teaching business law in this manner should be obvious.

A technical course in business law should be offered only to those individuals who intend to become practicing lawyers. Obviously, then, a course of this nature should not be offered to high-school students. The legal language itself often is a deterrent to learning for high-school boys and girls. Despite herculean efforts by the authors of secondary business law textbooks the technical language cannot be entirely eliminated or minimized.

Subject-matter mastery of detail in business law can also lead to another problem. Students (especially high-school students) might possibly develop an unwarranted confidence in their ability to interpret the law for themselves and for others. This is not only illegal but can be dangerous and can lead to much hardship and disillusionment because of failure to consult trained lawyers when the need arises.

Business educators generally subscribe to the principle that the subject-matter of the business law course should not be mastered as other subject-matter courses but that the primary purpose is for students to obtain an appreciation of the principles by which present-day business law is formed. If this concept is accepted, then the methods by which business law is taught will be materially directed toward this end.

Some Specific Techniques for Teaching Business Law. Although business law is a recitation-type course (as distinguished from a drill-type course), there are some specific techniques that may be used by the teacher, other than the classroom discussion, in order to make the course both interesting and stimulating. These techniques are:

1. The use of supplementary instructional materials
2. The use of community resources as an aid to instruction
3. The use of student experiences and their relationship to the principles found in business law

Supplementary Instructional Materials. Without question there is sufficient material in the typical business law textbook to keep both the teacher and student busy without the use of outside supplementary materials. However, for an enriched course and to illustrate the universality and importance of business law problems, the teacher will find it highly valuable to make reference to sources other than the text. It is almost mandatory in the well-taught business law class to use supplementary instructional materials and resources because of the proximity of the textual material in business law to the ordinary day-to-day living of the student.

One of the richest sources of supplementary material is the daily newspaper. Practically any newspaper picked at random will have news stories concerning such items as contracts, sales, or some other element of concern to the business law class.

Much of the content of a business law course can be developed around the use of case problems as a basis for discussion by the use of cases found in the newspapers and in magazine articles. These can certainly make the business law class more realistic and practical. In the foregoing illustrations, for example, very realistic discussions can be developed which will bring out vividly the principles of contracts, bailments, warranties, and torts.

Many other types of supplementary instructional materials are available to the teacher. Materials from trade associations, legal societies, and better business bureaus are just a few of these types of sources. Films, filmstrips, and bulletin-board materials for illustrative purposes are available for teaching the many concepts found in business law.

The Use of Community Resources. The community in which the school is located is an excellent source of reference for teaching business law. Regardless of the size of the community there should be some resources available for any school. Individuals in the community such as attorneys, police officers, businessmen, and the city officials can be of much help in making presentations to students. Discussions by these resource persons of the more common business law problems in which people become involved; the everyday principles of law with which the businessman comes in contact; the legal principles involved in operating a municipal or county government are all illustrations of the types of legal activities that can be explored.

The community is also an excellent source of information with respect to visitations to places where legal activities are carried on. The local court when a business trial is in session is quite valuable. In some communities the local bar associations have been following a practice of coming into the classroom and presenting a mock trial for the benefit of the students. Visitation to city council meetings to see local government in action, though of more interest to a government class, still can have many applications to business law. Such items as the awarding of contracts, or the legal implications of commercial zoning, are illustrative of the actions that may be observed.

Most communities are rich in resources for the business law class. It merely takes a discerning teacher to pick out those everyday activities which will be applicable.

Use of Student Experiences. One of the most successful techniques that can be used in the teaching of business law is the adapting of the instruction to the maturity level and experiences of the students in the class. Many activities experienced by the typical junior or senior in high school have a definite application to business law.

Many of the students will either own or drive automobiles. The implications found in buying a car through financing, the responsibility to other people through insurance coverage, and the element of torts might be applicable.

Because of the nature of our present economic condition, many boys and girls of high-school age are participating in business activities that formerly were not available to them. Examples such as employer-employee relationships, laws affecting both employers and employees, buying on credit, and borrowing money all have significance in business law. The responsibilities and legal requirements of minors and the difficulties that may be encountered by minors through ignorance of the law are other illustrative factors.

With these elements in mind the superior business law teacher will utilize the present experiences of students in developing the content of the business law class around these experiences. Not only should this type of instruction motivate the class, but it should have the valuable result of making the instruction meaningful and helpful to the students.

Although the use of discussion techniques will prove to be most successful in teaching business law and will be the most dominant method used, there are some other supplementary devices which the teacher will find useful and enriching to the class. The content of business law lends itself readily to stimulating student reports on topics appropriate to the subject. Mock trials dramatized by students, exhibits of student projects, bulletin-board and room displays and student debates can be used most effectively. By using a variety of devices and by using the many sources of supplementary materials around him the *dynamic* teacher will be highly successful in teaching business law.

Consumer Business

Consumer business or consumer education is commonly taught in the modern secondary school by the business education teacher. Sometimes this course is taught by the home economics teacher or it may be offered in the social science department under the title of *consumer economics.* Too often, business teachers are concerned if the course is taught other than by themselves. They believe that if consumer business is taught by other than a business teacher the course will not be taught properly. Needless to say, it is of no concern to the authors where or by whom the course is taught—it is sufficient to state that this course may be a valuable one for secondary-school students if taught correctly.

Consumer business may be classified as another course in the basic business area. The primary objective of the course is to provide general education values to high-school students. For this reason, consumer education may be considered to have value for all high-school students regardless of their educational or vocational futures.

In consumer business an attempt is made to bring together into one course much of the consumer information often taught in various courses in home economics, science, social science, and business education. The aims are to give students basic knowledges concerning available goods and services. No attempt is made to give specific information concerning the purchase of all commodities. Rather the course seeks to teach the consumer to choose discriminatingly in purchasing goods. The importance of such information comes from the fact that one's standard of living depends not only on the salary earned but upon the utilization of that salary and the values derived from the wise expenditure of income.

The common objectives typically listed for teaching consumer business are:

1. To develop in students a knowledge of basic economic principles with particular attention to the problems of consumption
2. To provide students with sufficient information to evaluate goods and services intelligently
3. To enable student consumers to make intelligent buying choices
4. To teach students the elements of personal financial affairs, including budgeting, saving, credit, insurance, and investment of funds
5. To provide students with the knowledge concerning the sources of aids for consumers and to develop the ability to choose wisely between true and false information
6. To instruct students concerning the part played by government and the contribution that government makes to the protection and advancement of consumer welfare

In order to meet these objectives, the typical consumer business textbook incorporates the following types of information:

1. Basic consumer problems
2. Aid for the consumer
3. Propaganda analysis
4. Advertising
5. Consumer cooperatives
6. Grades, standards, labels
7. Money and banking
8. Budgeting, credit, savings, investments
9. Insurance and social security
10. Education and advisory services for consumers
11. Housing
12. Taxes
13. Health services
14. Frauds
15. General buying principles
16. Current topics of interest to consumers

An analysis of the several topics of content reveals that much of consumer business is concerned with the personal financial problems of people. Appropriately enough, many high-school students today have personal financial problems that can be readily fused into the content of the course. Because consumer business is typically offered in the senior or combined senior and junior years, the several topics of content are usually of much interest to these students because of their level of maturity.

Methods and Problems of Teaching Consumer Business. Because consumer business is also another "recitation"-type course, the subject-matter lends itself most readily to the discussion method. It is another course in the business curriculum where student experiences can be used quite readily as a starting point for class discussion, since many of the students have experienced some contact with the topics of content.

There is a danger in teaching consumer business that an inexperienced teacher may inadvertently make the course a technical one, as there is a vast amount of technical information available for consumers. The dangers in this type of approach should be most apparent as nothing will kill interest more readily than concentration on technical detail.

The objective, then, in consumer business is to provide the student with the knowledges with which to make wise choices. Through the educational process it is hoped that he will use the tools that are provided him in making these wise choices. A student should not be compelled in the consumer business course to make detailed studies of the differences in values of one size can or another, or to make a chemical analysis of some type of cloth. Rather he should be given some basic principles of consumership plus sources of information which he may use in making his decisions. This, then, coupled with the ability to use his knowledge rationally, should prepare a well-trained consumer.

Resources for Teaching Consumer Business. There is a vast wealth of resources for teaching consumer business, of which the superior teacher will avail himself in teaching the course. Much of this material is free. Many businesses today realize that an informed consumer actually reduces their costs and increases their goodwill. A satisfied consumer is one of the best sources of advertising. Any good business educator's bibliography will provide many such sources of information. There are also commercial agencies such as the magazines, *Consumers Guide* and *Consumers Union.* In these magazines space is given to the study and reporting of information for consumers. Pamphlets from the federal government and from local agencies such as better business bureaus are also highly valuable sources of information.

Much help can be obtained from the local business community. Businessmen in the community can be very helpful in providing students with information on both good and poor consumer practices that they have observed in their own customers. As has been stated in preceding paragraphs, the American businessmen, contrary to the opinion held by some people, do not all subscribe to the principle of "let the buyer beware" and are desirous of having an informed consumer.

The consumer business course can be one of the most interesting classes taught in the business curriculum if the teacher will keep in mind the procedures mentioned above.

Business Arithmetic

Business arithmetic is one of the less frequently taught business subjects in the secondary schools. Most often this course is found in the curriculums of the larger or urban high schools as a part of the clerical curriculum.

Content of the Course in Business Arithmetic. Business arithmetic may be taught as either a one- or a two-semester course. Accordingly, the content of the course will vary with its length. In general the several items of content which are typically found are as follows:

1. Fundamental processes (addition, subtraction, and so on)
2. Common fractions and mixed numbers
3. Decimals
4. Payroll procedures
5. Weights and measures
6. Business charts
7. Percentage
8. Depreciation
9. Profit and loss
10. Interest
11. Bank discount

12. Commission
13. Insurances
14. Taxes
15. Public utilities
16. Transportation

Usually, the subject-matter is devoted to the arithmetical computations involved in the various topics with little attempt being made to include understanding of the business procedures in back of the computations. Since business arithmetic is usually offered to either freshmen or sophomores in high school much of the content behind the computations will be learned in subsequent courses or concurrently.

Methods and Problems of Teaching Business Arithmetic. A typical lesson in business arithmetic may begin with a pretest of the principles involved in the chapter. One purpose of this pretesting is to determine as far as possible the difficulties the students might have concerning the principles involved and which elements appear to be of no difficulty. In other words, the purpose of the pretest is to begin the teaching at the place where the students are. It is wasteful to teach what the students already know.

After the pretest, the narrative explaining the new principle is presented along with problems illustrating the new principle. These problems are usually completely worked out so that the students may see the procedure recommended for working the problems covering the principle. It is at this point that the teacher should explain and illustrate the new principle to the students and perhaps work out a few problems in class for the purposes of illustration.

Then comes drill. Problems that are worked in class by the students, perhaps some at the blackboard and the remainder at their desks, are used to drill on the procedures involved. It is during this period that the teacher can be most helpful as he walks about the room observing the students as they work the drill problems, giving aid and assistance as he sees it is needed. Finally come the homework problems, which are to be worked and handed in to the teacher for checking for remedial-instruction purposes. This, then, would be the basic day-to-day procedure for teaching the class.

Of course, the dynamic teacher will vary his procedure from day to day in order to maintain interest and stimulate enthusiasm in the class. The same routine followed day in and day out would become monotonous and boring with a resulting breaking down of instruction. Several procedures might be followed in order to vary the routine of the class.

One suitable procedure would be a general class discussion of the reasons why some of the computations must be made in business operations. For example, the class might discuss the principle behind the offering of cash discounts. Why are cash discounts offered by business firms? Does the businessman offering the cash discount really reduce his selling price by the amount of the discount or does he increase his selling price on the original quotation so that if someone does take the cash discount he will realize the price he wished to realize from the very beginning? Those who do not take the discount then, are they paying a carrying charge because of credit?

Another discussion might be of the personal type in which the arithmetic computations involved in the experiences of the students are illustrated. For example, most students are interested in automobiles. What are the various interest charges made by loan companies and banks on the financing of cars? How are these interest charges stated? Are they computed correctly to tell the true story? Is there a difference in finance charges made by different companies? Still another illustration is the determination of what various charges against the wages of a student are withheld for both tax and social security purposes. Are these charges computed correctly?

These are just a few of the methods whereby the alert business teacher can make the business arithmetic class more realistic and vital. The wise teacher will avoid routinizing his instruction and will use every device and technique at his command to avoid this pitfall.

Problems of Teaching Business Arithmetic. One of the most frustrating things found oftentimes by teachers of business arithmetic is the students' lack of ability in the fundamental arithmetic concepts. The typical response made by some teachers when it is found that students do not have the ability to perform well the simplest of arithmetic computations is to throw up their hands in despair and blame the teachers in the elementary school for not teaching the basic arithmetic fundamentals properly. It is highly doubtful that this is the reason. In any event, it does little good to place the blame on some other teacher—rather the business teacher should attempt to understand the reasons behind the problem and then attempt some constructive steps to solve it.

For one thing, it should be remembered that arithmetic is a perishable skill; that once learned the student must be working with it constantly in order to maintain a high rate of proficiency. Usually it will be found that some review and drill upon the basic arithmetic concepts will bring back a high degree of ability. However, there are those students who seem never to have learned some of the most basic skills in arithmetic. It is possible that these people do not have any special aptitude in working with arithmetic and as a result have built up a resentment against a subject with which they have always had difficulty. Generally speaking, the basic problem with these people is that from the earliest beginning they have never thoroughly understood the number concept of 10 upon which our numerical system is based. Their instruction has been by rote memorization with little or no understanding of our basic number concept. Modern-day instruction in the elementary schools has recognized this problem and is now taking steps to overcome it. The modern elementary teacher teaches numbers from the point of view of understanding why our number system is as it is, and she is accomplishing much in helping elementary students to visualize numbers rather than to accomplish strict memorization. For this reason the business arithmetic teacher may find it necessary, with some students, to start with the very beginnings of arithmetic and teach the reasons behind our number system based upon 10. Students' difficulty with arithmetic is a common one and should not be interpreted by the business teacher to mean that our educational system has gone to pot.

Another problem that sometimes faces the business arithmetic teacher, one which to some extent is based upon the preceding problem, is that of providing "crutches" for students. The teacher may ask herself, "Is it proper for me to provide my students with interest tables, discount tables, payroll tables, or other devices of this nature if students have difficulty in making the computations from the beginning?"

The answer to this problem is simple. By all means use all the so-called "crutches" that you can as long as the use of the "crutch" is based upon understanding of the principles involved in its construction. It is certainly a waste of a student's time if he is required to make one computation after another in arriving at the interest due on notes when he could simplify his computations and save much time by the use of a simple interest table.

There is nothing wrong with this type of device as long as it is used properly—that is, to supplement understanding and to save time rather than to support an inability to make the computation.

Business arithmetic teachers often ask themselves what part the element of speed should play in determining the ability of students in working problems. Obviously, a competent worker in business should work rapidly as well as accurately. There is little value in a worker who is rapid but inaccurate. Conversely there is little value in a worker who is highly accurate but works so slowly that the expense of his employment is prohibitive. The element of speed should be brought into the arithmetic course and an attempt made to make the student both accurate and rapid. It is difficult or useless to say which is the more important. One without the other is value-less; instruction should be adapted to develop both abilities. The drills used in business arithmetic should incorporate both aspects of speed and of accuracy.

Other Business Education Courses

In the preceding sections the business courses most commonly taught in the secondary school were briefly discussed. There are several other courses that can be classified in the business category; yet there are certain features about the content that verge into other areas of learning.

A brief description of these courses is found below. The methods and techniques for teaching them are similar to those used for other business courses. If the business teacher should find himself teaching one or more of these courses, an inadequate knowledge of the content would no doubt be his chief problem—not the methods whereby the course could be taught most efficiently.

Business Organization and Management. A course sometimes found in the secondary school at the fourth-year level is business organization and management. This course would probably be of most interest to boys and girls who hope to own or manage their own business after graduation from school. There may also be a secondary objective for students enrolled in this course since, by studying the principles behind the organization and management of a business enterprise, the students, who will eventually be working in a business, will have a better understanding and appreciation of business operation.

The topics of content usually included in a course in business organization and management are:

1. Problems of organizing and starting a business
2. Production and merchandising problems
3. Financial problems
4. Governmental relationships with business

This course can be an excellent supplement to the basic business offerings in the secondary school and can be used most effectively to integrate the principles found in such courses as business law, bookkeeping, general business, and office and secretarial practice. It is doubtful that its inclusion in the secondary curriculum in any but the larger high schools would be justified if it meant that one or more basic business courses would be excluded.

Business English. Another course sometimes found in the curriculums of larger high schools is business English. In this course an emphasis is placed upon a rapid review of grammar and sentence structure with a major emphasis being placed upon the principles of business letter writing.

This course has value for all types of student interests in business, both in the secretarial and the general business fields. Besides giving prospective stenographers a basic knowledge of grammar (as it may apply to business letters), it also provides them with a knowledge of the proper form and tone of business letters. For the clerical or bookkeeping student, business English can be helpful in providing understandings of report writing and the ability to express one's self clearly and concisely in terms of those documents typically found in business.

One problem with respect to business English is that in the typical high school a student will be enrolled in at least three years of English. A course in business English may duplicate to some extent the general English courses. However, if the terminology and form peculiar to business are stressed, it is doubtful that this overlapping will be particularly harmful.

Economic Geography. A course in economic geography is sometimes found in business curriculums; it is a type of course that can be very helpful for all students. The emphasis in this course is placed upon the natural and economic resources of the various countries of the world rather than upon their physical characteristics. However, it is difficult to distinguish between the two for economic purposes, because very often the physical and cultural characteristics to a large extent determine the economic factors. In any event, economic geography can be very useful in helping students to understand the political, cultural, and social characteristics of the various peoples of the world through the study of their economic forces.

Projects and Questions for Discussion

1. Create a visual aid or teaching device that would help students understand better the requirements of our society for the rapid and accurate processing of business data.

2. Develop a simple case problem in the area of business law which is based upon the type of experiences that a high-school student would be likely to encounter.

3. Make a list of the type of consumer problems which a high school might have. Suggest some ways you could weave these problems into the instruction of a course in consumer business.

4. Are there any ways in which the content of a course in business arithmetic could be useful in teaching data-processing concepts? If so, make a list of those items of content that could be used for this purpose.

5. Assume that you are a teacher of business law and in your class you have a student who constantly tries to argue about some of the legal points which come up in the discussion. In addition, the student tries to embarrass you by asking highly technical questions which you are unable to answer because of your limited background in law. What remedies might you use to counteract a situation of this sort?

6. In a consumer business class a student has made the statement that advertising is a bad thing because it adds to the cost of goods and also entices people to buy things they do not need. If you were the teacher in this class how might you answer the student?

7. A superintendent of schools wishes to offer a course in consumer business in the school in which you are teaching and is debating whether to ask you or the home economics teacher to teach it. What qualifications would you tell him you possess for teaching this course?

Case Problems

1. You are teaching business subjects in a large city high school, specifically, two classes in general business and two in consumer business. The superintendent of your school finds that it is necessary to add an

additional class in business arithmetic to the offering of the clerical curriculum. Noticing that your load is rather light he assigns this class to you.

After the second week of instruction, you are amazed and chagrined to find that at least half of your students have a great deal of difficulty in working with the simplest of arithmetic problems. Division is particularly difficult for them and in fractions they are lost. Realizing that the arithmetic concepts coming later in the course are much more difficult (percentage, aliquot parts, and so on) you are in a quandary as to what to do. In the past it has been considered highly important by your immediate supervisor that all of the content of courses taught in this department be covered in the time assigned. You realize that if you spend more time on the fundamental processes you will not be able to cover the textbook. On the other hand, if you don't try and obtain more skill in your students in the fundamental processes, you are confident they won't be able to comprehend the concepts coming later anyway. What can you do in a situation of this sort?

2. You have been teaching a business law class (which is just a one-semester course) for approximately four weeks. You have noticed that in the past few days the students in the class have been attempting to bring into the class discussions questions about some of the "sensational" items found in the newspapers. The students appear to obtain a great deal of delight asking questions about such things as murders, divorces, robberies, and the like.

You are perturbed because none of these illustrations relates very much to business law. You don't wish to discourage enthusiasm, but you feel that some of these topics brought up in class are just not appropriate for the classroom. Is there anything you can do in this situation to eliminate illustrations of this type without appearing to be too "stuffy"?

3. In a class in consumer business which you are teaching you have one small group of students who always want to argue about some of the principles found in the textbook. For example, in the unit on budgeting and saving this group stated that they did not believe it was necessary to operate under a budget because none of their parents did and they seemed to get along quite well. There have been other cases when the same sort of argumentative attitude prevailed. The students are not rude—just dogmatic. It is beginning to get on your nerves and some of the other students in the class are becoming irritated. What should be done here?

4. For the first time in your teaching experience you have been assigned to teach a course in business principles and management to a group of senior students. You have had such courses in your undergraduate training under excellent instructors. However, your business experi-

ence has been very limited and you realize that all you know about the organization and operation of a business enterprise is what you have learned in books. You would like to make this course very practical as most of the students in the class are actually interested in going into business for themselves sometime in the near future. Is there anything you can do to make this course other than a theory course?

Suggested Readings

Gawronski, James A., "Business Law—Technical vs. Non-Technical," *Balance Sheet,* January, 1963.

Hanna, J. Marshall, "Can Automation Be Taught in Bookkeeping?" *Business Teacher,* December, 1963.

Nadler, Charles D., "Arithmetic Project—Automobile Operation," *Journal of Business Education,* December, 1963.

Satlow, I. David, "Current Developments in Consumer Education," *Business Education World.* See 1963-1964 issues.

Wood, Merle W., "Another Community Service—Data Processing," *Balance Sheet,* December, 1963.

———— and Robert G. Espegren, "Data Processing Instruction in Secondary Schools," *Journal of Business Education,* February, 1963.

IV

EXTENDING
LEARNING
BEYOND
THE
CLASSROOM

No clear-cut line can be drawn separating good teaching "methodology" from the many other phases of good teaching. It is beyond the scope of a single text such as this to include everything of value in improving the work of a business teacher.

Yet there are some areas of the work of the business teacher so closely associated with and so greatly influencing his methodology that to ignore them would almost be to ignore a portion of common practice in methods of teaching business subjects. Part Four further broadens the teacher's concept of "methods of teaching" to include many of these important related concepts.

Much of the effectiveness of teaching in the area of vocational business education will depend on the available opportunity for effective practice or apprenticeship applications. The modern, educationally directed, cooperative part-time work-experience program is an important answer to this need. Every business teacher should know about such programs, since they materially alter teaching methods for advanced vocational students.

Likewise, although personal development, habits, traits, and attitudes are extremely important educational objectives, quite often extraclass activities provide superior media for teaching them. Thus the methods the business teacher uses in the classroom may be both supplemented and influenced by the presence of well-organized and expertly directed associated activities for the business student—such as a chapter of the "Future Business Leaders of America."

In Part Four are presented a number of these modern concepts which are materially influencing both the achievements and the learning procedures of today's business students. The business teacher will do well to include them in his plans for improvement of methods of teaching.

12

Cooperative Part-time Business Education Programs

"Work has always been at the center of man's total integration—social, emotional, cultural, and vocational"—Gold.[1]

The growth in the use of and participation in cooperative training is a notable development in business education. Ever since cooperative part-time training for the distributive occupations was formally recognized by the George-Deen Act in 1936 more and more youth have found cooperative training the real answer to their vocational preparation, both in the distributive and office occupations. The educator and the businessman should be commended for their encouragement of such programs.

When business firms were small the employees learned the business directly from the employer. But even before 1900 concentrations of population developed department stores, multipurpose offices, and other large business establishments. Personal contact between owner and employee was lost, and the beginning clerical or sales worker had to learn his job through trial and error or under poorly qualified, poorly motivated fellow workers. Expansion of many related fields demanding office and distributive workers paral-

[1] Milton Gold, *Working to Learn* (New York: Bureau of Publications, Teachers College, Columbia University, 1951).

leled the growth of stores and offices. As the field of business grew in size and importance, the need for training in all business occupations became necessary.

In order to provide the student who is going into business occupations with occupational counseling and supervision while he is adjusting to real work situations, various work-study programs were inaugurated. These programs were immediately successful; they have grown in number as the demands for trained distributive and office workers have increased.

Today more and more educators realize the importance of planned work in the education of greater numbers of youth who enter adult employment upon leaving high school. Many of those youth who are going on to college also have real benefits to gain by training under a school-work program. The extent of this practical education is reflected in United States Office of Education statistics. The number of high-school youth in work training programs, both federally reimbursed and the nonreimbursed, shows steady growth in our nation's high schools.

During the development of planned work programs in business education several different titles were used to indicate this type of training. The title that finally emerged and is now generally accepted in business education circles was *Cooperative Part-Time Training.*

What Is Cooperative Business Education? Cooperative part-time training programs for students interested in office or distributive (retailing, selling, service, and wholesaling) occupations operate in many high schools, large and small, in the United States; and they provide a unique opportunity for the secondary pupil to begin his career in business.

Cooperative programs enrolling business students can be classified into four basic types.

1. Straight Office Education Program—so called because the related classes enroll only students in office occupations. These office occupations may be of a secretarial, clerical, or bookkeeping nature.

2. Straight Distributive Education Program—so called when all students are in retailing, wholesaling, outside selling, or service occupations. The related class is made up only of students in these occupations.

3. Business Education Occupations Program—a combination of-

fice and distributive program wherein related instruction is given to a class made up of both office and distributive students.
4. Diversified Occupations Program—so called because students are in office, distributive, trade, and industrial occupations.

The cooperative part-time program operates on what is known as the *alternation plan*. Usually students spend the morning in school and afternoons on the job. Some notably successful programs, often in larger school systems, use a plan of alternating a week in the classroom with a week on the job. Students in programs obtaining state and federal reimbursement must meet the standard of fifteen hours minimum per week on the job. They generally have either two periods of related instruction in school for one year (called plan B in distributive education) or one period of instruction for one year plus meeting certain prerequisite courses (called plan C in distributive education). Some programs operate over a two-year period (called plan A in distributive education) in which students receive one period of related instruction during both the junior and the senior year. The related instruction hours may be taught by the coordinator, who knows firsthand the job-training needs and problems of the trainees, or by a teacher of a related subject. If circumstances permit, the teacher-coordinator role is preferred.

The heart of the cooperative program is the on-the-job training under the supervision of the coordinator, and the correlation of instruction in the related class with the job needs of the student. The chronological order of instructional units in the classroom is determined by the requirements of the student on his individual job. Much of the instruction is individual in nature since every student has different needs. His job duties, his firm, and his personal requirements are dissimilar from all others.

The uniqueness of cooperative part-time programs, therefore, presents the qualified teacher-coordinator with a need for methods and procedures not commonly used in classroom situations. The instruction is heavily individual, mostly vocational in nature, and in every case specifically pointed to and developed around an occupational area.

What Are the Advantages of Cooperative Business Education?
When any one program in a single field attracts over 95,000 students during a single year, and has had consistent enrollment increases since its beginning about 1935, we may justly say that it has enjoyed

a phenomenal growth. Such is the story of cooperative part-time programs in distributive and office education.

What is the significance of the high-school cooperative program? What advantages exist that make this such an attractive program for students, schools, and businesses? Here are some of the reasons:

For the Student

1. It furnishes practical training of the kind that makes the student more efficient and valuable to his employers.
2. It offers him a natural method of choosing an occupation. In doing so, vocational guidance opportunities are inherent. Moreover, the student is imbued with the desire to know the important everyday use of his school training.
3. The method that combines theory and practice has been found to be a sound, workable educational method.
4. It prolongs and makes meaningful the school life of many students who would otherwise not be receiving training toward an occupational goal.
5. It helps the student bridge the gap between school and the business world.

For the School

1. It brings together the business community and the school community.
2. The school learns the problems of the business community, and becomes better equipped to teach students how to cope with them.
3. Cooperative education has immense public relations value since the business world meets and tests the products of the school. Many of the projects carried on in the program result in favorable publicity.

For the Business Community

1. It provides for the constant and systematic infusion of desirable beginners into office and distributive work.
2. The school training "upgrades" the level of all other workers in the business firm and attracts a better grade of employee.

3. The school aids in the initial training, helping the business firm reduce its training problems and expense.
4. It reduces cost by increasing the efficiency of the office or distributive worker.

Education at public expense can be justified only in terms of the contribution it makes to the general welfare of society. A program of cooperative education under public supervision and control can be justified only when it provides training that enables those engaged in the business field to give better, more economical, and more efficient service. The social and economic benefits that will accrue from an adequate program in distributive and office education will be shared by business workers, business firms, producers, and consumers.

Terms Used in Cooperative Distributive and Office Education. Certain terms used in the field of cooperative education should be defined and understood so that all teachers and others connected with business education will be able to communicate adequately as well as comprehend fully the professional literature in the field.

Cooperative education is a method of education that integrates learning experience in the school with work experience made available in some cooperating agency outside the school. This is all under the regular supervision of a school representative called a coordinator.

Coordinator is a person who holds a secondary teaching certificate plus special technical and professional requirements in the office, distributive, or trade field, as well as a certain amount of actual occupation experience in his particular field. He is directly charged with the planning of the program as well as with the selection, placement, training, and promotion of students connected with a cooperative part-time training program. A *teacher-coordinator* is one who also teaches the related instruction class in school.

Related instruction is instruction provided under a vocationally competent instructor, and directly meaningful to the student enrolled in a cooperative program. This class is usually titled *Distributive Practices* in the Distributive Educational Programs and *Office Practice* or *Secretarial Practice* in the Office Education Programs.

Training station is a cooperating business that agrees to employ a student on a part-time basis and to provide this student with a variety of experiences and training necessary to develop occupational efficiency. The agreement is usually only for the period of a regular school year.

Sponsor is an employee appointed by the business firm to carry out the training and rotation of the student through a series of experiences. He supervises the training of the student, evaluates the student's progress periodically on forms provided by the school, and consults with the coordinator on the student's over-all training. He may be called a *training supervisor*.

Student Learner is a student who has elected to take part in the cooperative program. The student is usually a senior (some programs do start in the junior year) and has a sincere interest in a chosen business occupation. He is mature, employable, and has the necessary aptitude for the job for which he will be training. The student learner is either planning to enter the field upon graduation from high school or needs the occupational background in preparation for advanced study.

Advisory committee is a group of business people and others of the community who are interested in the welfare and advancement of the cooperative program within the school. They provide suggestions and advice to the school in matters concerning the cooperative program, especially in those phases involving business directly. They may also assist in the promotion, course determination, selection of instructors, and other matters pertaining to the adult program in the school.

Reimbursed program is a cooperative program that, by maintaining certain standards, receives state and federal moneys under provisions of the state and federal vocational legislation. The Vocational Education Act of 1963 provides reimbursement to cooperative programs and also to preparatory programs meeting vocational standards. Standards involve coordinator and teacher requirements, student selection, employment schedules, course content, facilities and equipment, and other factors which help assure an educationally sound program.

The Nature of Learning
in Cooperative Part-Time Training

One of the most important and difficult parts of the coordinator's job is the provision for school training directly helpful to each student trainee. Since the entire purpose of the cooperative program is to train youth, not just to find them employment, there is little excuse for operating a program unless it is prepared to offer the related instruction and coordination needed.

Importance of Coordination. Coordination is the integrating factor that unites all necessary elements of a cooperative program, and directs them toward a common purpose. Coordination is essentially a combining activity which brings in and fits together the various parts needed to make a complete and functioning cooperative program. Without coordination a training program ceases to be cooperative, and lacks the element that makes such training truly vocational.

A broad definition of coordination is "all activities carried on by the teacher-coordinator." These can be grouped as: (*a*) promotion, (*b*) organization and administration, (*c*) selection of trainees and training stations, (*d*) placement of trainees, and (*e*) instruction. Efforts in each of these areas must be blended together to produce a well-trained, fully qualified worker upon graduation. Lack of work in any one of the areas will seriously hamper the effectiveness of the program and the quality of the training. As we examine the nature of the learnings provided in cooperative training it must be remembered that for these learnings to be fully achieved they must be carefully coordinated with all other areas, especially on-the-job activities.

Categories of Learnings. The total learnings expected of a trainee can be classified into four areas: (*a*) general related learnings, (*b*) occupational group learnings, (*c*) specific job learnings, and (*d*) on-the-job learnings.

General related learnings are received in those subjects embracing problems common to all workers regardless of kind of work. This would include topics such as these: employer-employee relations, work habits and attitudes, human relations, employee benefits and protection, personal habits affecting work, government-business relationships, labor organization, and occupational planning.

Occupational group learnings would include auxiliary technical and nontechnical information that is necessary to the individual for confidence, understanding, and job pride. It would not be necessary for the student to study this area at the time he is actually performing the skills on the job. In office occupations this would include such subjects as typewriting, bookkeeping, shorthand, filing, duplicating, and office machines. In the distributive occupations this would include subjects such as store organization, color, line and design, speech, principles of display, store record keeping, and salesmanship.

Specific job learnings would include the technical information needed to perform skills and to make judgments. Office topics would include credit, office procedure, medical stenography, and dental-receptionist duties. The units for the distributive worker might include merchandise analysis, specific selling techniques, unit control, and salescheck systems.

On-the-job learnings include the technical information learned on the job such as special machines, special business forms, policies and practices peculiar to a single business, and other skills or knowledges that can be learned on the job under the supervision of the student's sponsor or training supervisor.

Categories of learnings provided in post-high-school cooperative programs are the same as in high school, although the content is designed to prepare the post-high-school student for middle-level occupations.

Ways of Presenting Learnings. General Related Learnings—these are usually learned through group-instruction methods with full use of community resources such as committees, informal discussion, resource persons, field trips, and visual aids.

Occupational Group Learnings—the content in this area is handled through group work—with allowances for individual differences, of course. In the Business Education Occupations program and the Diversified Occupations program, the class may be divided into broad fields of interest—office, distributive, or trades. Further breakdown may be made as the situation warrants.

Specific Job Learnings—this material is usually handled in small groups or on an individual basis according to its nature in the particular case. It may be provided through individual study guides as the Minnesota card system (also Ohio and Oklahoma) or through individual study manuals as those of Texas, Missouri, and Alabama. Students may also make individual manuals or notebooks about their job or the merchandise handled. Generally a combination of these devices is necessary. The sponsor or training supervisor assists in this type of training.

On-the-Job Learnings—coordinator, student, and training supervisor work out a job breakdown, also called a *schedule of processes* or *plan of experiences.* The various sections of the breakdown are placed in a suitable sequence, and the trainee performs one duty after another as he is ready for them. In training stations where all tasks are performed at the outset of the training period a sequence of study is planned.

In actual teaching practice the distinctions among areas of learning are not as fine as indicated here. A class period may be scheduled for related study, but the division of the class period among the different kinds of learnings is left to the discretion of the teacher. The teacher can correlate or integrate according to the dictates of his judgment.

Most students have the bulk of their general related learnings before reaching the senior year and their entrance to the cooperative program. Some of the occupational group learnings will be received in pre-employment classes, but much will be received in the related class. Specific job learnings are entirely taken in the related instruction class. On-the-job learnings are received only at the student's training station.

Because of the flexibility and adaptability of teaching methods, most can be used in two or more of the learning areas. The committee, for example, can be used just as effectively in general related learnings as it can in occupational group learnings. However, in order to give some core of focus to the cooperative training methods, each method is listed under the learning area where it is most often used.

The methods explained here should not be construed to be the only ones used or needed in cooperative training, but these are effective and common. The examples are given merely to show specific application. It is assumed that the teacher has a complete mastery of the methods needed in general classroom teaching.

Typical Curriculum Patterns in High School Cooperative Business Education Programs. In order that the reader may better visualize the curriculums, a sample curriculum pattern for each cooperative program is given. The patterns shown would be changed somewhat for the larger schools where more offerings could be made. The usual high-school requirements and electives are not shown.

The business education occupations program is found in the smaller schools where the total number of students enrolled in cooperative training is not sufficiently large to warrant a separate class for each group. A curriculum pattern for this type of program would

Distributive Education Curriculum Pattern

9th Grade	11th Grade	12th Grade
General Business	Bookkeeping	Distributive
	Salesmanship ½	Practices (2 peri-
10th Grade	and	ods if plan B, 1 if
Typewriting	Business Law ½ or	plan C)
	Consumer Education ½ or	Cooperative
	Business Arithmetic ½	Training (on the
		job)

Office Education Curriculum Pattern (Secretarial)

9th Grade	11th Grade	12th Grade
General Business	Bookkeeping	Secretarial
	Shorthand	Practice
10th Grade	Office Machines	Cooperative
Typewriting		Training (on the
		job)

Office Education Curriculum Pattern (Clerical)

9th Grade	11th Grade	12th Grade
General Business	Bookkeeping	Clerical
	Office Machines	Practice
10th Grade	Business Law ½	Cooperative
Typewriting	and	Training (on the
	Consumer Education ½ or	job)
	Business Arithmetic ½ or	
	Business English ½	

rest heavily on the school's current offerings. It is highly recommended that the pattern include general business, typewriting, bookkeeping, and occupations practice plus cooperative training.

The pattern for a diversified occupations class must be built around the offerings of very small schools. This is best worked out under the guidance of state supervisors of the fields represented.

Sample Distributive Practices Instructional Schedule. The following is a sample outline of what a coordinator may plan to provide in the distributive practices class. The general related learnings would be the most variable depending on what has been provided in other classes prior to the student's enrollment in the cooperative program in the senior year. This plan is based on a plan C distributive program. The plan B program, having two periods per day for the school year, would give approximately twice as much time for each type of learning. Plan A would also have about twice as much time for each learning, as it has one class period in both the junior and senior years.

Area of Instruction	*Number of Weeks* (*1 hour per day*)
General Related Learnings	6
Occupational Group Learnings	20
Specific Job Learnings	10
	——
	36
On-the-Job Learnings (15 hours per week minimum)	36

The coordinator would break down each of the learnings into a time schedule so he could draw up his units of study. The occupational group learnings might look like this.

Occupational Group Learnings Outline

Channels of Distribution	1 week
Basic Salesmanship (review)	4
Related Skills in Selling	2
Job Analysis	1
Store Operation	2
Store Organization	2
Merchandise Information	1
Problems in Selling	2
Advertising	1
Display	2
Fashion Merchandising	1
Buying	1
	——
Total	20 weeks

The general related learnings would be drawn from those units not covered in previous classes (these units are listed later under "Techniques in Providing General Related Learnings"). The specific job learnings would vary considerably from student to student, but undoubtedly would include a great deal of merchandise study as well as specific skills in advertising, display, merchandising, and buying. With this over-all view let us now examine methods that might be used for each of these learnings.

Typical Curriculum Patterns in Post-High-School Cooperative Business Education Programs. Post-high-school cooperative programs in distributive and office occupations vary considerably. Frequently they may be more specialized than the high-school programs and offer a greater depth of education in the occupation under study. The usual post-high-school program contains about sixty-four to sixty-eight semester hours of course offerings. The study typically is organized somewhat as follows:

First Year		*Second Year*	
Communication Skills	6	Occupational Analysis	3
Business Mathematics	3	Economics	3
Accounting	6	Field Experience	6-12
Psychology of Human Relations	3	Occupational Subjects (Marketing or Office Skills)	18-22
American Institutions	3		
Business Law	3		
Occupational Subjects (Marketing or Office Skills)	10		

Field experiences may be arranged on an alternating schedule of half day in school and half day on the job as in the high-school program, or may be blocked into periods of twelve to eighteen weeks alternating with semesters of full-time attendance at the post high school.

Techniques in Providing General Related Learnings

It has been pointed out that general related learnings are those common to all workers regardless of the field of work. Courses that usually present general related learnings would be: general business, English, business arithmetic, salesmanship, bookkeeping, and, to a lesser degree, nearly all other required classes in the secondary school.

The methods used in providing general related learnings are those common to any group instruction involving the use of community resources, audio-visual aids, reference work, discussion, and lecture. A sample list of the units or topics providing general related learnings is given below.

These units are found in the courses mentioned above or, in some cases, are grouped together and offered in a class called *Occupational Relations*. The merits of a separate course have been argued pro and con, and certain values do accrue from having such a class. However, the integration of these topics into several courses taken by nearly all high-school students is the current trend.

*Units Containing General Related Learnings for the Cooperative Trainee**

How Can I Find My Place in the World of Work?

How Can I Get the Job I Want?

How Can I Work Successfully with People with Whom I Come in Contact on a Job?

How Do Existing Labor Laws Affect Me?

How Will Labor Organizations Affect Me?

How Can I Advance in My Occupation?

How Can I Keep Healthy as a Worker?

How Can I Make Best Use of My Earnings?

How Can I Protect Myself and Others from Accidents and Injuries on the Job?

What Deductions Are Made from My Wages and Why Are They Made?

The teacher-coordinator will continually check to see which of these learnings have been covered in other classes. Those not covered will have to be scheduled for the related class. Oftentimes a brief visit with a fellow teacher will result in a change in classes to accommodate some part of the general related learnings.

For example, a unit in English on "Occupations" would touch on several of the above topics. A unit in a social studies class on "Labor Unions," if approached from the effect on the individual worker, would satisfy at least two of the above units. The bookkeeping class is a natural for discussion on taxes, social security, and other information about payroll deductions. The physical education classes would cover good grooming and personal health habits.

If the general related learnings are not being covered in these

---

* *Units of Instruction for the Occupational Relations Course* (St. Paul, Minnesota: Vocational Division, State Department of Education).

classes, it is seldom because the teachers will not do it, but more often because they are not aware that these units are desired by the coordinator for the students going into the cooperative program.

Techniques in Providing Occupational Group Learnings

Occupational group learnings are taught in the distributive practices class for distributive trainees, in clerical or secretarial practice class for office trainees, and in the occupations class for business or diversified programs. Half or more of the time in these classes is given to occupational group learnings, with the remainder of the time used for specific job instruction. It can be seen, then, that considerable attention should be given methods used in this type of instruction.

Instruction in this area of learning is built around units that apply to all students in an occupational field. In distributive practices all the students are employed in some distributive occupation, and the learnings provided are those necessary for all workers in distribution. The methods used in occupational group learnings, however, are equally applicable to all occupational fields—distributive, office, and trades. Several methods used in occupational group learnings will be explained briefly, and examples will be given.

Individual Reports. The use of the individual report combines several worth-while learning activities into one project. The student would carry out the following steps in preparing a typical report.

1. Define the problem on which the report is to be given.
2. Gather the information needed to satisfy the problem.
3. Draw together related facts and reach some conclusions.
4. Organize the report in a logical manner.
5. Present to the class the problem, findings, and conclusions.
6. Answer questions and defend conclusions.

For example, in a unit on store organization questions may arise as to local practice on such things as leased departments, receiving and marking, or chain-store managership. A student could be asked to prepare a report on one of these questions and present his findings to the class. After getting the problem clearly in mind, the student may draw background information. When the necessary information has been acquired a written report would be prepared and the findings presented orally to the class. Questions and discussion would naturally follow the report, thus providing the entire class with some understanding of the particular area that one student has studied.

A valuable part of the individual report is the experience the student gets from presenting his report to the class, answering questions and defending his conclusions. This skill is very important to those in selling and office work where they meet with customers and clients. It is not necessary that every student in class prepare an individual report at the same time. Reports have more meaning when they are assigned as the result of a recognized need rather than just as a problem "drawn from a hat."

Resource Person. A resource person is usually defined as a person who has, through experience and/or training, acquired a fund of information that he is willing to share with others. The resource person may take the form of a guest speaker in the classroom, a member of a panel, or someone who meets with students conducting field interviews.

The resource person can best be used to provide information needed by students in an area in which the coordinator has little or no background. The person usually has a clear understanding of the topic and can draw from many local examples that are real and interesting to the students. The students, through questions that may be prepared ahead of time, can clarify views they already have on the topic. The resource person also has been used effectively in introducing new units, or in climaxing a unit of instruction.

In order for the class to receive the utmost value from the resource person, the coordinator should be sure that the subject-matter dovetails satisfactorily into the objectives and learning outcomes that he desires. When selecting an individual the coordinator should make sure that the person will present information in keeping with the philosophy of the community. Above all it should be kept in mind that the resource people should be used only if they can present additional information or clarify information already covered.

Case Study. The case-study method is the relating of some story, anecdote, or the like, usually in the third party, often used to add variety and human interest to a classroom situation. It probably has its greatest usages in illustrating a particular point or opening a new subject or unit.

When either a true or a hypothetical case is presented by the teacher the students have alternative solutions from which to choose, and it is up to them to select the most appropriate one. A case is most effective if the student is asked what he would do if he were in the particular situation. It is recommended that the coordinator write the facts of the case on the blackboard before beginning the class period so that the student will be able to use them as a frame of reference.

In using this technique the instructor asks the students to put themselves into a pseudosituation, and decide what they would do if confronted with a specific problem.

The case method often shows the teacher what knowledge the students lack and creates or instills in them the desire to continue with the subject until they have mastered it.

Field Interview. A field interview is an activity wherein a student contacts an employer, co-worker, customer, consumer, parent, government official, or any other predetermined person in an informal situation for the purpose of securing authentic opinions and facts related to a problem that he is studying. It is ordinarily a question-and-answer process which can be altered to fit the circumstances.

The interview is much more important than the space that has been allotted to it in recent publications would indicate. Because virtually all distributive workers employ the method, and because a very definite skill is involved that is valuable in many life situations, it should have a prominent place among the learning activities of students in cooperative training. Through the field interview, the student will gain confidence in himself and in the community. When the interview is well executed those who have been interviewed will acquire respect for the school and the program.

The planning of the field interview should be a cooperative activity between the teacher-coordinator and the individual, committee, or entire class. Arrangements should be made well in advance of the interview. Frequently the teacher will "scout" the persons to be interviewed. This may or may not be known by the students involved.

In teaching salesmanship, the field interview might well be used to study the sales practices of various types of stores or service enterprises, to examine company policy concerning particular merchandising situations, or to investigate customer reactions to sales procedures. In the retailing course, it might be applied to the study of store organization, store system, merchandising policies, or advertising procedures. In the area of occupational relations, it is appropriate to an investigation of the desirable traits of workers in the several fields of distribution, common deficiencies of personnel, human relations problems, and safety practices. The opportunities for using the field interview are very many indeed.

Role Playing. Role playing is an unrehearsed, spontaneous dramatization stressing the role of the individual. The primary purpose of role playing is to have a student achieve successful technique for handling a given situation. Two or more students may re-enact a problem situation that actually occurred or has been observed on the job. They may take their own roles or assume the role of some one else. Pseudosituations may also be created in which special problems are dramatized. The role-playing activity can be presented to the entire class or carried out as a group activity while other students are conducting sales practice or individual study.

The degree to which a role-playing situation is structured is a matter of choice depending upon your objectives. If you are using role playing to present information or facts, you may want a rather carefully controlled situation. If, on the other hand, your main purpose is to develop confidence, control, or skills in the student, a spontaneous portrayal may suit your needs.

The more important purposes of role playing are: to develop specific skills; to develop an appreciation of work standards; to present information and facts; to try out new techniques; to develop desirable attitudes; to point out common problems; to improve communication; to develop self-confidence; to correct undesirable attitudes and habits; to provide practice in adaptability; to motivate learning; to reduce emotional tension; and to evaluate progress and achievement.

Like most new learning devices, role playing must be introduced gradually with a great deal of tact and salesmanship. A full explanation of what is to be accomplished, along with coordinator participation, helps to make it a valuable device.

Demonstrations. Demonstrations take two basic forms: teacher demonstrations and student demonstrations. Appropriately used, the demonstration elicits high interest and attention, which other devices may not do. It can be used in nearly all cases where a skill, technique, or procedure is to be taught or practiced.

The teacher demonstration can be used to introduce a topic for discussion, to highlight a unit, or to create interest in an area that students may feel is unimportant. Through the medium of a demonstration the teacher can introduce a great deal of showmanship, and point out the need for finesse in a particular skill or technique. Naturally the teacher will want to make sure the demonstration is motion perfect before presenting it to the class.

Student demonstrations offer the students an opportunity to show what they have learned in class or on the job. It can be used equally well by students of both high and low ability, merely by controlling the complexity of what is to be demonstrated. The sales demonstration is the most common type in the distributive field. In this two students take part, one as a customer, the other as a salesperson. These points can be well demonstrated by this method:

Steps of the sale	Receptionist duties
Handling customer complaints	Operation of a machine
Taking telephone orders	Human relations problems
Demonstrating merchandise	Nonselling skills
Customer viewpoints	Job instruction
Telephone procedure	Service procedure

Certain props are sometimes necessary in order to present an effective demonstration. A well-equipped distributive or office classroom will usually have enough variety of equipment to provide everything except in the very special case. In cases where additional merchandise or equipment is needed it can quite often be borrowed from a local business firm for a short time. With a little encouragement students can develop very workable props for demonstration purposes. The creative coordinator will not hesitate to use the demonstration method, for he recognizes that it often can be the final clincher to a good lesson.

Committee Work. The committee is a device wherein students are divided into small groups for the purpose of working out activities, topics, problems, or assignments instead of working on them individually or as a class. It allows more opportunities for the individual student to participate actively in the learning situation. Learning is greatest when the student gets response from others to his ideas and actions. Responses of a committee to a member's ideas will stimulate his thinking, help him to evaluate himself as a person, and see himself as others see him. During the course of committee work the student develops skills for effective group participation and individual expression.

In office education the committee could be used for topics such as business forms, reception procedures, recording procedures, and office practices. In distributive education the committee has been successful in nearly all of the courses in the field—salesmanship, retailing, occupational relations, merchandise information, and display. How to treat the various kinds of customers—silent, talkative, hard of hearing, indefinite, shopper, and so forth—lends itself to committee study. Surveys of various kinds, such as shopping habits, window display, store practices, personnel policies, consumer preferences, generally call for committee treatment if the projects are to be adequately covered. In the occupational relations field, certain aspects of labor legislation, labor organizations, employer-employee relations, social security, safety, health, and management of personal affairs are suitable to this method.

Shopping Reports. The shopping report is used to evaluate and record the activities of salespersons and their physical environment as observed in an actual buying situation. The report is a prepared form listing the information to be secured, reactions to be noted, and points to be observed with provisions for a graduated system of evaluation by the shopper. The form and content of the report may vary according to the purpose for which it is used and the particular points to be emphasized.

This method is generally used when the student is being shopped or where he is rating another salesperson. The shopping report can be incorporated as an activity in various types of units of instruction. Inasmuch as it involves a complete sales transaction, it is pertinent to practically all areas of training in retail selling, including customer relations, sales steps, merchandise handling, display, and pre-employment units.

The shopping report develops the customer's point of view in the student. By introspection and subjective analysis the customer's reaction can be analyzed. He can better appreciate the value of cordiality, tolerance, and willingness to serve in his relationship with others. The report can also be used as a means of evaluating and measuring the student's progress in his learnings.

Field Trips. The field trip is "any kind of definitely organized trip with a primarily educational purpose, made by a group of pupils as a part of their regular school work." [2] It has no definite time duration and may include several incidental activities. Most generally it takes the form of a class visit to a business firm, industrial plant, office, or other institution exposing the student to firsthand experiences in the everyday world of work and business.

In cooperative training where students are regularly working in business on a part-time basis one might feel that field trips would have little value. Actually this is not true. The field trips add much to the experience of those already engaged in "live" contacts.

The field trip is a wonderful device to provide a preview of forthcoming work. It is question-provoking and a discussion stimulator. However, if used as a preview it will naturally be limited to primary observation. When used as a means of instruction the trip is probably operating at its best. In the distributive field it would allow the coordinator to teach specific retail techniques to a large class. This is especially appropriate where facilities such as window display, advertising make-up rooms, ticket machines, and others are not available in the classroom. The field trip can also be used to tie together phases of a unit already studied—for example, pulling together all phases of store operation.

In the office occupations the field trip could be used to show the various ways offices are organized, special types of office machines, progression of work through an office, and many other important office learnings that could not be provided for in any other way.

Field Observation. The field observation is a learning activity in which the individual student procures firsthand information by intelligent observation of real-life situations outside the classroom. It frequently takes the form of an assignment in which one or more persons bring information of interest back to the group. On the other hand, it may be used by a particular student for an individual study purpose. In the distributive occupations field the learner gets his information by actually going into the store, warehouse, shopping center, or other place with the express purpose in mind of noting or observing certain previously determined items, practices, or situations. In the office field such observations may be somewhat more

---

[2] Henry C. Atyeo, *The Excursion as a Teaching Technique* (New York: Teachers College, Columbia University, 1939), p. 27.

difficult, as many offices are not open to the public; nevertheless, this device can be used effectively.

Field observation differs from the field trip in that a group does not visit a single place at one time. Each student is on his own. Were it not for the fact that the field observation does not entail a special excursion, it might be termed an *individual field trip*. In reality, when the field observation is modified it blends into the field trip or the field interview.

The field observation differs from the field interview in that personal contact with an interviewee may be entirely lacking. On the other hand, a few questions asked of a person in charge would not disqualify it as a field observation.

Techniques in Providing Specific Job Learnings

One of the cardinal features of the cooperative part-time training program is the aid it offers in the adjustment of the student to the business world. "It bridges the gap between the school and the job" is a statement frequently used. Adjustments of students to their jobs involve individual problems and, thus, we must work with these students as individuals. We should seek out the abilities and inabilities, habits and attitudes, that contribute to the success or failure of each student. This section deals with the procedures and methods we can use to help individual students with their particular job problems and adjustments.

Individual Study Methods. Specific instructional needs of individual students should be determined from (*a*) occupational needs of the student and (*b*) personal needs of the individual. For example, the occupational needs of a trainee in a men's specialty store are definitely different from those of a trainee in a hardware store. The specialized knowledges for each job would be completely different. The personal needs will vary with the background of each student, and could consist of a need for emotional adjustment as well as for instruction in some basic skill such as arithmetic, salesmanship, or speech.

The *Evaluative Criteria for Distributive Education*[3] indicates that

---

[3] Special Committee of Distributive Education, *Evaluative Criteria for Distributive Vocational Education* (Washington, D.C.: American Vocational Association, 1954), p. 12.

up to half of the related classroom time should be given to specific related instruction. Individual study then does have a major place in the instruction for cooperative trainees.

The use of a job study guide often provides motivation for the student worker in the classroom and on the job. Some of the reasons for this might be: the material is immediately applicable to the student's work; it frequently leads to favorable recognition by the employer; the student works relatively independently of the other students; the quantity and quality depends entirely on him; the student can see his progress; he knows where he is going and where he has been; and the on-the-job trainer can give specific help and encouragement in training the student.

Two basic plans of individual study are currently in wide use. Both plans have certain features that make them desirable and each, of course, has certain weaknesses. Coordinators in Minnesota, Ohio, and Oklahoma have developed a "Card System." With this type of study guide the content is placed on variously colored cards 5 x 8 inches in size. The cards, in order of usual use, are Index Cards, Bibliography Cards, Unit Cards, Information Cards, Activity Cards, and Key Cards. One set of cards is placed in the coordinator's file, and a second set is set up for student use. If a card from a trainee's set is lost a copy of the missing card can easily be made from the coordinator's set. Cards are coded and additional material is easily added. References must be purchased in addition to the cards.

The second type of individual study guide is the individual study manual. Several states have produced these manuals, which typically follow a pattern of outlining the area to be studied, referring the student to certain readings, and then assigning questions and activities to be completed. Many coordinators have found that manuals containing an information section, such as those produced by the University of Texas, are very easy to use. With a "Texas manual" no other references are needed, and the student has just one piece of material with which to work.

Perhaps the strongest appeal in the use of job study guides is to good teaching practice. It is one place where the teacher-coordinator can give real proof to the claim that cooperative education provides a separate curriculum for each student. The job study guide is geared to the needs of each particular student in that it is written for one particular kind of work. It is flexible because only the parts needed by the student worker are selected for study. The student may draw from several guides if his position cuts across two or more occupational fields.

The actual procedure for using individual study guides will vary according to the type of guides used. Many coordinators set aside one or more class periods each week for individual study. The coordinator can work with individual students checking work, answering questions, assisting them in locating reference material, and explaining further assignments. Individual study can be used when a special need arises on the job for the student to learn a skill in order to move along on his learning program. Individual study is especially useful because it is flexible and can be used at any time without prior preparation. The alert coordinator will follow the professional writings to keep up to date on this phase of instruction.

Job Manuals, Merchandise Manuals, and Scrapbooks. What is a job manual? It is a manual containing the basic facts a learner should know about the business place in which he is working. It is, in effect, an orientation to the store policy, procedure, organization, and other fundamentals every good employee should know about his firm. Most manuals are merely outlined by the teacher, and the student is obligated to fill in the manual with information about his place of employment. Sample outlines of job manuals would be:

For a Distributive Occupation	*For an Office Occupation*
Facts about My Store	Facts about My Office
Store Rules and Policy	Office Rules and Policy
List of My Duties	List of My Duties
Store Layout	Office Layout
Sales Check System	Office Jobs Breakdown
Personnel Policies	Filing
Advertising-Display	Telephone
Customer Services	Typing
Credit Policies	(and others as needed)
Nonselling Duties	Receptionist Duties
Technical Terms	Handling Mail
Store Maintenance	Record-Keeping Procedure
My Store and My Community	Technical Terms
	Office Housekeeping
	My Office and My Community

What is a merchandise manual? It is a manual prepared by the student including whatever information a salesperson needs to know about his merchandise to sell it effectively. A merchandise manual is a logical means of directing the learner's efforts specifically to the knowledges needed to sell. It would include brand-name understanding, merchandise knowledge, how to display or demonstrate the merchandise, plus information needed to talk to customers in terms of their enjoyment or use of the product. A sample outline of a merchandise manual would be:

Introduction

What Your Customer Wants to Know

Qualities Customers Look For

How to Recognize Merchandise Factors

Steps in Making the Sale

Learning Your Products' Language

Summary of General Information

List of Information Sources

A similar manual is used in the office field; the student prepares a manual on material used in the office such as paper, machines, or the products handled by the company.

What is a scrapbook? Typically a scrapbook is a collection of pertinent articles, advertisements, labels, reports, samples, and other items concerning a product, job, business organization, or other factors about an occupation. The scrapbook is a long-term project wherein the student gathers information that will help in his future development as a distributive or office worker. There appears to be no special outline for scrapbooks. The organization, layout, and content are left to the creativity of the student.

Additional Suggestions for Specific Instruction. Individual study guides and various student-prepared manuals are the two major means of providing specific instruction. Many other techniques can also be used. A few of these will be described briefly.

Demonstrations—planned demonstrations provide an opportunity to assign individual instruction.

> *Example:*   A person who has proved proficient in gift wrapping through class or on-the-job training may demonstrate dexterity to other members of the class who may not perform this skill as part of their work.

Displays in the classroom—

> *Example:*   A trainee who has learned how to display hardlines through specific instruction for his job may, as a part of his training, prepare a display for other members of the class to evaluate.

Preparation of reports to be presented to the class—the organization of a report may be used as specific instruction. This report may have valuable basic information useful to other members of the class.

The service of other teachers—other teachers may be asked to help with certain problems.

> *Example:*   The home economics teacher may be willing to talk with the students on textiles. The English teacher could assign students projects that will help them meet their occupational requirements. The science teacher may help students in technical information on merchandise qualities.

Student project—each student may be assigned a project. It should be one that will benefit the student in his specific situation.

> *Example:*   A student may develop a notebook-scrapbook combination of "tricks" that help him in his particular job. Typing tricks, magazine articles, lists of often-misspelled words, display techniques, personality suggestions, or lists of selling phrases are projects that would be worth-while. To be educational these projects should apply to the person making the book.

Coordinator-student interviews—planned interviews at stated intervals will serve as a means of discussing individual problems, especially those of a personal nature.

> *Example:*   An interview could be held to discuss how the student could get the most out of a new experience to be undertaken on the job. It may also serve as a means of drawing together several pieces of study carried out on an individual basis.

Procedure for Providing On-the-Job Learnings

Instruction on the job is usually handled by a sponsor or training supervisor appointed by the store or office management. Seldom does the teacher-coordinator do any great amount of actual instruction at the place of the student's employment, and then only if it is with the approval of the trainee's employer. The coordinator does have the responsibility, nevertheless, of making sure adequate training is given the student. The coordinator should be sure the sponsor understands his role in the cooperative program, and just what things he should be training the student to do. Only a close and well-planned program of instruction can make on the job experiences worth-while.

When the coordinator places a student in a training station, it is the result of previous evaluation of the business, acceptance of the cooperative program by management, and an understanding of the duties and obligations by all concerned. In small business firms the training supervisor may be the owner or manager. In larger firms a sponsor is usually appointed by management. In either case this person is the one that the coordinator will work with in the training and evaluation of the student.

At the beginning of the student's employment, the coordinator and the sponsor plan a series of job experiences that will lead to the ultimate goal of giving the student learner a complete and well-rounded background in a particular occupation. If possible, the student should be introduced to each phase of his job as he is ready for it. Some students will thus progress rapidly on a job while others will progress more slowly. A student in a small business firm may have to work in all phases of the business the first few days of employment; therefore, the sponsor and the coordinator will have to use considerable judgment as to which part of his work will receive classroom study first.

There are several methods used to insure the sponsor's being ready and able to give the instruction needed by the student. The amount of direction that the coordinator gives the sponsor will depend on that need, the cooperation of the training firm, and the ability of the student. The use of a sponsor handbook, advisory committee action, training profile, and sponsor meeting to facilitate training will be explained.

Sponsor Handbook. The coordinator will give a handbook to the sponsor as soon as a student has been assigned to the cooperating firm. One coordinator prepares a handbook for his sponsors by assembling the following materials into a manila folder.

The Youth You Supervise, Bulletin 174, United States Department of Labor

Employer's Confidential Rating Report for Cooperative Trainees
Trainee's Progress Report
Training Profile Sheets with Instructions
High School Publication on Cooperative Training
Complete Set of Forms Used in Selection of Cooperative Trainees
Summary Sheet on the Student the Sponsor Is to Train.

The coordinator and sponsor discuss this material, and plan the student's learning experiences in the store or office. One copy of this plan will be added to the folder. Such a handbook provides the sponsor with a reference to turn to during the training period for information on how to work with youth, how to fill out rating forms, and other questions that come up during the year. The coordinator may remind the sponsor from time to time to review some part of the contents for ideas on training the student.

Advisory Committee Action. The advisory committee is an integral part of the cooperative training program. It is a body appointed by the superintendent of schools to assist in smooth functioning of the cooperative program. The membership is usually made up of leaders in the business community, and, thus, carries a great deal of weight with all businesses in the community. It deals with such things as student-trainee wages, evaluations, selection of training stations, instructional materials, placement procedures, and training assistance. From time to time during the school year it may find material or information that it feels should go to businesses training students. In such cases this material can be obtained or duplicated and sent to each sponsor and cooperating firm. The coordinator can then follow up such action, and help the sponsor carry through on the advisory committee's suggestions.

Training Profile. The training profile is a listing of job duties, experiences, or procedures the trainee in an occupation must generally learn to become a proficient worker. Trainees are asked periodically to rate each item on the list in terms of how much training they have received. This list can then be used as a measure by the coordinator and the sponsor of what has been accomplished, and to what degree the student feels he has learned each of the items included in the profile. It provides the sponsor with a check sheet on his training efforts, and gives the coordinator a picture of how the training is progressing in a certain business or situation.

Sponsor Meetings. Holding meetings of all sponsors to discuss job training is not currently a common practice in cooperative training. It is being used very effectively by some coordinators, however. Such a meeting at the beginning of the training period does provide the coordinator with the opportunity to orient the entire group of sponsors to the program, and to answer the various questions they might have. Meetings during the school year can motivate sponsors to do a better job of training as well as inform them of new ideas in training and supervision.

Coordinator-Sponsor-Trainee Conferences. Whenever questions arise about on-the-job training a three-way meeting should be arranged to discuss possible solutions. Most often only two-way discussions are conducted, coordinator-student, coordinator-sponsor, or student-sponsor, on problems that are of importance to all three. Naturally some cases would merit only two-way discussion, but the value of all three parties discussing progress, problems, weaknesses, and strengths cannot be overlooked.

In Conclusion

The teacher-coordinator of a cooperative training program should not assume that the foregoing devices are the only ones to be used in presenting the learnings needed by cooperative students. These devices are presented only to give some idea of how they can be used to provide special instructional needs. The effective teacher will modify, adapt, combine, add to, and in many ways improve upon these devices to fit his own particular abilities, and the needs and desires of the students.

In no case will any amount of special methods and devices take the place of adequate classroom preparation based on the students' needs and blended together with interesting and meaningful content. Sound classroom procedure should be the teacher-coordinator's first goal. The use of additional methods will then add meaning and depth to a worth-while base.

Projects and Questions for Discussion

1. Some educators have been known to object to cooperative part-time programs on the grounds that they "cannot justify excusing students from school in order that they may go to work." What answers might be given to this objection? Is the objection valid?

2. Occasionally educators have been known to object to having cooperative part-time students receive wages for the work they do on the grounds that it is an educational program for which the students receive school credit and that it is wrong for them to receive both pay and credit for their work. What answers might be given to this objection? Is the objection valid?

3. It has been claimed that students on cooperative part-time programs mature in citizenship more rapidly than do other students. Is there any real basis for such a claim?

4. Why is it that some schools operate cooperative part-time programs without receiving state and federal financial aid?

5. Student learners in cooperative programs constantly are exposed to business practices at their training stations. Many of these practices do not conform to recommendations found in texts or trade periodicals. How should the teacher-coordinator handle resulting student inquires about "the correct practice"?

6. Learning activities used in cooperative education frequently involve interviews, observations, or collecting materials outside the school proper. What procedure should the teacher follow to assure that students carry out these learning activities in a tactful and business-like manner?

7. How important, relatively, are the consumer-citizenship learnings of the student trainee in a cooperative part-time program as compared to the learning that is of a vocational nature?

8. Proper selection of students for a vocational distributive or office program is essential. Prepare a list of things the teacher-coordinator might do to aid and facilitate the proper selection of students by the guidance staff.

Case Problems

General:

1. The student has been at the training station about four-and-a-half months and according to the employer he is doing a good job. The coordinator has felt for several weeks that the student was not being exposed to new learnings with his present tasks. (This was confirmed by the student in conference.) What steps should the coordinator take to get the trainee back to a learning situation?

2. A coordinator who regularly visits every training station (and feels that everything is going well) receives a phone call wherein an employer of a P-T coop student says "that trainee has been coming in late half the time for the last five weeks. Either get that trainee here on time or

keep her in school!" What information would you want and what steps should be taken to appease this situation?

3. On the six-week report a sponsor rates a trainee *very poor* on personal grooming. Upon discussing this deficiency the coordinator finds that the trainee has a severe case of body odor and bad breath. It is so bad that it has caused considerable comment by fellow workers. The sponsor has tried several times to get the trainee to do something about the problem but without success. He wants you, as coordinator, to do something about it. What action would you take?

Office:

1. A P-T coop trainee has completed the unit on mimeographing and seems to have done quite well. During a regular visit the coordinator finds that the employer is unhappy with the trainee's mimeograph work. A check reveals that the training station has the same type of machine used at school. What steps should be taken?

2. A trainee in carrying out her work must answer and use the telephone. The sponsor reports that although he has tried to teach her proper procedures she still is difficult to understand, because of her poor diction, but oftentimes she ignores set procedure for handling a telephone call. The result has been some confusion and misunderstanding both in this office and to those that have called. What can you as the coordinator do?

3. An employer states that unless the trainee "straightens out" he will have to let her go. The trainee is an "A" student in school and does an excellent job in the office-practices class. On the job, however, she is flighty, prone to giggle, and in general not very responsible. List the steps the coordinator should take to correct this.

Distributive:

1. The employer of a student learner tells you the student has made excellent progress in the men's clothing department. The student has worked in the stock room, sold men's accessories, and put in displays. The employer now would like to have the student move into selling men's slacks, sport coats, and possibly suits in about three weeks. What learning activities would you assign the student to prepare him for these new activities?

2. The employer of a trainee reports that many of the trainee's high-school friends stop at the store after school and talk with the trainee, sometimes as long as forty-five minutes. The employer doesn't want to kick these students out but is concerned over the trainee's not waiting on "paying" customers during this time. He has mentioned this to the

trainee but the condition still exists. What action can the coordinator take?

3. Millard Cooper is the coordinator of a distributive education program for the Kingston High School. He has conducted an excellent program there for five years and has received strong backing from all businessmen associated with the program. In the spring of 1964 Mr. Cooper was contacted by a representative from a new shopping center that is planning to open in September of 1964. The representative asked Mr. Cooper to provide twenty student learners for the various stores opening in the new center. Most of the stores were businesses new to the community. Mr. Cooper had tentatively placed all but eight of his twenty-four students for the 1964-1965 school year.

Mr. Cooper told his advisory committee of the request. Five of the eight advisory members were against placing any students in the new shopping center; the other three were noncommittal. Animosity of the established business community toward the new shopping center was quite evident. What action would you suggest Mr. Cooper take in this situation?

Suggested Readings

American Vocational Journal, American Vocational Association, Inc.

Business Education Forum, National Business Education Association.

Clark, Harold F. and Harold S. Sloan, *Classrooms in the Stores.* Sweet Springs, Missouri: Roxbury Press, Inc., 1962.

Haines, Peter G. and Herbert Tedder, *Distributive Education Training Guides.* Cincinnati: South-Western Publishing Company, 1963.

Mason, Ralph E., *Methods in Distributive Education.* Danville, Illinois: The Interstate Printers and Publishers, Inc., 1962.

Meyer, Warren G. and Wayne G. Little, "Distributive Education Facilities 1964," *American Vocational Journal* (January 1964), pp. 19-21.

National Study of Secondary School Evaluation, *Evaluative Criteria,* "Distributive Education," Section D-5. Washington, D.C.: National Study of Secondary School Evaluation, 1960, pp. 93-100.

Raines, Pearl L., "Standards for Selecting Work Stations for Cooperative Part-Time Students," *Business Education Forum,* May, 1964, pp. 34-36.

U.S. Office of Education, "Preparation of Teachers," *Office Education,* May, 1960, p. 24. A report of a national conference.

U.S. Office of Education, *A Study of Curriculum Development in the*

High School Cooperative Program, OE-82000, Vocational Bulletin No. 281. Washington, D.C.: Government Printing Office, 1960.

U.S. Office of Education, *Distributive Education Post-High School Cooperative Programs*, OE-82001, Vocational Bulletin No. 283. Washington, D.C.: Government Printing Office, 1960.

Venn, Grant, *Man, Education and Work*. Washington, D.C.: American Council on Education, 1964.

Willis, Benjamin C., "Recommendations for Improvements," *Education for a Changing World of Work*, Chap. 11. Washington, D.C.: U.S. Office of Education, 1963. Report of the panel of consultants on vocational education.

13

Adult Programs in Business Education

Adult education in its many forms continues to grow and to gain in relative importance in the United States. Owing to the rapidly increasing percentage of our population classified as adult, as well as other factors, this trend can be expected to continue and perhaps to accelerate. Business education will continue to be a major factor in adult educational programs.

When teaching adults the business teacher must fit his instructional materials and his teaching methods to the felt needs and desires of his students; must adjust his psychology to recognize and make use of the experience and mature judgment of his students; and must constantly recognize that these adults *are there for a purpose.*

Great numbers of business teachers conduct adult classes each year; many of them even do so during their first year of teaching. It is the purpose of this chapter to provide for the beginning business teacher an orientation toward adult education that should enable him to approach more intelligently the responsibility of preparing for and teaching adult classes when called upon to do so.

This is not a complete treatise on adult education; that is a broad field! Rather, this chapter serves to direct attention to those factors which are of major importance to the business teacher who hopes to *successfully* prepare for and teach adult classes in the field of business education.

Adult Education in General

What Is It? The term *adult education* is not an easy one to define in a meaningful manner; it is too broad. However, our question may well be answered by taking a look at some of the well-recognized characteristics of adult education. At the same time this listing of important characteristics can form the background on which one may base his preparation for teaching any adult class.

The Department of Public Instruction of one state has listed these characteristics for us as follows:

1. It is general and vocational education on the adult level.
2. It has to do with voluntary learning acquired outside the conventional school program.
3. It includes those activities with an educative purpose carried on voluntarily by adults usually on a part-time basis, such as adult evening classes, forums, discussions, round-tables, and institutes.
4. It is self-education starting with an adult student where he is and taking him in the direction he wishes to go.
5. It involves purposeful learning on the adult level which tends to give a new zest to life.
6. It usually results in action on the part of the group that participates.
7. Its students are students by volition who participate in its courses so long as these courses give them what they desire.
8. Its students come to select from its offerings and are not told which courses they are required to take.[1]

Obviously, then, adult education means much more than simply classes held for students who are adults! It involves, also, the use of an additional professional psychology distinct and different from that customarily used in the classroom education of adolescents.

What Are its Purposes? Obviously, if adult education is to be de-

---

[1] State of Iowa, *Adult Education Handbook for Iowa Schools,* published by the State of Iowa, 1947, p. 5.

signed to take the student "in the direction he wishes to go" the purposes of adult education are as broad and diversified as are the desires of the adults to be served. However, here are a few of the purposes more commonly served by adult education:

1. Occupational training or retraining—in one form or another this is applicable to any occupation or vocation one might mention.

2. Pure enjoyment through broadening one's viewpoint and interests—music, art, literature, psychology, and sports are illustrative media.

3. Personal enlightenment regarding world affairs and social and political trends

4. Increasing one's knowledge in specific fields, or fulfilling some specifically felt deficiency—this may range all the way from learning to read or write, through learning to typewrite, learning business law, or learning accounting, to learning a foreign language or learning how to repair electric appliances in the home.

The purposes of adult education also are well summarized by George C. Mann, Chief of the Bureau of Adult Education, California State Department of Education, in these two sentences:

> People generally are increasingly convinced that adult education must be designed to meet the interests of adults and the needs of society, which can be met by education and which are worthy of being met at public expense. There is firm agreement that adult education must offer a program which makes important contributions to those aspects of life which have long been held in high merit by the American people.[2]

Beginnings of Adult Education. The beginning business teacher, when first confronted with the problem of teaching an adult class, all too often looks upon it as something relatively new which is being added to his professional work and endeavors. This rather hazy concept should be corrected, for adult education has been recognized and practiced in the United States since early colonial days.

Originally these adult evening schools were private undertakings conducted for profit; thus the early history of adult education has

---

[2] *Public School Adult Education,* a publication of the National Association of Public School Adult Educators, 1956, p. 1.

much in common with the early history of business education. Such evening schools are known to have been in operation in New York State as early as 1661, and were in operation in Boston, Philadelphia, and Charleston, South Carolina before 1750. These evening schools, institutes, and lyceums continued to grow in number and expand in functions so rapidly that by the early 1880's demand was arising that adult education be conducted at public expense.

As early as 1857 there were twenty-five evening schools in New York City conducted at public expense and operating classes five evenings a week. Probably the first state to pass a general legislative enactment providing for evening schools at public expense was Ohio, which passed such legislation in 1839. However, as early as 1823 public funds were appropriated by the state of Massachusetts for use in evening schools, and by 1869 the major cities in Massachusetts all had opened evening schools. Similarly we find that publicly supported evening schools were established in Pittsburgh and San Francisco in 1856, St. Louis in 1859, Chicago in 1862, and shortly afterwards in larger cities throughout the nation. By 1900 at least 165 major cities of the United States had established evening schools whose primary function was to meet the educational needs of adults.[3]

Modern Scope and Trends. There is no universally accepted classification of areas in which adult education today is offered. Courses of various types and contents have been developed in the various states and communities to meet desires and needs. However, to the extent that states and the federal government have given financial aid there has tended to be some uniformity in the general curriculum form and practices.

Today many states prescribe courses that will meet with approval of the state department of public instruction. At least two states, New York and California, have classified the accepted fields of adult education in this manner:

Agriculture	Industrial and Trade
Americanization	Remedial
Arts and Crafts	Miscellaneous
Business and Distribution	Civic and Public Affairs
Safety and Driver Education	Engineering and Technology

[3] Further details relative to the development of this field of education may be found in *Public School Adult Education,* published by NASPSAE, a department of the NEA, 1955.

Elementary	Homemaking
Parent and Family Life	Health and Physical
General Academic	Music

Thus the business teacher must realize that any contribution he may be able to make to adult education is but a relatively small part of the entire field of adult education throughout the nation. A larger city school system may even include all of these diversified branches of adult education in its one program. Yet, on the other hand, it sometimes happens that in a smaller community the *only* adult education offered is the evening classwork taught by the business teacher!

A greater uniformity of course offerings and instructional practices tends to be found in the vocational areas of adult education. This has been influenced by the greater availability of state and federal funds for vocational education, as evidenced by educational developments fostered by legislation such as the Smith-Hughes Act of 1917, the George-Deen Act of 1936, the George-Barden Act of 1946, the National Defense Education Act of 1958, and the National Vocational Education Act of 1963. In fact, it may be pointed out that over half of the funds used in providing vocational education of all kinds comes from direct state and federal appropriations; and the general field of vocational education has always been one of the major areas of adult education.

National studies of adult education[4] indicate that between the years 1946-1947 and 1950-1951 the enrollment in adult education in small cities increased by 100 per cent while that in medium-sized cities increased by nearly 188 per cent. In the NEA study of 1952 it was found that the three most important aims of adult education then reported by the cities being studied were as follows:

> To train for vocational competence and economic efficiency; to provide for the enrichment of life, and to make adults aware of the civic responsibilities.

Today we are living in a rather complicated economic world. We are a part of a population that has a rapidly increasing percentage

[4] Edward B. Olds, *Financing Adult Education in America's Public Schools and Community Councils* (Washington, D.C.: National Commission on Adult Eduction, 1954).

National Education Association, Division of Adult Education Service, *A Study of Urban Public School Adult Education Programs of the United States* (Washington, D.C.: N.E.A., 1952).

of adults. We are a part of a society that maintains a high standard of living and that strongly favors excellent educational opportunities for all. Thus it seems relatively certain that adult education will continue to expand and probably in all of its areas. Certainly the fact that we live in and largely exist by means of a "business economy" can only mean that the business teacher should be prepared to witness an increasing demand for adult education in the field of business and distributive education in the future.

Applied Psychology for Adult Business Education

Younger business teachers frequently hesitate to accept evening classes or other classes intended for the education of adults. Undoubtedly this is partly because one just isn't accustomed to the idea of older people turning to younger people for instruction and leadership in the classroom. Certainly this situation doesn't exist during the twelve years of elementary and secondary education in the nation's schools with which everyone is quite familiar. Similarly, in our homes we grow up accustomed to the idea that leadership and instruction come from those who are older, and not from "young" people. Thus the hesitancy on the part of younger business teachers is a normal one.

To some degree this hesitancy also is a logical and rational one; after all, it is *true* that these older and more experienced adults will know many things pertinent to the subject being studied that the younger business teacher will not know!

In spite of these facts, the younger business teacher who is competent, well prepared, and fully qualified for his profession need have no fear of conducting adult classes. This is not to say that preference shouldn't be given to older and more experienced business teachers in taking responsibility for adult classes when they are available, for often they definitely are in position to conduct the classes more successfully. Yet even the younger teacher has in his favor the powerful factor of "know-how" in applying appropriate psychology to the learning situation!

Basic Adult Psychology. It seems almost trite to mention that adults belong to the same species in the animal kingdom as do adolescents; both are human beings and, as the saying goes, "like father, like son!" Both have the same types of sensory apparatus, the same types of nervous systems, the same types of musculature, the same internal glands, and the same native capacities at birth. Thus one should never forget that the various basic psychological factors affecting learning (such as those outlined in Chapter Three of this text) are just as much in evidence in an adult class as in any other class.

Thus, as in any other educational situation, learning is a matter of *individual* growth; it takes place best when *motivation* is best; it wanes when attention or interest is lost, or when fatigue or boredom is present; and it thrives under the influence of knowledge of results, of rivalry and competition, and of attainable goals. Also, among the members of any adult class is likely to be found the usual wide range of individual differences in ability.

Yet, by virtue of the very fact that the class members are adults, (*a*) they bring to class an important background of experience not possessed by younger students and (*b*) they attend class only because—and when!—they *want* to and not because they are required to attend. These two important factors must be given heavy weight in planning for a successful adult class. They materially influence the methods used in *applying* the basic psychology of learning.

Build Courses Around Adult Needs and Interests. In the final analysis, it is the individual adults to be served who determine the nature of an adult course that is to be successful. That is why communities with well-developed adult education programs make use of advisory councils or similar groups of adults; one of the duties of such a group is to help decide the nature of courses needed or desired by adults of the community. The advice, *know your students,* is especially applicable to adult classes, for only then can the teacher intelligently decide on the best content and procedures for any given adult class.

In determining the needs and interests of adults of the community, it is desirable to go somewhat into detail; otherwise there is risk that the *contents* of the course planned by the instructor will be far from that which the interested adults may expect it to be. For instance, a group of housewives might make it known to school authorities that they would like to study family bookkeeping. In due time word reaches the business teacher that an adult class in bookkeeping is requested. The teacher probably would make a serious error should he therefore conclude that the regular text he uses in his high-school double-entry bookkeeping could serve as his lesson plans for the course!

When adults voluntarily seek educational aid—and all adult education is entered into voluntarily—the motivation obviously already is present. Thus the teacher immediately is relieved of one of his most persistent and troublesome problems found in classes of young people. Although the motivation may be very strong in the case of these adults, it must also be recognized that it is *very specific*. The housewives, for example, strongly wished to learn better methods of helping to keep the family records. As a result, failure to offer a course that will satisfy the objective of that strong desire almost certainly will stifle and kill the enthusiasm and motivation that brings the housewives to class. The result: they simply quit coming to class!

Hence, perhaps the number one guide for the teacher of adults who desires to have a successful class is: Know your individual students, their needs and their desires, and then build your course around those needs and desires.

Maintain an Atmosphere of Informality. The formalized class with the instructor being the "center of attention" and perhaps the authoritarian has little place in adult education. Occasional exceptions do occur, mostly in the area of skill-development such as typewriting and shorthand classes. For the most part, though, the students should themselves be the center of attention. They should actively participate in discussion and in bringing new ideas to the class.

In developing this friendly, informal atmosphere most adult teachers prefer to be on hand before it is time for the class to start in order to greet and get acquainted with individual class members. The informal conversations that develop enable the class to begin with a far different feeling from that which customarily is present when, as the class is about to start, the teacher walks in to his "station" in front of a hushed and "cold" class! In planning to develop this informal atmosphere some adult teachers have been known to deliberately arrange to be putting the finishing touches to equipment and teaching aids just prior to class; this often permits getting one or more of the class members to assist, or getting them into conversation about the materials being prepared, thus starting active participation of the class in a normal and informal situation. Once the ice is broken, future class participation comes easily.

In keeping with this desire to encourage individual participation by class members, it frequently is desirable to have them grouped around a conference table where all are face to face. This encourages each to talk to the entire group and also to listen to what other members of the group may have to say. At the same time the resulting interchange of ideas among the class members relieves the instructor of the pressure of carrying the entire burden and permits him better to be the true *leader* that he should be; he can then devote thought to directing the discussions into most desirable channels, to seeing that each class member has appropriate opportunity to contribute, to raising pertinent questions, to offering needed periodic summaries, and to many other factors that can contribute heavily toward a successful class.

Make Use of the Knowledge of Adult Students. The combined knowledge of the adult enrollees on most subjects is almost certain to exceed the knowledge of the teacher. Each adult enrollee is likely to have had experience giving him knowledge that is relatively unique and distinct from that gained by the other enrollees. And at the same time the instructor is almost certain to possess knowledge that none of the enrollees possess. Thus in most adult classes maximum benefits will be derived from a pooling of the experiences, ideas, and knowledges of everyone there—with the instructor, of course, always playing the role of leader and skillfully directing the contributions and discussions toward the desired goal.

This again suggests the desirability of having most classes grouped around a conference table. This physical arrangement often materially aids the group in becoming acquainted and thus further encourages active individual participation, especially if a name card is prominently displayed in front of each enrollee so that all may see the name of each person at the table. The name should be in print sufficiently large to be easily read by all. If regular card holders are not available, the cardboard on which the name is printed can be bent to form its own support.

Make the Course Functional. Most adults have little desire to learn merely for the sake of learning; thus they are not inclined toward learning mere facts. Instead, they want information that they *feel* will *actually function* in their lives. Special attention is directed to the word *feel* in the preceding sentence. In the final analysis the actual content of a course that is "functional" may be essentially the same as that found in one that is nonfunctional; the difference lies largely in the way in which the material is presented and developed.

Thus if the housewives previously mentioned were informed at their first meeting that they would begin their study of bookkeeping by learning the names of typical assets and by learning what a balance sheet is and how it is constructed, they probably would fail to see any connection between the lesson and their own special needs— and might well tend to rebel at what to them seemed a waste of their time. On the other hand, the housewives might well feel that this same information was important and would immediately function in their lives if the first meeting of the class were to start off with a thorough discussion and identification of their record-keeping needs and problems; under the guidance of the instructor they might then well arrive at the conclusion that one of the first steps in deciding how to classify information and in learning how to properly differentiate between expenses and investments, or assets, would be to study assets and the balance sheet.

Actually there is nothing new in the idea of keeping the course functional; quite likely that is a good rule to follow in almost all classes, adult or otherwise. Yet failure to do so is not always as fatal to success in regular school work as it is in adult work, since younger people are less insistent that all of their learning seem meaningful to them in terms of their own less-well-defined objectives—at times, at least, they will proceed with their learning merely because the teacher tells them to! Even regular classroom work results in more efficient learning, though, if it is made functional.

Another way of expressing this same idea is to say that the adult class should be devoted essentially to "learning to do" rather than to "learning about" something.

Use Visual Aids Liberally. Success in teaching adults demands alert, efficient, and meaningful teaching. Most teachers already recognize the great value of visual aids in effective and efficient teaching. Often teachers simply do not have the time to prepare all of the special aids they would like to use in regular classroom situations; when each course meets daily and the teacher has four, five, six, or even more classes to teach daily there isn't adequate preparation time for developing the needed aids. But in many situations the adult class meets only once or twice each week, and this relative infrequency of meetings makes it all the more imperative that each one be the best possible. This also tends to give the teacher greater opportunity to fully prepare for the next class meeting.

Though certain types of visual aids are more useful with certain types of adult classes, on the whole adult programs may be said to make great use of just about every possible type of aid. In addition to the available commercially prepared films, filmstrips, exhibits, pictures, charts, maps, replicas, and other aids, adult group instructors typically make much use of their own specially prepared charts, diagrams, chalk-board illustrations, flannel-board aids, and mimeographed or duplicated materials.

Perhaps there is little justification for finding more evidence of better preparation and better teaching in adult classes than in other classes, yet that seems to be the situation and the business teacher who assumes adult education responsibilities should be aware of it. This probably is partially brought about by the motivation felt by the teacher in dealing with adult minds, and by his knowing that these students are there for a purpose and, moreover, knowing that they will not hesitate to drop out of class at any time when they fail to feel they are in some way profiting by attendance. Incidentally, they often do feel they are profiting when they find the class to be interesting—and they probably are right! And appropriate visual aids certainly do add considerably to gaining the participants' attention and interest.

Use a Variety of Teaching Techniques. Sameness in anything is likely to become monotonous and boring. This is especially true when your students are adults with ambition and a purpose. It is true that some one teaching method or technique may be especially well adapted to a given subject or adult group; if so, then that technique should be given a major role in the conduct of the class. Nevertheless, this does not preclude the introduction of variations or of completely different techniques at times in order that new interest and renewed attention may be achieved and the chance of monotony diminished.

Knowles lists and discusses nine possible methods of instruction that might be used in adult classes: lecture, question and answer, discussion, project, laboratory, apprenticeship, demonstration and visual aids, individual investigation, and drill.[5] It is quite conceivable that all nine might be used at various times in a single adult course.

Moreover, even though one method seems best and basically is used most of the time, various techniques may be introduced within that method. The discussion, for instance, is quite widely recognized as being most effective for the purposes of most adult classes. Yet there are many ways of inaugurating and conducting a discussion.

---

[5] Malcolm S. Knowles, *Informal Adult Education, A Guide for Administrators, Leaders, and Teachers* (New York: Association Press, 1951), pp. 38-47.

For example, the discussion may start with a symposium, or a presentation made by several class members who may hold different ideas or points of view. This may be followed by questions and comments from the rest of the class and, depending on the circumstances and size of the group, lead directly into an excellent discussion. A variation might be to start with a panel and an informal conversation before the group, or, if preferred, with a more formal debate type of presentation. At times the discussion might well follow a lecture presented either by the instructor or, preferably, by some authority —or it might follow the viewing of a relevant film or other visual aid.

Special Administrative Considerations

It is the responsibility and prerogative of the properly constituted educational authorities in any given community or school system to determine what adult courses, if any, shall be offered; also to determine the pertinent conditions under which the courses shall be offered and to select and employ the instructional staff. Such arrangements usually will be made by or through the local school board, or the superintendent of schools, or the director of adult education, or some teacher designated to assume this responsibility. Thus administrative considerations are not the immediate concern of the individual teacher.

Nevertheless, the individual teacher chosen to teach an adult class must complete his work within the governing administrative framework. Since the administration of adult education involves a number of rather special considerations, it is highly desirable that potential teachers of adult classes have some awareness of the more important ones; otherwise misunderstandings and irritations are likely to arise.

Meeting Financial Needs. Certainly the small fees usually paid by enrollees in adult classes do not cover the total costs involved. On an average, the fees paid account for less than 10 per cent of the total costs of adult education in the nation. The teacher should understand, then, that some administrators first take the necessary steps to assure availability of adequate funds to cover costs.

Over the nation as a whole between one-fourth and one-third of the cost is being met through local taxes. Thus it may be that the local school board allocates funds for adult education; however, this is not always true. In perhaps a dozen states direct aid is available from state funds for adult education. And in certain types of adult education additional funds are made available as a part of state and federal vocational aid and through Veterans Administration Educational Benefits. These last two, taken together, account for much more of the funds than do local taxes when the nation as a whole is considered.

The teacher interested in holding an adult class should consult with his principal or superintendent and should realize that the financing problem may be one that requires considerable thought and work on the part of some administrator.

Salary Paid to Instructor. The major financial cost of adult education is the salary paid the instructor; it accounts for approximately 70 per cent of the total cost. However, the rate of salary paid varies extremely among the various cities and communities. In larger cities the median salary in 1954 was about $3.50 per hour, but today it will vary from a low of around $1.50 per hour to a high of $25.00 or more per hour.

In the state of Iowa during the 1955-1956 school year a total of 168 public schools offered adult education programs, according to statistics issued by the Iowa Department of Public Instruction.[6] In twenty of these programs the instructor received no additional pay for teaching an adult class, this having been included in the teacher's regular salary. The pay of other instructors ranged from a low of 50 cents per hour to a high of $10 per hour, and, on a term basis, from a low of $5 per term to a high of $500 per term. The most typical rate of pay was from $2 to $3 per hour (this had increased to $5 per hour in 1964).

Fees Charged Students. There is no common pattern of fees for adult education courses; some courses are offered free of charge, others charge only a nominal fee, and still others depend on the fee for defraying the cost of the course. In the Iowa report just mentioned twenty schools reported no fee charged, twenty charged $3, twenty-seven charged $5, nine charged $10, and one charged $15. Still other schools charged from 10 cents up to $1 per class meeting.

Length of the Course. The length of any specific adult education course will vary with its purposes and contents, the season of the year in which it is offered, the availability of the potential students,

---

[6] *Iowa Public School Adult Education Programs.* (Des Moines, Iowa: Iowa Department of Public Instruction, 1955-1956.)

and any other related local factors. Occasionally an adult group may be brought together for a discussion or a special lecture or demonstration that may be completed in one evening. On the other hand, some courses run practically continuously, with students entering and leaving at various times. Thus one should have no preconceived idea that there are definite limits to the length of adult courses.

On the other hand, it frequently is true that the total time available for a course will be quite limited. Thus in some communities and in some states many adults find they have more time to devote to furthering their education during about three months of the winter season. In such cases a teacher might be asked to offer a beginning shorthand class, for instance, but will find that instead of having the usual nine months in which to teach it he will have only about twelve weeks. Moreover, these adults probably will be able to attend class only one or possibly two evenings each week! Obviously this teacher has a difficult problem on his hands.

However, this apparent limitation on time is somewhat offset by the fact that adult evening classes customarily meet for a longer period of time each time they meet. Thus, in the Iowa report previously mentioned, it appears that two hours is the customary length of class meeting; ninety-four schools reported class meetings of two hours in length, while thirty-four reported class meetings to be ninety minutes in length. Others varied considerably, but almost all reported meetings of from one hour up to three hours in length.

Records and Reports. Although the factors of grades and credit earned do not enter into most adult classes, the instructor nevertheless must give attention to certain records and reports. Usually attendance records are important. Often the financial aid to be received from sources other than enrollees will depend somewhat on the number of students in attendance at each meeting; this figure then becomes extremely important to the administrator charged with the responsibility of financing the course. And in many instances appropriate certificates are awarded to those enrollees who have maintained a designated attendance standard.

Even aside from these immediate practical reasons, rather complete records are needed to assist in numerous reports and studies that the administrator is likely to be called on to prepare in the future. In fact, such information is quite likely to become important in guiding the future plans for adult education in that community.

Public Relations. To a very great extent today the success of any undertaking is measured by and dependent upon the opinion of the general public. No matter how good a program or an undertaking may be in the opinions of those who may be in best position to evaluate it, if the public acquires and maintains the attitude or opinion that the program or undertaking is poor, or bad, or unworthy, or unsuccessful—then it is doomed to eventual failure! Since adult education directly serves a relatively unorganized and heterogeneous section of the public who participate entirely voluntarily, good public relations becomes especially important for its success.

In brief, public relations consists of keeping the public informed. This is a simple yet basic concept of public relations. However, getting the public to intelligently absorb or acquire information frequently is even more difficult than having a class do so! In both situations perhaps the key word to success is *interest*. If he will but take advantage of it, the teacher, with his professional knowledge of human psychology, is in an especially favorable position to assure good public relations for his adult education program. Interesting and appropriate news items, announcements, pictures, and "doings" of the class definitely need to be released to the general public from time to time if the continued interest, backing, and financial support of the general public is expected in the future.

Business Classes for Adults

One cannot generalize with any great degree of helpfulness about the specific business subjects that are offered or should be offered for adult classes. Rather, it must be recognized that (*a*) the demands of the local community should determine which subjects to offer and (*b*) the resulting course titles may well be very different from the ones customarily offered in high school. For instance, in writing about the adult offerings of the business education department of the Emily Griffith Opportunity School of Denver, Colorado, the coordinator of business education recently had this to say:

> The curriculum shifts constantly. As the needs of the people of Denver are learned, through the expression of individuals, of business, and of advisory committees, classes are opened and closed. Every class in school is represented by a lay advisory committee, actively at work, so that instruction in all areas, at all times, is guided by people in the city who are best equipped to know the

type of training that will meet the needs of the community in the home life, the economic life, and the sociocivic life of its citizens.[7]

The Emily Griffith Opportunity School is the adult and vocational division of the Denver Public Schools, and thus is tax-supported. When it was established in 1916 the course offerings were limited to typewriting, shorthand, bookkeeping, spelling, telegraphy, and subjects for foreigners. "Today the course offerings number more than 300 in fields of general self-improvement, business, distributive, homemaking, apprenticeship, and trade and industrial education, with students enrolled in about 700 classes." [8] The school annually enrolls more than 35,000 persons under a staff of more than 400 full- and part-time instructors.

In schools such as the Emily Griffith Opportunity School (of which equivalents are to be found in many large cities) various courses to meet *specific needs* in the areas of typewriting, bookkeeping, and secretarial work continue to be a major portion of the offerings in business education. But there are *many other* courses in business education, including courses in filing, clerical practice, comptometry, accounting machines, posting machines, key-punch operation, tabulating machines, transcription, voice-writing machines, duplicating machines, business writing, business speaking, selling, personnel, office supervision, business law, real estate, insurance, and others. In the area of distributive education alone, dozens of special adult classes are held annually; typical course titles often are such as these:

Advertising	Purchasing Policies
Window Display	Supervisory Training
Interior Display	Customer Service
Layout	Retail Salesmanship
Cashiering	Textile Fibers
Package Wrapping	Mark-up and Pricing
Inventory Control	Sales Psychology

Smaller Schools. In smaller school systems, where many business teachers start their professional careers and also teach their first adult classes, the community does not have sufficient demand to support

---

[7] Mrs. Carlene Samson, "Business Education Conducts Appropriate Adult Programs," *The Business Education Program in the Expanding Secondary School* (Washington, D.C.: UBEA, 1957), chap. 15.

[8] Samson, *ibid.*

highly specialized courses. In such situations the course titles are much more likely to be somewhat similar to titles of courses offered in the regular high-school classes. Even so, time limitations and the interests and needs of the enrollees usually result in a content and a procedure considerably different from that found in the high-school classes bearing similar titles.

Many Western, Midwestern, and Southern states have numerous small communities. (See Chapter Two, section on "The Small High School," pp. 34-37.) The state of Iowa may be used as an example. In Iowa in 1956 there were 788 separate high schools; the typical (median) high-school enrollment was approximately eighty students. Obviously, most of these small high schools are serving relatively small business communities. What adult education do they offer?

For the 1955-1956 school year, the report *Iowa Public School Adult Education Programs*[9] summarizes reports received from 168 Iowa public schools offering adult education programs and scheduling from 1 to 113 courses per school. These schools were asked to list the five popular courses determined on the basis of enrollment. Out of the 112 separate courses listed as being popular, typewriting headed the list; this subject was so reported by ninety-three of the reporting schools! The following list shows the number of schools reporting each of various "business" subjects as being popular:

Typewriting	93
Commercial Law, Business Law, Laymen's Law, Egg Law, Farm Law, Law, and Legal Problems	17
Bookkeeping and Accounting	10
Shorthand	8
"Commercial" and "Business"	4
Business Machines	2
Personnel Management	1
Investment Forum	1
Consumer Buying	1
Economic Development of the Community	1
Sales Clinic	1

---

[9] Wayne L. Pratt, *Iowa Public School Adult Education Programs, School Year 1955-56* (Des Moines: Department of Public Instruction, State of Iowa, 1956), 17 pp. Mimeographed. No comparable reports have been issued in Iowa during more recent years. However, consolidations had reduced the total number of public high schools in Iowa to less than 500 by 1964.

Thus in this state typewriting far exceeds all other business courses in popularity as measured by enrollment in the course. It should be noted that quite probably many other Iowa schools also offered typewriting to adults, but that for one reason or another it was not so popular in those schools. Various courses in law, bookkeeping, and shorthand also enjoyed considerable popularity, but certainly rated far below typewriting.

One of the difficulties encountered when offering an adult class in a smaller community is the natural tendency to accept into the course enrollees with widely differing objectives and backgrounds. This is done in order to assure a class enrollment of reasonable size. Yet each enrollee is likely to come with rather specific individual needs or desires in mind. The result is that instead of conducting one class the instructor finds himself almost conducting a separate class for each individual! In some types of learning this may be done quite satisfactorily, but in others it causes difficulties.

An adult class in Beginning Typewriting, for instance, likely would attract a different group of enrollees than would one in Advanced Typewriting, or in Typewriting Review. However, should it seem advisable to merely offer one course under the general title of Typewriting, the instructor in all probability would find it necessary to plan his teaching to include some enrollees who had no previous typewriting training along with others who may have already had a year or more of high-school typewriting! Yet this is exactly what some smaller communities find is a desirable type of adult class. When possible, more satisfactory learning certainly is likely when beginning and more advanced students can be scheduled in separate classes.

Course Content and Instructional Materials. Frequently the contents of the course for adults and the instructional materials used must be specifically tailored or composed to meet the needs of the particular group of students enrolled. As already pointed out, time limitations alone often demand this. In addition, the wishes of the enrollees must be considered. Yet at other times, as when the course is one in beginning typewriting, it is quite possible to make use of regular commercially available text material.

Yet even in a subject such as beginning typewriting the instructor has available a relatively large selection of instructional materials and should use judgment in making his choice. Thus it may well be that for a beginning typewriting course consisting of no more than ten weekly two-hour classes it would be better judgment to select one of the briefer texts (frequently referred to as Personal-Use Typewriting or by other names implying a shorter course) rather than to use a more complete text that proceeds at a slower and more thorough-going pace. Yet the experienced typewriting teacher can readily select from the longer regular texts those materials which will best serve the needs of the adult class; certainly, though, he would need to eliminate and reorganize much of the material in order that his adult group may feel that it has accomplished its purpose in the ten meetings scheduled.

In the attempt to teach beginning shorthand to adults in a limited number of class meetings, a serious mistake will have been made if the course ends with only a portion of the shorthand theory having been presented! This makes it an especially difficult task for the instructor to teach some types of symbol shorthand and frequently results in the use of some system in which the fundamentals may be mastered in a shorter length of time. It should be observed, however, that instructors can be found who claim real success with either type of shorthand; thus much still depends on the instructor and on his ability to properly organize and present his materials to the class.

Office Machines and Clerical Practice illustrate other business courses that are commonly taught in adult classes and that require time devoted to drill. In these courses, however, it frequently is possible to actually have each student working continuously on his own chosen machine or special project and thus to actually achieve rather substantially in his learning. This is greatly aided by the use of job sheets and special projects. Recommendations previously given relative to introducing variations in procedures into the class still apply even though the class work may be mostly drill.

In most nondrill business subjects taught in adult classes it usually is desirable to choose only specific units or applications or areas of the subject. This then permits greatly needed group discussions within the available class and course time limits. Frequently, too, it is necessary for the instructor to pull together pertinent materials from many sources, to make liberal use of reproduced materials, and to prepare special teaching aids in order to successfully teach such adult courses.

Checklist of Procedures. Good teaching in adult business education includes the same principles, procedures, and practices that good teaching requires in the ordinary classroom. Yet, owing to each enrollee's experience and his adult situation, many practices become *especially* important in conducting almost any adult class in business. Not all of the suggestions given in the following checklist are equally applicable to every adult course, but most of them are. Thus this list is presented to the business teacher as a guide and as a means of checking on the completeness and appropriateness of his preparation and procedures in teaching any adult class in business.

Advance Preparation

1. First determine whether there is a demand for the course proposed.
2. Identify the potential enrollees. Know their needs and desires.
3. See that necessary administrative questions are cleared with your administrator.
   a. How many weeks may be used for the course?
   b. Will a minimum enrollment be required?
   c. How many class meetings per week?
   d. How long should each class meeting last?
   e. What fee must enrollees pay?
   f. Must enrollees pay for supplies in addition to paying the fee?
   g. Will the cost be supplemented by local, state, or federal aid?
   h. How much will the instructor be paid?
   i. What records are required?
   j. Will regular school facilities be made available for use?
   k. Where, to whom, and when must enrollees pay their fees?
   l. Will certificates be awarded? If so, on what basis?
   m. Will special instructional materials be obtainable? How?
   n. Who will be responsible for proper publicity?
4. Confer with an appropriate advisory committee relative to the course.
5. Plan the course to meet exact needs of probable enrollees, but keep it flexible.
6. Aid in getting proper publicity released about the course.
7. As needed, see that sufficient texts and supplies are on hand or ordered sufficiently in advance of the first meeting.
8. Prepare needed charts, flannel boards, outlines, mimeographed materials, and other instructional aids.
9. Order needed films, filmstrips, records, free handouts, pictures, or other aids you will need but cannot make yourself.
10. See that needed equipment will be available and in good condition.
11. Arrange for any outside speakers or special discussion leaders you may need.

12. Secure additional special information you may need; much of this usually should come from your own community.
13. Plan in advance for the comfort of your enrollees in matters such as coffee breaks, smoking facilities, and having the room opened, heated, ventilated, and lighted.
14. Decide which major instructional techniques will best apply to the needs of your class most of the time; prepare to use them.
15. Provide yourself with suitable additional techniques for needed variety.

Classroom Procedures and Reminders

1. Start on time—always!
2. Stop on time—always!
3. Be there in advance of your students; put each at ease as he arrives.
4. Have all instructional materials and equipment ready and convenient.
5. Be prepared to care for needed registrations at the first meeting.
6. Look your best.
7. Be business-like.

Projects and Questions for Discussion

1. Collect printed folders, newspaper announcements, or other published statements about adult courses offered in selected communities in your state and prepare an appropriate bulletin-board display.

2. Inquire of the state supervisor or teacher-educator for distributive education and/or office education in your state about the adult courses offered throughout the state; report to your class.

3. Investigate and report on the types of adult education offered in your state through technical institutes, area vocational schools, junior colleges, and similar types of post-high-school education.

4. Check with the local chamber of commerce in your community or some other community and determine whether or not it has cooperated in promoting or organizing any adult classes during the past few years.

5. Interview one or more personnel managers in large businesses and determine what type of educational work they may have conducted during the past few years for employees of the business.

6. Would you say that the psychology the teacher of adults should use is predominantly a rather uniquely adult psychology or one that is essentially regular psychology of learning? Defend your choice.

7. Which would you say is more important to include in an adult

course—that which the class members need, or that which they desire? How would you justify your choice?

Case Problems

1. Velma Higgins is teaching her first year at Planora Consolidated School. She teaches all of the business education classes and has a relatively full schedule, including her fair share of extracurricular activities. When she accepted the position nothing was said about teaching adult classes. In November her principal, Mr. Stephens, reminds her that "as is customary in Planora" she will be expected to teach an adult class in beginning typewriting on Wednesday evenings for ten weeks beginning early in January. He says nothing about any additional pay. What should Velma do about it?

2. Jim Baughman is teaching an adult class in Small Business Records. Twenty students are enrolled, most of them being young owners or managers of small local businesses. One of them, Tom Thorpe, graduated from a university with a major in accounting and has now taken over his father's business, the Thorpe Dairy; it maintains its own herd of dairy cows, processes milk, and sells directly to local customers. Tom is a friendly, congenial student, but he falls into the habit of doing too much of the talking—since no other class members seem to have any formal knowledge of accounting. He does not realize it, but other members of the class are tending to resent his continual suggestions. How can Jim Baughman best handle this situation?

3. Edith Horton is an experienced secretarial teacher in a large high school in Minneapolis, Minnesota. She also has had considerable secretarial experience. One evening the office manager of a large Minneapolis concern asks her whether she could arrange to hold a special series of late-afternoon classes for about fifteen of his younger secretaries. He primarily is interested in getting them to improve their transcriptions. He offers to furnish meeting facilities in his office rooms and to pay Miss Horton a rather substantial fee. She is interested in his proposition. What advice would you offer Edith?

4. While chatting informally at the weekly luncheon of his Lions Club, Bruce Campbell, a high-school business teacher, is told by a fellow Lion that many young men of the town are entering local business careers but lack the "know-how" necessary for promotion and real success. Bruce feels that if this is true he might be able to help them some through special adult evening classes. Since the community is only of medium size, he believes it might be well to start with an evening course in

Business Management. Accordingly, he draws up a tentative general outline for such a course and then goes to his principal and superintendent to get permission to offer such a course. They, too, like the idea but tell Bruce there are no local funds available to help defray costs and they feel it would be unwise to assess the total costs against the enrollees. Bruce now is undecided as to whether to drop the idea until financial aid can be secured in the future or to go ahead and offer his services free or practically so. What would seem best?

Suggested Readings

Cook, Fred S., "Typewriting for Adults," *Journal of Business Education,* December, 1956.

Dorr, Eugene L. and Albert L. De Mond, "Adult Preparatory Education for Careers in Distribution," *Business Education Forum,* April, 1964, p. 16.

Lee, Dorothy E., "Teaching Shorthand in Adult Programs," *Journal of Business Education,* January, 1956.

"Problems of Teachers of Adult Business Education," *American Business Education,* January, 1961, pp. 155-56.

Public School Adult Education, A Guide for Administrators and Teachers. Washington, D.C.: National Association of Public School Adult Educators, 1956.

Samson, Carlene, "Business Education Conducts Appropriate Adult Programs," *The Business Education Program in the Expanding Secondary School,* pp. 86-89. Washington, D.C.: National Business Education Association, 1957.

Satlow, I. David, "Investment Clubs are Here to Stay," *Journal of Business Education,* February, 1964, pp. 201-203.

Sherrill, Hunting, "A Statewide Program of Adult Classes in Business Education," *Business Education Forum,* January, 1961, pp. 17-19.

Stadel, Emil J., "A Study of Materials and Methods in a Beginning Typewriting Course for Adults," *National Business Education Quarterly,* October, 1962, p. 64.

U.S. Office of Education, *Distributive Education for Adults; Guide for Part-Time Instructors.* Washington, D.C.: Government Printing Office, 1955.

Zancanella, James, "Adult Classes in Business Education," *Business Education Forum,* January, 1962, p. 2.

Pamphlets of the Adult Education Association of the United States of America:

"How to Lead Discussions," Leadership Pamphlet No. 1.
"How to Teach Adults," Leadership Pamphlet No. 5.
"How to Use Role Playing and Other Tools for Learning," Leadership Pamphlet No. 6.

14

Business
Student
Organizations

Although formal classroom learning still constitutes the backbone of education and still is considered of major importance in acquiring an education, today's educators realize full well that learning is taking place at all times. Many of us even are quite sure that more often than not things learned outside the classroom, and in no way directly a part of formal education, make a more lasting impression and influence one's habits, ways of thinking, attitudes, and future life to a greater extent than do the more formal classroom learnings.

Accordingly, the modern school makes appropriate plans to assist in channeling nonclass, or extracurricular, activities of students into various desirable group activities. Participation usually is completely on a voluntary basis and is entered into primarily because the student enjoys doing so. This enjoyment may be derived from doing something that itself is enjoyable to the young person. It also may be derived from a naturally gregarious nature and from being a part of a group. Associated with both may be the enjoyment derived from social approval, either as a part of a recognized group or as an individual performer of merit.

The important factor is not that the school assist the students in finding enjoyment, but that it assist them in finding enjoyment through an activity that in itself is helping to develop them into more desirable and useful and satisfactory individuals and future citizens.

Today nearly everyone is familiar with some types of organized group—or so-called extracurricular—activities sponsored by our public secondary schools for the benefit of students. It would be both useless and difficult to attempt listing all of them; the more common ones range from activities such as athletics to activities such as music, Future Farmers of America, camera clubs, dramatics, student councils, teen-age dances, debate, pep organizations, secretarial clubs, Latin clubs, Future Business Leaders of America, Future Homemakers of America, Distributive Education Clubs of America, junior chambers of commerce, class organization, bridge and purely social clubs, and hundreds of other activities organized to meet special needs and interests. Serving especially the young people interested in the field of business are groups such as commercial clubs, secretarial clubs, junior chambers of commerce, junior sales clubs, retailing clubs, and, on the national level, the Future Business Leaders of America (FBLA), Distributive Educational Clubs of America (DECA), and Junior Achievement, Incorporated. The latter organization usually is not directly affiliated with the secondary school, however.

The Psychology of Student Organizations

What urge is it that causes students by the thousands to voluntarily associate themselves with these various student groups—and often to spend many hours working for the good of the group with an energy and purpose which the classroom teacher all too often must sorrowfully admit is not apparent when it comes to studying for regular classroom assignments? The answer, of course, is a many-sided one. It will vary somewhat with individual students and among the various types of group activity. However, the teaching profession recognizes psychological drives that are at work. Many of these drives are quite familiar to the student of educational psychology;

others are more closely associated with social psychology and the psychology of personality development.

It is true that the *skillful* teacher makes use of these same psychological drives in connection with his regular classroom work. Yet no teacher can achieve perfection in his profession or even approach it at all times. These voluntary student organizations provide a sort of "self-feeding" process by which the individual student frequently and almost automatically satisfies some of these drives which otherwise are becoming relatively starved. And when his activities in the organization are well directed through competent leadership, much supplementary learning of direct value is taking place. In fact, owing to the presence of strong motivational drives the learning may be unusually efficient and effective!

Desire to Excel. The desire to be recognized for our excellency is so strong in all of us that failure to excel in *some* way is almost sure to result in a frustrated individual who is unhappy and dissatisfied with his place in life. Such individuals create serious problems for society, as well as for themselves and their immediate families. On the other hand, it matters little what medium affords an opportunity for the individual to excel so long as it is recognized and approved by others. If it can be approved by all of society, so much the better, but, failing in this, some individuals do not hesitate to attempt excelling even in unsavory activities so long as the approval of even a few can be obtained. Certainly this drive has much to do with recent juvenile gang activities.

When one considers the fact that our secondary schools typically require all students, regardless of abilities or interests, to spend half or more of their time and endeavors in the same common core of required subjects, it is not too difficult to understand that many students must almost necessarily find themselves unable to "excel" to an appreciable extent in the usual classroom activities. Of course, we must remember that this is not the *only* drive at work, and these same subjects may aid in satisfying other important drives for almost all students.

Extra voluntary activities, such as athletics in its various forms, frequently provide ideal opportunities for individual students to gain the feeling of importance and well-being that comes so largely from recognition of their excellence in some facet of life's activities. And this feeling of success, importance, and recognition is extremely vital to the development of a well-adjusted and desirable personality.

It is pertinent at this point to mention that psychologists quite generally agree that most lasting and most effective good results come from a recognition of excellence when that excellence can be associated with an area or activity that is to be one's life work; a secondary choice would be an area that may become a hobby or form of relaxation during one's lifetime. Since the world of business is going to provide the vocation or life work for a very sizable portion of today's secondary students it is a most serious mistake to deprive them of opportunity to voluntarily participate in extracurricular activities associated with this major interest in life.

Students interested in business most assuredly also should be encouraged to develop interests in other things, such as music, dramatics, and athletics. Yet it must be recognized that when they are *limited* to these other types of activities they also are being forced to *limit* their chances of special recognition to areas in which they actually are in competition with other students who have a major *interest* or ability in those areas! Thus failure to provide them *also* with suitable voluntary clubs or other organizations in their major field of interest or business, certainly is stacking the cards *against* the business students in any endeavor to develop excellency in an activity associated with their chosen life work.

Gregariousness and Belongingness. It is well-known that man is a gregarious creature; he enjoys being with others rather than by himself. Owing to this natural trait it is practically inevitable that young people are going to voluntarily associate themselves together in groups of one kind or another. That being the case, education much prefers that these voluntary groups be socially approved groups appropriately organized and directed for maximum natural benefits to the members.

Closely associated with this gregarious trait of mankind, and in fact growing directly out of it, is the negative feeling of uneasiness and discontent when one does not "belong" to a group—when one has *failed* to be accepted by his fellow students as a recognized equal. This often is described as a desire for the satisfaction of a feeling of "belongingness." Thus, again, we find all secondary students naturally feeling more comfortable and satisfied with their lot in life if they can "belong" to one or more groups.

Again it is pertinent to point out that this feeling of belongingness also has its most beneficial and long-lasting effects when it can be associated with something that is to be a part of one's life activities.

Thus again we find strong psychological reason for providing business students with opportunity to belong to and participate in some voluntary activity associated with their chosen major interest of business, such as a business club or a chapter of Future Business Leaders of America or some other appropriate organization.

Self-Assertion. Though not always fully agreeing as to whether to label it an instinct or not, psychologists for many years have considered self-assertiveness to be one of the common characteristics of all mankind. Certainly the desire to assert one's self is a universally recognizable trait, and opportunities constantly appear for observing it in action among young children! And the urge or drive is one which remains with us throughout life.

Undoubtedly one major reason for the success of democracy is the great opportunity it gives its participants for freely asserting themselves. Each knows that his vote is as important as the vote of anyone else; that he is free to speak his mind and assert his views; that he may choose his own religious activities and beliefs and his own economic activities and way of life. Democracy provides us with maximum opportunity for self-assertion.

All too frequently the student feels he must somewhat restrain himself from complete self-assertion in the regular classroom; in fact, the rules, regulations, semiregimentation, and supervision customarily and necessarily associated with today's mass education at the secondary level very largely are admittedly restraints on the self-assertiveness of youth! Nor is the situation too much different in the normal home, for there, again, youth feels it is being restrained by adult authority.

But what a difference exists when the adolescent (or young adult) finds he is largely "on his own" in his own student organization! Here he expresses his views and "asserts" himself quite freely. He then feels that, just as in any adult democratic society, his opinions are important and his vote counts. Moreover, he then feels more like giving expression to his thoughts and feelings—and usually does so. In fact he not only expresses them but not infrequently asserts them in words, gestures, and connotations so powerful that no doubt is left in the minds of his associates as to the point he is making!

Again it is appropriate to point out to the business teacher that the business students are at some disadvantage in selecting their extracurricular activities if they do not have available an appropriate student organization within their own sphere of special interest from which to choose; it is but natural that one feels less restrained in asserting his ideas—in asserting himself—when he is on the familiar ground of his own major area of interest and knowledge. And failure to find suitable opportunity for asserting himself in approved situations (such as approved student organizations) can readily lead to finding nondesirable media for an outlet for this self-assertion urge.

Other Psychological Factors. It is to be recognized that many other psychological factors do enter as a part of the basis on which student organizations are built. Thus some groups may provide media for pure enjoyment of the competitive urge, others may provide suitable settings for the urge to mingle with the opposite sex, still others may help satisfy the urge to gain special approval through excellence in vocational ability, and so on. It thus is quite appropriate to develop student voluntary groups that make use of and cater to various other additional psychological bases. As a whole, however, probably the most basic psychological reasons underlying successful student extracurricular or cocurricular organizations are the desire to excel, the tendency toward gregariousness, the desire for belongingness, and the urge toward self-assertion. It is important that the teacher who acts as sponsor for a student organization or activity be at least partially guided by these psychological factors at all times if he wishes to be successful in his job as sponsor.

Causes of Unsuccessful Activities. Not infrequently a given student activity, such as a chapter of the Future Business Leaders of America or a local business club, will be a comparative failure in one school while a similar organization in another and perhaps nearby school will have the reputation of being one of the most active and valuable organizations in its school. Why is this?

Frequently the cause is attributed to "lack of leadership." Probably that is right—in one sense or another. It might be more exact, however, to say it is due to misdirected or ill-advised or uninformed leadership, since in all probability the sponsor actually is trying. And usually careful analysis of the situation will indicate some situations or practices that directly thwart or are opposed to the free operation of basic psychological drives through participation as members of the organization.

The most frequent causes of lack of success in a student organization may be identified if the sponsor will but ask himself certain types of questions relative to the functioning of the organization. The following list may be used as a guide.

1. Who makes the decisions? Is it the sponsor or the members? Within a minimum framework of regulations the members should be free to make their own decisions in a democratic way. It is the sponsor's job to assist them in knowing *how* to do this successfully, but it should be the responsibility of the individual members to decide *what* is to be done. Authoritarianism on the part of the sponsor, although necessary in upholding school regulation, is fatal when applied to decisions that should be the prerogative and the responsibility of the student members.

2. Is every member given something to do? Students belong to an organization because they feel the urge to be *doing* things—to have opportunity to "work with" others in an adult fashion and to gain approval of others for what they do. This does not mean that the sponsor must dole out duties; under skillful suggestions of the sponsor the members will themselves see the desirability of having actively participating members and will develop their own methods of providing desired activities for all.

3. Is the sponsor contagiously enthusiastic about the organization? This situation may not always be possible, yet its absence does tend to unwittingly detract from the importance of the activity in the minds of the students. What student is likely to voluntarily enter enthusiastically into something that doesn't seem to be recognized as important even by those who sponsor it?

4. Is the opinion and judgment of every member sought *and respected?* Only in that way can the real feeling of "belongingness" be fostered. Moreover, the student enters the organization partly to satisfy his urge to be considered important; when he feels that he is a respected and important part of the organization he has fulfilled his need for "belongingness." He also is then further encouraged to assert himself and to attempt to excel.

5. Are students in other organizations gaining more credit, or public acclaim (publicity) than are members of your organization? If so, your organization by comparison is *felt* to be a failure, regardless of how well it may be functioning or how much good it may be doing.

6. Are business-like procedures used comparable to similar situations in adult life? When members recognize the presence of slipshod methods they unwittingly lose respect for this immature situation; instead, they seek activities where they can feel they are being adult. True, many members will go right along with unbusiness-like proce-

dures and actually give overt evidence of approval; subconsciously, though, they are likely to be building up a psychological distaste for the whole organization!

In addition, it is important that the organization and its activities have inherently worth-while values; such values may be assumed to exist in almost any organization that would meet with the approval of the sponsor and the public school. These values will be further identified in the following section.

Worth-While Concomitant Learnings

In the well-advised extracurricular student organization care is taken to see that members have every possible opportunity to develop desirable and improved habits, attitudes, skills, knowledges, and understandings. Failure to properly guard such aspects of their activities can easily result in actual damage to the personalities and futures of the individual student participants.

Opportunities for these important developmental learnings will vary with student organizations, but most such groups will find it worth-while to give due attention to nearly all of the following items:

Development of correct techniques, habits, skills, and attitudes—

1. In keeping financial records.
2. In recording minutes of meetings.
3. In participating in and conducting discussions, programs, and various types of group meetings.
4. In cooperating and working with others.
5. In orally presenting viewpoints and arguments.
6. In meeting and solving practical problems "on their own."
7. In assuming leadership responsibilities over others.
8. In preparing and giving special reports and recommendations.
9. In participating in social gatherings.
10. In working within the framework of specified regulations.
11. In arranging details of business transactions.
12. In arranging details connected with program responsibilities.
13. In carrying on membership or sales campaigns.
14. In paying attention to and respecting opinions of others.
15. In spending money.

16. In using various communication media, including telephone, mail, and telegraph.
17. In maintaining files.
18. In the use of various appropriate types of equipment.
19. In interpreting constitutions, by-laws, and other official documents and writings.
20. In connection with membership in a local or national organization.

Objections to Student Organizations

On the whole there are few serious objections to good voluntary student organizations that meet with approval of adults concerned. In fact certain types of student extracurricular activities, such as music, athletics, and dramatics, practically are demanded by entire communities today. Thus objections usually do not involve anything inherently objectionable about the organization as such.

However, it is true that most public schools of today already do have a relatively large number of well-established student organizations. Thus the objections one is likely to encounter are not so much objections to an organization as they are objections to *another* organization. The business teacher who wishes to start a chapter of FBLA, for instance, often is told by his principal that the students already have so many organizations they haven't any time left for study; that they already have more organizations than the school can justify; or that they have many organizations now doing an excellent job and that the school does not wish to decrease the effectiveness of present organizations by encouraging students to spread their endeavors over additional ones.

The viewpoint of the principal, as indicated above, is quite understandable and has much logic. Yet it is not necessarily the final and best answer to the problem. In fact, we know that one of the faults of education that must be guarded against is its definite tendency to protect the *status quo* and its vested interests. It is a well-known fact that in many, many instances educational practices lag far behind those of society in general.

Moreover, in these years of rapidly expanding enrollments in our schools it is more than likely that an actual need is developing for *more* student organizations in order to maintain the former standards of opportunities for each student to actively participate. And with a larger student body it also seems logical that a greater variety of personal interests will be found among those students—again pointing toward the desirability of *new types* of student organizations catering to interests not now represented among existing organizations.

Thus the business teacher desirous of forming a new student activity group in the area of business education should not hesitate to seek approval; he may very well be aiding in the filling of a most important need in our expanding schools of today. Perhaps of even greater importance than the increased enrollments are the psychological reasons already mentioned indicating the need for business students to have opportunity to channel their extracurricular activities into organizations related to their chosen life work.

One must recognize, though, that in the smaller schools it often is only too true that an additional student organization merely means one more organization for the *same* students to join; too few students and too many organizations can do real harm to the students! In such situations choices often must be made.

Occasionally objections are made to the costs involved in connection with student organizations. Certainly costs to the students—and thus to their parents—are important considerations. It is inadvisable to approve plans that are excessively costly. All too frequently the financial situations of some students dictate that they refrain from participating in activities that involve additional unnecessary expense. Perhaps it would be better if the costs of all approved activities could be paid by the general public rather than by the individual participants, so that none would be deprived of opportunities to participate. Since this usually is impracticable, we must realize that it is equally unjust to deprive other students of opportunities at reasonable cost simply because a few cannot afford even the reasonable cost.

We should also recognize that business teachers themselves quite often raise an objection of a different type; sometimes they object to an organization on the grounds that it will require considerable extra time and effort on their part and they feel that they already are doing a full day's work or more and should not burden themselves further with the task of organizing and sponsoring an additional organization. Sometimes such objections are well founded.

If the teaching profession is going to approve and advocate the development of student organizations—as it does—then it follows that the development and sponsoring of such organizations is one part of the professional work of the teacher. This work then deserves equal consideration along with classroom and other work in determining the total work load of the teacher. This customarily is the practice in well-administered schools of today.

It might be mentioned in connection with this objection, though, that business teachers who do organize and sponsor successful student organizations (such as FBLA or DECA) everywhere are most enthusiastic about that part of their work. Many of them actually feel that they are doing more for their students through such activities than they are able to achieve for them in the formal classroom.

National Organizations for Business Students

There are three national organizations for students and young people interested in business that deserve special mention; they are the Future Business Leaders of America, the Distributive Education Clubs of America, and Junior Achievement, Incorporated. Business teachers should be familiar with all three of them.

In adult life we have no doubt about the merits of voluntarily associating together into a national organization those groups of people throughout the nation who have comparable interests and purposes. America seems to thrive on voluntary national organizations and we deal with them in our daily lives. They include all types of human interests such as mutual insurance associations, religious and charitable associations, chambers of commerce, hundreds of national trade associations, and innumerable national professional associations. In the business world of today we are accustomed to national chains of stores, national advertising, and big-scale factory production for national distribution. National political parties and national TV programs and national labor unions and various other activities that are national in scope provide a daily diet of news for the American public. Thus we are being very unrealistic when we occasionally question the advisability of permitting American students to associate themselves together in national organizations.

No attempt will be made to enumerate all the potential advantages to be derived from being a part of a national organization. Obviously, the major advantages accrue from strength resulting from united numbers. It is only sufficiently large and "strong" organizations that can afford the efficiency and effectiveness of a full-time executive director and his staff, of a paid editorial staff and an acceptable and recognized printed publication issued regularly, and of dozens of other highly desirable and effective aids and activities that only such a national headquarters is capable of furnishing consistently.

Objections often are raised on two major points—both of which also exist in connection with our adult American national organizations: one is the objection that it raises costs, and the other is the objection that "outside" control or influence will be brought to bear. Perhaps both are more in the nature of "excuses" than of "objections." In terms of achievements and of learnings derived from a student organization per dollar spent, it may easily be much more expensive *not* to belong to a national group. Just as the more successful and professionally minded business teachers feel they *cannot afford not to belong* to their voluntary national professional associations, so also do many local student organizations feel that they cannot afford not to be a part of an available national association. At the same time it must be admitted that we cannot expect to receive values without paying for them.

As to "outside" controls and influences, in the final analysis the shoe is on the other foot; these American voluntary associations typically are democratic forms of organization and the basic power lies in the individual votes of the members throughout the nation! And experience in exercising this power as students in a national student organization can go far toward preparing them to do a much better job of exercising the same type of power later as adults.

Future Business Leaders of America. It may properly be said that FBLA is sponsored by the business teachers of the nation. This is done through their professional association, the National Business Education Association, which is one of the departments of the NEA. Besides the several thousand individual teachers holding NBEA membership, over 200 colleges and universities engaged in the preparation of business teachers form one division of NBEA through institutional memberships; thus they, too, aid in sponsoring FBLA.

The first high-school chapter of FBLA was chartered in 1942 at Johnson City, Tennessee, and the first college chapter was chartered that same year at the Iowa State Teachers College, Cedar Falls, Iowa (now the State College of Iowa). Although a purely voluntary organization, by June, 1964, over 3,000 local chapters had been organized throughout the entire United States (including Hawaii) and in Puerto Rico, and the official publication *FBLA Forum* was being sent to over 70,000 individual members. Over thirty states have state chapters organized and usually hold annual state conventions. The first national FBLA convention was held in Chicago in 1952, and national conventions have been held annually since then. Over 1,200 representatives and sponsors registered for the thirteenth national FBLA-PBL convention held in Washington, D.C. in June 1964.

The approximately 300 college chapters chartered by 1964 have their own College Division of the Future Business Leaders of America, known by the Greek letters Phi Beta Lambda. Although PBL has its own separate national officers, its national convention customarily is held at the same time and place as that of FBLA.

The purposes of the Future Business Leaders of America are admirably stated in the National FBLA *Handbook* as follows:[1]

1. Develop competent, aggressive business leadership.
2. Strengthen the confidence of young men and women in themselves and their work.
3. Create more interest and understanding in the intelligent choice of business occupations.
4. Encourage members in the development of individual projects and in establishing themselves in business.
5. Encourage members to improve the home and community.
6. Participate in worthy undertakings for the improvement of business and the community.
7. Develop character, train for useful citizenship, and foster patriotism.
8. Participate in cooperative effort.
9. Encourage and practice thrift.
10. Encourage improvement in scholarship and promote school loyalty.
11. Provide and encourage the development of organized recreational activities.
12. Improve and establish standards for entrance upon store and office occupations.

The FBLA pledge taken by each member consists of the following simple statement: "I do solemnly promise to uphold the aims and

---

[1] *Future Business Leaders of America Handbook,* Third Edition, National Business Education Association, N.E.A., Washington, D.C., 1963, p. 3.

responsibilities of Future Business Leaders of America, and as an active member I shall strive to develop the qualities necessary in becoming a Future Business Leader."

The Creed that has been adopted as a guiding philosophy for business students belonging to FBLA is indeed an excellent one; in fact it might also well be adopted as a guiding philosophy by every business teacher. It is reproduced in full below.

The organization is served by a full-time paid executive secretary and his associated staff with well-equipped permanent headquarters provided in the NBEA national headquarters at the fine new NEA Building in Washington, D.C. It is here that the *FBLA Forum* is published and various services to local chapters and members originate, such as membership cards, official seals and plaques, official pins and emblems, official handbooks, and numerous suggestions and aids for organizing and successfully conducting a local chapter. Business teachers who are not already familiar with this organization through information received from their own professional association, NBEA, should request FBLA information from the headquarters office at Washington, D.C.[2] The current cost of a local charter is $1 and the annual national fee (dues) for each student member is 50 cents; annual national dues for members of Phi Beta Lambda, the college division, are set at $1.00.

CREED

FUTURE BUSINESS LEADERS OF AMERICA

I believe that free education is the right of every young person in America.

I believe that the future of America depends upon mutual understanding and cooperation of business, industry, labor, the home, the church, the school, and by the peoples of our own and other lands. I agree to do my utmost to bring about better understanding and cooperation on the part of all of these groups.

I believe every young person should prepare himself for a useful occupation, and that he should carry on that occupation in a manner that will bring the greatest good to the greatest number.

I believe every young person should be actively interested in better social, political, community, and family life.

I believe every young person has a right to earn his living at a

---

[2] The address of the national executive secretary of FBLA or the national executive director of NBEA is 1201 Sixteenth Street, N.W., Washington 6, D.C.

useful occupation and that this right should not be denied him because of race, color, or creed.

I believe every young person should take responsibility for carrying out assigned tasks in a manner that will reflect credit to himself, his associates, his school, and his community.

I believe in my own ability to work efficiently and to think clearly, and I pledge myself to use these abilities to make America a better place for everyone.

Among the competitive events encouraged by FBLA and customarily used on local, state, and national levels are the following:

1. Best chapter project
2. Most unique chapter project
3. Best chapter exhibit
4. Extemporaneous speaking contest
5. Public speaking contest
6. Selection of Miss FBLA and Mr. FBLA (high schools) and of Miss Future Business Executive and Mr. Future Business Executive (colleges)
7. Spelling team contest (high schools) and vocabulary team contest (colleges)
8. Outstanding chapter award (state and national levels)
9. Parliamentary law team contest
10. Selection of Miss Future Business Teacher and Mr. Future Business Teacher (colleges)

Various other events are sponsored from time to time by local and state chapters. One of the very interesting and valuable features of the national convention is the National Delegate Assembly at which currently the delegates cast their ballots for national officers according to a roll-call of states very much in the same fashion that our great American political parties select their candidates for national offices.

Distributive Education Clubs of America. The recognized meaning of the term *distributive education* already has been presented (see Chapters Ten and Twelve). Distributive Education Clubs of America is a national organization open to all students enrolled in officially recognized distributive education programs. However, membership of the individual student in DECA must be achieved through his membership in his local DE Club.

High-school distributive education programs were started in various parts of the nation in 1937 following the passage of the George-Deen Act. From the very first, local clubs were being formed for students enrolled in these programs. As early as 1940 these clubs had formed state associations in some states and were operating as local clubs in a state organization. The movement has been distinctly successful and has expanded rapidly. The seventeenth annual national convention of state distributive education clubs was held at Chicago in the spring of 1964, the national organization having been initiated at Memphis, Tennessee in 1947.

The national constitution of the Distributive Education Clubs of America states (Article III, Section 1) "The Distributive Education Clubs of America is an association of state distributive education clubs each operating in accordance with and by the legal authority derived from a charter granted by The D.E.C.A., INC." The administration is vested in a Board of Governors elected by the chartered state clubs. There is a national Representative Advisory Committee consisting of the state supervisors of distributive education from states having state clubs, professional personnel from the U.S. Office of Education who are working directly with distributive education, six leaders from the field of distributive education, and the Executive Committee of the National Association of State Directors of Vocational Education. In 1950 the American Vocational Association became official sponsor of the Distributive Education Clubs of America.

Thus DECA differs from FBLA in a number of ways. In the first place it is intended to serve only those business students enrolled in the vocational DE programs whereas FBLA is intended to serve all business students, both vocational and nonvocational, and in the areas of both office and distributive occupations. A second major point of difference is the fact that DECA, quite properly, leans heavily upon the guidance and advice of professional vocational personnel located in various state departments of public instruction and in the U.S. Office of Education, whereas FBLA similarly turns to the advice and guidance of professional personnel associated with the NEA and its business education department, the NBEA.

The purposes of DECA are set forth in its national constitution (Article II) as follows:

a. To develop progressive leadership in the field of distribution that is competent, aggressive, self-reliant and cooperative.

b. To provide for an intelligent choice of occupations in distribution through exploration of opportunities in the field.

c. To create in each member an abiding interest in his chosen occupation through an appreciation of the opportunity it offers him to contribute his share in worthy home and community membership.

d. To encourage the use of high ethical standards in business.

e. To provide for mental and physical health through satisfactory social and recreational activities.

f. To foster a deep feeling of responsibility for contributing through business activities to the civic, social, and moral welfare of society.

g. To develop an appreciation of the influence of the fine arts in business.

h. To engender a healthy respect for vocational education, and a desire to keep abreast of current developments in business through the use of the training facilities it offers, both in school and adult life.

The Creed of the Distributive Education Clubs of America, "The Distributor's Creed," is reproduced below. It certainly sets forth an excellent philosophy for young people about to engage in careers in distribution.

THE DISTRIBUTOR'S CREED

I BELIEVE in the future which I am planning for myself in the field of distribution, and in the opportunities which my chosen vocation affords.

I BELIEVE that by rendering the highest measure of service to my customers, and by cooperating to the fullest extent with my fellow workers, I will be rewarded with a feeling of inward satisfaction as well as with material wealth.

I BELIEVE in the democratic philosophies of private enterprise and competition—that these philosophies allow for the fullest development of my abilities and the fullest use of individual initiative.

I BELIEVE that the ethics of conduct laid down by The Great Distributor of all good gifts should apply to my personal relationships in the field of business.

I BELIEVE that by doing my best in every way to live according to these high principles, I will be of most service both to myself and mankind.

Currently the annual membership fee for each student is $1.00. The cost of the official magazine *The Distributor* is $1.00 to DECA members and is included in their national dues; it is issued eight times during the school year. In 1964 DECA clubs were serving approximately 50,000 students through local and state clubs in forty-eight states and in Puerto Rico. Coordinators of distributive education programs usually are kept informed of the availability and activities of DECA through their state supervisors and teacher-educators of distributive education, but they also can obtain complete information by writing to Distributive Education Clubs of America, 1510 H Street, N.W., Washington, D.C.

Among the activities commonly sponsored by DECA and in which competitive events are held at state and national conventions are these:

1. Best chapter display
2. Best sales talk
3. Best sales demonstration
4. Best advertising layout
5. Best merchandise manual
6. Best job application and interview
7. Public speaking contest
8. Essay contest
9. Best club activities manual
10. Best window display
11. Best state newspaper and newsletter

Since DECA members are students participating in distributive education programs they all hold part-time positions in the business world. One of the very important and significant activities of each chapter customarily is an Employer Appreciation event, frequently a dinner, to which the students invite their employers as their guests.

Junior Achievement, Inc. Next fall probably more than 5,000 new corporations will start business—and all will be completely staffed, from workers up through management and including the president of the corporation, by American boys and girls between the ages of fifteen and twenty-one. All of these young people also will be stockholders in these corporations. By the end of the school year all of the corporations will have completed their business, balanced their books, settled their accounts, and closed their doors forever. And many thousands of American young people will have gained for the first time a clear understanding of and insight into our American economic system of free private enterprise and its interrelated problems of labor, management, and capital.

Occasionally a business teacher is heard to say that business will not cooperate and back good business education; certainly Junior Achievement, Inc. disproves such statements completely. Here is one of the nation's outstanding educational organizations for young business people and, instead of being sponsored by professional educators, it is completely promoted, sponsored, and backed financially through time, effort, and money contributed voluntarily by business and business people.

The movement was started in 1919 in Springfield, Massachusetts, by Horace A. Moses, then chairman of the Strathmore Paper Company. Cooperating closely with him during these early years was the president of the American Telephone and Telegraph Company, Theodore N. Vail, and Senator Murray A. Crane, of Massachusetts. The movement was incorporated in 1926 and later, in 1942, organized on a national basis with headquarters in New York. During the 1964-1965 school year JA will be serving some 110,000 young people through approximately 17,500 JA companies located in some 400 communities throughout the United States, Canada, and some foreign countries. They will be served by 17,500 adult business advisers, and will have available sixty-four national and hundreds of local scholarships. Today information about JA and assistance in getting new groups organized and conducted may be obtained by writing to Expansion Department, Junior Achievement, Inc., 51 W. 51st Street, New York, N.Y., 10019. It is a movement with which every business teacher should be acquainted.

The company is organized through the assistance of local branches of Junior Achievement, Inc. It may be started when ten to fifteen boys and girls (usually juniors and seniors in high school) decide to manufacture and sell some product or business service and have the proper sponsors as arranged through Junior Achievement, Inc.

Each Junior Achiever must own one share of stock in the miniature company and may not own more than five, at 50 cents a share. These student owners must decide upon the exact product or service to be marketed, select a name for their company, decide upon the capital to be needed, and take all the necessary steps to incorporate, including the sale and issuance of real certificates of stock. Junior Achievers become the board of directors, decide all general policies, elect officers from among themselves, and delegate powers as they believe best. They also become the labor force in producing and selling their product or service. They usually work two hours during one evening at the Business Center which cooperating businesses provide for them at a nominal rental of $2 per month.

Complete double-entry books are kept, wage and labor disputes are settled, additional stock is sold when needed, dividends are declared (if earned), equipment is purchased, raw materials and supplies are purchased and used, customers are found, sales programs are mapped out, bottlenecks and breakdowns are encountered and solved, competition is met, stockholders' reports are issued—in fact, everything that must be done by any comparable regular-sized corporation is done by this miniature corporation, and it all is done by these Junior Achievers themselves. The final act is the issuance of the liquidating dividend to cancel the outstanding stock.

The real purpose of Junior Achievement is to give youth a realistic but clear understanding of how American free enterprise works. In the process it is true that they become sold on our American economic system; this is in spite of the fact that, realistically, many of these miniature corporations fail to make a profit and around 10 per cent of them actually fail before the year is ended. Evidence that the organization is accomplishing its purpose well is overwhelming. Illustrative of this is the fact that 1,500 Junior Achievers registered for the National Junior Achievers Conference at Indiana University, Bloomington, Indiana, August 18-23, 1964.

Evidence of the widespread interest that has been shown in Junior Achievement throughout the nation is to be found in the following *partial* list of publications in which descriptions of Junior Achievement activities have appeared from time to time. In addition, metropolitan and local newspapers constantly carry items and pictures dealing with local, state, and national awards won by Junior Achievers.

The Business Education World	*Open Road*
Dun's Review	*American Paint Journal*
Coronet	*Pageant*
People Today	*Investment Dealer's Digest*

Catholic Digest	*Bankers Monthly*
Better Homes and Gardens	*Railway Age*

Over the years the types of different products that have been manufactured and sold by these miniature student-operated companies have been legion, of course. Some idea of the variety of products may be gained from this illustrative listing.

Toys	Stain removers
Aluminum products	Hand-decorated items
Water softeners	Charcoal grills
Candy	Insulated glasses and coasters
Leather goods	Personalized matches
Wooden products	Memo pads
Lamps	House signs
Plastic products	Various chemical products
Jewelry	Newspaper and cookbook holders
Cookies	
Neckties	

Among the service fields in which Junior Achievement companies have operated are the following:

Advertising	Photography
Art and decoration	Printing
Banking	Publishing
Broadcasting	Sales
Business services	Silk screening
Entertainment	Stenography

Definite effort is made to have most of the products handmade so far as possible. Nearly as many girls as boys are Junior Achievers.

As an incentive to outstanding high-school Junior Achievers who have above-average scholastic ability, Junior Achievement provides a broad college scholarship program. More than 100 scholarships are available each year; most of them provide free tuition to specific colleges, although others are cash awards supplied by business in lieu of tuition and other expenses. The New York Stock Exchange, for instance, provides a trip to New York each year for the president and treasurer of the Junior Achievement company that prepares the best stockholder report.

Since Junior Achievement is business-sponsored, the first important requisite for starting a JA company is a community sufficiently strong in business developments and business personnel to assure (1) adequate interest and financial backing by business, and (2) the necessary business personnel with "know-how," ability, willingness, and time to provide approved sponsorship. Each Junior Achievement company must have three advisors: a business advisor to advise on financial matters, accounting, and business practice; a production advisor to give counsel relative to efficient production techniques; and a sales advisor to give guidance in selling, promotion, advertising, public relations, and other marketing factors.

Projects and Questions for Discussion

1. Obtain a list of all FBLA chapters in your state, together with the names of all current state FBLA officers. Prepare a map bulletin board showing the locations of these chapters. Also indicate any college chapters of Phi Beta Lambda.

2. Similarly investigate and prepare a bulletin board showing the DECA chapters in your state.

3. Arrange for a committee to visit some FBLA, DECA, or JA chapter, or several of them, and to report to class on the chapter activities.

4. Invite several sponsors and/or representatives of FBLA or DECA chapters to visit your campus for a special meeting to discuss their activities with your class and other business education students.

5. Set up a display of FBLA (or DECA or JA) publications and other materials. (*Note:* Write to headquarters addresses given in this chapter and request appropriate free materials and a price list of other materials. Many excellent "career" folders are issued by FBLA at 10 cents each.)

6. How does the learning that takes place through extracurricular activities compare with classroom learning as to quality and future value to the learner?

7. Should a business teacher be willing to sponsor an extracurricular activity in his own major area in addition to a full load of regular class work?

8. Do most of today's college graduates who are prepared for careers as business teachers have appropriate preparation and "know-how" to act as sponsors and advisors for business student organizations? In what ways may they be weak in such preparation?

9. Discuss the values of each of these learnings which are presumed to be a part of the student's experience in most extracurricular activities. Are these learnings being properly achieved in most such organizations?

How to keep financial records
How to properly conduct a business meeting
How to work cooperatively with others
Effective presentation of oral arguments before others
How to effectively direct the work of others
How to plan and conduct membership or sales campaigns
How to properly conduct various business transactions

10. If a business teacher is convinced his school and students should have a chapter of FBLA but his principal is opposed on the grounds that the school already has enough student activities, what should be done about it?

11. Show how the Distributor's Creed or the FBLA Creed might provide a valuable basic philosophy by which a business teacher might well be guided in his professional career.

12. Which do you feel are in better position to provide the most effective guidance and advice for a student organization—business teachers who are members of UBEA and NEA, educators within AVA, or business people?

Case Problems

1. For a number of years the Blue Mound High School has had a local student organization known as the Commercial Club. Its membership has been restricted to students who have earned a grade of "B" or higher in shorthand. All members are girls. With expanding high-school enrollments it has now seemed advisable to add other business subjects to the typewriting, bookkeeping, and shorthand already offered, and a second business teacher has been secured for that purpose. New courses now include general business, salesmanship, retailing, and clerical practice. In the near future the school plans to add a third business teacher and to start an approved cooperative program for both office and store occupations.

The second business teacher now feels that a chapter of FBLA is needed which will serve all business students, but of course the other business teacher objects strenuously to discontinuing her Commercial Club, which she says has been extremely successful. She especially feels that "standards" are important, and objects to the fact that FBLA admits all business students regardless of academic achievement. The principal points out that very soon a DECA club might be appropriate. What would seem to be the best solution to the problem?

2. Esther Jones is having difficulties as sponsor of the Springer High School chapter of FBLA. The chapter president, Ed Powers, quite

properly believes in assuring democratic decisions made by the membership of the chapter and feels that the organization belongs to the student members and that they should be protected from having "pressures," as he calls it, brought on them to do things in ways that the sponsor feels would be better. Miss Jones has been trying to encourage her president to suggest that the various committees get their plans completed early and do their work in a more business-like manner prior to the last available minute. Ed feels that this is the sponsor's idea and not the idea of the students, and hence refuses to do anything about it. Who is correct? What should be done about it?

3. At a state convention of one of the national business student organizations recently a certain high-school girl won a state competitive honor which entitled her to represent her state at the national convention. She very much wanted to enter the national competition and was encouraged by others to do so. However, the national convention met at a city some distance away and, in spite of rather nominal financial assistance toward her expenses provided by the state and national organization, she simply was financially unable to make the trip. Sensing the girl's embarrassment, her teacher, who was sponsor for the local organization, arranged to drive her own car to the national convention and take the girl along without personal cost to the girl. Actually, though, this did result in an expenditure of around $100 by the teacher which she had not intended and which she could ill afford. Could the development of this situation reasonably have been avoided in advance? If so, how?

Suggested Readings

"Administrative Organization at the State Level," *Business Education Forum*, March, 1954, p. 49.

Applegate, Harry A., "DECA—Prepared for New Challenges," *American Vocational Journal*, March, 1964, pp. 22-24. *Note:* see other youth-organization articles in this issue also.

Arnold, Cecil B., "How D.E. Contests Benefit Businessmen," *Business Education World*, April, 1964, pp. 20-21.

Atkinson, Virginia S., "FBLA's Contributions to the Department of Business Education," *Business Education Forum*, January, 1962, p. 23.

Bender, Ralph E., "YOUTH ORGANIZATIONS—A Significant Part of Vocational Education," *American Vocational Journal*, March, 1964, p. 6.

Clanton, Richard D., "The Future Business Leaders of America," *National Business Education Quarterly*, May, 1962, pp. 77-81.

Forkner, Hamden L., "A Call to Service—Proposed Plan for a National Organization of Youth," *Journal of Business Education*, November, 1940, p. 30.

――――, "How FBLA Got Its Start," *Business Education Forum*, May, 1957, pp. 30-32.

――――, "Why Your Students Should Belong to FBLA," *Business Education Forum*, November, 1955, pp. 41-42.

Future Business Leaders of America: see *Business Education Forum*, October, 1963, p. 39; November, 1963, p. 31; December, 1963, p. 31; January, 1964, p. 22; February, 1964, p. 31; April, 1964, p. 33; and May, 1964, p. 1.

Future Business Leaders of America *Handbook* (3rd ed.). Washington, D.C.: National Business Education Association, 1963.

Phi Beta Lambda *Handbook* (1st ed.). Washington, D.C.: National Business Education Association, 1964.

Rupple, Ray, "How Clubs Provide for Individual Differences," *American Business Education*, December, 1956, pp. 96-98.

Sheridan, Ardis F., "Preview the Need for an FBLA Chapter," *Balance Sheet* December, 1961, pp. 154-55.

"Wanted: Teachers of Free Enterprise," *Forbes Business and Finance*, July 1, 1963, p. 1. *Note:* description of Junior Achievement work.

Webb, Mary D., "The Preparation of Sponsors for FBLA Chapters and Other Activities in Business Education," *Business Education Forum*, February, 1954, pp. 37-38.

Yerian, Theodore, "OPERATION ECON—Career Competency," *Business Education Forum*, November, 1963, p. 1. An editorial.

INDEX

ABC system of shorthand, 187
Accuracy drills, typing, 144, 146-47 (*exhibit*)
  adjacent-finger, 147
  alphabet (words, sentences, paragraphs), 144
  call-the-throw for control, 145
  difficult material, 144-45
  difficult reaches, 147
  double-letter words, 147
  figure and symbol, 145
  one-hand words, 147
  opposite fingers, same reach, 148
  repetition, 145, 147
  unison typing, 148
Adult education, Iowa handbook for, 476*n.*, 487*n.*
Adult programs: *see* Business education, adult programs
Advisory committee, cooperative part-time program, 448
American Business Education Yearbook, 18, 354
American Vocational Association, 18, 28*n.*, 399
Approaches to keyboard, 127-29
Attention, interest, desire, 53-58
  attention-killers, 54-56
  fatigue and boredom, 56-58
Atyeo, Henry C., 462*n.*
Audio-visual aids, 347
  See also Visual aids
Austin, Minnesota, business education program, 37-39 (*table*)
Automation and clerical work, 268-70
Awards, use of, 50-51

Bookkeeping:
  equation, 371-72
  instructional materials, types of:
    miscellaneous, 366
    practice sets, 365
    textbooks, 364-65
    workbooks, 365
  in secondary school:
    course content, 363-64
    grade placement, 363
    objectives, 359-60
    point of view, differences in, 360
    reasons for teaching, 360-63
    types of courses, 363
  teaching of:
    evaluation techniques:
      examinations, 389-91
      homework assignments, 391-92
      practice sets, 392
    general topics:
      bookkeeping equation, 371-72
      books of account, 374-75
      closing the books, 379
      financial statements, 379
      getting started, 371-73
      theory of debit and credit, 373-74
      use of "T" accounts, 380
      worksheet, 376-79
    goals, 266-67
    manual and machine bookkeeping, 382-83
    methods:
      discussion, 367-68
      individual instruction, 370
      problem-project, 369-70

motivation techniques, 388-89
special problems:
  income tax, 381-82
  individual differences, 383-85
  paper work, 385-86
  payroll bookkeeping, 381
  weaknesses of students in fundamental processes, 385
visual aids, 386-88
  films and film strips, 386-87
  teacher-made, 387
why vs. how, 392
Boredom and fatigue, 56-58
Brewington, Ann, 203
Briefhand system of shorthand, 187
Business arithmetic:
  course content, 431-32
  methods of teaching, 432-33
  problems in teaching, 433-35
Business education:
  adult programs, 15-16, 475-97
    administrative considerations:
      fees charged students, 487
      financial aspects, 486-87
      length of course, 487-88
      public relations, 488-89
      records and reports, 488
    checklist of teaching procedures, 493-95
    course content, 492-93
    curriculum, 489-90
      in smaller schools, 490-92
    definition and description, 476
    history, 477-78
    instructional materials, 492-93
    modern scope and trends, 478-80
    psychological factors:
      atmosphere of informality, 482-83
      basic factors, 480-81
      building course around needs and interests, 481-82
      making course functional, 483-84
      using knowledge of students, 483
    purposes, 476-77
    teaching opportunities in, 15-16
    teaching techniques, 485-86
    visual aids, 484-85
  changed setting, 5-6
  cooperative part-time programs:
    advantages:
      community, 446-47
      school, 446
      student, 446
    alternation plan, 445
    categories of learnings, 449-50
    curriculum patterns, 451-52
      in post-high-school programs, 454
    definition, 444-45
    distributive practices instructional schedule, 452-54
    general related learnings, 449, 451, 454-56
    history, 443-44
    importance of coordination, 449
    nature of learnings, 448-54
    occupational group learnings, 449-50, 456-63
    on-the-job training, 445, 450-51, 467-70
    specific job learnings, 450, 463-67
    techniques in providing learnings, 454-70
    terms used in, 447-48
    types, 444
    ways of presenting learnings, 450-51
  definition of, 24-25
  field of, 27-28
  former setting, 4-5
  general, characteristics of, 30
  in medium-sized city, 37-41 (*table*)
  objectives:
    general, 30-32
    Iowa, 31-32
    South Dakota, 32
  twofold classification, 28-30
  vocational, characteristics of, 29
Business Education Forum, 18
Business Education Manual for Pennsylvania, 284, 308, 309
Business Education—Part II, Typewriting (Virginia), 122*n*.
Business Education in the Secondary School (Illinois), 294
Business Education for Secondary Schools (Dallas, Texas), 291
Business Education—Secondary Schools (Iowa program), 31*n*.
Business English, 417, 436
Business law:
  course content, 424-25

Business law (*Cont.*)
objectives of teaching, 424
specific teaching techniques:
community resources, use of, 426-27
student experiences, use of, 427-28
supplementary instructional materials, use of, 426
Business organization and management, 435-36
Business student organizations: *see* Organizations, business student
Business teachers: *see* Teachers, business
Business Teaching Aid No. K-1 (Porter), 306*n.*
Buzz sessions, 340

Carnegie units, 33
City programs in clerical practice teaching, 284-92 (*tables*)
Civil service examinations, 315
Class recitation, evaluation of, 101-2
Classroom:
human relationships (discipline), 77-79
organization, 76-77
physical arrangements, 75-76
Classroom discussion:
advantages, 341-42
disadvantages, 342-43
factors to consider in, 343
techniques, 338
Clerical activities, nonspecialized, 271
Clerical duties, classification of, 271-72
Clerical practice:
and automation, 268-70
description of, 267-68
electric typing in, 302
equipment and supplies for, 277-79
filing in, 306-7
job instruction sheets, 294-98 (*exhibits*)
methods of teaching:
battery plan, 279
cooperative plan, 284
integrated or model office plan, 283-84
rotation plan, 279-83 (*exhibit*)
objectives of course, 273-74

office machines in, 303-4
prerequisites for course, 274-75
record keeping, 307
standards in, 314-15
state and city programs in, 284-92 (*tables*)
teaching suggestions, 292-301 (*exhibits*)
units for one-semester course, 301-7
units to be included, 275-77
Clerical typing, 302
Clerical work, factors constituting success in, 272-73
Clerical workers, duties of, 270-73 (*table*)
Commercial education: *see* Business education
Competition and rivalry, 61-62
Concentration drills, typing, 148-50 (*exhibit*)
copy including instructions, 149, 150
deleting repetitions, 148
difficult contextual materials, 150
eyes on copy, 150
omission of vowels or words, 149, 150
spelling and punctuation, 149, 150-51
Consumer business:
course content, 429-30
methods and problems in teaching, 430
objectives of teaching, 429
resources for use in teaching, 430-31
Consumers Guide, 431
Consumers Union, 431
Controlled Reader, 136
Conversion table for dictation speeds, 223
Cooperative part-time training: *see* Business education, cooperative part-time programs
Coordinating teaching with transcription, 237-42 (*exhibits*)
Coordinator, cooperative part-time program, 447
Criteria for Certification of Business Teachers (NABTE Bulletin), 11*n.*
Curriculum:
business education:

characteristics of, 30
definition of, 28
goals of, 28
part-time cooperative programs, 451-52, 454
high school program, 32-34
elective units, 34
required units, 33-34
medium-sized high school, 37-41 (*table*)
minimum program (general education), 35-37
small high school, 34-37
vocational curriculum:
characteristics of, 29
definition of, 28
goals of, 28
illustrations of, 40
in small high school, 34

Dakins, J. Gordon, 399*n*.
Data processing:
in business education curriculum, 418-19, 423
curriculum of Des Moines, Iowa, high school, 420-22
selected bibliography, 419-20
suggested teaching techniques in, 423-24
Data Processing Management Association, 269-70
Data Processor, 424
Davenport, Elizabeth, 209-10
Dealey, W. L., 112*n*.
Debit and credit, theory of, 373-74
Definitions of Terms in Vocational and Practical Arts Education (AVA), 28*n*., 399*n*.
Desks, typewriter, 112-13
Dictation:
conversion table for speeds, 223
how to give, 211-15, 220-21, 222
material, 211
of new matter, 220-21
postviews, 212
progressive, 215, 218 (*exhibit*)
rate, 210-11
reasons for giving, 209-10
speed-building, 215
spurt, 213-16 (*exhibits*)
tapes and records, 151, 218, 226-27
tests, 221-22, 229
timing of, 21

Dictation for Transcription (Zoubek) 223*n*.
Dictionary of Education (Good), 5*n*.
Discipline, 52, 77-79
procedures to minimize difficulty in, 78-79
Discussion method:
in bookkeeping teaching, 337-38
in business law teaching, 427-28
in distributive subjects, 404
techniques, 338
types:
classroom, 336, 337-43
committee or roundtable, 336
group dynamics, 336
Distributive education:
areas of subject-specialization, 6
definition, 399
evaluative criteria, 463-65
part-time programs: *see* Business education, cooperative part-time programs
state plans for, 400
Distributive Education Clubs of America (DECA), 10-11, 500, 513-16
Distributive occupations, definition of, 397-98
Distributive subjects:
bases for teaching, 396-97
cooperative part-time programs, 413
measurement of achievement in, 402-4
names of courses, 398-99
purposes of courses, 401-2
techniques of teaching:
case studies, 408
of local businesses, 412-13
demonstration, 404-6
field trips and speakers, 411-12
group discussion, 404
miscellaneous aids, 413
posters and displays, 410-11
sales skit, 407-8
precautions in using, 408
sales talk, 406-7
shopping tours and reports, 409-10
Diversified occupations, part-time programs: *see* Business education, cooperative part-time programs
Duplicating machines, 302-3
Dvorak, August, 112*n*.

Economic education, 352-55 (*fig.*)
Economic geography, 436-37
Educating Youth for Economic Competence, 354n.
Education for All American Youth, 25
Educational Developmental Laboratories, 129
Educational Policies Commission of NEA, 25, 26
Educational psychology, 46-47
Electric typewriting, 176-79, 302
    changing from electric to manual, 178
    changing from manual to electric, 178-79
    first lessons in, 177-78
Electronic computers: *see* Data processing
Emily Griffith Opportunity School, 489-90
Essay-type questions, 96-98
Evaluation:
    in bookkeeping, 389-92
    and grading, 91-102
        bases for assigning grades:
            class recitations, 101-2
            examinations, 93-101
            student projects, 102
            typical problems, 91-92
    and measurement: *see* General business
Evaluation criteria for distributive education, 463-65
"Evaluation of Outcomes" (N.Y. University and Council on Economic Education), 349n.
Evening classes: *see* Business education, adult program
Examinations:
    essay, 96-98
    objective, 93-96
    performance, 100-101
    problem, 98-100
Eyster, Elvin S., 354

Facility drills, typing, 151
Fatigue and boredom, 56-58
FBLA Forum, 11
Felter, Emma K., 271n.
Field trips:
    cooperative part-time programs, 462
    distributive subjects, 411-12

general business, 346-47
Filing in clerical practice, 306-7
Financial statements, 379
Financing Adult Education (Olds), 479n.
Forkner system of shorthand, 187
Foy, Sister Mary Antonine, 272n.
Fuller, Donald C., 131n.
Functional method, shorthand, 195-97
Future Business Leaders of America (FBLA), 10-11, 18, 51, 500, 510-13

General business:
    college courses of aid in teaching, 329
    course content, 328-29
    definition and description of, 327
    evaluation and measurement, 348-52
        tests in measurement of:
            abilities, 349-50
            understandings, 350-51
    instructional materials:
        bibliography of free and inexpensive material, 358
        community as source of, 333
        extent of, 330
        methods of using, 330-33 (*fig.*)
    methodology: *see* Methodology, general business
    objectives of, 327-28
    problems of teaching, 333-35
    teaching methods, 333-35
General related learnings, cooperative part-time business
    education programs, 449, 451, 454-56
George-Barden Act, 11, 400, 479
George-Deen Act, 400, 443, 479
Gibson, E. Dana, 424
Glidden, Carlos, 112
Goals:
    of secondary education, 25-27
    and subgoals in learning, 62-63
Gold, Milton, 443n.
Good, Carter V., 5n.
Grading: *see* Evaluation, and grading
Gregg shorthand, 187, 191, 226
Group and individual projects, 345-46
Grubbs, Robert L., 215
Guide for Vocational Office Training for Virginia, 288

Handbook in Business Education for South Dakota, 32n.
Headphones, 80
Homerow approach, 127
Human relationships: *see* Discipline

Income tax, as special problem in bookkeeping, 381-82
Individual differences in students, 66-67
in bookkeeping ability, 383-85
in shorthand ability, 218-19
Individual instruction in bookkeeping, 370
Informal Adult Education (Knowles), 485n.
Instructional equipment, specialized, 79-81
Instructional Guide for Typewriting in Junior and Senior High School (Los Angeles), 122n., 172
Instructional materials, general business:
bibliography of free and inexpensive material, 358
community as source of, 333
extent of, 330
methods of using, 330-33 (fig.)
Iowa Public School Adult Education Programs, 487n., 491n.

Job instruction sheets, 294-98 (*exhibits*)
Joint Council for Economic Education, 354
Junior Achievement, Inc., 500, 516-20

Knowledge of results in learning, 58-59
Knowles, Malcolm S., 485n.

Learning:
attention, interest, desire, 53-58
attention-killers, 54-56
fatigue and boredom, 56-58
goals and subgoals, 62-63
individual differences in students, 66-67

as individual growth, 47-49
knowledge of results, 58-59
problem solving, 65-66
psychological factors of:
goals and subgoals, 62-63
individual differences, 66-67
individual growth, 47-49
knowledge of results, 58-59
motivation, 49-53
problem solving, 65-66
rivalry and competition, 61-62
skill development, 63-65
whole vs. part learning, 59-60
Learning process, teaching techniques applied to, 72-107
Leslie, Louis A., 195, 222n.
Lesson plans, 82, 87-88, 90
Liles, Alton B. Parker, 272
Lloyd, Alan C., 120n., 159n., 171n.
Longhand transcription tests, 228-29

Machine shorthand, 187-88
Machine transcription, suggestions for teaching, 304-6
Mann, George C., 477
Manual and machine bookkeeping, 382-83
Manual method, shorthand, 194-95
Manuals, job and merchandise, 465-66
Methodology:
factors to consider in using, 102-3
Methodology, general business:
discussion, 335-43
advantages, 341-42
disadvantages, 342-43
factors to consider, 343
miscellaneous techniques:
audio-visual aids, 347
field trips, 346-47
group and individual projects, 345-46
methodology in general, 347
problems in, 333-35
question-and-answer method, 343-44
Minor in business education, 8-9
Motivation, 49-53
artificial, 50-51
praise and encouragement, 51-53
real, 49-50
techniques in bookkeeping, 388-89

Murphy, Glen, 209-10

National Association for Business Teacher Education, 11n.
National Association of Public School Adult Educators, 477n.
National Association of Secondary School Principals, 25
National Business Education Association, 4, 11, 17-18
National Business Education Quarterly, 18
National Business Entrance Tests, 18, 315
National Education Association (NEA), 4, 11, 17, 18, 479
New-matter dictation, 220-21
Nonskill subjects, 325-439

Objective tests, 93-96
Occupational group learnings, cooperative part-time business education programs, 449-50
    techniques in providing, 456-63
    case study, 457-58
    committee work, 460-61
    demonstrations, 459-60
    field interview, 458-59
    field observation, 462-63
    field trips, 462
    resource person, 457
    role playing, 459
    shopping reports, 461
Office education part-time programs: *see* Business education, cooperative part-time programs
Office Equipment Industry, 303
Office machines, 303-4
Office practice:
    state and city programs, 284-92 (*tables*)
    teaching of, 264-67, 447
Olds, Edward B., 479n.
One-minute speed building plan, 213-15
On-the-job learnings, cooperative part-time business education programs, 445, 450-51
    procedures for providing, 467-70
    advisory committee action, 469
    coordinator-sponsor-trainee conferences, 470

sponsor handbook, 468-69
sponsor meetings, 470
training profile, 469
Organization, classroom, 76-77
Organizations, business student, 51, 499-520
concomitant learnings, 506-7
national organizations:
    Distributive Education Clubs of America, 10-11, 500, 513-16
    Future Business Leaders of America, 10-11, 18, 51, 500, 510-13
    Junior Achievement, Inc., 500, 516-20
objections to, 507-9, 510
psychology of:
    desire to excel, 501-2
    gregariousness and belongingness, 502-3
    miscellaneous factors, 504
    self-assertion, 503-4
types of, 500
unsuccessful activities, causes of, 504-6

Part learning vs. whole, 59-60
Payroll bookkeeping, special problems in, 381
Pens in shorthand, 211-12
Performance tests, 100-101
Physical arrangements, classroom, 75-76
Pipe-organ method of typing numbers, 153
Pitman shorthand, 187
Planning, 82-91
    daily lesson plans, 87-88, 90
    long-range, 83-84
    team teaching, 88-89
    unit, 84-87
Planning for American Youth, 25
Plates, reading of, 203-5
Porter, Leonard J., 306
Posters and displays, distributive subjects, 410-11
Postviews in shorthand, 212
Practice sets, bookkeeping, 365
Pratt, Wayne L., 491n.
Pretranscription training, 229-30
Problem-project method in bookkeeping, 369-70
Problem solving, 65-66

Problem tests, 98-100
Production typewriting, 165-70 (*exhibits*)
Programmed instructional materials, 81
Projectors, 80
Proofreading of typing: *see* Typewriting, proofreading
Psychology:
of skill, 63-65, 326
of typewriting, 115-20
Public School Adult Education (NAPSAE), 477*n.*, 478*n.*
Punched card processes: *see* Data processing

Question and answer method, 343-44

Reading Factors in Typewriting (Fuller), 131*n.*
Record keeping, 307
Reimbursed programs, 448
Related instruction, 447
Related typing knowledges, 160-62 (*exhibits*)
Remington, E. & Sons, 112
Resource person in cooperative part-time programs, 457
Rhythm drills, typing, 142, 151
Rivalry and competition, 61-62
Role playing in cooperative part-time programs, 459
Rotation plan in clerical practice, 279-83 (*exhibit*)
Rowe, Clyde E., 163

Sales skit, 407-8
Sales talk, 406-7
Samson, Carlene, 490*n.*
Satlow, I. David, 271
Scrapbooks, 466
Secretarial office practice, 307-11, 447
Selectrics, 177*n.*
Shoales, Christopher, 112
Shopping tours and reports, 409-10, 461
Shorthand:
blackboard, use of, 200-202, 212
classroom procedures, ways to vary, 198-200
course, length of, 192-94

dictation equipment, 224
dictation of new matter, 220-21
dictation practices, 208-24 (*exhibits, table*)
homework assignments, 205-8
amount, 207
reading, 206
theory, 205-6
writing practice, 206-7
individual differences in students, 218-19
methods:
functional, 195-97
manual, 194-95
similarities and differences in, 197-98
objectives, 188-89
one-year program, 193
penmanship practice, 208-9
plates, reading of, 203-5
standard word count, 222*n.*
standards in, 230-34
student, qualifications of, 190-91
systems, 187-88, 191-92
teacher, qualifications of, 189-90
teaching suggestions, 198-229
tests, 228-29
dictation, 221-22, 229
longhand transcription, 228-29
word, 228
theory, teaching of, 202-3
Skill development, 63-65, 110
in typewriting, 115-20
Skill subjects, 58, 109-324
Skip-around approach, 127-28
Small high school, 34-37
adult programs, 490-92
business teacher in, 12-13
vocational curriculum, 35-37
Smith-Hughes Act, 479
Society for Automation in Business Education (SABE), 424
Sociobusiness subjects, 58
Specific job learnings, cooperative part-time business education programs, 450
techniques in providing, 463-67
demonstrations, 466
individual study methods, 463-65
interviews, coordinator-student, 467
job manuals, 465
merchandise manuals, 465-66

Specific job learnings (*Cont.*)
  preparation of reports, 467
  services of other teachers, 467
  student projects, 467
Speed drills, typing:
  balanced-hand words and sentences, 139
  call-the-throw drills, 142
  easy words, sentences, paragraphs, 139
  flash words, 141
  goal writings, 141-42
  preview drills, 141
  repetition of similar sentences, 144
  repetitive three-three-three plan, 144
  repetitive writings, twelve-second to one-minute, 139
  rhythm drills, 142 ,151
  syllable drills, 141
  word- and phrase-level typing, 139
Speedwriting, 187
Sponsor, cooperative part-time program, 448
State programs in clerical practice teaching, 284-92 (*tables*)
Stein, Eric Sedwick, 399*n.*
Stenograph, 188
Stenographic office practice, 266, 307-8
  objectives of, 308-9
  units in, 309-11
Stenographic practice, teaching suggestions for, 311-13
Stuart, Esta Ross, 314
Student learner, cooperative part-time program, 448
Student organizations, business: *see* Organizations, business student
Student projects, evaluation of, 102
Students, qualifications for success in shorthand, 190-91

"T" accounts, use of, 380
Tachistoscope, 136
Teacher, business:
  acquiring professional stature, 16-19
  adult and evening classes, 15-16, 486, 487
  extracurricular activities, 10-11
  future career possibilities, 19-20

in large high school, 13-14
modern, 3-4
personal characteristics:
  democratic, 74-75
  dynamic, 73
  realistic, 74
  scholarly, 73-74
position in community, 3-4
position in teaching profession, 3-4
in post-high-school work, 14-15
preparation of:
  business experience, 11-12
  general and liberal arts, 7
  minor in business education, 8-9
  minor subject-specializations, 7-8
  personal development, 9-10
  professional preparation, 9
  subject-specialization, areas of, 607
qualifications for shorthand teaching, 189-90
in small high school, 12-13
subject-specialization, areas of, 6-7, 7-8
as a technician, 75-81
Teaching machines, 81
Team teaching, 88-89
Technique drills, typing, 138, 139-41 (*exhibit*)
  backspace key, 139
  carriage throw, 139
  eyes-on-copy, 130-31, 141
  left-and-right hand, 141
  margin release, 139
  reach, 141
  shift key, 140
  stroking, 130, 141
  tabulator key, 140
Ten Imperative Needs of Youth, 25
Tests: *see* Examinations
Textbooks, bookkeeping, 364-65
Thermofax copy machine, 80
Training station, cooperative part-time program, 447-48
Transcription:
  building skill in use of materials, 250-51
  building speed and accuracy in, 242
  drills in, 242-43
  errors, analysis of, 243-45
  grading, 243
  introducing machine transcription, 234, 236

length of course, 253-56
mailability, 243
office style dictation, 253
plan for integrated program, 255-56
power drive, 244 (*exhibit*)
program in advanced shorthand, 245-48 (*exhibit*)
program in six weeks' course, 248-49 (*exhibit*)
punctuation in, 237-41 (*exhibits*)
rate of, 237
standards in, 252
stenographic notebook, use of, 251-52
teaching of, 234-56
Typewriting:
  accuracy and speed in, 134-36
  composition at the machine, 162-64
  courses of study:
    content of, 121-27
    length of, 120-21
    Los Angeles, 122, 125-27
    Virginia, 123-25
  desks and chairs, 112-13
  developing correct techniques in, 129-34
  drills:
    accuracy, 144, 146-47 (*exhibit*)
      See also Accuracy drills
    alphabet, 144
    balanced-hand, 139
    concentration, 148-50 (*exhibit*)
      See also Concentration drills
    key location, 128-29
    rhythm, 142, 151
    speed, 139, 142-43 (*exhibit*)
      See also Speed drills
    technique, 138, 139-41 (*exhibit*)
    warm-up, 137-38 (*exhibit*), 154
  electric, 176-79
    See also Electric typewriting
  equipment in typing room, 112-13
  erasing, 164-65
  errors:
    analysis of, 154-58
    causes of, 155-57
    types of, 157-58
  with eyes on copy, 130-31
  figures and symbols, teaching of, 151-54
    drills on, 145
  grading: *see* Typewriting standards
  invention of, 112

keyboard, introduction to, 127-29
  homerow approach, 127
  skip-around or word-pattern approach, 127-28
  vertical approach, 127
  whole-keyboard approach, 128
knowledges, related, 160-62 (*exhibits*)
machine manipulations, 131-32
machine parts, teaching of, 129
objectives, 114-15, 121-22
  personal use, 114-15
  vocational, 114-15
production, 165-70 (*exhibits*)
proofreading, 158-60
  classification of errors, 159
  methods of, 159
  procedures for teaching, 159-60
psychology of, 115-20
reading habits in, 131
room, 112-14
simplified keyboard, 112*n.*
skill development in, 115-20
speed and accuracy in, 134-36
speed-building suggestions, 135-36
standards, 170-76
  Los Angeles high schools, 171-72 (*exhibit*), 173, 175 (*exhibit*)
  production, 175-76
  straight copy, 172-75 (*exhibits*)
stroking, 130
tables, 112-13
teaching aids, 136
techniques:
  development of, 129-34
  drills, 138, 139-41 (*exhibit*)
  error charts, 132-34 (*exhibit*)
tests:
  centering, 162 (*exhibit*)
  English and typing usage, 161 (*exhibit*)

Unit plan for general business, 84-87
Units of Instruction for the Occupational Relations Course (St. Paul, Minn.), 455*n.*

Van Derveer, Elizabeth T., 227, 271
Vertical approach, 127
Visual aids:
  in adult education, 484-85

Visual aids (*Cont.*)
    in bookkeeping instruction, 386-88
Vocational Education Act, 15, 400, 423, 479
Vocational Education Bulletin No. 1 (U.S. Office of Education), 297*n.*, 397*n*

Warm-up drills, typing, 137-38 (*exhibit*), 154

Whole-keyboard approach, 128
Whole vs. part learning, 59-60
Word pattern approach, 127-28
Word tests, shorthand, 228
Workbooks, bookkeeping, 365
Working to Learn (Gold), 443*n.*
Worksheet, 376-79

Zoubek, Charles E., 223*n.*